The Royal Court Theatre and the modern stage

The Royal Court Theatre is arguably the major influence on the development of post-war theatre. The English Stage Company at the Court commissioned and performed some of the most influential plays in modern theatre history, including works by Arden, Bond, Churchill, Hare, Storey, Wertenbaker and Wesker. The story of the Royal Court is also the history of the contemporary stage. In this absorbing account of the Court's evolution from 1956 to 1998, Philip Roberts draws on previously unused archives in both public and private collections and on a series of interviews with people who were prominent in the life of the Court. The book also includes a foreword by Max Stafford-Clark, to date the longest-serving Artistic Director of the Company. The result is an intimate account of the working of the foremost producing house for new work both in Britain and abroad.

PHILIP ROBERTS is Professor of Drama and Theatre Studies at the University of Leeds. He is the author of a number of studies of modern theatre, including *The Royal Court Theatre, 1965–1972* (1986).

The Royal Court Theatre and the modern stage

Philip Roberts

CAMBRIDGE
UNIVERSITY PRESS

PUBLISHED BY THE PRESS SYNDICATE OF THE UNIVERSITY OF CAMBRIDGE
The Pitt Building, Trumpington Street, Cambridge, United Kingdom

CAMBRIDGE UNIVERSITY PRESS
The Edinburgh Building, Cambridge CB2 2RU, United Kingdom
http://www.cup.cam.ac.uk
40 West 20th Street, New York, NY 10011–4211, USA   http://www.cup.org
10 Stamford Road, Oakleigh, Melbourne 3166, Australia

© Cambridge University Press 1999

First published 1999
Printed in the United Kingdom at the University Press, Cambridge

Typeset in Trump [CE]

A catalogue record for this book is available from the British Library

Library of Congress cataloguing in publication data

Roberts, Philip, 1942–
The Royal Court Theatre and the Modern Stage / Philip Roberts.
      p.   cm. – (Cambridge studies in modern theatre)
Includes bibliographical references and index.
ISBN 0 521 47438 8 (hardback) – ISBN 0 521 47962 2 (paperback)
1. Royal Court Theatre – History.   I. Title.   II. Series.
PN2596.L7R5173   1999
792'.09421 – dc21   98–53258   CIP

ISBN 0 521 47438 8 hardback
ISBN 0 521 47962 2 paperback

For Kate, Martha and Chloe

The worlds of pop music, broadcasting, football, the cinema, politics, and love, all have lost domains occupied by the memories of great past performances, which are sought out for solace or to shame the shabbiness of the present – 'When Churchill was Prime Minister' ... 'When we were in the World Cup Final' ... 'when we were first married' ... David Hare calls the curators of these golden worlds the 'whenwes'. They guard their territory with a dogged devotion. The theatre isn't immune from the virus – 'The National Theatre under Laurence Olivier' ... 'The Royal Court under George Devine' and 'Joan Littlewood at Stratford East' are particularly robust strains.

(Richard Eyre, *Utopia and other places*)

The Court, of course, has never actually been what it used to be.

(Rob Ritchie, *Plays*, January 1985)

Contents

Foreword by Max Stafford-Clark   page xi

Preface   xiii

Acknowledgements   xv

List of abbreviations   xvii

Biographical notes   xix

Introduction: abortive schemes, 1951–1954   *1*

1 Coincidences, 1954–1956   *17*

2 The struggle for control, 1956–1960   *45*

3 Conflict and competition, 1961–1965   *79*

4 A socialist theatre, 1965–1969   *105*

5 A humanist theatre, 1969–1975   *129*

6 Changing places, 1975–1979   *151*

7 Theatre in a cold climate, 1980–1986   *170*

8 Holding on, 1987–1993   *195*

   Afterword   *219*

   Notes   230

   Select bibliography   254

   Index   277

Foreword

I recall attending an academic conference at Baton Rouge, Louisiana, in the early eighties which took the history of The Royal Court as its subject. A number of us had been flown in at considerable expense to the heart of bayou country.

After three days of genial bickering and disagreement about almost every aspect of the Royal Court's provenance and history, one of our gracious hosts asked if there was any aspect of the Royal Court we could agree on. It turned out that there wasn't, so the requirement for an objective and comprehensive history of this important theatre is well due.

It is hard to write about such a passionate theatre in a dispassionate and accurate way, but Philip Roberts' rich account, which covers the history of the Royal Court from its inception in 1956 to the end of the millennium, is invaluable to anybody interested in theatre, and is intriguing for those of us who had the pleasure of playing some part in those events.

No other theatre in England attracts more passion to itself than the Royal Court. Several generations of writers and directors have held the mirror up to their society and defined their times on its stage. In 1993, the year I left, it was called both 'Europe's most interesting theatre' by the *New York Times* and 'a dump' by our own *Sunday Times*. I hoped that both statements contained an element of truth.

Many directors, writers and actors feel they have left the best part of themselves at the Court. The youthful idealism and best hopes of several generations are somehow caught up in its walls. In the day-to-day running of the Royal Court it is easy to forget this, but when you go wrong you are reminded. People you've never met write to tell you how badly you've let them down. It is this measure of passionate identification that makes the Court a great theatre. When it reopens it will no longer be 'a dump' but it may well continue to be 'Europe's most interesting theatre'.

Max Stafford-Clark

Preface

This book chronicles the life of the English Stage Company at the Royal Court Theatre. The Company is in its fifth decade of work. The years reflect the growth and development of the Court from precarious beginnings in the mid-fifties to the battles with censorship in the sixties, the troughs of the early seventies, the wars of attrition of the eighties and the movement of the Company into the West End in the nineties. In 1964 George Devine could not afford to perform other than cosmetic surgery on his beloved theatre. Thirty years later, Stephen Daldry, armed with a huge subvention from the National Lottery, determined that the theatre in London's Sloane Square should remain essentially Devine's theatre. In the meantime, however, the Court had become central to theatrical life in Britain and many other countries. For many, it had become an institution. Analysing this institution is the purpose of this account, for to define the Court is in many ways to define the modern stage. No other company has had a comparable effect on post-war theatre writing and production. Without the Royal Court, the emergence of what became the Royal Shakespeare Company, the Royal National Theatre, together with the growth of a myriad smaller theatres, might not have been possible.

The struggle to demonstrate Devine's belief that theatre could equal the seriousness of other artistic forms engendered a tightly knit, fiercely defensive group. The Court family was exclusive and uncompromising. It still is. It provoked external anger and hostility at its stance. It still does. It has survived, often barely, as the most important producer of new writing in the history of the theatre. That is its glory.

xiii

My approach has been to try to tell the story of the Court as it evolved as an institution over the decades via many of its principal figures and, in particular, its Artistic Directors. What determines the stance of a theatre is not preconceived theoretic notions. Rather, it is the ability, practically, to make judgements and to sustain the consequences against the odds. No one at the Court would offer an identical answer to a question about house style, but everyone would know what should not play there, even if eyes were closed to the occasional, and usually failing, pot-boiler.

The story makes use of material from interviews with virtually all the major figures involved in running the Court, together with archival material from a number of important sources. This has not been used before and frequently offers an intimate and inside account of what, publicly, might appear very different, for the Court excelled at closing ranks. Throughout its history, the Court has striven to represent contemporary life and culture, and its current Artistic Director, Ian Rickson, expresses the credo in a way Devine himself would surely have approved:

> We're not particularly interested in plays with wigs or plays set in drawing rooms. We want to put real life on stage in all its complexity, and we look for actors who can do that.
>
> (*Independent on Sunday*, 20 September 1998)

Acknowledgements

I have many people to thank for their help. The principal collections of papers in private hands are those of the Earl of Harewood, Jocelyn Herbert (papers of George Devine) and Greville Poke (who also holds the archive of Neville Blond). These three distinguished contributors to the story of the English Stage Company allowed me to study their archives in Sheffield. I am deeply grateful for their trust. Others were equally generous: Max Stafford-Clark allowed me to consult his diaries; the late J. E. Blacksell gave me his Court papers, as did Stuart Burge; Matthew Evans loaned his papers for study; the Council of the English Stage Company agreed to my consulting company records.

The following gave their time for often extended interviews: Lindsay Anderson; Stuart Burge; Graham Cowley; Stephen Daldry; Matthew Evans; William Gaskill; Margaret Harris; Jocelyn Herbert; Clare Jeffery; Oscar Lewenstein; Greville Poke; Max Stafford-Clark; David Storey; Alan Tagg; Nicholas Wright. The staff of the following institutions were most helpful: Sarah Newman, Arts Council of Great Britain; Judith Leigh, Authors' Licensing and Collecting Society; Diane Arnold, Central Library, Birmingham; Christopher Robinson, The Theatre Collection, University of Bristol; Neil Somerville, BBC Information and Archives, Caversham; Dean Proctor, National Sound Archive, the British Library; Claire Hudson and Andrew Kirk, the British Theatre Museum; Tracey Brett, Condé Nast Publications Ltd; Linda Poole, Partnership Archivist, the John Lewis Partnership; Anna Trussler, Archivist, the Ronald Duncan Papers: the New Collection, University of Plymouth; Neil Cobbett, the Public Record Office; Melissa Miller, Cathy Henderson and Pat Fox, the Harry Ransom

Humanities Research Center, the University of Texas at Austin; David Ward, Chief Librarian, Royal Holloway, University of London; Stella Hawkyard, the John Rylands Library, Manchester; Helen Gardner, the Society of Authors.

Many individuals helped provide information or guidance. I do not value them the less for listing their names alphabetically: Jane Baldwin; Christopher Baugh; Edward Bond; Richard Boon; Emma Bradley; John Bull; Matthew Campbell; Helen Dawson; Keith Dewhurst; Christine Eccles; Jim Emmet; Lindy Fletcher; Angela Fox; John Haffenden; Billy J. Harbin; Vikki Heywood; Donald Howarth; Jacqueline Labbe; Patricia Lawrence; Sandra Lousada; Patricia MacNaughton; Ian MacKillop; David Meyer; John Mortimer; P. H. Newby; Charles Osborne; Anthony Page; Natasha Richardson; Rob Ritchie; Dominic Shellard; Michael Thomas; Sue Vice; Martin White; Oliver Wilkinson.

I am obliged to the British Academy and the University of Sheffield for financial aid. The latter also granted me leave to complete this book.

Victoria Cooper, my editor at Cambridge University Press, and David Bradby, my general editor, were both helpful and patient, as was Margaret Flower, who had the difficult job of deciphering my handwriting.

Abbreviations

(i)   People

JEB	James Blacksell
SB	Stuart Burge
ME	Matthew Evans
GH	George, Earl of Harewood
JH	Jocelyn Herbert
OL	Oscar Lewenstein
GP	Greville Poke

(ii)   Places

BTM	British Theatre Museum, London
RDA	The Ronald Duncan Archive, University of Plymouth
JLP	The John Lewis Partnership Archive, Stevenage
HRHRC	The Harry Ransom Humanities Research Center, University of Texas at Austin

Note: The English Stage Company at the Royal Court is variously referred to as: ESC; Court; RCT. AD is Artistic Director.

(iii) Books

Doty and Harbin	Gresdna A. Doty and Billy J. Harbin (eds.), *Inside the the Royal Court Theatre, 1956–1981. Artists talk* (Baton Rouge, Louisiana University Press, 1990)
Findlater	Richard Findlater (ed.), *At the Royal Court. 25 years of the English Stage Company* (Amber Lane Press, 1981)

| Lewenstein | Oscar Lewenstein, *Kicking against the pricks: a theatre producer looks back* (Nick Hern Books, 1994) |
| Wardle | Irving Wardle, *The theatres of George Devine* (Cape, 1978) |

(iv)   Letters

Ownership of letters and other documents cited in the Notes or listed in the Bibliography is indicated by the following abbreviations within brackets.

LA	Lindsay Anderson
JB	Jane Baldwin
JEB	James Blacksell
BTM	British Theatre Museum, London
SB	Stuart Burge
RDA	The Ronald Duncan Archive, Plymouth
ME	Matthew Evans
WG	William Gaskill
GH	Lord Harewood
JH	Jocelyn Herbert
JLP	The John Lewis Partnership, Stevenage
GP	Greville Poke/Neville Blond
PR	Philip Roberts
MSC	Max Stafford-Clark
HRHRC	The Harry Ransom Humanities Research Center, Austin, Texas

Note: All unattributed quotations are from the joint archive of Greville Poke and Neville Blond, in the possession of the former.

Biographical notes

The principal figures involved in this study are:

LINDSAY ANDERSON. Film and stage director. Assistant Director at
    the Royal Court from 1957. Artistic Director 1969–72. Left the
    Court in 1975. Directed many of David Storey's plays and the
    films *If* and *O Lucky Man*. d. 1994.

NEVILLE BLOND. First Chairman of the English Stage Company
    1955–70. OBE 1945. CMG 1950. Married 1944 Elaine Marks,
    daughter of the founder of Marks and Spencer. d. 1970.

STUART BURGE. Artistic Director 1977–80, thereafter a member of
    the Court's Council. Artistic Director of the Queen's,
    Hornchurch, 1951–53 and of Nottingham Playhouse, 1963–74.
    CBE 1974. Important television director.

STEPHEN DALDRY. Artistic Director 1993–98. Formerly Artistic
    Director of the Gate Theatre, 1989–92. Celebrated for his
    direction of Priestley's *An Inspector Calls* (opened National
    Theatre 1992).

GEORGE DEVINE. Founder of the ESC and first Artistic Director
    1956–65. Manager and resident producer, London Theatre
    Studio, 1936–39. Director of Young Vic Company and co-
    director with Glen Byam Shaw of the Old Vic School. CBE,
    1957. The father of modern British theatre. d. 1966.

JOHN DEXTER. Joined ESC 1957. Noted for his direction at the Court
    of Wesker's trilogy. Associate Director, National Theatre,
    1963–66. Director of Production, New York Metropolitan
    Opera for seven years. d. 1990.

RONALD DUNCAN. Writer, librettist and founder with Oscar

Lewenstein of the company which became the English Stage Company. Worked with Britten and for Beaverbrook. Founded the Taw and Torridge (later the Devon) Festival 1953. Resigned from ESC Council 1966. d. 1992.

ALFRED ESDAILE. Businessman. Leased Royal Court to ESC 1955. Vice-Chairman of the Company. d. 1975.

MATTHEW EVANS. Chairman ESC 1984–90. Managing Director of Faber and Faber, 1972–93. Chairman of Faber's 1981– .

ROBIN FOX. Impresario and theatrical agent. Brought in by Blond as General Manager, 1957. Council and Artistic Committee member 1957–70. Co-Chairman with Lewenstein, 1970–71. d. 1971.

WILLIAM GASKILL. Artistic Director who succeeded Devine, 1965–69; thereafter one of the trilogy of Artistic Directors with Anderson and Page, 1969–72. Joined ESC 1957. Associate Director 1959. Associate Director, National Theatre, 1963–65. Devine's chosen son. Resigned 1987.

GEORGE, EARL OF HAREWOOD. Son of HRH the Princess Mary. A director of the Royal Opera House, 1969–72. Artistic Director, Edinburgh Festival, 1961–65. President of the English Football Association 1963–72. Original member of ESC Council from 1955; Chairman Artistic Committee 1955–72. President of the ESC 1972–76.

JOCELYN HERBERT. Internationally renowned Stage Designer. Trained in theatre design at the Slade. Joined London Theatre Studio 1936. Worked with Michel Saint-Denis, Devine and Motley. Joined the ESC 1956. Associated particularly with Beckett and Storey.

ROBERT KIDD. Joint Artistic Director with Nicholas Wright 1975–77. Assistant Director 1967. d. 1980.

OSCAR LEWENSTEIN. Impresario. Established with Duncan the company that became the ESC. General Manager of the Court for Esdaile, 1953–54. Suggested Devine's name for Artistic Director's post. Member of Artistic Committee and Council. Chairman 1971–73. Artistic Director 1973–75. Resigned 1977. d. 1997.

JOHN MORTIMER. Chairman ESC 1990– . Novelist, playwright. QC
1966. CBE 1986. Knighted 1998.

HOWARD NEWBY. Chairman ESC 1978–84. Managing Director BBC
Radio 1975–78. First Booker prize winner 1969.

ANTHONY PAGE. Artistic Director 1964–65. One of the trilogy of
Artistic Directors with Anderson and Gaskill, 1969–72.

GREVILLE POKE. Hon Sec ESC 1955–73. Chairman 1973–78.
Currently President, appointed by Mortimer. The longest-
serving member of the ESC.

TONY RICHARDSON. First Associate Director and founder member of
the ESC with Devine. Principally a film director. d. 1991.

IAN RICKSON. Artistic Director 1998– .

MAX STAFFORD-CLARK. Longest serving Artistic Director, 1979–93.
Artistic Director, Traverse Theatre Company, 1968–70. AD,
Traverse Workshop Company, 1970–74. Co-founder with
Gaskill of Joint Stock Theatre Company, 1974. Currently AD
of Out of Joint Theatre Company, 1993– .

NICHOLAS WRIGHT. Joint Artistic Director 1975–77. Assistant
Director 1968. First Director of the Theatre Upstairs 1969.

Introduction: abortive schemes, 1951–1954

I have lucid moments when the background of the past and the great possibilities of the future stir me, and the old pulse begins to beat with thoughts and ideas ... But until I feel the future near at hand, *the* future that is, I cannot think these ideas will develop ... What shall I do, dear Michel? Will I be wrong in my fears, or must I decide to take up some administrative work in the theatre and leave the stage to others? I beg you to write to me, as I have never done before, because I really do need to hear from you.

(Devine, Letters to Saint-Denis, October 1943 and June 1945)

When George Devine wrote the letters from which these extracts are taken, he was on active service in India and Burma during the Second World War. The letters are to his mentor and friend, Michel Saint-Denis, who had already formulated draft plans in London for what was to become the Old Vic Theatre Centre. On returning home in November 1945, Devine became effectively responsible for the development of the Centre. Saint-Denis, Devine and Glen Byam Shaw – the 'three boys' as they were known – set out to create a post-war version of the London Theatre Studio, which, directed by Saint-Denis and Devine, had closed after four years with the outbreak of the Second World War, despite Devine's efforts to save it.[1]

The Old Vic Theatre Centre eventually came under immense pressure from those powerful figures whose overarching objective was the creation of a National Theatre, with the Old Vic at its heart. Principal among these was the Chairman of the Governors, Lord Esher, who succeeded Lord Hambledon in March 1948. Esher, in a spectacular display of the kind of ignorance commonly found in chairs of theatre boards, refused to renew the contracts of Olivier, Richardson and Burrell, the three directors of the Old Vic Company, and made his views known as to the unstable situation of the Vic

I

Centre. A steady attrition ensued of the most important post-war theatre experiment at that time and, with the hostility evinced by Esher and Hugh Hunt, brought in as a fourth director by the Governors, to Saint-Denis, both in terms of his theories and his foreignness, it was only a matter of time before the scheme collapsed. Early in 1951, the Governors decided that only three directors could be afforded, though Hunt's contract was extended to June 1955. In May, the three boys offered their resignations, which Esher accepted. The following month saw the arrival of Tyrone Guthrie as General Manager. Guthrie promptly acted to recommend the closure of both the School and the Young Vic. By 1952, no trace of the structure remained.[2] Despite a huge outcry in the press, the resignations of fifteen of the Vic Centre's teachers, a unanimous resolution condemning the Governors by the British Drama League, a letter to *The Times* of 25 May 1951, signed by ninety Vic students, a call by Equity for an independent enquiry, a joint letter by such as Cecil Day Lewis, E. M. Forster, Dingle Foot, David Garnett, Rupert Hart Davis, Geoffrey Keynes, Siegfried Sassoon and other distinguished figures (*The Times*, 1 June 1951), the Governors remained adamant. The affair reached the House of Commons on 17 July with questions from Anthony Wedgwood Benn and Philip Noel-Baker to the Financial Secretary of the Treasury. Noel-Baker powerfully indicted the Governors who, he maintained, 'have lost money, lost the best directors and producers, lost the best artists, closed the Young Vic and now have closed the School' (*The Times*, 18 July 1952).

The disaster was keenly felt and stayed for a long time in the memories of those involved. Peggy Ashcroft's view was that 'If it were not so tragic, it would be ludicrous ... I have never been so shocked and disillusioned by anything in my twenty-five years in the theatre.'[3] For many theatre people, the villains of the piece were Esher, Hunt and Guthrie. Ashcroft's distrust of Guthrie is now a matter of record.[4] Jocelyn Herbert's view is that the three boys were gradually squeezed from the Centre until their voices became ineffectual:

> up until then the three boys, or one of them, had always gone to
> the meetings and talked things through ... There was always

2

this terrible jealousy that these three brilliant directors were tied up in the School and wouldn't work in the West End or anything. And the powers that be kept voicing the idea that Michel wanted to become the head of the National Theatre and there was this conspiracy that he shouldn't. A lot of people didn't like the teaching, the improvisation, the movement, the sound, all that. So they weren't allowed to go to meetings any more. They had to write letters. They never got any answers. They discovered that their letters weren't being read in the Governors' meetings. Finally they said things can't go on like this and they resigned. I can remember terribly well our saying, for God's sake explain to the papers and for some reason they wouldn't. They thought that they [the Governors] wouldn't close the School, we mustn't antagonise them, it will all blow over. They thought Tony Guthrie would speak up for them and he didn't. He didn't back them. He agreed with the Governors and it was a terrible betrayal because he had supported the London Theatre Studio. It never occurred to them that he wouldn't support them ... Esher was the big monster ... It was such a wonderful School. The shows were amazing.[5]

Margaret 'Percy' Harris of Motley, who taught at the School, is equally clear about the causes of the collapse:

I think the Governors thought this is going to become the National Theatre and we cannot have it run by a Frenchman. That was their basic reason for engineering Michel's resignation and when he did the whole thing collapsed. Everybody else resigned and the students said they wouldn't go on without these people. Michel was the first to decide to go and then the other two of course immediately went. Then the whole staff of the Vic School left. And then Hugh [Hunt] tried to establish a company and couldn't do it because nobody wanted to know. That's my assessment, but they never talked about it very much, silly boys, because I think they felt they must not destroy the Vic Scheme ... Hugh was very difficult because he used to talk about himself in relation to the Vic Scheme and he never mentioned the others at all. He never spoke about them. I felt he'd been extremely disloyal by trying to take the honours of the plan on himself. It was nothing to do with him.[6]

In October 1965, George Devine began compiling an autobiography for Faber. From page one, the memory of the Vic Scheme disaster is apparent. He refers to 'the unfortunate incident at the Old Vic when the three of us were intrigued out by an unscrupulous co-director, in the face of an impercipient chairman, Lord Esher, and a weak and cowardly intervention by Sir Tyrone Guthrie. The Arts Council, floundering about under its chairman, Sir Ernest Pooley, allowed six years of serious work to be torpedoed in so many months.'[7] However, with the pragmatism and tenacity which characterised his artistic life, Devine drew from the *débâcle* certain lessons. If they appear to be tinged with cynicism, they also appear to be accurate. Referring to the time immediately after his resignation in 1951, he dissects the implications:

> I was still smarting under the humiliation of those incidents. Certain of them were to serve me in the future. I had learned, for example, that to carry out one's job seriously and with dedication, producing the results was not enough in subsidised ventures in England. A more generous application of soft soap, a few lunches and dinners with the right people would have safeguarded our interests. I had learnt that even in artistic enterprises a certain kind of snob success was still essential. I had learnt that the theatrical profession was essentially conservative and not to be trusted to take collective action until it was too late. All this experience was to fortify my cunning for the future.[8]

As the outcry subsided, the three boys split up. Byam Shaw joined Anthony Quayle at the Stratford Memorial Theatre. Saint-Denis went to Strasbourg as Director of the Centre Nationale Dramatique de l'Est. Devine went freelance. Over the next few years, he directed, amongst other productions, five operas at Sadler's Wells and five plays at Stratford.

There was no shortage of work, but little of the kind Devine wanted. He graciously declined an offer from Laurence Olivier to both himself and Byam Shaw in the immediate aftermath of the collapse of the Vic Scheme to manage Laurence Olivier Productions because 'I am bound to bend every effort next year to get something else going before the frighteningly imminent dissolution of our partnership, which is naturally more fused than ever by the fire of our recent experience. It is not only a question of loyalty to Michel. It is even more an attachment to certain precise ideas which we have evolved together.'[9]

On holiday in the south of France in September 1951 Devine visited Edward Gordon Craig and told him the story of the Vic Scheme and his determination to continue:

> The word 'unhealthy', as used by Lord Esher, made him roar with laughter, and suddenly go black with rage. The story of the resignation of the staff delighted him most. He said he knew it all – and that things did not change. That those wealthy socialites who ran the Arts must be run out of it by the scruff of their necks ... All individuals and groups should get together and drive out these parasites who had got a grip on the purse strings and thought that entitled them to interfere in the theatre.[10]

Despite Devine's efforts to perpetuate the ideas of the Vic Scheme, as expressed in his letter to Olivier, by the middle of 1952 he was no further forward. According to Jocelyn Herbert, 'He kept himself going financially but he was planning all the time.'[11] The planning then took an extraordinary turn when Devine met Tony Richardson, a young BBC producer:

> I had a telephone call from the BBC to say would I appear in a television play? I said, 'Oh no, I can't be bothered, the thing bores me to hell, forget it', and put down the phone. Half an hour later, the phone rang. 'This is Mr Tony Richardson's secretary speaking. He's very disappointed that you don't want to do the play, as you haven't even seen the script.' I said I was

not interested. Would I meet Mr Richardson for a drink? I said, 'All right'. This was how I met this extraordinary young man who, of course, persuaded me to do this short TV play. At the end of it he rang me after we had shot the thing and said, 'Can I come and see you? I want you to criticise my work.' Well, I blenched at this because nobody ever asks you to criticise their work these days ... Anyway, from that there grew a great friendship.[12]

This alliance mystified Devine's friends, but with it came the work which was eventually to provide the foundation of the modern British stage. Devine appears in a short time to have moved to a large extent away from some of the priorities of Saint-Denis and very much towards the idea of new theatre work. He was not by this stage seeking to continue the central focus of the three boys: 'No, not at all. It was a complete break. His only interest was to have a theatre to encourage new writers. That was the basis of it ... It was a break. It was his thing.'[13]

Richardson imported all the enthusiasm of a younger generation and a wealthy patroness. She was Elaine Brunner.

> We went to see Mrs Brunner in Addison Road and she appeared in a Japanese kimono and we had brandies and all that and finally Tony said, 'This is the man who is going to run the theatre.' She said to me, 'What can I do?' and I said, 'I want to have a contemporary theatre. I have been all my life in the classical theatre. I want to try to make the theatre have a different position and have something to say and be part of the intellectual life of the community.' To which she said, 'I quite agree' and then disappeared off the scene.[14]

Richardson himself cannot explain the partnership: 'I don't know whether some subconscious calculation – to ally myself with the mainstream of the British theatre to which I was a complete outsider – underlay the decision. Whatever, it was one of the best – no *the* best – I ever made.'[15] The combination of Devine's theatrical pedigree and Richardson's unfettered energy was potent. They agreed about their

6

objective and began to look for a theatre. There was, of course, no money forthcoming at this stage.

Just as Devine and Richardson were looking for a new theatre, an old one was surfacing. *The Times* of 16 January 1952 reported the acquisition of the Royal Court, Sloane Square, by Alfred Esdaile: 'It will begin its new lease of life in about two months' time as a theatre club ... Work in making good the war damage is now in full swing.'[16] The Court was associated with legendary figures and events, of which perhaps the most celebrated were the four seasons of 1904–8 run by Granville Barker and his business manager, J. E. Vedrenne. The seasons both established Shaw and also produced contemporary British and European plays.[17] According to Jocelyn Herbert, for Devine 'it was the theatre of Shaw ... He tried to get it for years before he did. He never wanted to leave it.'[18]

Esdaile, for First Investa Securities Ltd, signed the lease of the Court on 23 May 1952 by agreement with Cadogan Settled Estates for the term of forty and a half years, running from 29 September 1951. On 15 January 1953, Esdaile concluded another agreement with the British Transport Commission for the lease of land between the Court and Sloane Square underground station, for the same term. The plan was to open the theatre as a club with a limited membership of 3,000 at a subscription of five guineas per head per annum. Use of the club rooms and restaurant was included. Members of the general public could, on payment of five shillings per annum, see the productions without joining the club. On re-opening, the theatre seated 450 people and was, according to *The Times* of 22 March 1952, 'being redecorated in the red and gold of its Edwardian period'.

The Council of the club, which was to be responsible for overall artistic policy, included Giles Playfair as Artistic Director, Dame Sybil Thorndike, Sir Lewis Casson, Joyce Grenfell and Ellen Pollock. A play called *The Bride of Denmark Hill*, about John Ruskin, opened at the Court in the first week of July 1952. The theatre, in *The Times* review of 3 July, is described as 'elegantly intimate in crimson and gold'. By 7 August, the Court was in crisis, as the entire Council resigned. In a statement, the Council, which had advisory powers only, argued that such a position 'is not a practical method of guiding the policy of the theatre'. Playfair's successor as Artistic Director of the club was Oscar Lewenstein. After *The Bride of Denmark Hill*, which transferred to the West End, Frank Baker's play, *Miss Hargreaves*, opened. Lewenstein arranged to import a production of *The Comedy of Errors*, which opened on 27 August 1952.[19] The last show in this sequence was *A Kiss for Adèle*, which opened on 20 November 1952, after which the Court closed for work to be done to gain a licence for public performance.

While Esdaile modernised and improved his theatre, Devine was mapping out his ideas for his theatre and trying to find the money to launch it. The years of 1953 and 1954 saw immense activity and immense frustration. Devine wrote to his friend Mary Hutchinson on 15 March 1953:

> Some months ago you urged me to try and take the Court. I am now working hard on a scheme to do so. My introduction to the idea came about in a very strange way which I will tell you when we meet. Meanwhile, I enclose for your interest, a first draft of our scheme ... I need all the help I can get to raise the necessary capital. I have more or less a promise from the Arts Council for some, but nothing like enough.[20]

'The Royal Court Theatre Scheme' runs through four drafts. The first is dated 16 March 1953; the fourth 13 August 1953. In between, there is a version prepared for The John Lewis Partnership, of 12 April, and another of 10 August titled 'The Mark Turner plan'. The Scheme announces its central beliefs in all versions, although the phrasing is softened on occasions and the opening paragraph of the first version was subsequently left out. It reads: 'The policy of the Royal Court will be to encourage the living drama by providing a theatre where contemporary playwrights may express themselves more freely and frequently than is possible under commercial conditions.' Devine, after all, needed financial backers. The fourth puts it thus:

> Although the major classics are now well catered for by the Old Vic, the Shakespeare Memorial Theatre, Sir John Gielgud's productions, etc, there is no theatre in England which

consistently presents the whole range of contemporary drama. Modern movements in music, sculpture, painting, literature, cinema and ballet all have reasonable circulation, but the comparable body of work in the theatre has no outlet ...

For dramatic development, the urgent need of our time is to discover a truly contemporary style wherein dramatic action, dialogue, acting and method of presentation are all combined to make a modern theatre spectacle, as definite in style as it has been in all the great periods of theatre ...

Of all the theatres in central London, the Royal Court is by far the best suited to such a purpose. The work of Harley Granville Barker, his revolutionary productions of the classics and his presentation of a new school of dramatists give the Royal Court a fine and appropriate tradition.[21]

Devine proposed a three-year period of operation, with Richardson as his assistant. The repertoire would contain as many original plays as possible; a club would be established; training schemes developed; and connections made with comparable enterprises in the other arts.

The scheme both reflects some of the priorities of Michel Saint-Denis and departs from others, especially in its insistence on the primacy of new work. Devine's movement into the area of living contemporary theatre did not suddenly occur. In a British Council lecture in Bristol of October 1948, Devine defined the present as 'a period of transition and reaction – war brought theatre into focus as a popular art – a slow and tardy change of ballet, cinema, radio and television'. The role of the producer as 'the conductor of interpretation [is] to find the heart of the play, to represent the author, to relate the play to the audience so that the impact is real and not theatrical'. Above all, coterie theatre should be banished. Productions 'must be up to date – methods must change. The producer must know his time and be in touch with it – a *popular* art – not for a few special intellectuals.'[22] The significance of these statements of 1948 is that Devine was beginning to develop his own, quite distinctive voice, a voice ironically liberated by the demise of the Vic Scheme and the accident whereby he did acquire the Court.

Throughout 1953, Devine and Richardson looked for funding from any likely source. Richardson wrote to Arnold Goodman for suggestions. Devine contacted Selfridges, Duncan Openheimer, Jean Rowntree, the Hulton Press, T. R. Grieve, and the Peter Jones Theatre Group.[23] The most promising source appeared to be The John Lewis Partnership, owners of Peter Jones, the store opposite the Court in Sloane Square. During the course of a series of letters between Devine and O. B. Miller, Deputy Chairman of the Partnership, a prime example of Devine's pragmatic approach became apparent. Miller, in his letter of 5 May, worried away at the diet of plays proposed in the scheme:

> The first thing that strikes me about it is that most of the plays which I recognise seem to be what I might call rather gloomy in type and my general impression of contemporary drama is that it runs very much to tragedies of the introspective and obsessional types, and to maintain satisfactory audiences year in and year out you would need to have a sufficient admixture of lighter plays as well as other presentations of various kinds.

To which Devine, a day later, replied with all the aplomb of a seasoned handler of potential sponsors:

> I was grateful for and interested in your remarks about the repertoire. I think that this is a justifiable criticism which applies more to the memorandum and the way a repertoire is presented than to our intentions. We are very aware of this danger in the modern 'Art Theatre' and are most anxious to counteract this tendency. We are amending our Memoranda accordingly to include some of the light fare, comedies, farces and musical dramas that we have on our lists.[24]

No such emendations were made, but the reply illustrates the absolute determination of Devine to get his theatre. Anthony Lousada, husband of Jocelyn Herbert, worked tirelessly on Devine's behalf to sort out the legalities of any and all arrangements.[25] However that avenue closed when it became apparent that the Partnership, though keen in principle to help, lost a great deal of money in its dealings during the period of the Korean War.[26] Devine had asked his old friend, Sybil Thorndike, who was also close to Spedan Lewis, founder of the Partnership, to act as go-between with O. B. Miller, then the Chairman Designate. Sybil Thorndike's reaction to the Royal Court Scheme was that it was:

> awfully good – not wildly original as you say but there *is* no theatre in London with these aims in view, is there. I see the [Court's] opening again. Will it make any difference, I wonder, if it's a success to his [Esdaile's] wanting to rent it or sell. I should like to know this before seeing Mr Miller because we would not want to go so far then Esdaile not want to give it up. And an intimate revue might be just the thing to make a success.[27]

She was absolutely right. On 22 April 1953, with Lewenstein now the Court's General Manager, Laurier Lister's *Airs on a Shoe-string* opened at the Court and ran for nearly two years. The revue was said by *Theatre World* (June 1953) to have 'put Sloane Square back on the theatrical map'. It was 'a happy choice to re-open the Royal Court as a public theatre'. Esdaile had a success on his hands and would clearly not be inclined to listen to attempts to buy or rent his theatre. On 1 May he signed an agreement with Clement Freud for a further period of management of the club by Freud.[28] This deal was to cause immense difficulty in the early years of the English Stage Company.

On 12 May 1953 Devine wrote to Esdaile to tell him of his failure to gather the money:

> I have, however, re-opened the matter in detail with the Arts Council and have had a very enthusiastic reception from the highest people there. At the same time I am pursuing other financial possibilities. I just want you to know that I am still determined to make all possible effort to find the money and launch the scheme at your theatre. I would like to ask you, therefore, to be kind enough to inform me if you are at any time thinking of any major deal which would preclude the possibility of my taking the theatre.[29]

In fact the Arts Council's initial suggestion was that Devine might take his scheme to the Westminster theatre, where the London Mask Theatre, under Thane Parker, was sub-letting. Bill Williams, Secretary-General of the Council, liked Devine's scheme and 'felt it to be worth some kind of Arts Council support'.[30] Parker wrote in a lukewarm way to Devine about this on 18 June 1953. The letter is annotated by Devine: 'I have a strong feeling that (a) Thane is getting old and lazy (b) he does not really want to do the scheme but does not want to offend anyone or lose the A.C. £5,000.'[31] On 12 May, the Chairman of the Arts Council, Sir Kenneth Clark, wrote to Devine to praise the scheme: 'I have read your Memorandum which says exactly what I have long hoped that someone would say ... From my memory of the Court Theatre I agree that it would be more agreeable than the Westminster. On the other hand, the Westminster has size and nearness to recommend it and I fancy we should look to whichever one can be had on the best terms.'[32]

Devine's next move was to propose a link with Stratford, a somewhat desperate act, given his manifesto assertion that his principal interest was in new plays, but there seemed to be no alternative. As Devine tells it:

> we sold them the idea of their having a London theatre and we went to Stratford and saw them and said, 'Well you must have an outlet in London – the main problem is that you just perform in Stratford. If you want to get more interesting actors you must have a London outlet.' 'Splendid idea.'[33]

Anthony Quayle's version of this is that Stratford was impelled to try to get a London base because it was becoming 'more and more clear that the Old Vic looked destined to become the National Theatre ... We had to find a London theatre where we could present every sort of play, then change round and bring our own productions into London.'

> We called George Devine in on our discussions and plans, and he was enthusiastic about them. The idea was that Glen would continue to run [Stratford] and while George would be in charge of the London end of things, I would act as a link between the two theatres ... George was asked to go and find a suitable

theatre that might be available ... A month or so passed and we
all met in a friend's flat in Sloane Square. We asked George if he
had found himself a theatre as yet.
'I have indeed,' he said.
'Where? Which one?'
He said, 'Come here'. He led us to the window and pointed
down to the far end of the square. 'That one.' It was the Royal
Court.
'But it's surely not big enough for our needs.' He shrugged.
'Perhaps not. But that's the theatre I want. And that's the
theatre I'm going for. I know it's not any good to you at all, but I
have to follow my own course.'[34]

It's not clear whether Devine was conducting an elaborate bluff to
push Stratford into agreeing to take the Court. What does appear to be
the case is that Quayle and Devine visited Esdaile to open negotiations.
The scheme was backed unanimously by the Arts Council on 14
October 1953.[35] However, by this time Esdaile was very content with
the success of *Airs on a Shoestring* and announced he was unwilling to
let the Court but would sell for £70,000. 'This preposterous figure was,
of course, beyond the bounds of possibility.'[36] The Arts Council
contacted Esdaile who was reported to be unwilling to negotiate. 'I
subsequently had a telephone conversation with Esdaile ... and came
to the conclusion that the Royal Court Theatre was out.'[37]

   This was not only a huge blow to Devine but also to a scheme
proposed by the Arts Council for a theatre 'grid'. A Council report of
16 July 1953 outlined a link between the large repertories in the major
cities of Britain and another link between that group and 'the big No.
1 theatres which work with permanent companies in their own
buildings'.[38] In a colourful metaphor, the report envisaged that 'an
improved and revitalised theatrical current can be generated which
can ... supply the needs of the whole country ... the urgent need is for
more big generating plants evenly spread over the country, or the
London generators may wear out from over centralisation, and their
current of ideas cease'. The scheme proposed by Devine clearly fitted
part of the emerging policy:

This means the creation of one or more 'Art' theatres where a
live and faithful public can be built up for a short run or
repertoire policy for new plays. Such a theatre could very well
form a very profitable part of the 'grid' for all parties concerned,
especially in exchanging new plays that might only warrant
short runs, between London and the provincial cities.

The driving force behind the idea of a grid was the Secretary-General
of the Arts Council, Bill Williams, who spoke for figures like Devine
when he asserted that:

the theatre in London is dominated by show business organised
on strict commercial lines. There are some specially obnoxious
features about the London theatre. One is the profiteering in
bricks and mortar by speculators ... The consequence ... is that
any show which does not reveal immediate signs of a long run
is whipped off at once. The twin mottoes of the London Theatre
are: long run or sudden death.[39]

Early in 1954, Williams offered a personal impression of the
grid proposal, and it becomes clear that the original idea came from
Benn Levy. In a passionate denunciation of an Arts Council drama
policy as 'ineffectual and timid', Williams characterises the contemporary
theatre as being run:

on a lottery basis, and most of the men and women who work
in it have no sort of security. The consequences of this
desperate insecurity are manifold; the wastage or
misapplication of talent; the unwillingness of actors to go to the
provinces lest they miss their bread-and-butter engagements
with the BBC; the broken hearts behind the fancy waistcoats;
the artistic squalor of weekly repertory; the almost total
extinction of studio theatre and similar experimental efforts.[40]

Williams concludes his paper with a scornful glance at a policy
which Devine was to follow for a time at the beginning of the English
Stage Company's history: 'And our latest gropings for a policy find us
toying with dubious schemes for making playwrights out of novelists

and journalists; an endeavour which recalls Swift's satirical project for extracting sunbeams out of cucumbers.'

Williams' analysis echoed the view of John Whiting, who wrote to Devine on 23 August 1953:

> Many thanks for sending me the scheme for the Royal Court Theatre. I've read it with the greatest interest. It's a fine plan – a most exciting and oh so necessary scheme. It is something which must come into being. It must! Such a theatre, I know, would provide such a stimulus to so many people in the theatre in this country. I know because I first read the plan on a train and spent the rest of the journey staring out of the window and dreaming about the kind of plays you could do in such a theatre. And that, my God, is what's needed ... As a playwright – you mentioned this at dinner the other night – there is a play I'm wanting to write which might interest you ... I'd like to talk further. I don't think I've been so excited for ages as when I read what you call your 'screed'. Hell! I wish I had pots of money.[41]

Devine began 1954 with no prospect of realising his dream. The scheme was in abeyance. Devine was asked by John Gielgud, on behalf of the Arts Council, if he might be interested in participating in the establishment of a Sunday Producing Society, but it was small beer.[42] Devine reflected on failure in a letter of April 1954 to Michel Saint-Denis, written from his new home in Lower Mall, Hammersmith:

> I had a rather bad year last year, waiting and hoping for this damned Court scheme and refusing to do anything which might get in the way should it have come off ... and although there have been at least four or five alternative schemes, it all finally came to nothing and I am really left exactly where I was a year ago. I cannot go into all this in a letter: it would take too long but it has been a bitter blow for me and a terrible loss of time. Things were so far advanced that I indicated to the Arts Council I would probably be doing my plan with Stratford and now I have to face Williams again with this fizzled out failure. I am slightly suffering from this setback at the moment but I am

going to start again when I have re-orientated myself. I still
think the scheme is good and right for me but maybe I shall
approach it in a different way.[43]

Nothing better illustrates the absolute stubbornness and determination which is the hallmark of Devine's work than this letter. He
could have been forgiven for simply abandoning the project and
remaining a freelance artist. That he did not is remarkable. That he
gained the Royal Court in a massively ironic context is even more
remarkable. On the day Devine wrote this letter to his great friend,
Oscar Lewenstein was writing to a librettist and playwright, Ronald
Duncan, about plans to launch a management for the performance of
non-commercial plays. The two utterly different theatrical strands
were to combine and allow Devine to take the Court and create the
English Stage Company.[44]

1   Coincidences, 1954–1956

Ronnie was at Cambridge with Eric Bessborough, as indeed I was ... Eric and I had adjacent rooms in 16 Jesus Lane so we got to know each other and then Ronnie suggested I come into the English Stage Society, as it was then ... a few days later I bumped into Eric and he said, 'Oh, I hear we're going to join up company with the English Stage Society'. 'Oh', I said, 'Have you been asked on it too?' He said, 'Yes'. So I said, 'What fun'.

(Interview with Greville Poke, March 1994)

The emergence of the English Stage Company came about by a combination of unpredictable and bizarre circumstances. As Devine regrouped, one strand of the combination was forming in Devon. *The Times* for 22 April 1953 reported the creation of the Taw and Torridge Festival of the Arts. The prime mover in this was Ronald Duncan, a playwright and librettist, together with Lord Harewood and Edward Blacksell, a Barnstaple schoolmaster, both Duncan's friends. The Festival offered in July E. Martin Browne's production of Duncan's *Don Juan*, Britten's *Let's Make an Opera* and his version of Gay's *The Beggar's Opera*, together with Eliot reading his own work and a 'Soirée Musicale' with Peter Pears and Britten himself. The Minutes of the first meeting of the Festival Council, held on 5 December 1953, saw Harewood appointed Chairman, Duncan and Blacksell Council members and a galaxy of prominent figures becoming Vice-Presidents, including Britten, T. S. Eliot, Jacob Epstein, Robert Helpmann, Henry Moore, Ezra Pound, Jeremy Thorpe and Henry Williamson.

The 1954 Festival saw productions of *The Cocktail Party* and Duncan's *The Death of Satan*. These were created by a local group as opposed to the works performed by the English Opera Group. It was the inability of the Festival to attract to Devon professional theatre companies that created in Duncan the desire to establish a theatre

17

company analogous to the English Opera Group. Such a company would concentrate in part on plays having difficulty in finding a production with commercial companies. This included work by Ronald Duncan himself, thought by some to be a major talent. Blacksell wrote to Harewood on 4 January 1954 to say that 'I think it is most important to put on a play by Ronnie if at all possible. I believe his work is a major contribution to our time so that the Festival performs an important function in giving him an audience ... since it is difficult to see how he can out-Rattigan Rattigan in the West End.'[1] Blacksell further tells Harewood that the Festival was trying to promote Duncan's *Don Juan* and *The Death of Satan* by writing to Donald Wolfit, the celebrated actor-manager, and by arranging a series of performances at other theatres and festivals. It is clearly the case that the promotion of Duncan's plays formed the main impetus towards establishing a company. It is equally clear that what evolved was in no one's mind at this point. Thus, while it is true that Duncan began a process which eventually turned into the ESC, it is not true that he founded the ESC.

Duncan began at this stage, April 1954, a lengthy correspondence with Oscar Lewenstein, now Alfred Esdaile's General Manager at the Royal Court. Attempts had been made to secure a production of the two Duncan plays either at the Embassy Theatre or in the West End. Lewenstein felt that the plays should be strongly cast and had asked Alan Badel and Claire Bloom.[2] This intriguing letter also demonstrates that the primary backer of the venture was Sir Reginald Kennedy-Cox, who was taking advice from Hugh Hunt. Kennedy-Cox, Chairman of the Salisbury Arts Theatre, had put up £2,000, with a proviso which was to cause difficulty in the early years of the Court, that a young protégé of his, George Selway, play a major part. In speaking of this years later, Devine described Kennedy-Cox as a 'weird man ... who was friendly with Ronnie and he was a sort of rather a rich, old queer, and he said he would support the thing because it was going to give encouragement to new, young talent. I said to Tony, "I know what that means." And of course, sure enough, three days later there came a letter saying he was very interested in this young actor called X.'[3] Also evident here is Lewenstein, the budding impresario. It

was an aspect of his work which caused some uneasiness later at the
Court. Here he advised Duncan that they should

> First get Sir Reginald's money tied up. Second see if we can cast
> either or both plays in such a way as to justify a West End
> production ... Thirdly, if we cannot get West End names, then
> arrange a production at the Embassy and, if we are still in time,
> also combine this with a production at the Festival.[4]

By 29 April, the position was that Bloom, Badel and Michael
Redgrave had turned the offer down. Paul Scofield was next and
Trevor Howard after that. Hugh Hunt, still very much on the scene,
gave the plays to Donald Sinden, who was apparently keen. This was,
however, not for an Embassy production; the initial drive was to the
West End and not any form of fringe or experimental theatre.[5] By now,
Lewenstein was moving towards presenting the work himself at the
Embassy. He also, importantly, proposed that a company be formed.
The question of a name for the company arose. Lewenstein suggested
the 'English Theatre Group' but Hugh Hunt felt the name was too
close to the 'English Opera Group' to be accepted. Lewenstein offered
'Contemporary Theatre' or 'Modern Theatre' and described a seven-
strong directorate of himself, Duncan, Harewood, Duncannon,
Britten, and possibly their legal advisor, Isador Caplan.[6] A seventh
figure was to be found. Four of these names appeared on the list of
members of the Court's first Council.

On 2 June 1954, Lewenstein reported to Duncan that there
already was a company called the 'English Theatre Guild', which
meant that anything with 'English Theatre' in it was not allowable by
the Registrar of Companies.[7] In the same letter, the original notion of
Duncan's plays being presented is expanded to include *The Threepenny Opera* (a favourite of Lord Harewood's) and *Cock-a-Doodle-
Dandy*. Esdaile is to be put on the board and will allow the new
company to use the Royal Court as an office. Thirteen days later, *The
Crucible* was added to the list.

The negotiations for a theatre and for a star continued. Lewenstein lunched with Hugh Hunt on 13 July to find that Scofield was
still deliberating, but that Thane Parker of the London Mask Theatre

would be prepared to lease the Westminster for £150 per week. At the same time, Brecht's representative told Lewenstein that the rights for *The Threepenny Opera* were available 'but since the play's success in Paris and New York, Brecht has set a higher value on it!'[8]

By 16 July 1954, the company had become 'The English Stage Society Ltd' and by 21 July the seven directors were Lord Harewood, Duncannon (now Earl of Bessborough), Sir Reginald Kennedy-Cox, Alfred Esdaile, Ronald Duncan, Oscar Lewenstein and Greville Poke.[9] This in fact comprises, with one name to be added, the Council of the English Stage Company later. Duncan set about building his list of Vice-Presidents, including Christopher Fry who replied saying, 'I should be delighted to be included as a vice-president of the English Stage Society if it's any help.'[10] In essence, the structure of the Taw and Torridge Festival was to be imported as the structure of the new company, together with, implicitly, the Festival's beliefs and objectives. However, an early blow was the decision by Lord Harewood not to be Chairman. Apart from being very occupied with many other artistic schemes, Harewood, astutely enough, pointed out his lack of 'practical experience of how any theatrical enterprise is run, apart that is to say from those connected with opera ... it must be someone who can be frequently in London, and someone who is prepared to take on the responsibility for the running of the company.'[11] As he later commented, 'I then performed the greatest service I ever did for the ESC, by refusing to be its Chairman.'[12]

On 16 October 1954, the *Memorandum and Articles of Association of the English Stage Society Ltd* was published. Finally there were eight directors of the Company, with Blacksell's name added to the original list. Less than a month later, the company name was changed. It was pointed out by Sir St Vincent Troubridge of the Lord Chamberlain's Office, apparently with some strength of feeling, that using the chosen name more than trespassed on the Stage Society of the early years of the century. The Company then proposed two alternative names but

> It is not possible for the Registrar (of Companies) to approve the name 'The English Stage Guild Ltd', because it conflicts with

the existing organisation 'English Theatre Guild', and accordingly we have fallen back on our second choice, which is 'The English Stage Company Ltd'.[13]

If the combination, eventually, of the Devon group and the Devine/ Richardson partnership, is to be seen as wonderfully coincidental, it is surely a further irony that the 'society' and the 'guild' gave way to the 'company'. It is a further example of the amateur in the best sense confronting the highly professional. When Devine met this group, it is unsurprising that he regarded it with suspicion, since it carried in many ways the marks of the theatre attitudes he most resented and from which he wished to free the English theatre. These attitudes ran through the new Council even as far as the appointment of a Press Officer. George Fearon, who was to clash frequently with Devine, had been Press Officer for the Taw and Torridge Festival and, as will be evident, regarded Devine as an employee much like himself. The freeing of the Artistic Director from hireling to policy maker, together with the gradual diminution of the executive function of the Council, formed one of the great struggles of the early years of the Court. It is a constant feature but one most in evidence when Devine was Artistic Director.

The Council of the Company held its first meeting on 26 October 1954. Poke was appointed Honorary Secretary; A. T. Chenalls & Co were to be Auditors; and Forsyte, Kerman and Phillips were to be the Company's Solicitors. Current plans included *The Threepenny Opera* with Peter Ustinov; the presentation of plays at Aldeburgh, Glyndebourne and Devon; and obtaining the use of the Westminster or Embassy Theatre. There was as yet no formal Chairman of the Company, but in the Minutes of its second meeting on 19 November, the name of Neville Blond appears for the first time.

Blond's name was suggested by Blacksell and, it is thought by some, by Blond's solicitor, Isador Caplan.[14] Blacksell's connection with Blond was via the Blonds' support for the plastic surgery work at the Queen Victoria Hospital, East Grinstead, by Archibald McIndoe. Blacksell was a wartime sergeant there. Whichever is correct, it is certainly the case that Blond was invited to lunch by Duncan and

Poke after being asked by Council to approach him. Duncan had lunched with Blond two days earlier and both had gone to see Esdaile in his Park Lane office. Poke recalled that

> I arranged a lunch party at the Garrick consisting of you, Neville and myself. In your article[15] you say you wondered if you had enough money to pay for the lunch. You never did! I did! It was over that lunch – historic in its way – after you had explained the aims and objects of the English Stage Company that Neville bowled us over by saying that without a London theatre as a base, our ideas would not work, and if we could find such a theatre he would join us. We reported our conversation to the Council and Alfred Esdaile then offered to sell us the derelict Kingsway Theatre which he owned ... Neville joined us and he, Oscar and I bore the brunt of the negotiations with Alfred and eventually bought the property from him. It was a matter of some excitement that this was to be the first new theatre after the war in London.[16]

On 30 November, Blond was elected Chairman of the ESC at a Council meeting. He had studied a memorandum by Esdaile about the Kingsway Theatre. Esdaile maintained that he had suspended negotiations with an American at the request of Mr Blond. His discussion with Mr Blond therefore was not with the idea of material gain to himself, but with a view to helping the English Stage Company (Minutes, 19 November). The self-justifying tone of these remarks is entirely characteristic of Esdaile's association with the Court.

Blond by now had begun the kind of work he was good at. A private meeting between him, Duncan and Esdaile had been held on 12 November to discuss the circumstances of the Kingsway. Esdaile's projected costs were between £65,000 and £75,000. He was prepared to let the theatre for forty-two years at a rental of £5,000 per annum for the sum of £60,000. Writing to Blond on 12 November, Esdaile's solicitor, said that 'Mr Esdaile knows that the English Stage Co Ltd have no finance as yet but ... he could, no doubt, arrange for a substantial part of the consideration to be left on mortgage ... if they could get together £15,000–20,000 they could, in six to eight months' time have the theatre themselves'. On 29 November, Blond received a positive report on the Kingsway from an estate agent. By late December, however, no licence was apparent, and Blond, in his element, was telling the Company lawyers that 'Mr Alfred Esdaile ... is of no interest to us unless we are satisfied he has in fact the licence.'[17]

If the best service Harewood did for the ESC was to decline to be its Chairman, the best service Lewenstein did was to find the ESC's Artistic Director. Recalling Devine's earlier approaches to Esdaile, Lewenstein went in the autumn of 1954 to the Westminster Theatre where Devine was playing Tesman in *Hedda Gabler*. From nowhere within the theatrical establishment had Devine been able to develop his plans. Now, it appeared, the offer was available from the most unlikely source. This case was inadvertently strengthened by a glowing account of him as 'a complete man of the theatre'.[18] The portrait was occasioned by his production of Walton's *Troilus and Cressida* at Covent Garden. It is an account of Devine which would without doubt have appealed to the Council of the ESC. Indeed, when Devine accepted the part of Artistic Director, thousands of copies of the piece were ordered for publicising purposes.

Lewenstein accurately points up the ironies of the situation and the offer to Devine to become the first Artistic Director of the ESC:

> George had to be interested, though it came from such an
> unlikely source. I say 'unlikely' because George Devine's career
> had been at the centre of English theatrical life. Starting off as
> President of OUDS, he had worked with all the great names:
> Laurence Olivier, Peggy Ashcroft, Michael Redgrave. Although
> there had always been an unconventional side to his character,
> he was basically an 'insider' whereas we of the ESC, even
> Ronnie, were theatrical 'outsiders'. George Devine belonged to
> the central magic circle, we did not.[19]

Clearly, the perception of Devine as an establishment figure would appeal to the ESC Council. Equally clearly, Devine did nothing to dispel it. He lunched with Duncan and Harewood on 20 January 1955. The following day, Duncan wrote to Devine to say that 'George

Harewood and I enjoyed very much talking to you the other day at luncheon. It's very gratifying to know that we think on similar lines.'[20] On the same day Duncan wrote to Blond to say that Devine 'is full of ideas and most anxious to see a plan of the Kingsway stage with its dimensions'. The idea that Duncan and Devine would agree on policy is feasible only if it is remembered that Devine was ruthless in pursuit of an objective, as was evident in his earlier dealings with The John Lewis Partnership. There is no record of the lunch but Duncan was demonstrably deceived. At a later date he reflected sourly that Devine said 'he was in complete agreement. I believed him. I was never a judge of character.'[21] As Harewood put it, Devine 'told the truth but not the whole truth'.[22]

Before Devine met Duncan and Harewood, he had checked on Blond. A friend of his 'made some enquiries in the city and my friends do not know much about him as he comes from the North of England but he is supposed to have large textile interests ... They think that he would be a reliable man to deal with but nobody can, of course, say whether he is sympathetic to the Arts. PS. One rumour said he was rather attracted to the [drawing of a whisky bottle].'[23] At the same time, Devine began to write a series of notes, between 6 January and 15 February, all theoretical, all to do with the requirements of a new theatre and a new stage. He was very clear about one essential:

What is needed, however, is not adaptability, or a synthesis of the past but for the theatre to create a new milieu in modern terms which will be a completely fresh restatement of the old traditions. In fact, we have once more to sweep the stage clear as Copeau did with his *Trétau nu*, and to rethink the whole conception of the stage as an acting space. In what kind of space can the words of a dramatist both live and create the poetic world of the drama?

The stage must have space and air and freedom from the trappings which are used to pretend that it is something which it is not. In an indoor theatre must be created the same state of frankness and clarity which appertains to an architectural open air theatre.[24]

24

'Percy' Harris's comments are incisive. She agreed about illusion: 'discard all things destroying illusion but consider the question of distraction and have a point of view about this ... Can such a performance as you give as Tesman work as completely without the illusion of reality, especially in costume? What would be the point of view about costume?' Harris's main theme is

> not to try and conceal construction but to make it part of the
> design: in fact to feature it as being the leading part of the
> design because in fact it is. And not decorate it or hide it or put
> something on the other side to balance it or pretend it is
> something else: in fact *not to pretend at all*, which is something
> to do with the basis of your idea.[25]

Tony Richardson's notes react strongly and positively to Devine's notion, as expressed on 6 January, of giving the stage 'air and freedom'. As he puts it, 'This seems to me the first major attempt to re-evaluate the theatre design in contemporary terms.' For Richardson, the notes by Devine 'conceive the theatre in our terms and align it with the whole contemporary movement in architecture and it's there I'm sure the future must lie'.[26]

By 23 January the notes achieve some sort of synthesis. Devine is also, from hard-won experience, realistic: 'I use the words "fought for" advisedly because I am sure it will be difficult to convince people that it will be worth while to do the work, and to find the way to fit such ideas into a theatre which will, in all likelihood, be structurally conventional.'[27] He still had not received the plans of the Kingsway. The final version of the memorandum was sent to Harewood and Duncan. They were extremely enthusiastic and proposed 'a drawing of our own which would then give Esdaile and his architect a precise idea of what we want.'[28]

Devine, however, was only a potential employee of the ESC and had no say in policy at this stage. Indeed, the Council meeting for 17 January 1955 resolved that staff for the Kingsway be engaged 'in the following order of priority: (a) Club Manager (b) Artistic Director (c) Theatre Manager'. Moreover, when Lewenstein suggested that Devine be invited to the Council's next meeting he was told that Devine could be invited when the Kingsway work was nearer completion. The manner in which Devine and some of his artistic colleagues were regarded was another area of struggle in the next few years.

News of the renovation of the Kingsway began to circulate. The BBC interviewed Esdaile on 21 January, on which occasion he said that he 'would like to see the Kingsway as another centre of London play-going in the old style – a place reminding you of the good old days with people dressing for dinner and regularly and devotedly going to their old, friendly little theatre'.[29] Given this view, a clash was inevitable, and it was to last until Devine resigned. It is the case that Esdaile was utterly unused to any director having views about the running of a theatre. Such a person was hired to produce the play and not formulate policy, still less draw up plans for the redesigning of a theatre. He obviously objected to Devine's memorandum since, on 9 February, Blond sent him a sharp note: 'What is something theoretical and idealistic might well be something practical and I do not think we should treat this project for a new stage lightly.'[30] On the same day, Blond affirmed to Devine that he had spoken to Esdaile 'and he says he will be delighted to work with you in regard to the theatre and the decor'.[31] Devine had still not agreed to accept the job at the ESC and Blond worked hard to keep all the parties together. To Blacksell he wrote privately that 'I hope they do not land me with the whole thing – that is the only thing I am afraid of. As I have informed the noble Earl, I am not "carrying the can back" and I am going to exploit him in the fullest.' He then asked Harewood to look after the artistic side while he looked after the business side. It should be remembered at this point that Blond knew nothing about theatre or theatre people. He had this in common with the majority of the ESC Council, but he was shrewd enough to leave that to Harewood. In so doing, he unwittingly enabled the ESC to survive, for Harewood proved to be both a protector of Devine and a formidable and clever negotiator with Blond. Without such a talented buffer figure, the enterprise would not have lasted.

At the 7 February Council, the membership of committees was decided. An Artistic Sub-Committee, chaired by Harewood, would also have Duncan and Lewenstein as members, and a Finance Sub-

Committee was to consist of Esdaile (Chair), Poke and Lewenstein. The Arts Council representative made a first appearance at this meeting. This was Jo Hodgkinson, recently appointed to head drama.[32] Two days later, Devine lunched with Harewood, Duncan and Blond 'and it looks to me that Mr Devine is going to work for us – I only hope he does not ask for too much money'.[33] Devine asked for another meeting with Blond before finally committing himself and it is not difficult to imagine Devine's excitement but also caution. He had been in this kind of situation before, either as part of a scheme which was destroyed (the Vic Scheme) or a scheme which had collapsed (the earlier Court) and he was now close to yet another attempt to go on with his work. Also on offer was the Headship of the Royal Academy of Dramatic Art. This he turned down, and he received a letter from Harewood expressing his delight that Devine was 'disposed' to join the ESC. Harewood also refers to Devine's final memorandum on the Kingsway:

> I think your new memorandum is explicit and helpful, but it
> has put the wind up Mr Esdaile who, all the same, eats out of
> Blond's velvet-gloved but definitely iron hand. I think we shall
> get a bit of what we want if we can formulate reasonably exact
> demands.[34]

The general feeling was that Esdaile was not entirely to be trusted. Blond pushed the affair along, asking Devine for a model of the new stage, for 'It is of the utmost importance that we know where we are and that we are not presented with a "fait accompli" ' (Blond to Poke, 23 February 1955).

Blond duly lunched with Devine on 24 February and Devine laid out his terms on 26 February. He accepted a minimum salary of £1,560 p.a. (£30 per week) but reserved the right 'to study the planning and the budget' before confirming. The salary was very low for such an appointment and Devine insisted that it be reviewed at the earliest opportunity,[35] and that Tony Richardson become his Associate. Blond was pleased with his bargain and, in a nicely ironic letter to Poke of 23 February, his pleasure is apparent: 'I was very much impressed with his approach to our problem and I really think this is just the kind of fellow we need to have. I hope you will all be as happy as I am with him.'

The ESC now had its major figures in place. As negotiations for the Kingsway proceeded, *Airs on a Shoestring* closed at the Court on 5 March after 770 performances. Devine was officially appointed two days earlier. The significant fact for the ESC was that the next show at the Court, also brought in by Lister and called 'The Burning Boat', began on 10 March and was withdrawn after only a few performances. Its replacement was 'Uncertain Joy', which opened at the Court on 31 March and transferred to the Duchess on 20 June. While *Airs on a Shoestring* ran so well (Poke's view was that 'Alfred thought it was going to become a sort of *Mousetrap*, and it was going to go on forever'[36]), Esdaile comfortably dealt with the ESC in relation to the Kingsway. He changed his view once his 'Mousetrap' ended.

It was at this stage that the ESC produced the brochure containing its 'Aims and Objects'. The first of these had been prepared on 3 December 1954. The aims were to present plays by modern authors; to present 'from time to time' a London season; to visit other festivals; to play at venues which could not support a theatre; to tour contemporary English plays abroad; to stimulate new unity; 'to encourage the theatre of imagination and poetry as against the theatre which predominates today'. Versions in early 1955 carried illustrations of the Kingsway Theatre, complete with limousines, chauffeurs and a doorman. Devine is described as the 'Art Director'. A brochure dated 5 April 1955 replaces the Kingsway illustration with John Piper's version of the top part of a monument erected at Stowe in honour of Congreve. It shows a monkey looking in a mirror, representing, according to Piper, the stage as a mirror of life.[37] Reaction to the monkey was swift. Blond wrote to Poke on 14 March: 'The brochure looks very good apart from the drawing by John Piper which I hope to speak to you about.' Lewenstein asked for it to be removed in a letter to Poke of 8 April and it eventually was.

More indicative of the struggle to come was the action Duncan was taking. A Council of 21 February had authorised him to contact Eliot, Fry and others 'to discover whether they would be willing to offer a play to the English Stage Company'. On 11 March, Duncan wrote to John Whiting and Peter Ustinov on the matter,[38] in terms which indicate how well he thought of himself and his role in the company: 'As you may know, I have formed the English Stage Company.' There's no reference to any consultation with Devine, since the idea that Devine should be consulted would not have arisen. Equally, on 21 March, Duncan sent off to the printers of the brochure the celebrated statement of artistic support: 'The following artists support our aims, and the Company hopes to present their work: T. S. Eliot, Christopher Fry, Peter Ustinov, John Whiting, Ronald Duncan, Berthold Brecht, Gabriel Marcel, Benjamin Britten, John Piper.' This brought a rapid response from Lewenstein (Devine was abroad with *Hedda Gabler*). On 8 April he wrote to Poke objecting to the list and, in particular, to the inclusion of Brecht's name. This was partly because he was concluding agreements with Brecht's agent to produce *The Threepenny Opera*. He also states bluntly that 'I am sure we have never been asked to pass this wording.' Though 'support' in the statement was replaced by 'in sympathy with', the names, with the exception of Brecht, remained. None of the writers, except Duncan himself, ever had work done at the Court and when, in 1960, Duncan famously inveighed against Devine for breaking his promise, he conveniently forgot that he alone made the list and had it put in the 'Aims and Objects'. Council had been told by Duncan on 21 March that Eliot had suggested the ESC consider optioning *The Family Reunion*, and that Whiting would send the play he was currently writing. It's worth stressing that Devine did not at this stage go to Council meetings. The relationship between Council, which made executive decisions, and its Artistic Director was that of employer and employee and remained so for some time. Devine made his first appearance at a Council meeting on 28 April. He had returned from Europe on 24 March.

It was at the 28 April Council that the Artistic Sub-Committee made its first report. It proposed a plan of operation of true repertory, with eight plays in the repertoire over a forty-week period. These plays would consist of three original plays by British authors, a British revival, two translations, a mixed bill of short plays and a classic. The report was approved, as was Lewenstein's budget. Esdaile assured

Council that by 17 July he would be able to give a definite date for completion of the work on the Kingsway. This would enable the first season to begin on 23 January 1956. Esdaile further undertook to approach the Masons, who owned the adjacent bombed site, with a view to renting it to provide a workshop and storeroom for the ESC. Finally, Blond guaranteed Esdaile against any loss incurred in the structural alterations of the Kingsway if the ESC failed.

Devine instinctively mistrusted Esdaile. On 4 May, he drafted a prophetic note to Blond: 'I am far from convinced that he wants all this, although in front of you he always sings to your tune. It is not to his taste and, as he took some pains to explain to me *after* you left, from *his* point of view, the more conventional the theatre, the better.' Devine felt that Esdaile was going to carry on as though the ESC did not exist until the contract was signed and the money in the bank: 'To be obliged to listen to my advice or opinion is useless, as he will wriggle his way out of anything, unless constrained.'[39] As Devine voiced his growing concern, elsewhere Osborne recorded in his diary for 4 May 1955: 'Began writing *Look Back in Anger* ... Friday, May 13th: Went to see *Hedda Gabler*.'[40]

Towards the end of May, Harewood wrote to Blond about Esdaile's choosing a House Manager. Esdaile wanted a certain Herbert Ray. When Devine asked to meet Ray, Esdaile said bluntly that it was not Devine's business. Harewood and his committee 'were really seriously concerned to hear of such a show of hand from Esdaile, which confirms the fears that I for one have had all along ... how can we accept such an appointment without the backing of our Artistic Director – and why should we? It seems to me crucial that Devine should be concerned in the selection of *all senior personnel*.' This worry is critical. The struggle involved here stands for the overall struggle of the emerging job of Artistic Director of a theatre in the modern world, and Harewood, as always, was sensitive to it. Esdaile has

> so far acted exclusively as the vendor of the property we want to acquire, not at all as one of our directors. I myself can only view this latest effort to force one of his nominees on us *without an*

interview with the artistic head of the enterprise as something to be strongly resisted. We – and that includes Esdaile – have chosen Devine as the man to give practical and artistic expression to the Company's objects, and we must rely on his enormous theatrical knowledge and experience to help us.[41]

Harewood further urged Blond to import a consultant architect to supervise the decorative scheme. If this isn't done, 'We shall have Esdaile's gilt-and-plush everywhere (I started to type "guilt", so you can see the way my mind is working!).'

Blond replied to what he called Harewood's '*cri de coeur*' letter and assured Harewood things were all under control. He also soothed Esdaile, 'who wanted to resign, but I told him that it was very silly to take his wickets [*sic*] home and not play with us' (2 June). To some extent, Blond was in his element. However, he appears not to have realised how close he came to losing his Artistic Director over the question of who ruled the roost in some areas. Poke reported to Blond on 6 June that Esdaile was in the habit of saying to Devine, 'I am the Gov'nor around here', not a sentiment likely to appeal to Devine. The problem was compounded by the fact that Devine was even then beginning a seven-month tour for Stratford with *Much Ado About Nothing* and his remarkable production of what became known as the 'Noguchi' *Lear*.[42]

In early July, there occurs the first reference to the Royal Court. At a Council held on 5 July, a piece of paper was circulated on which is scribbled: 'How do you react to leasing the Royal Court Theatre from December as an alternative pending the Kingsway being built?' This is in Lewenstein's hand. Below it, Duncan's reaction is 'Not worthwhile if Kingsway can open early 1956.' Harewood's note is: 'The point is if; we ought not to open in any other theatre than the Kingsway, *unless* there will be a long stay, and the Kingsway not ready until, say, mid-1956.' This thought is clearly occasioned by the delays in work on the Kingsway and the fact that the Court was not enjoying a long run. Working with Esdaile did not get easier. As reported by Poke to Blond on 18 June, Esdaile refused to show his lighting plans to Devine because he did not want them vetted.

Despite talk of the Court, the work on the Kingsway went on and a party to launch the Company was announced for 20 July in the Kingsway itself. The Council for 18 July was introduced to a Paul Anstey who undertook to decorate the theatre in 'an appropriate way'. He had a plan 'for making the auditorium look as if the builders were really in, with ladders, pots of paint, odd bits of scenery and builders' materials lying around'. An elaborate deception was about to take place. In the same meeting, Esdaile offered the ESC its eventual home. This means that the famous occasion when Blond passed Poke the note which read 'Alfred says would we like the Court instead of the Kingsway and I scribbled on the note, "not half" and handed it back to him' must have taken place at a Council meeting earlier than 18 July.[43] It was not realised at the time that Esdaile had a very good reason for the offer. It became apparent that the Masons 'wanted the Kingsway to extend and they made Alfred a fantastic offer, which made him want to get out of his obligation to us'.[44] It was perfect for Esdaile. He made money from selling the Kingsway; he could appear to be acting generously in offering the ESC the Court. And he could off-load a theatre which, since *Airs on a Shoestring* had closed, had not done particularly well.

Devine, on the other hand, having had a model of the new stage prepared by Jocelyn Herbert, saw the prospect of a new theatre from the floor up, disappear, even if the new offer was for the theatre he had most wanted. Harewood met Devine before 15 July 'and I then explained the position about the Kingsway Theatre and the Court Theatre, and found that he inclined to my own view – that we are publicly committed to the Kingsway Theatre, and ... Only if it seems unlikely that it will be finished in time should we consider the Court Theatre' (to Poke, 15 July). Poke, however, could see some advantages: 'The more I think of the Royal Court, the more I like it. To have a theatre without having to find a heavy capital sum is attractive' (to Blond, 30 July).

In fact, Devine knew about the offer. He received a telephone call from Esdaile on 4 April. His notes record 'incl. bars ... the whole shoot ... Says no structural alterations ... absolutely perfect'.[45] In 1965, he recalled the moment. Esdaile telephoned him with the offer:

I flipped naturally, with the history of that theatre and said, 'sure' ... I went round and the place was in a frightful mess. It was very poorly re-installed. Esdaile kept saying, 'It's a lovely theatre, beautiful condition, the switchboard ...' Well you couldn't touch the switchboard without getting a 1,000-volt shock ... But I wasn't telling them ... I wasn't really going to be fool enough to tell them what it was going to cost them to put the place in order.[46]

By this stage, the launch of the ESC had taken place in the shell of the Kingsway on 21 July, at which gathering the purpose of the new venture was explained. By 8 August, the ESC had formally accepted the invitation to move into the Court. The lease was for thirty-five years at the rate of £5,000 per annum; a capital payment immediately of £5,000, and the repayment of another £20,000 over ten years. Devine had concerns and requests very quickly; on 15 August he wrote to ask Blond about the chances of acquiring the derelict cottages at the back of the theatre.

The meeting of the Artistic Sub-Committee of 24 August noted that *Look Back in Anger* had been read by Devine, Duncan and Lewenstein 'and it was thought to be a very promising find, although a difficult play to swallow'. Osborne was to be offered £25 for a short option.[47] The play was one of 675 received in response to an advertisement by the ESC.[48] Other writers discussed by the Committee included Sean O'Casey with *Cock-a-Doodle-Dandy*, Miller's *The Crucible*, Brecht's *The Good Woman of Setzuan* and a Lorca play. Whiting's new play would not be ready for the season but, as Duncan reported, Eliot had given permission for the Company to do *Sweeney Agonistes*. Devine proposed to open the season with the O'Casey. It was objected that he was not British. Devine had opted for Brecht and Lorca. It was objected that there were not translations. Devine also conceived the notion of novelists writing plays. One of the authors he had contacted was Nigel Dennis who had replied in September 1955 to say that he 'very much appreciated your letter: thank you for your interest. The only play I have ever written is 'The Prince of Antioch' in *Cards of Identity*. Is there any hope of your being interested in that?'[49] Another writer was suggested by John Lehmann of the *London Magazine*:

> my very best wishes for the success of your venture. During the last ten years or more I have frequently tried to persuade such writers as V. S. Pritchett and Henry Green, whose skill with dialogue is particularly outstanding, to write for the theatre, but without much success. If you can persuade them that it's going to be much more rewarding than it looks, more power to your elbow ... Angus Wilson has just had a play accepted by the Bristol Old Vic; he might be very good indeed.[50]

At the beginning of September, Devine proposed to the Artistic Sub-Committee a number of Sunday rehearsed readings for promising but not yet performable plays. These became the 'Sunday Nights' which began in May 1957. He also wrote an important document about the stage at the Court. He knew that he would have an opportunity when back on tour for Stratford to see Brecht's theatre but

> Before I see the Brecht theatre, I want to develop my own mind about the stage of the Royal Court. This is a small stage in a small theatre. It will be difficult to 'work', being small. Elaborate or complicated mechanisms will be an encumbrance and defeat their own ends ... The problem is how to create, in that limited and encumbered area, a feeling of space and air. It is an architectural/sculptural/stage design problem ...
>
> Some form of masking is essential for reasons of economy and time ... How flexible must it be? And how rigid? Too much flexibility means nothing, too much rigidity kills ... Our solution must appear to be essential, as opposed to ideological, functional as opposed to decorative, natural as opposed to theoretical ... We do not want to say, 'Look, there is nothing up our sleeve' BUT 'Yes, there is plenty up our sleeve but we do not want to pretend that we have nothing' – for the pretence starts in the scenery, lights, costumes, acting and words, all specifically inspired by the dramatic action. It is these thoughts

which bring me back always to the idea of suggesting solidity without actually having it ... There are two main ways in which this idea of space/air may be created on a limited stage inside a building; by the shape and direction of the masking – suggesting that the limiting planes do not end but lead to further space; by the material of the masking – suggesting that air can pass through, that the solidity is conventional rather than pictorial/actual ... We want something that will seem as impermanent and of the moment as the life that takes place on the stage, which lives and dies in less than a second ... Next instalment – all the answers![51]

Not only is this paper written before Devine saw Brecht's theatre, but it, together with his theoretical papers focused on the Kingsway, establishes him as a theatre thinker of importance, perhaps a good antidote to the avuncular image sometimes thought accurately to characterise him.

By 13 September the first season consisted of O'Casey, Miller, Duncan, Osborne and Brecht. Devine was due to meet Brecht on 18 September. Given the objections to the O'Casey opening, Devine was at pains to stress that at that stage the ESC did not have an opening play. Duncan, Harewood and Poke were strongly of the view that the opening season should contain a preponderance of English plays: 'Authors like Brecht are no doubt of some importance in their proper place but he is German ... Speaking personally, having read *Cock-a-Doodle-Dandy* I am against its inclusion altogether because it is a mad Irish play which in my opinion can only be done by Irishmen with that wonderful flair for putting over the blarney' (Poke to Blond, 22 September). Clearly the relationship between Devine and some members of the ESC would never be resolved in some areas, particularly to do with taste. Many issues were being raised which would take a long time to resolve. The question of play-reading was central and begins to appear as an impending conflict. Another was publicity. No one had told George Fearon, the Press Officer, of the move to the Court. He was, not unreasonably, angry at going ahead with publicity for the Kingsway, only to find it a waste of time. It is one of the few times Fearon was entitled to sympathy. He wrote to Poke on 5 October to say he was 'Furious! More Furious!! Most Furious!!!'.

At the 19 October Council, the central issue was that of the opening play. Blond was obviously nervous that a play was not in place and good publicity time was being wasted. Esdaile, who at this meeting was confirmed as the ESC Vice-Chairman, 'urged that the Company should obtain the services of two good stars to open. Lord Harewood pointed out that Mr Devine had this matter well in hand.' If Esdaile wanted stars, Kennedy-Cox wanted to make a star. It was for this purpose that he had put up his £2,000 for Duncan's original venture. Letters from Kennedy-Cox to the ESC run through 1955 and 1956 and raise a serious matter of principle, for the money was conditional upon George Selway playing second lead parts in ESC productions. Devine, unsurprisingly, objected strongly. Poke reported to Blond in a letter of 24 October that he felt Devine was 'taking an entirely unrealistic view of this matter. Nobody admires anyone more than I do for acting on principle ... and quite rightly, he says he is not going to have bad actors and actresses foisted on him for money [but] People who can put up £2,000 are not found on every tree [and] Selway is practically Sir Reginald's adopted son.' Eventually, Devine was persuaded to see Selway and some other actors so lauded by Kennedy-Cox. Devine wrote to Kennedy-Cox on 30 January 1956. He turned one actor down flat, thought another might eventually be useful and went to see Selway in a play: 'To be frank I am of the opinion that this actor has a great deal to learn. He is uneasy, constricted and vocally tight.' Devine refused to give Selway good parts but offered to help him in his acting if he would come to the Court in small parts. Selway played in The Crucible, the Duncan double bill and Cards of Identity and nothing after that. It was a kind of compromise, except that Devine clearly would not allow an actor of whom he disapproved to take second leads.

On 15 November, Devine sent to Harewood 'Plan Z set out properly: no longer Z, I think, but THE plan! I think it is good.'[52] The note makes clear that Devine and Harewood were allies, and that Duncan was already a problem. After asking Harewood to get it typed (Devine was on tour in Newcastle), the letter says 'If you do so, I would leave out the last para of the second page ... It might upset him.' Devine's plan insists that success lies in the 'sheer compelling potency of our programme of plays: this will be much more important than stars or productions or publicity. If we can find these plays from English writers, so much the better but this will take time and "digging". Meanwhile we must not dither on the sidelines but hit hard and with conviction.'

The paragraph Devine asked Harewood to keep from Duncan nails his colours to the mast:

> It will be important to show the kind of thing we are after and to achieve enough success to keep going. The so-called highbrow public now seeks a new form of nostalgia in the 'new intellectual theatre theatrical' (Betti, Beckett, Eliot, Fry, Whiting). We have to drive beyond this point to keep going.

Duncan's notion of theatre was thus comprehensively destroyed before the ESC gave its first performance. Harewood clearly did not show him the paragraph – there is no record of the inevitable explosion it would have provoked. What is remarkable about 'Plan Z' is that the tone is passionate, committed and imperious, almost as if another opportunity such as this will never arrive. Devine inveighs against the 'rubbish' he has been sent: 'On the whole the standard of insipidity ... is remarkably high and there is a lot of "phoney" drama – phoney "poetry"; phoney "theatrical situations"; turgid wallowings in the mud of the "poetic soul" which is just as bad, worse, than conventional ineptitude – such plays have no human interest.'

His first six plays now were: Brecht, *The Good Woman of Setzuan*; Nigel Dennis, *Cards of Identity*; the Duncan double bill; Miller's *The Crucible*; *Look Back in Anger*; and Sartre's *The Devil and the Lord*. Being held in reserve at this stage were Wilson's *The Mulberry Bush* and Dennis Johnstone's *The Golden Cuckoo*. These were to be considered if the Dennis was not adequate. As Devine remarks in 'Plan Z', the problem with the Dennis 'is that the script does not exist. I am confident that there is a dramatist here and think that a play can be made out of this book. He agrees and I and my assistant are working on a scenario with him.' Devine commented that the Brecht should do well with Ashcroft in the lead, and the Duncan plays were planned as a masque and anti-masque: 'I would propose some cuts. Is this a good idea? I am not sure that the dramatist is keen.'[53] This last sentence is something of an understatement, and Devine had no more interest in the Duncan plays than he had in what they represented, but at this stage he was unwilling to provoke the inevitable confrontation that would ensue if he left the plays out of the bill. The Miller would attract attention since the author was well known. Of *Look Back in Anger*, Devine says: 'A complete "shot in the dark" but a completely new dramatist and a powerful play'. The Sartre, it was thought, would do well. The earlier objections to the O'Casey had resulted in its being dropped, although Devine eventually directed it at the Court in 1959.

A problem for Devine at this stage, and subsequently, was to do with the ignorance or the hostility of his Council. Blond, for example, wrote to Harewood on 23 November to say that he had been at a meeting of the Incorporated Society of Designers and they said 'if we could have a decent play, something like *The Second Mrs Tanqueray* when Gladys Cooper looked so wonderful, they would be willing to dress the show. This would be all the top twelve boys starting with Norman Hartnell which the Americans would love to see, and to the Americans no-one looks nicer in evening dress than an English Woman.'

Hostility continued to emanate from Esdaile, inevitably. He accused Harewood and Devine of wasting money and he condemned the idea of a workshop. Poke wrote to Blond on 23 November to say that if he went on like this, 'fur will fly'. Devine had to try to surmount this, but the very problems he was finding at the Court were denied by its owner. From Liverpool on 23 November, Devine sent 'Plan Z' to Poke and told him that the lighting equipment and the board were useless. At the same time, Lewenstein asked to lease the Court from February 1956, when the ESC officially took the theatre over, until the ESC season opened, in order to present *The Threepenny Opera*. Lewenstein had been negotiating for the rights from mid-1955. The production functioned as a kind of pre-season run.

Devine next produced a document on the Court's stage

lighting, arguing rightly that the lighting currently installed was so poor that Laurier Lister had imported hired lighting as a consequence. Blond lined up behind Devine about this and pressured Esdaile to sanction new estimates from the Strand Electric Company. Esdaile, of course, fought back and suggested that Devine, widely respected as one of the best lighters in the profession, did not know what he was talking about: 'All I can say is that he is making very, very heavy weather about this switchboard. In the first place he has got his facts wrong ... so his twenty-five years experience has not taken him very far' (to Blond, 15 December). Devine got his way. Esdaile sulked.

As well as fighting for new lighting, Devine was in touch with Brecht over *The Good Woman of Setzuan*. Negotiations with Brecht were always potentially difficult. This one was complicated by the fact that Lewenstein was given the rights independently of the ESC. Brecht wrote to Lewenstein on 8 December revoking the rights – it was all a misunderstanding – and referring to the proposed Devine–Ashcroft production and to Devine as 'one of the most outstanding English directors to whom I already spoke about it when he visited me in Munich four years ago'.[54] Lewenstein then acted for the ESC rather than independently. Devine wrote to Brecht on 22 December to say that H. M. Tennant was interested in transferring the production. All looked well except for the translation. Brecht had suggested that Devine send a playwright to Berlin to work with him on a translation. Devine proposed to send Osborne:

> The regular poet dramatists like Fry and Whiting are not
> suitable, in my firm opinion ... This young chap has the right
> humour and social feeling, I think, and you could mould him as
> you wished. He does not speak German but none of them do,
> except Auden, and he is in America, has not answered my letter
> of two months ago, and would probably not be available to
> come over.[55]

Discussions about an English version of the play continued into 1956.

The underlease was signed on 22 December and the ESC officially become owners of the building. Three days earlier another letter had arrived this one from Esdaile's solicitors, saying that 'It appears that it has been suggested in certain quarters that he is doing a very good thing for himself in granting the lease.' Continuing in a comparably unlegal manner, the letter went on to report that Esdaile had said the ESC was free to withdraw if it so wished. The letter was ignored; there were more important matters. On 23 December, Devine distributed an account of some of the personnel he needed and their tasks. Reference is made specifically to a General Manager, a Stage Director and an Assistant Director, i.e. Richardson. This latter post included in its specification 'Producer of some plays'. It resulted in the drafting of a letter, signed by Blond, which suggested that if an Assistant were necessary, one should be engaged as and when needed, but the core of the objection was, once again, about who runs what. Blond admits to 'a great feeling of malaise at the gloom you cast over our last meeting by what seemed to be your desire to take full control ... I do not want to feel as I do, that once you have got your budget you are just going ahead without reference.' This is crucial. Scribbled on the back of a letter of 19 December, in Devine's hand, is 'Therefore I cannot be expected to and I cannot accept that the Manager should be responsible directly to anyone but myself.'[56] Some Council members became alarmed at the degree of autonomy demanded by the Artistic Director. Devine phoned Poke on 30 December to say that he had interviewed a candidate for the General Manager's job (Poke to Blond, 31 December). Poke could clearly see control being taken from the Council. Accordingly, he wrote to Duncan on 31 December: 'My fear is that unless we have a cut and dried scheme of our own George will create his own which might be difficult and embarrassing to alter.' Poke asks Duncan to propose at the next Council that a sub-committee be formed to appoint the General Manager. The sub-committee, pushed by Devine, duly appointed Gordon Hamilton Gay in February 1956. He was not a success. Devine wrote to Poke on 28 February: 'I give you full and entire permission to kick me hard on the backside next time we meet! Mr G. H. Gay is a wash-out! He is a first-rate pfaffer (?!) – everybody dislikes him for his gas-bag inefficiency ... All the rest of our people are first rate and working splendidly.' Devine tried to educate Blond in a letter of 6 January by distinguishing between the operation in a commercial as opposed to an 'art' theatre.

In the former, 'where the basic object is to make money, the financial side maintains control throughout. But in an art theatre, the artist is given control provided (and this is the essence of the arrangement) he keeps within a certain agreed budget. The artistic policy and the budget are therefore entirely wedded.' Devine never quite achieved this objective but his successors profited from his efforts.

By the turn of the year, *The Mulberry Bush*, rewritten by Angus Wilson, was scheduled to open the season. No one was keen on the version which had played at Bristol. At best, some felt it needed stars such as Thorndike and Casson to make it work. They were unavailable. The new version of the Wilson was still being worked on into the new year, as was *Cards of Identity*. Dennis sent Devine Act I on 19 January with the comment that 'It is important that you should see it before we sign a contract, and if you find it disappointing and don't want to proceed, I assure you that I shall not feel injured.'[57] In February, Dennis wrote to Devine and Richardson to say that 'Act II wrote itself in 10 days ... Act III is soaring along at the same pace and needs about one more week ... I am in the middle of Father Orfe at the moment.'[58] Dennis was still revising at the end of May. At about the same time, Devine was trying to persuade Orson Welles to accept the leading role in Brecht's *Puntila and his Man Matti* ('just made for you, I think').[59] He was also having to deal with the fact that Ashcroft wanted to put back playing in the Brecht until the autumn. Since there were still problems about the translation, Devine recommended agreement to the Council on 20 January. While he kept tightly focused on his first season, he nevertheless was sent plays from all quarters. Some came via the Chairman who told Devine he had lunched with Benn Levy: 'He is very much attached to you and he thinks you can have nothing but success ... So look kindly on his play' (25 January). Devine agreed that he 'certainly will look kindly on his play but in the final count, I am sure you will agree we must be impartial' (27 January). Blond wrote to Benjamin Britten to ask for a 'Pantomime (or Christmas Entertainment) ... it would be of the greatest interest to us here, if we could put on such a show in our theatre ... it would be well in accordance with our policy' (30 January). The letter was copied to Poke, but not to Devine. From another source, the new Chairman of The John Lewis Partnership, O. B. Miller, who was considering putting money into the Company, asked about leasing the Court for some of the Partnership's own productions (Miller to Devine, December–January 1955–56).

On 17 February, Glen Byam Shaw, Devine's former partner in the Old Vic Scheme, now at Stratford, wrote with 'all good wishes at the start of your exciting and most important venture ... the realisation of your plans that you have had in mind for so long has come about at exactly the right time both for you as a person and for the English Theatre'.[60] And Gordon Craig asked Devine in a letter of 24 March for a programme for each of the Court's productions: 'I'd be very happy to follow it all at a distance.'[61] *The Times* devoted a leader to the opening of the ESC at the Court (31 March). Byam Shaw wrote again to say 'I believe that such work cannot fail' (31 March). He further remarked that on his visit of 30 March, 'It seemed to me that you were in a perfectly balanced state. In full control of the entire situation. Outwardly calm and relaxed. That may not be so, but if you can make *me* feel that then I am sure all those who are working with you feel it too.'

Not all of them did. Poke wrote a worried letter to Duncan on 28 March about what was to happen after the first season. No plays had been circulated as Poke thought had been agreed. Neither he nor Lewenstein had read a script for months. Plays, however, had been rejected by Devine and by Richardson. Poke was right to be concerned since the Artistic Director and his Assistant were effectively conducting the Court's artistic policy and the Council was not. The lines were drawn for a fierce battle in the near future.

As far as the artists at the Court were concerned, particularly those working on the technical side, it was as if the London Theatre Studio and the Old Vic family had come together again. It included Richard Negri and Alan Tagg, as well as 'Percy' Harris as designers; Sophie Harris as costume designer; and the workshop group of Jocelyn Herbert, Clare Jeffery and Stephen Doncaster.[62] In some respects, therefore, the initial link between the Court and the Vic School, the London Theatre Studio and, via Michel Saint-Denis, the Quinze of Copeau, was maintained. In others, however, it was not, for Devine's pursuit of his ambitions led to a distancing between him and his teacher:

> George moved away from Michel's method of production in
> that Michel was terribly strict and planned his productions with
> the greatest meticulous care and stuck to that and George ...
> didn't plan his productions so carefully. He planned them, of
> course, but he allowed much more freedom in development and
> I think that he felt that the whole theatre needed much more
> freedom than Michel would give it. Michel did not allow
> freedom to his actors or to his designers very much ... George
> was much more malleable. He would say, 'Well, it doesn't quite
> work, let's change it.'[63]

Jocelyn Herbert's view is that Devine 'wasn't trying to repeat anything and that was one of Michel's sadnesses when he came to see shows at the Court, that visually it wasn't the same sort of thing at all, except the bare stage. George was very much more concerned with the quality of the play than the visual aspect.'[64] And Richardson from a different generation remarked derisively on the Vic School's training: 'They were doing mime and sub-Copeau jumping about, which wasn't at all the sort of acting that was required.'[65] Richardson, of course, wasn't family and caused some irritation: 'there were people who were Old Vic School who resented him because they thought they might have got there ... a lot of people who had just finished the directing course at the Old Vic were peeved.'[66] Devine was clearly moving on, taking the best of the schools he had been involved with, but boldly taking as his number two a figure who had nothing at all to do with recent theatre history.

The creation of the short-lived surround by 'Percy' Harris was in response to Devine's earlier series of theoretical notes, made on 8 September 1955. The objective remained a setting which implied space beyond it, and one which allowed light and air to pass through it:[67]

> George and I designed it together ... It related to the fact that at
> that time almost everything was done with a black surround

because a black surround was supposed not to exist. It was supposed to be something that you didn't know was there and we thought that was out of date and untrue and we decided that it would be better to have a light colour surround. We invented that sort of shape because we hoped it would be less strict than a perfectly plain wings and border, so we had these 'S' shaped wings and it didn't do what we'd hoped it would do, really, and it didn't last very long ... It was new. It was going away from the conventional thing, to try to put things in a space which was not too nebulous, which led an existence of its own and which was light so that you didn't have all this gloom of black all round.[68]

It's difficult now to capture the tension and excitement as the opening drew closer. Herbert speaks of the 'real excitement, anxiety and fun' with everyone totally involved'.[69] 'Percy' Harris can remember 'swaying about on a ladder having terrible panics because I was all right when I was going up the side of the proscenium but in the middle of the proscenium there I was with nothing to hold on to, trying to paint it ... we painted it all ourselves, the proscenium and the stage'.[70] And Clare Jeffery recalls making props under the stage, and

John Osborne very kindly helping us make a bush for The Mulberry Bush out of dyed green hessian and getting green dye all over his teeth ... he was absolutely unknown then, and he was an actor in the company and he came and helped but I've always felt guilty because he ended up with green teeth.[71]

2   The struggle for control, 1956–1960

They all used to draw up schedules of the kind of plays that they would like to do – Sternheim, Wedekind, Lorca, Pirandello – a whole body of European work ... An art theatre of some kind was certainly in their minds in the preparation stage [but *Look Back in Anger*] came from a quite different area than the poetic kind of art theatre envisioned, and once that had happened, it swung the whole movement in a completely different direction. Immediately, everyone realised that what they had been dreaming of, this European art theatre, was no longer the kind of theatre that would be realised, but that the writers themselves would dictate the character of the new theatre.

(Gaskill, in Doty and Harbin, 30–31)

We have only just started. We have no time for memories, only for experiences.

(Devine, 'English Stage Company. A record of two years work', 1958).

The English Stage Company's opening production on 2 April 1956 was Wilson's *The Mulberry Bush*, known in the Court as 'the Wilson'.[1] A conventionally built play of ideas, sitting in the middle of the all-purpose surround, produced reviews ranging from the polite to the irritated. While most critics welcomed the overall enterprise of Devine's company, none saw, yet, anything to become either excited or enraged about. Privately, others were keener. 'Binkie' Beaumont was 'thrilled' by the play: 'Angus will obviously be a major playwright ... I am absolutely convinced he will really write a magnificent play in the very near future.'[2] Nigel Dennis was similarly enthusiastic: 'Of course *The Mulberry Bush* is good – a clear, firm line of development from start to finish with no monkey-tricks; only the first ten minutes seem contrived and clumsy'.[3]

As the Company prepared to offer the second play in the repertory, Miller's *The Crucible*, an issue was developing which was to cause great difficulty in the coming years. It was to do with the reading of plays as they arrived and it was essentially an argument, once again, about artistic control. At a meeting of the Artistic Committee on 4 April, it was clear that some felt left out of the decision-making process. Poke suggested he take on the job of circulating scripts to the members of the Committee. Devine was having none of this. He wrote to Poke on 6 April to say that he proposed to appoint Osborne as an initial reader of scripts. Anything of interest would be read by Devine, after which it would go to the Committee: 'I think the use of a playwright on the spot to read will help us immensely', particularly a playwright whose priorities accorded with those of Devine's and not, say, Duncan's. Poke immediately contacted Duncan about the matter and the struggle began, intermittently at first. It could be said to climax with the rejection by Devine of Fry's *Curtmantle* in 1960, but the years in between saw bitter in-fighting.

The Crucible, which opened on 9 April, attracted better reviews generally, including one which suggested that it, and not *The Mulberry Bush*, should have headed the bill. In some ways, the production more closely realised Devine's ideas about staging and production values than the rest of the season's plays. Within the permanent setting and with, virtually, a permanent company, there were the costume designs of Sophie Harris. These were originally to be a form of permanent costume for the season, but the time the season opened, the idea of permanent costumes had gone. Consequently, *The Crucible* saw their only outing. It was also the only time that Devine, faced with a text he greatly admired, and with a credo entirely to do with the supremacy of the writer, tampered with a play. He cut the character of Giles Corey. According to Tony Richardson, it was a matter of money.[4] According to Devine, it was to improve the play. He wrote to Miller on 11 April that he had taken the action 'for strong artistic reasons because I thought it would strengthen the play ... You may feel that this is an appalling presumption.'[5] Miller did and cabled his English agent on 25 April to the effect that Corey should be reinstated or the production must close. Devine's action was entirely uncharacteristic and not repeated. However, it allowed those who were uncomfortable with Devine's role some satisfaction. Duncan noted in a memorandum of 29 April that 'such a ghastly error' has made him feel that 'as a result of it Devine is now very much more manageable'. Esdaile was busily fulminating about high costs. He told Blond on 26 April that 'The whole thing is costing too much and we are getting a ten shilling article for which we are paying a fiver ... I told you that these fellows can ruin anybody if they are not held tightly on the bit.'

Towards the end of April the feeling arose in the Council that *The Mulberry Bush*, which was playing to a half-empty theatre, should come off. Blond wrote to Poke on 24 April to say that Blacksell felt the play should finish. Blond was all for it so long as the ESC didn't 'lose face if we take it off too quickly'. Eric Bessborough felt similarly but Devine's reaction was that 'it means going against printed publicity and is a slight loss of face so early in our career'. It is significant that Devine was told it should come off, rather than consulted. As the employee, he was not allowed to take the decision. A Finance Committee meeting of 30 April decided to allow the play to run its allotted course because of the potential 'loss of prestige'.

Blond began to worry, as he did regularly, about the lack of scripts to follow the current productions. Britten had replied in his letter of 30 January to say that 'there is not a ghost of a chance that I could do a Pantomime this year'. Blond had contacted Charles Miller of the Music Corporation of America, who held the rights to Williams' *Cat on a Hot Tin Roof*, to ask for the play. The view was that the author would be unwilling 'to do the play in a theatre as small as yours'.[6] Devine continued his own enquiries. He lunched with Stephen Spender, out of which came a suggestion from the latter that Devine and he take Buchner's *Danton's Death* 'and radically rewrite it – just do a new play based on Buchner'.[7]

Look Back in Anger joined the repertoire on 8 May. The sole survivor of 750 plays sent to the Court in response to its advertisement, it evoked an immediate reaction from Devine and Richardson. Lord Harewood, reading the play on the train from London to Leeds 'with mounting excitement' gave it to a weekend guest, Dicky Buckle, who 'found it a thrilling experience, but ... we could never put such a thing on in the theatre. One could not insult an audience in this kind of way.'[8] Buckle's remark is unintentionally revealing about the expectation of audiences when watching a play. It is a remark about theatre as confirmatory of the audience's *status quo*. The notion that the theatre should be in any way disturbing, let alone bad mannered, was inconceivable. Such a script as *Look Back in Anger* directly challenged the Buckles of the world as well as, for that matter, most of the members of the Court's Council. The play thus functioned paradoxically in its context, apart from the Artistic Directorate, who knew that it had to be done, even if the very set for the play, positioned within the original surround, effectively stated its rejection of the earlier design and ideology.

The opening night of the play bizarrely set the world of the play against that of the Council, all of whom attended at Devine's insistence, all of whom wore evening dress, all of whom had as a Council sent flowers to the actresses. If 'Binkie' Beaumont had liked *The Mulberry Bush*, he had a very different view of the Osborne. It is said that at the interval Beaumont announced his dislike of it and his intention to leave. Terence Rattigan, about to follow, was persuaded by the critic, T. C. Worsley, to stay.[9] After the performance, Rattigan remarked to John Barber of the *Daily Express* that the play said simply, 'Look, Ma, how unlike Terence Rattigan I'm being.' The quotation duly appeared the following day and Rattigan hurried to repair the damage. In a letter to Devine, he insisted that he 'greatly enjoyed my evening and all I meant by the rather feeble wisecrack was that I felt occasionally the author was being a little self-conscious about his "modernism"'.[10] Rattigan was of course right in his remark, for the play served notice that work which Dicky Buckle would approve of was no longer quite at the centre of things.

That some of the reviews were very hostile; that Tynan's *Observer* review identified a young audience; that the play moved slowly in box-office terms until an eighteen-minute television excerpt on 16 October, introduced by Harewood, produced a huge upturn in the demand for tickets, as did the transmission of the entire play by Granada Television on 28 November – all of these things are known, as is George Fearon's inspired use of the term 'angry young man'.[11] What is not perhaps so obvious is to do with the audience. After the television excerpt, 'the theatre became filled with people – young people in their later teens or early twenties – who, from the way they were behaving, hadn't been to the theatre at all before . . . At that time, young people had virtually no relationship with the theatre.'[12] The clear implication was that young people watched television but did not regard theatre as in any way referring to their lives. Consequently, such people would not read theatre critics and would not consider a television excerpt as something relating to the act of going to a theatre. *Look Back in Anger* impelled them to a radical action, that of going to see the play. An activity regarded later as perfectly natural was offered by the Court to an audience which confirmed its relevance. A letter arrived at the Court from four young members of the audience:

> May we, as four members of the vast and usually phlegmatic British public, write and express our wildly enthusiastic appreciation of your production of *Look Back in Anger*. It seems to us the first time that our home-grown brand of mixed up kid has been presented on any stage . . . and can only applaud the complete truthfulness and alarming realism of the whole production . . . as contemporaries of the characters in your play [we] are delighted to endorse the veracity of the whole business.[13]

If Dicky Buckle reacted honestly to the play, so did the reviewers. If theatrical fare of a particular kind dominated the pre-Court stage and set out its own parameters, then it is also the case that reviewers were used to reacting in a particular manner, especially the older ones. Their world, as fundamentally as that of Rattigan, had altered with the advent of work such as *Waiting for Godot* in 1955 and now with *Look Back in Anger*. A process of education had begun. The problematic relationship between the Court and the press runs consistently through the Court's history and was always extremely sensitive.

If the Court had found its *raison d'être*, it had also to deal with its other resident playwright. Ronald Duncan's *Don Juan* and *The Death of Satan* had appeared on the original list put together by Duncan and Lewenstein. Duncan's work represented powerfully the kind of theatre Devine loathed. It is typical of Devine that he undertook to direct the double bill, but there is no reason to believe Duncan's accusation of deliberate sabotage.[14] The production opened on 15 May, lasted for eight performances, and was withdrawn. The occasion was both good and bad for the Court: good because it banished Duncan's work and that which it represented from the new theatre; bad, because it muddled the audience perception of what the new theatre was. It thus illustrated the perennial difficulty of most innovative theatre. Producing new plays logically means the production of available new plays. The theatre is driven by what arrives. What has to be done erodes what might be done and with it the identity of a specific theatre. What is available dictates what is done. What is unavoidable (Duncan) damages the constancy of a particular audience. Sometimes, what is done is done for economic reasons (*The Country Wife*, December 1956, or, disastrously, *Look After Lulu*, July 1959). In all this, an artist such as Devine must work to maintain his purpose. To say it was an uphill struggle is to put it mildly. Throughout its years the Court has never found a consistent audience, only audiences.

By May 1956, running in repertory was coming under pressure. Figures like Lewenstein, always more of an impresario than the others, were dubious from the beginning:

> because I believe that running a theatre, which was principally devoted to productions of new plays and trying to run in repertory, without large funds, was an impossibility. First of all, we wanted to do a wide selection of plays, so that you'd have needed a very broad company ... there would always be a struggle between casting the play as well as possible and the use of a small permanent company.[15]

Harewood put it more bluntly: 'we had to give it up because we wanted to be able to transfer. Simple as that'.[16] At an Artistic Committee meeting on 22 May, the alternatives to true repertory were discussed. One was to finish the season at the end of July and let the theatre; another was to produce an additional play (the suggestions were Joan Plowright in *The Country Wife*, *Nekrassov* or Marilyn Monroe in *Lysistrata*: 'It was agreed that Miss Monroe should be

contacted at once'); a third was to continue with the existing programme and keep it under review. Despite the fact that at this stage,
average takings were 39 per cent as opposed to a budgeted 50 per cent,
'it was also agreed that it would be fatal to retract our policy'. This did
not stop Blond's constant pressure on Devine to find plays which
would succeed financially. After lunching with Barber of the *Daily
Express* on 31 May, Blond came up with a Rattigan, an Edith Bagnold
'and plays by someone called Kingsley Amies and John Wayne'. On
other occasions, Blond would bombard Poke with questions about
finance, committee meetings or Council meetings. It was unusual for
him to be in the position of losing money and face: 'If *Cards of
Identity* does not turn out to be a financial success we will have to
take it off before the end of the programme as we cannot afford to keep
it. What about another play?' The reaction is one of irritation at
indifferent merchandise; all his business instincts were being out-
raged. It was during this period that Blond held the first of his annual
critics' lunches, an event which tended to leave the Artistic Directors
somewhat cool. On 27 June, Blond reviewed his theatre's progress in
front of a group of critics whom he described as 'highly intellectual
people', and he took it upon himself to announce that if no native
writers emerged the Court would look to foreign plays. It is not
difficult to imagine the faces of Devine and Richardson at what was to
become an annual trial by critic.

Before the season began, Lewenstein and Richardson thought
that *The Crucible* would produce the biggest success and that the
Osborne 'would be lucky to cover itself'.[17] In a different way, *Cards of
Identity*, which opened on 26 June, carried a good deal of hope on
Devine's part, since Dennis was a novelist he had courted to adapt his
book.[18] Despite good reviews, it managed only 46 per cent at the box
office. Devine, nevertheless, was to keep faith with Dennis for two
more plays before the relationship broke down irretrievably. He also
kept faith with the belief that novelists could write plays. A list
submitted to the Artistic Committee of 29 June included Wyndham
Lewis, William Plover, Iris Murdoch, John Wain, Evelyn Waugh and
others. In the absence of playwrights, this seemed the only feasible
route. Devine's appraisal of the situation in early July was that six

plays had been mounted in twelve weeks at a cost of approximately £4,700. The running losses were approximately £3,400. He had only two plays to juggle with, the Osborne and the Dennis, before the Brecht opened at the end of October. Both could run until October; on the other hand, the Dennis play may fall out. In opting for an additional show, Devine listed the possibilities to fill the gap to October. These were Michael Redgrave's version of *The Aspern Papers* or Ionesco's *The Chairs* to run as a curtain-raiser to Michael Hastings's *Yes – and After*. After the Brecht and for the following six months, the choices were *The Country Wife*; new plays by Osborne, Dennis, Wilson; Sartre's *Nekrassov*; and Ionesco. Devine had, in view of the nature of his Chairman, to appear to be in control of a situation which was not controllable but dependent on a variety of factors, not the least of which was delivery of scripts.

In addition to internal pressure, Devine had to negotiate with Brecht over the translation of *The Good Woman of Setzuan*, which had begun in late 1955. Brecht had written to Devine to say: 'I would be delighted if Peggy Ashcroft would play the title part.'[19] The translation in question at the time was by Ella Winter, to whom Devine wrote on 8 December to say that neither he nor Ashcroft liked it. Two days later, Devine told Brecht they preferred the translation by Eric Bentley. Elisabeth Hauptmann-Dessau wrote on Brecht's behalf to say that both translations were being studied. On 10 April 1956, John Willett wrote to offer a collaboration with Winter. Complications arose when Hauptmann-Dessau told Devine they liked Willett's version, but on 5 July, Devine told Hauptmann-Dessau that both he and Ashcroft wanted to use the Bentley version. By 24 July it was agreed: a telegram from Brecht read: 'If you and Peggy Ashcroft approve of Bentley translation, Brecht agrees.' By this time, the Berliner Ensemble was preparing for its first and celebrated visit to London. And Brecht died. On 17 August, Devine wrote to Bentley: 'What a blow about Brecht's death. Far too young and far too disturbing to be allowed to disappear. I fear his posthumous reputation and his supporters as much as I admire what he has actually done.' Four days later, Devine wrote again to Bentley: 'The Ensemble arrives here next Monday. What a strange and ironical business. I can't really get over it. Tragic'. Devine had agreed to a request from the British Centre of the International Theatre Institute to host a party for the Berliner at the Arts Theatre on 30 August. The writer (10 August) ironically says 'There is still some doubt as to Brecht's state of health, but everyone seems optimistic enough.'[20] Late in September Hauptmann-Dessau wrote to Devine: 'We of the Berliner Ensemble wish to thank you for the warm welcome you extended to us when we were in London. We are looking back to those days as a wonderfully important human and professional experience.'

The Brecht opened on 31 October. Devine had already worried about Ashcroft. He had written to Hauptmann-Dessau on 1 October to say that 'Peggy Ashcroft is in a good state and I think, although in a *way* she is *miscast* (ie by type) in another way (ie by nature) she is perfect and this is most important.'[21] The production was not well received. Even within the Court, Richardson criticised 'this drab, hopeless copy of an Ensemble production'.[22] Devine wrote to Bentley on 12 November and called the reviews 'murderous in many cases. There is clearly a strong anti-British feeling here. With the international situation and the poor press, business has been seriously affected.' To Helene Weigel on 4 November, he wrote, enclosing the main notices: 'There is little doubt that there was considerable hostility in the audience from the start as the company went into the show very confident and happy but found the going very hard indeed.'

By the end of July, business at the Court was not proceeding well. Blond complained more or less daily to Devine who responded in a letter of 30 July that although he continually appreciated the 'precariousness of our financial position ... I equally feel that any lowering of the sights as far as our artistic policy is concerned would be highly dangerous. The prestige value of ... the Brecht or the *Nekrassov* which cannot be undertaken commercially because of their size is very important to us.' Devine also threw the sop of producing these plays 'with a big star name'. On the same day he contacted Harewood to urge a presentation for Christmas of *The Country Wife* with Plowright. On the other hand, the editor of the *London Magazine*, John Lehmann, wrote on 24 August to congratulate Devine on his achievements so far: 'You have certainly gone beyond *my* expectations of what one year's work could produce.'[23] And the first of the theatrical knights began, albeit with some reluctance, to show an interest. Poke informed Blond on 26 September that Olivier had been with Arthur Miller and Marilyn Monroe to see *Look Back in Anger*. Miller told Olivier he was wrong in his dislike of the play. After Olivier had seen the play a second time, 'Olivier asked John Osborne to write a play for him ... George Devine followed this up later to find that Olivier was quite sincere, and has tentatively suggested six weeks during April and early May of next year' (Poke to Blond, 26 September). Olivier agreed to play in what became *The Entertainer* after reading Act I. The Council was delighted. Poke's letter ends with a long list of producing possibilities which 'is almost embarrassing'.

The Council would obviously have been pleased with a consistent diet of Oliviers. Devine seemed quite content to have the occasional star, but the overall quality of the work and its representation was of paramount importance. One of the ways in which this showed itself had to do with photographing the work. This caused a protracted clash with Fearon, the Press Officer. Devine liked the work of Julie Hamilton: 'A new kind of photography, and everyone said, "Oh, the editors will not take them, they are coarse-grained" and I said, "Go out and sell these damned pictures." I was not having all that old stuff of two people next to each other and a sub-title underneath. I wanted a really modern, direct impression of what happens on the stage in each particular play ... it was a whole *attitude* about the theatre which expressed itself as much as was possible'.[24] Between Fearon's hostility – he maintained that he could not sell Hamilton's pictures – and the Council's desire for extensive publicity, Devine could not win what for him was an important matter, a statement about his theatre. After using Hamilton's work up to and including the Brecht, Devine surrendered while Fearon remained an employee. Poke, typically for the Council, thought Devine should use Stratford's photographer, Angus McBean.

If Fearon was a formidable obstacle to Devine, so was Esdaile, who had been so from the inception, despite being Vice-President of the Company. This time, he drew a very angry response from the normally urbane Harewood. Esdaile wrote to Blond on 12 November to report adverse criticism of the Brecht in the 8 November issue of the *Stage*: 'I have said all along the line that we have given a certain dictatorial gentleman too much power. I was dead against this from the commencement. Mr Opinion is, and it has been proved, not as brilliant as he would like us to think he is.' Poke copied the letter to Harewood who felt that it:

> is exactly the sort of letter that could have been written about Esdaile rather than by him; he started as a troublemaker and he will go on as a troublemaker, and the thing that exercises us is when Neville is going to lose his temper with him ... Esdaile is completely out of sympathy with everything that we are doing, and he has not even a glimmering of understanding ... This sort of letter makes me furious, and I should have thought the sort of person who thinks *Look Back in Anger* a failure ... is the sort of person from whom we don't want to accept advice.

The year ended with Devine's production of *The Country Wife*.[25] Coincidentally, Richardson had directed the play at Stratford East in July 1955, the first London production since 1936. Its star at the Court was Lawrence Harvey 'who was a big star and the last person most of us would have thought of casting. And it gave Joan Plowright her chance so it served the company in that way, too. But certainly it was done with an eye to being much safer than what we had been doing.' Devine's designer was 'Percy' Harris, whose set came about by an accident:

> I did a model for George and we decided how we wanted to do it and I used perspex and drew the sets on it. We wanted to make them of a very fine metal, so I drew them in ink on perspex. George came and saw it and said, why don't we do it like that? It would be much cheaper and better ... they had terrible trouble with the lighting because when the perspex was vertical the lights went into it and straight back into the audience ... it was purely fortuitous that it was done that way.[26]

The Country Wife played to nearly 95 per cent and established

Plowright as a star. It also kept Blond quiet temporarily. But there was still a price. The policy of true repertory was to be suspended 'through expedience'. The same brief for Blond to send to the Arts Council adds optimistically: 'It will be re-introduced during the period under review' (18 December). By 20 December, Blond was telling Poke not only that 'everyone is happy' but that he had agreed to fund two assistant directors 'in order to train up young men'. This became the basis of hiring the Assistant Artistic Directors in 1957. Lewenstein was to be paid to act as General Manager of the Court and Ronald Duncan's new play, *The Catalyst*, had arrived. Predictably, neither Devine nor Richardson liked it: 'There appears to be such controversy and the Artistic Committee have not discussed it, that I hope the censor rejects it', said Blond plaintively in a letter to Poke of 21 December. The end of the year reviews were on the whole reasonable, if patronising. J. W. Lambert described the Court as 'an able little repertory company' and Devine as 'tousled and determined'. The productions consisted of 'An old-fashioned Galsworthian play of self-critical liberalism, a tight, strong melodrama, a dose of Shaw and water [and] a tentative excursion into the new nihilism'.[27] A more thoughtful view believed that 'The next generation of playwrights is on the move, and at last there is a theatre in London open to them.'[28]

In January 1957, Devine reviewed the list of writers with whom he was in contact. There were thirty-two. Twelve of them had plays produced at the Court over the following two years. The rest, including Christopher Fry, John Whiting and Peter Ustinov, were not produced. Angus Wilson, unsurprisingly, 'is giving up playwriting for a while'. Those playwrights performed included Beckett, Dennis, Giradoux, Hastings, Ionesco, O'Casey, Osborne and Sartre. The range of the work was part of a deliberate strategy by Devine:

> when we had a success with the Osborne, I said I am not going
> to pursue that line exclusively. I am going to introduce this
> other line, the line of Beckett and Ionesco and all that, because I
> believe that the truth lies somewhere between these two
> points. So I took a sort of dialectic and educative attitude
> towards the thing. From the audience's point of view it is not so

56

easy because . . . one minute it is Beckett, the next minute it is Osborne, the next Arden, then Jellicoe, then Brecht . . . In fact the two major events that have transformed the British theatre in my opinion were [Hall's] production of *Waiting for Godot* in 1955 and the production of *Look Back in Anger* in 1956. These are what I call the two lines . . . these were the two main influences [which] changed the face of the theatre.[29]

In effect, Devine's original notion of a European art theatre, referred to earlier, was to survive as the other major partner to the hoped-for arrival of new British plays. The modern British theatre was to look to modern continental European theatre for its contemporary masters, Beckett and Brecht. The catholicity that has marked the Court during its years was implicit in its beginning phase. The mix, when it developed, placed the British theatre in the mainstream avant-garde of Europe.

The opening show of 1957 was Carson McCullers' *The Member of the Wedding*. Richardson had sent copies to the Artistic Committee on 7 September 1956. Lewenstein held the rights but would release them and the play was provisionally scheduled for early in the new year. Poke liked it but was cautious about the fact that 'it is so essentially American in atmosphere, phraseology and sympathy. Whether all these factors would appeal to a British audience is anybody's guess' (Poke to Richardson, 16 September 1956). Richardson wrote to McCullers on 2 January. Having said how thrilled he was to be directing the play, Richardson asked for some alterations. McCullers replied: 'I'm so pleased that you're going to do my play. I wish I could be present at the London opening. At this time I don't have the money to come over and I am working very hard on a second play.'[30] In fact, the play did poor business and was replaced after thirty-seven performances by the first revival of *Look Back in Anger*. It remained for Richardson a play he loved 'as I've loved no other play ever'.[31] The production also illustrated what became a running strain between the Court and Lewenstein. As an impresario with his own business (Oscar Lewenstein Limited), it was his duty to find the best deal for those plays he held the rights of; as a member of the Court's Council and of the Artistic Committee, he may be said to have had different priorities. These occasionally clashed and it was well known that a certain animus existed between Lewenstein and Blond. On the occasion of the McCullers, and of Sartre's *Nekrassov*, which opened in September, Lewenstein threatened to withdraw both if the Court did not agree his terms. Lewenstein, later to become Chairman, briefly, and Artistic Director in the early seventies, was never, despite the large number of plays he brought to the Court, thought of as 'family', and never really accepted.

On 3 April for a week, Beckett's work appeared at the Court for the first time, but by a curious set of circumstances. Devine had asked Beckett for permission to pair his *Act Without Words* with Ionesco's *The Chairs*. The French company then rehearsing *Endgame* and *Act Without Words* for the Théâtre de L'Oeuvre in Paris suddenly found itself without a theatre. Devine saw Beckett and Roger Blin in Paris and secured a week's run at the Court as part of a 'French fortnight' in London, organised by the Union Française des Industries Exportatrices.[32] A gala performance, black tie obligatory, was attended by the French Ambassador and other notables. Programme-sellers included Phyllis Calvert, Anna Massey, Rachel Kempson and others. Beckett was, characteristically, nowhere to be seen. It was an important moment. The Court paid for the French production and Beckett undertook to translate *Endgame* and to allow the Court to put on the English première.

In late March, Devine told the English Stage Society (the Court's support group, formed in the autumn of 1956) of his intention to put on productions of plays 'considered too risky for the Company to undertake' (Minutes, 27 March). These pieces would be rehearsed up to the final run-through and staged on the main stage in a 'simple way without scenery'. These were eventually known as the Sunday Night Productions without décor. They served several purposes: they could provide a means whereby promising writers could see and hear their work and profit by it; they could be used to try out work about which there was a certain unease; and they could be quite ruthlessly used to fob off work which could not simply be dismissed. Devine was by now receiving a great many scripts, most of which were useless, some of which would work, and some of which he did not particularly warm to. An example is Wesker's *Chicken Soup with Barley*, 'an obvious Sunday night'.[33]

The Sunday Nights could also be used to try out new directors and 1957 saw the débuts of John Dexter, Lindsay Anderson and William Gaskill, with a Sunday Night of Hastings's *Yes – and After*, Kathleen Sully's *The Waiting of Lester Abbs*, and Simpson's *A Resounding Tinkle*. All three became celebrated directors, as did Anthony Page, who arrived in 1958 to make up the quartet. The family was becoming an extended one and often squabbled. The younger directors quite frequently resented the closeness between Devine and Richardson, even when recognising the extraordinary contribution of the latter. According to Gaskill:

> Tony was a very influential figure. He was very ruthless and would dominate George. And George would completely buy it ... I'm not taking anything away from George in saying that because Tony was himself a man of extraordinary contradictions ... all the time we thought we're here, building a home for these writers and then Tony would sweep in and say, we're going to do this instead. I remember one occasion, absolutely typical ... and he said, 'Now, go and see John Gielgud and ask him if he'll do *The Rehearsal* of Anouilh for us and we'll get Laurence Olivier and Edith Evans for it' ... and then he'd say, 'Go and see Margaret Leighton and Lawrence Harvey and see if they'll do *The Taming of the Shrew*.'[34]

They were also protective of their own writers. Of Beckett, Gaskill felt 'One admired him but I think we were so excited about our own writers that we thought it was wonderful having Beckett here but we didn't think it was that extraordinary.'[35] Jocelyn Herbert recalls that 'they used to come bellyaching round to the Studio, the three of them ... And I'd be up on my balcony working away ... and they never could agree about a single actor'.[36]

One matter needed to be settled before *The Entertainer* could be added to the bill. This was the situation which arose when the Artistic Committee discussed the play. Devine, Richardson, Hare-

wood, Duncan and Lewenstein were there, the latter three making up
the Committee, and

> after very lengthy discussion, it emerged that Ronnie and Oscar
> were against doing the play, George, Tony and I for it. I said,
> 'Well, that's three of us for and two against. I will tell the
> Council.' 'But only you, Ronnie and I are members of the
> Committee', said Oscar, 'and that makes two against one for. So
> we *don't* do it!' He was of course technically right, but I am
> afraid I told Neville the story forthwith and suggested that he
> and I should overrule the vote. Democracy went out of the
> window, we took a step towards a balanced budget, and
> incidentally put on one of the best plays we ever sponsored.[37]

Lewenstein's version of this highlights the coming crisis about who
ran the theatre. He asserted that 'Ronnie and I had started the English
Stage Company determined that it should not be a theatre for stars ...
I think disappointment with the play, plus thinking that George, by
giving it to Larry, had by-passed the Artistic Committee, made us
make what I am now quite sure was a foolish mistake.'[38] Both of
them, however, were right about Devine's pre-emptive strike.
Devine's response was to pack the Artistic Committee with his own
people – Ashcroft and Osborne – and, eventually, to win the right to
choose plays without consultation. It still took another two years to
achieve.[39] Devine defends his use of stars in his fragment of autobiography, where his view of *The Entertainer* seems a little muted:

> Osborne had not turned out another stunning work until
> *Luther*, although we made a pile out of *The Entertainer* ... It
> made us a few thousand at the Palace Theatre, in the provinces
> and in America. We tried a series of star productions to fill in
> the gaps and make money. They didn't always work and we
> were said to be betraying our cause, although we never declared
> an anti-star policy at the beginning [but] it seemed implicit in
> our attitude. These misunderstandings always occur when you
> are dealing with idealists.[40]

Devine's fascination with French theatre showed in the production following *The Entertainer*. He was searching for a play to go with Ionesco's *The Chairs*. After consultation running from October 1956, he settled on Giraudoux's *L'Apollon de Bellac*.[41] The production saw the further establishing of Joan Plowright as a major actor. It also marked the début for the ESC of the great designer, Jocelyn Herbert, although she had supervised the building of the set for *The Good Woman of Setzuan*.[42] With this production, Jocelyn Herbert set a bench mark for design which was to influence most subsequent designers at the Court and beyond. The Giraudoux did not meet the standard of the Ionesco and it was subsequently dropped. *The Chairs* was paired initially with Wilkinson's *How Can We Save Father?* from 5 August, and subsequently with another Ionesco, *The Lesson* (June 1958).

Nigel Dennis's second play for the Court, *The Making of Moo*, a fierce attack on organised religion, opened on 25 June. It was in many ways Devine's kind of play, a scathing, satirical attack on a major sacred cow. It also made the Lord Chamberlain nervous and elicited the following from his office: 'I am desired by the Lord Chamberlain to write to you regarding the above play and to ask for an assurance that the "Cardinal's hat" placed on the butler's head, will not be a replica of a Roman Catholic Cardinal's hat.'[43] The play achieved only 40 per cent at the box office, and it was not long before Blond started gunning for Richardson on the grounds that the McCullers, the French double bill and now the Dennis had all averaged a loss of £3,000, which 'reflects greatly on one producer' (Blond to Poke, 16 July 1957). In contrast, Blond hardly seemed to notice that Devine was still earning only £1,700 per annum, compared to Stratford directors, who earned £5,000 per annum.

The French link with the Court continued with the production of Sartre's *Nekrassov*, played first at the Edinburgh Festival. Sartre had given the play to Unity Theatre in January of the previous year. Harewood liked the play, but felt in his reader's report that it needed 'a Guinness or a Trevor Howard for the title role'. In the event, it was played by Robert Helpmann. Devine's direction seemed, according to the October *Theatre World*, 'keyed for laughs rather than for the pungent satire of Sartre's original'. By 20 September, Blond was agitating for the production to come off. It ran for its allotted time. If Blond was constantly exercised about finance, Harewood could tell the Council on 7 October that *Look Back in Anger* was a success in New York, that Devine was taking *The Country Wife* to New York and that *The Entertainer* would follow suit. He further said that the Osborne would be revived on 28 October, followed by Faulkner's *Requiem for a Nun*[44] and then *Lysistrata*.[45] He also noted the first Arden play, *The Waters of Babylon*, and Simpson's *A Resounding Tinkle*, both Sunday Nights, both by writers who in different ways would be of real significance to the Court. The Council also heard a proposal for a festival season of guest repertory companies for July 1958.

Before Devine left for New York, he had to contend with a row over the launch of *Declaration*, a book of essays by, among others, Osborne and Anderson, Colin Wilson and Doris Lessing. It ran through three impressions in as many months, no doubt aided by the fact that the Court Council cancelled the launch party which had been arranged to happen at the theatre. Osborne had typically attacked royalty; Council had typically disassociated itself from the remarks. The Court, now a natural venue for such enterprises, was made to look rather silly in its reaction. Some of its responses generally to events exhibited a forlorn notion of things past. 'Wouldn't it be nice if the Artistic Committee came along with equal enthusiasm for some play praising some of the good things Old England stands for' (Poke to Blond, 16 October 1957). On 8 November, Poke wrote to Blond to say that he and Duncan were concerned about the 'leftish' politics of the plays done at the Court and that perhaps some action was needed. At about the same time, the action being taken by the Artistic Directors was to commission the play by Arden which became *Live Like Pigs* and which was to cause uproar late in 1958.

The year began with an attempt by Blond to retire. He wrote to Blacksell on 24 January that the company was 'really on the way to success. We have got £20,000 on deposit on which we are earning 8 per cent per annum, and we have got £5,000 in the bank ... Frankly I do not think I could come off at a better time. I am trying to find another chap. My first try was a bad one, people did not like him. I find myself doing all the work, making my own agendas etc., and I am just fed up to the teeth'. Who the 'chap' was is not known, but it was not the case that Blond did all the work. If anyone did, it was Poke as Honorary Secretary. Blond stayed as Chairman until his death.

Meanwhile, Gaskill's first main bill production was an early Osborne, *Epitaph for George Dillon*, which, surprisingly, transferred to the West End, and was a great success in New York, thus providing the nice irony that the first show by Gaskill on the main stage was a powerful commercial success.[46] It was followed by what nearly everyone agreed was the first really experimental play at the Court, Ann Jellicoe's *The Sport of My Mad Mother*.[47] The play had won third prize in the competition run by the *Observer*, the results of which had been announced on 18 August 1956. For Jellicoe it was an extraordinary time and Devine was most supportive: 'First of all, he let me direct [it]. He put his name with mine to protect me, but he only came in to about one rehearsal in five. By putting his name there, he made it possible for me to direct that play.'[48] The notices were mainly poor and the play came off after fourteen performances, to be replaced by *George Dillon*. It was, however, a significant moment in the Court's development.

Another significant development was an idea Devine had but managed to persuade Blond was originally his. On 2 January 1958, Devine wrote to Blond to say that the idea of a writers' group 'certainly is a development of your scheme, only it is to be a small group of young writers ... I am particularly anxious not to ask Ronnie Duncan.' The Writers' Group began in 1958, met every Wednesday, and lasted for two years.[49] Initially it existed as more of a talking shop for writers whom Devine and others liked and who had been given a pass to shows at the Court. Gaskill then took it over. The early meetings saw a session by Devine on the use of comic masks. Some early meetings were attended by Michel Saint-Denis, but gradually under Gaskill's influence the event became a practically based teaching session for writers such as Arden, Wesker, Jellicoe, Soyinka, Bond and Cregan. Others, including Simpson, Howarth and Osborne, stayed away.

On 19 March, *The Times* celebrated nearly two years' work at the Court. Drawing a direct parallel with the Vedrenne–Barker seasons of the early twentieth century, it praised 'the marauder on the frontiers' of the London stage: 'Between the extremes of Beckett in French and Olivier in vaudeville there has been a steady output of sophisticated cosmopolitan drama and pilot staging of work by home authors of promise ... When the voice of Porter was heard in the land, annoyance and approval mingled, as if *avant-garde* conversation had invaded the servants' hall.' Such approbation did not prevent riots at the Sunday Night of Stuart Holroyd's *The Tenth Chance* on 9 March,[50] or completely divergent opinions about Doris Lessing's *Each his own Wilderness*: 'an excellent play' (Harewood); 'a beastly play' (Poke). Nor did it prevent Alec Guinness worrying about playing *Endgame*: 'I wouldn't want to interfere with the play *at all* – but for what it's worth I thought there was one too many references to pissing (rather tedious and self-conscious in English) and something in me (perhaps my religious convictions) would prefer "He doesn't exist. The bastard!" to the other way round as it is in the script.'[51]

Meanwhile, the bill of fare was as mixed as ever. The Court presented Duncan's *The Catalyst* at the Arts Theatre Club, conveniently out of the way; a Simpson double bill, rapturously welcomed by Kenneth Tynan;[52] and celebrated its second birthday. Devine summarised the work so far and said explicitly that the Court was not 'a tryout theatre in the sense of putting on plays with an eye cocked on West End production ... We are a theatre with an attitude, but it is non-political and non-sectarian.' Devine openly owned himself 'increasingly impatient in front of literary theatre. I believe the future lies somewhere in a triangle between Brecht, Beckett and Ionesco.'[53]

Barry Reckord's play, *Flesh to a Tiger*, with Cleo Laine as Della (the play's original title), opened on 21 May and lasted for only twenty-nine performances at a disastrous 15 per cent box office. A brave and adventurous work simply did not appeal. This production also saw the original surround disappear. After a revival of *The Chairs*, paired with *The Lesson*, came the, to some, ill-fated guest repertory season. According to Devine, he told Blond, a Manchester man, that the Court ought to do something about the provinces. Devine wrote to all the provincial repertory companies and 'the product of this was so lamentable that we could hardly raise four weeks. In fact we couldn't raise four weeks because I finally said to Tony we will have to send these people some of our scripts.'[54] The four companies involved were Glasgow Citizens, Salisbury Arts, Leatherhead Repertory, and the Belgrade at Coventry, which had opened on 27 March 1958. The experiment was not repeated.

By 13 June it was estimated that overall losses on productions, excluding Sunday Nights, amounted to nearly £28,000. Blond's characteristic way of putting it refers to 'the larder being pretty empty', 'sluice gates being opened', and 'seeing a red light'. In consequence, a production of *Major Barbara* was proposed as a money-spinner, though the Artistic Committee was doubtful if the show would hold up without a star. Following that would be *Live Like Pigs*, about which the Committee's report said 'There is a division of opinion in the Committee' (15 July). The Council became more alarmed as the year wore on. Poke told Duncan on 21 July that the plays being discussed, which included *A Taste of Honey, Chicken Soup with Barley* and *Live Like Pigs* 'are all about poor people living in sordid conditions. People felt bored ... if they are having this dreary, sordid seamy side of life continually thrown up'. Duncan, for his part, slightly bafflingly felt 'At the moment we are playing at being H. M. Tennant in a theatre too small for the Binkie game' (to Poke, 24 July). Blacksell joined in the chorus, drawing from Devine a tart response to his complaint that he never received any scripts to read. Blacksell's opinion 'is of no value at this level and so it is a waste of time' (to Blond, 8 August).

Major Barbara was not financially successful and produced just under 50 per cent. What followed it did only half of that figure. Back in April, Harewood called *Live Like Pigs* 'a strong candidate ... *certainly* not a Sunday evening show'. In May, Arden was trying to find an alternative title and sent lists to Devine, which included: 'Don't put your muck in *my* dustbin'; 'Sawney's walk alone'; 'Just because we live'. By the end of July, he was rewriting sections at the demand of the Lord Chamberlain's Office.[55] Arden was clear about his allegiances; in his contract, he stated that the agreement should operate 'only for as long as George Devine and/or Tony Richardson ...or an artistic direction with which I feel in sympathy, remains as artistic directors of your company'.[56] On the day the play opened (30

September), Poke wrote to Blond to voice his growing unhappiness with the direction the Court was taking, 'for I can see nothing in it of a cheering or uplifting nature'. Duncan walked out of the dress-rehearsal in disgust and complained that Wilfred Lawson was drunk.[57] Arden's play attracted ruinous notices and the unrest and discontent felt by the theatre's administration erupted. Letters to Blond attacked the failures of the guest repertory season onwards. Devine replied strongly to Blond on 3 October that he felt 'very depressed abut this . . . The work I am doing here is difficult enough but if all members of the Artistic Committee do not support me as entirely as George Hare-wood and Oscar do, I feel the work is being hampered.' It's worth noting that at no stage does Devine threaten to resign. Harewood, as ever, was supportive. He told Blond on 8 October that 'I must repeat that I was in favour of doing the play, and judging by the notices I cannot regret the decision.' Also rallying to the defence of Devine was Robin Fox, who had been drafted in at the beginning of the year to replace Lewenstein as General Manager. A close friend of Blond's, he was, with Harewood, a buffer between the Council and the Artistic Directorate. Devine contacted Poke on 10 October to suggest that he was obsessed with the idea of sordidness: 'For me it is a question of values. Cecil Wilson's notice . . . contained the word sordid in its headlines, and next to the column containing this notice there was a three column ten inch photograph of a young lady who was about to marry a man who was to be hanged in ten days' time . . . to me *Live Like Pigs* is a rose garden in comparison'. To Osborne, Devine wrote on 15 October: 'I am afraid the jolly old critics have slaughtered *Live Like Pigs*, and we have not been able to pull it out of the mire. It is very sad.' Devine was perfectly capable of looking after himself, but his workload was colossal and, quite often, Richardson, Gaskill and Page were away, leaving Devine to handle all of the events.

At the same time, Devine opened on 28 October in *Endgame*, playing Hamm, in a double bill with *Krapp's Last Tape*. Guinness had declined the role and so Devine did it, to a surprisingly hostile press.[58] Devine had written to Poke four days earlier to say 'I really am going flat out . . . I shall be glad to see at least Gaskill back – not to mention Tony. This *Endgame* is a *great* work – but proportionately the heavier

responsibility to make the public accept and see its greatness ...
Beckett has come over and this has been immensely helpful.' Towards
the end of the letter, his fatigue shows:

> I have fought myself to my knees. I know everyone feels
> desperate but to someone in the thick of it every day, ructions
> at 'Whitehall' don't help. We are better off than we were when
> we started – we have a world wide reputation ... a proud record,
> and financially we have more than we started with ... let's have
> a little rejoicing too! Must rehearse.

To Gaskill in New York on the same day, he wrote 'I must have a
breather ... I want to plan the future on the lines of alternating "star"
shows and "experimental" – six weeks at a time ... I need you back as
soon as possible. I am very isolated.'

Typically, Devine wrote to Blond on 11 November and set out
his stall. After paying what are clearly real compliments to Blond for
his tenacity and support, Devine asks simply: 'Do the Council want
me to continue or not? If they do I may as well declare right now that I
shall continue to want to find and present the hard hitting well
written play ... to run a theatre of no compromise'. Devine's view of
the world at the end of 1958 is one of 'no confidence in the changing
mood now talked about. For me it is a political trick prior to election.
The problems are still there and no amount of refrigerators, TV sets or
motor cars are going to relieve them ... as long as I am running the
theatre a certain kind of policy is bound to continue ... Is the Council
going to support me or not?' When the Old Vic Scheme crisis broke in
1951, Devine and the other two did not, in spite of being urged, do
other than keep quiet for fear of damaging the Scheme. Now Devine
says bluntly that he wants support if he is to continue. Devine also
wants Richardson's position resolved: 'He has been in the past of
immense value to the organisation, although at one time no-one liked
him; now he is not there everyone regrets his absence ... If Tony does
not return as my associate I will have to find another assistant on his
level. It is not possible to run the theatre as I have to do, have ideas
and carry them out.' He also wants a proper manager, which harks
back to what Craig had told him in 1951.

Poke's reactions to receiving a copy of Devine's letter are predictable, but he sharply and rightly picks up Devine's reference to running the theatre: 'Is he running the theatre? ... The people running the theatre are the management committee' (Letter to Blond, 13 November). The matter is not yet resolved. For Poke, in spite of Devine's assurances, the direction of artistic policy has not changed. Rather, in doing *Live Like Pigs*, the policy remains the same. The threat that ensued, to give Devine only a one-year contract, produced a strong letter from Peggy Ashcroft. Writing to Blond on 12 December, she is 'disturbed that such a decision – which seems to me tantamount to a vote of no confidence – should have been taken without the agreement of the whole Council' (of which Ashcroft had become a member). Ever passionate and sane, she asked for an early Council meeting to discuss 'not only this question but also the clear divergence of opinion on artistic policy inherent in it'.

The new year began with the main stage début of Lindsay Anderson. He directed *The Long and the Short and the Tall* by Willis Hall. Anderson 'thought the title was too severe and asked the taciturn Yorkshire author if he'd object to me retitling it ... "You're the fucking director", said Willis, meaning consent'.[59] Devine had warned Blond on 11 November that 'we may be criticised for lowering our sights ... It is not really up to our standards though it has some good writing in it.' The play had been done in Edinburgh and Nottingham; Lewenstein had bought it and suggested a co-production. For Devine, the play was one which might hold the fort for a while and give him a chance to breathe. It was to have starred a young Albert Finney who, on the discovery of appendicitis, was replaced by Peter O'Toole. Harewood perhaps describes it accurately in a letter to Blond of 2 February: 'it was an excellent and remarkable evening. The play is good, though perhaps not great, but the performance seemed to me a most startlingly brilliant affair ... I think we have an excellent addition to the theatre in Lindsay Anderson.' It made O'Toole a star overnight.

The play transferred to the New Theatre on 8 April and gave Devine a little breathing space, only for him to have to use it up in dealing with complaints. Kennedy-Cox had complained to Blond that only two designers were being used for Court productions, i.e. Jocelyn Herbert and Alan Tagg. It was obviously not so and in Devine's reply to Blond of 14 January he found himself 'sick to death of carping criticism of this sort from people who do not know their facts and are artistic nit-wits'. On 16 January he was forced to write to the *Stage* to refute an item which suggested the Court was 'trying to pinch' Pinter from his current agents: 'Mr Pinter is quite often around when he is in London, and is in touch with some of the younger writers here . . . and reads plays for us from time to time. He is also a holder of one of our writer's passes.' He also had to deal with Blond's objecting to his playing opposite Vivien Leigh for Granada Television, despite having reminded Blond of his inadequate salary (to Blond, 13 February). Nor did it help when W. A. Darlington wrote in the *Daily Telegraph* for 16 February accusing the Court of restrictive practices in their choice of play. Devine vigorously defended his policy, which of course was internally under pressure. The Earl of Drogheda, a Council member, sent Blond a copy of Darlington's article on 23 February and opined that 'I do rather agree with him that nothing is admitted on the boards of the Royal Court unless it is calculated to put the audience into a suicidal frame of mind (or to give them a list of pot-boiling eighteenth century smut).' It is not difficult to calculate the pressure on even Devine of this sort of ignorance.

It became apparent that *The Long and the Short and the Tall* was nearing the end of its natural run. Inserted therefore into the bill before Richardson's production of *Orpheus Descending* was Howarth's *Sugar in the Morning* (originally called 'Lady on the Barometer', and given a Sunday Night the previous September). It did no better than 20 per cent. Richardson's continuing love affair with America produced *Orpheus Descending* on 14 May. In some ways, the Sunday Nights were producing more interesting material, including, on 26 April, a double bill of Christopher Logue's *The Trial of Cob and Leach*, together with 'Jazzetry', both directed by Anderson. Devine thought the latter to be 'one of the most interesting experimental shows to be done on a Sunday Night' (to Blond, 11 May). Kenneth Allsop's review for the *Spectator* of 1 May gives a vivid account of Logue reading his poetry to music from the Tony Kinsey Quintet. The show reflected New York-based poetry–jazz experiments and to some degree anticipated the influence of American work on London in the sixties. A further Sunday Night, on 19 July, was *Eleven Men Dead at Hola Camp*, put together by Gaskill and Johnstone. This improvised around the beating to death of eleven detainees in Kenya. Gaskill called it 'a dramatised protest. We had never done anything as positively political as this before and the Council were shit-scared.' The evening was 'a strange mixture of inadequate improvisation, political passion, beautiful songs by Wole Soyinka ... It was way ahead of its time.'[60] The British influence was, however, still very apparent when on 28 May, *Look Back in Anger* was the Royal Film Première 'in the gracious presence of H. R. H. Princess Margaret'. The Countess of Harewood, chairing the Gala Committee, had written to ask the Princess if she would appear. On 23 March, the Princess agreed to appear if any proceeds were divided between the Court and her charity, the Docklands Settlements. She told Blond she would leave the whole organisation to him: 'he had been saying how good at it he was and laughing our little attempts to scorn, rather' (letter to the Countess of Harewood, 23 March). Blond initially offered the Princess some seats to sell and any cash from the advertisements, rather than half the proceeds: 'I then told him that, alas, I feared that I couldn't possibly come under those sorts of conditions, at which he immediately took back all he'd said and agreed.' Blond had clearly met his match.

Elsewhere, an ambitious Peter Hall was looking for a London theatre. He joined a plan proposed to Stratford by Olivier, which involved co-operation, or even merger, between the projected National Theatre and Stratford. Stratford, the Old Vic and the National would be run by Hall, Devine and Olivier, and 'the players would circulate in a way salubrious to their well-being and constructive to their development'.[61] A committee was formed, called 'The Joint Council of the National Theatre'. Hall told Devine on 3 May that the Stratford governors 'received my plans with great enthusiasm ... you and I should talk further about sharing a theatre'.[62]

As well as dealing with Blond and the Council, Devine had the problem of training and encouraging his younger directors. In 1959, two categories were established, of Associate Director and Assistant Director. Associates were not on permanent contracts but received a fee when working. Assistants were staff and received £10 per week, plus a directing fee.[63] One of the Associates was Lindsay Anderson, who wrote to Devine in 1959 to argue that the Associate Director scheme should be terminated 'at least as far as I am concerned'. Anderson felt the title was no more than nominal, since it didn't carry a vote on the Artistic Committee: 'Temperamentally I am not good at accepting a limited involvement. I like to be – or to try to be – an essential part of anything I am involved in.' This earned a withering reply from Devine which is aimed to some extent at all his assistants:

> I have known, of course, of your bad relations with most of the staff and your irrational behaviour and bursts of temper with 'inferiors' [but] what has surprised me more than anything is your lack of drive and initiative. A man in my position responds to dynamism almost more than anything else, since this is my main function and I need to share it ... when I announce the building of a mingy hut in your yard, most people look gloomy because it is so small. But who, may I ask, has done anything else?

Devine's fatigue is very evident. His supreme qualities as an all-round theatre figure effectively left him with all of the chores:

> I had hoped that all of you would do such things, as much for your own benefit as ours. Instead I find you remain as a figurehead that talks and bellyaches but does nothing. You wear a workman's cap but you don't work. You look like a workman but despise people who work – otherwise you could not be so abominably rude to people who work hard and do their best.[64]

Anderson, whose story and influence winds in and out of the story of the Court up to and including the appointment of Stephen Daldry in the 1990s, was never rebuked so powerfully again, professionally. It may be one reason why he loved Devine above all others at the Court.

On 30 June, *Roots* arrived at the Court from the newly opened

Belgrade, Coventry. Wesker suffered the disadvantage of not eliciting a strong response from Devine:

> George didn't like Wesker. Then when *Roots* was a success in Coventry, he brought it in and then the following year he was again against the Trilogy being done. And Lindsay and John and I met and said, we must push it through, and we did. George had his enthusiasms and he would respond to the enthusiasms of one of us to some extent.[65]

According to Poke, 'George simply had no really hostile feelings but no great feelings for them either. They were just there. He referred once to a group of second string writers. He included Wesker. And he certainly included Edward Bond and Keith Johnstone, who, he thought, weren't quite going to make the grade.'[66] Harewood's response was reflective: 'I vastly enjoyed *Roots* last night. How odd it is that the things that we think merely good enough to put on at the theatre so often turn out better than those in which we have great confidence. I think the play is remarkable and the performance exemplary.'[67]

Since plans for the immediate future included Arden's new play, *Serjeant Musgrave's Dance*, and with *Roots* set to arrive from Coventry, the Artistic Committee of 2 June had decided to go ahead with what was called 'the Lulu project'. This was the most obviously commercial decision made at that time at the Court in order to try to reduce the undoubted losses of the Arden. *Look After Lulu*, starring Vivien Leigh, and in association with Laurence Olivier Productions and Tennants, did well at the Court, transferred and lost the Court £1,500. So much for a 'dead cert'.

Devine had proposed, at the beginning of the ESC's life, to open with *Cock-a-Doodle Dandy*. It finally made its appearance on 17 September. O'Casey wrote to Devine about the play: 'Remember, though, George, that *Cock-a-Doodle Dandy*, being a criticism of Lourdes, will probably raise a storm, more fierce and angry than the one previously banned by the Archbishop'.[68] Devine sent O'Casey the cast list, which O'Casey described as 'as good as you could hope to get ... it will feel odd to me to have a big production like this in Britain.

With fervent good wishes for success from all of us, from Eileen and from me'.[69]

Wesker's *The Kitchen* made its appearance as a Sunday Night on 6 September.[70] No doubt much to the displeasure of the Council, *Serjeant Musgrave's Dance* made its appearance on 22 October. It was almost universally attacked in the notices, and almost universally regarded by the artists as an extraordinary work. It took 25 per cent at the box office. Anderson's hostility to critics – a perennial feature of his relationship with the Court – began essentially with their response to Arden's play, which he defended publicly and vehemently, to the alarm of the Court's publicity people. The Arden play, at the end of the fifties, was absolutely the statement Devine had been waiting to make about his theatre.[71] If Osborne had opened up the possibilities for the Court, Arden had stated unequivocally what the Court was for. Devine, by now rehearsing *Rosmersholm* with Ashcroft, wrote to Poke on 2 November that 'All our trials and tribulations come from the fact that we are making these kinds of investments in artists because we believe in them. The dividends we will just have to risk, and they certainly won't be in terms of cash.'

The cash came from the two final productions of the year on the main stage; *Rosmersholm* and Simpson's *One Way Pendulum* did 93 per cent and 87 per cent respectively. This did not prevent a gathering movement to replace Devine. He had told Duncan on 22 December that he did not like his new play, *Blind Man's Bluff*. Duncan, typically, accused Devine of double dealing and complained. On 23 December, Robin Fox wrote to Harewood that he was

> worried by one or two remarks of Neville's about George
> Devine. I get the impression that we are coming up for another
> attack on George and another attempt to unseat him. This time
> Neville claims that the Arts Council feel George is 'stale' and
> are recommending Frank Hauser from Oxford Playhouse. When
> I asked him who at the Arts Council, he said, 'the top boy –
> well, all of them'. I feel very strongly about this ... I haven't the
> faintest doubt that George *is* a bit stale and would say so and
> which of us isn't. To my mind the right way to deal with this

would be to try and find a period of two, preferably three, months, when Tony Richardson would take over and give George a really decent break ... there is some fairly shabby lobbying going on, and we ought to take some action, before the situation tends to get out of control.

Harewood agreed completely. His analysis was that there were Council members strongly against Devine's policy and one or two others who 'would not be averse to a change. I doubt if we can influence the first group, although we can presumably fight them. On the other hand we can certainly influence the second lot.'[72] The following year, 1960, was to be crucial in respect of Devine's theatre and the forces hostile to it.

Trouble was not long coming. On 5 January, Poke asked Lewenstein to try to pacify Duncan a little. Duncan's response was to tell Harewood that he intended to absent himself from Artistic Committee meetings. Blond, meanwhile, was telling Devine 'in front of Tony, that the Arts Council thought he was stale and not keeping up to standard. I told him that I equally felt we were being used as a tool for Oscar Lewenstein' (to Poke, 6 January). Devine's response is not recorded, except for a reply to Blond on 18 January: 'I know how you feel about Oscar but he has been instrumental in bringing us the following: *Member of the Wedding, Nekrassov, The Long and the Short and the Tall, The Lily White Boys* and John Arden, first introduced to us by him. Don't let's forget these things!' Whether the Arts Council said what is alleged is unclear. Poke noted to Blond on 22 March that Williams, the Council's Director-General, at lunch was very much in favour of Devine.

On 7 January, the trigger for the row arrived in the form of Fry's *Curtmantle*. The play had come via Olivier and it was sent to Harewood by Devine. However, at an Artistic Committee of 12 January 'It was decided, after long discussion, to inform Sir Laurence that we did not want to produce this play at the Royal Court.' If there is such a thing as a defining moment in the Court's history, this was it. Duncan ironically wrote that 'This is the kind of play the English Stage Company was formed to present.' Perhaps so, but the English Stage

Company Duncan was referring to no longer existed. While Duncan prepared to go public over the issue, *The Lily White Boys* opened the year after acrimonious exchanges between the author, Harry Cookson, Anderson and the Council. Cookson alleged that his play had been severely distorted to become the opposite of what he had written.[73] A double bill of Harold Pinter's *The Room* and *The Dumb Waiter* opened on 8 March. Hobson, reviewing the Bristol production, had urged Devine to take the plays to the Court. According to Gaskill, 'Hobson [said] these are wonderful plays and they must be done at the Court, and George would not be told by Harold Hobson what he should do in his theatre. So that was one of the reasons why he was so strongly against. It's silly, I know.'[74] In 1960, the plays were in fact directed by Page and James Roose Evans of the Hampstead Theatre Club. Pinter had no need of the Court subsequently. After the Pinter double bill, *The Naming of Murderer's Rock*, formerly a Sunday Night, came into the main bill as a filler to Orson Welles's direction of Olivier in Ionesco's *Rhinoceros*.

By this stage, two issues dominated discussion at the Court. The first was Duncan's last attempt to reclaim the Court. The second was the earliest attempt of the Court to take over a bigger theatre, on this occasion the old Metropolitan music hall, Edgware Road. This was in partnership with Laurence Olivier Productions, Oscar Lewenstein Ltd., and Granada Television. The scheme failed when it was discovered that a road was to go through the site. It was, however, only the first of many attempts to move. Subsequent attempts caused a deal more acrimony. On this occasion, draft notes of a meeting of Council for 5 July make it clear that Devine supported the scheme: 'G.D. said opportunities for a larger audience. Few cheap seats at Court. Artistic Committee feels that once we have got a dramatist, then give him an opportunity to speak to a larger audience. Launch him into a bigger field.'

The first issue saw Duncan producing on 1 March a document, 'Notes on the artistic policy of the English Stage Company'. It is a document which contains the injured tones of a writer already clear that the world has moved on. Consequently, the accusations are a mix of the patently untrue and the nostalgic. To say, for example, that

75

'Artists are not impressed with our achievement' is meaningless; to say that the Court has 'departed from the original aims and objects' is to forget that Duncan himself inserted those aims and objects, most particularly to do with which writers and which styles.[75] In one sense, neither Duncan nor Devine could have foreseen the events of the last four years, but if Devine adapted willingly, even at the expense of formerly held views of theatre, even if it marked a distancing from his former mentor, Michel Saint-Denis, Duncan could not. The tragedy for Duncan was that for him the emergence of modern theatre was the end of an era. Where Duncan became a spent force, although he remained at the Court until 1966, Devine produced a new 'Aims and Objects' for the Artistic Committee of 13 May. This was carefully rewritten by Harewood, as ever the skilful negotiator. Devine, in his triumph, tailored the 'Aims and Objects' to suit him and to make further demands:

> The English Stage Company still remains the only theatre with
> a consistent policy towards dramatists and modern theatre.
> This has only been achieved by sacrificing certain artistic
> principles and living a hand-to-mouth existence. The new
> programme calls for a recognition of these facts and a vigorous
> activity to put right the deficiencies of our organisation which
> can no longer be borne if the Company is to continue to be
> creative.

There was still a theatre to run. *Rhinoceros* achieved 99 per cent and transferred to the Strand Theatre, to be followed by the Wesker trilogy. It was as well that all of these shows succeeded financially, since 11 September brought Arden's *The Happy Haven* which over twenty-one performances managed 12 per cent. Gaskill, who directed, described how the masks used in the production grew from the classes given to the Writers' Group by Devine, so that the development of a new writer like Arden was linked via Devine with Saint-Denis and Copeau. Devine, in taking these classes, testified to his pedigree, that which Richardson was wont to call 'that Saint-Denis rubbish'.[76] The play, dismissed by, among others, Greville Poke ('cut to a one act farce and put on as part of a University rag, I think it might be amusing to an undergrad audience'), was predictably damned by the critics and defended by Devine, who wrote to Blond on 27 September to assert that 'Arden is probably the most important dramatist next to Osborne we have produced, and if we are going to occupy ourselves with presenting Rex Harrison in *Platonov* (not really our business at all), we must justify it by continuing to support the people we really believe in, *especially* if they don't have critical appeal ... Failures cannot be avoided. *Lulu* did our reputation more harm than all the plays of Arden put together.'

Platonov with Harrison duly attracted large audiences, though the Court's investment with him was to have disastrous consequences the following year. John Blatchley, looking after the Court while Devine stayed with Richardson in Los Angeles, wrote on 19 August about the difficulty of casting with Harrison's agreement. Harrison 'has been coming up with all sorts of mad suggestions' when the Court wanted Elvi Hale. Harrison, described by Blatchley as 'Sexy Rexy', was aware that his career had reached something of an impasse and on being asked why he was going to the Court for £60 per week suggested that he liked to think 'that the money I make in films enables me to take uncommercial chances in the theatre'.[77]

Devine then took a break to work in New York and left John Blatchley in charge. While he was away, the Court brought back *Cob and Leach*, first seen in 1959, and added *Trials by Logue*, both directed by Anderson. Devine was told on 19 November of a fuss by Anderson over the use of the word 'arse' and of a plot to play the National Anthem after the interval, despite a Council ruling that this should be done at the beginning. Devine's reply was to say 'Sorry the boys are troublesome. Hope they justify it'. On 23 November, Devine was told that 'Lindsay gave Neville Blond, Eric Bessborough and Robin heart attacks by instructing an actor, dressed as a stage hand, to smoke a cigarette during the playing of The Queen'.[78] A silly joke actually began to have repercussions. Greville Poke was said to be 'dithering with fury'. Fox was 'livid'. The Establishment was up in arms. Anderson enjoyed it all and solemnly warned the Court as to the consequences of employing 'progressive artists' (to Blatchley, 25 November). On 1 December, Anderson resigned from the Artistic

Committee, the first of many such resignations. Devine, still in New York, could not escape Anderson's opinions on the running of the theatre and policy. On 8 December, Anderson wrote to tell of his resignation, complain of the 'pylon' policy with stars – somewhat ironic in view of his later feeling – and of Richardson's constant absences from the theatre. Anderson declined frequent invitations over the years to become the Court's Artistic Director and consequently never had to manoeuvre and change faces as Devine did. To be critical from the sidelines became in Anderson's case a fine art.

The last show of 1960 was Delaney's *The Lion in Love*. Devine's view was that, after Osborne, Lewenstein and himself had seen the play in Bristol, it 'should be given a showing in London as an act of artistic faith in Delaney's talent and that we were the people to do it'.[79] Though the production did only 40 per cent, 'the act of artistic faith' was a powerful affirmation of the Court's work so far and of its hard-won victories. At the same time, a writer who was to become one of the Court's greatest, Caryl Churchill, was asserting her presence in a piece published in November 1960:

> When *Look Back in Anger* came out it was exciting, but already the working-class intellectual cracking at his wife's caricatured Daddy is a stock character. We know the English are still snobbish about accents, we're not happy about the British Empire, suburban life is often dull and many middle-aged men are unfulfilled. We can't communicate with each other, have a lot of illusions and don't know what if anything life is about. All right. Where do we go from here?[80]

3   Conflict and competition, 1961–1965

George wanted to run a theatre and here was his opportunity ... Once you've got the thing, it's not always all right because it's an illusion. I know from experience. You think, you're going to run a theatre, great, you can do the work you really aspire to, but you very rarely achieve that ... in the end you just have to be rather political and do what keeps the finances just in order.

> (Stuart Burge, interview with the author, 9 July 1996).

I suppose the Royal Court has many identities and one is thorough, high-born English-liberalism. It's a complete muddle.

> (Nicholas Wright, interview with the author, 3 October 1996)

Devine's own description of 1961 is brief and to the point:

> The year starts with a financially disastrous FRENCH SEASON – IONESCO, SARTRE, GENET – looks good but lost a lot. WESKER's THE KITCHEN much admired, especially DEXTER's direction. The mainstay of the year was TONY RICHARDSON's production of OSBORNE's LUTHER with FINNEY – Continental tour, Royal Court, Edinburgh Festival, West End and, subsequently, Broadway. HARRISON appeared in NIGEL DENNIS' AUGUST FOR THE PEOPLE but deserted it for the CLEOPATRA film, although TWENTIETH-CENTURY FOX paid for his release. GWYN THOMAS turned up with THE KEEP. ANN JELLICOE's second play THE KNACK gave much pleasure, and LINDSAY ANDERSON's production of THE FIRE RAISERS by MAX FRISCH was reckoned a big success but lost £6,500. I suffer a minor nervous breakdown.[1]

The early months of 1961 saw Devine defining the next stage of the Company's life in a series of policy documents.

Thus, in January, Devine put up a scheme which would have provided the Court with a provincial try-out theatre. Though the idea

79

may have been promoted as the creation of a theatre grid, his memorandum of 6 January says plainly that the scheme affords 'The advantage of a permanent try-out theatre, as opposed to, say, the Belgrade'. The Court, according to Devine, 'is badly in need of a studio or auxiliary theatre to develop the talent it has discovered ... The Sunday Night shows are not completely satisfactory because the rehearsal time is limited and it is becoming increasingly difficult to persuade actors to appear unpaid.' The project, which eventually became known as the Cambridge Arts Scheme was to be run by Gaskill, who had left the Court in 1960 to work elsewhere. Though *Plays and Players* for May hailed the concept as revolutionary, enabling provincial companies to send productions to the Court, none of this was envisaged by Devine. He wanted an overflow, not a conduit, one run by a Court director who would guarantee delivery of work within Court policy.[2] The scheme was scheduled to begin in October.

Also in January, Devine submitted a memorandum on artistic policy to do with programme planning. Plays would be categorised as 'Star shows; Normal shows; Experimental shows'. The first would be booked for a minimum of eight weeks, the second for six but with the possibility of extension, and the third for three weeks only, with three weeks' rehearsal. The memo contends that 'over £20,000 could have been gained by pursuing this policy from the start of the Company'. This attempt to systematise the Court's output, 'proposed as a working basis' and 'subject to amendment where necessary' seems to have been noted but not implemented.

Devine reflected on the position of his theatre in an interview he gave at the beginning of the year: 'I feel that the first statement of the Court has now been made, and all sorts of people are looking to me and saying "What are we going to do next?" It's terribly difficult to know for sure because there are so many things to do, so many fields which are quite unexplored.'[3] He defines the Court as 'a sort of *school*, after all', and targets secondary schools as part of the Court's perennial quest for an audience. In addition, he states that 'I'm going to make a big effort this year to start collecting a permanent company', and expresses a feeling that writers like Osborne, Wesker and Delaney will move away from 'modern dress naturalism. To begin with, they had to write what was close to them, from their own experience. Now they're starting to explore a much wider territory.'

Before the French season got under way, Richardson directed *The Changeling* with Jocelyn Herbert designing. Richardson's elaborate productions were clearly a source of irritation to the aesthetic increasingly apparent at the Court and in the work of Herbert. She 'used to get very angry and George used to say he's got to get it out of his system because George had done all that. It caused a lot of problems in the theatre of course.'[4] In fact, this production was the first time the two had spoken since Herbert refused to paint the set of *The Making of Moo* in June 1957. It had been designed by Audrey Cruddas. Herbert, at that stage, was still in the paintshop. It is an interesting reflection of Herbert's training in the London Theatre Studio that she took a stand early in the Court's career. It is also a telling example, perhaps, of Richardson's unconcern with such a pedigree.

Devine took a big step towards artistic autonomy at a meeting of the Artistic Committee on 22 February. With Ronald Duncan effectively silenced, he moved towards the notion of a consultative Artistic Committee. At the meeting, it was stated that 'where once we were likely to be the only management interested in certain types of plays, now our success has created a new climate in the theatre and other managements are in hot competition with us'. The point being forced is to do with the delay involved in scripts and artistic discussions wandering around all the members of the Committee. It is also clear that the point is about control. The group finally agreed that the Committee 'should in future be treated as consultative rather than executive'. The draft Minutes, subsequently modified by Harewood so that they were fit for the eyes of the Council, play the financial as well as the aesthetic card: 'When one considers how tenuous is our life-line in terms of new plays and how a simple success can turn a poor season into a good one, the importance of a decision which could lead to our securing plays we might otherwise miss will be obvious.' The appropriation of decision-making by the Artistic Directorate is of crucial importance. It also reflects the extent to which Devine was moulding conditions towards his sense of the modern emerging theatre. This was not without its disadvantages for he had demonstrated to other managements that new work could be capable of commercial success. It was still a good way from the Artistic Director having complete control. Poke, reporting the Committee's discussion in a letter to Blond of 24 February, recorded Richardson's belief 'that we were running the thing in entirely the wrong way, that the Council should give executive power to the Artistic Director and leave him to get on ... and that from time to time the Council should meet, consider what he had done and if they didn't like it fire him or if not let him carry on'. Small wonder that Council was a little chary of Richardson's sense of the correct way to go about matters.

Devine's sense of the necessity of a new beginning shows in a confidential letter he wrote to Blond in late March 1961. The first objective, 'to open up the field for the contemporary dramatist', the letter says, has been achieved but 'The next five years need a fresh impulse and a second objective.' Devine then analyses the current state of the English theatre and lists the following 'gaps'. There is

A. An outmoded and moribund attitude to the production of the classics especially Shakespeare.

B. The 'new movement', except through the medium of the rapidly reforming cinema, does not reach the 'new public'.

C. The 'new movement' is not attracting enough new writing – it is living on old capital.

D. The 'new movement' is limited by its own lack of 'dramatist education', and living in a world of its own.

E. The 'new movement' needs educating. It knows little or nothing about the varieties of theatrical style at its disposal, has no relationship with the other arts, and intellectually and theatrically it is lively but ill informed.

F. The 'new movement' managements – ourselves, Theatre Workshop and the progressive reps, are rapidly becoming try-out houses for the new managements (Codron, Lewenstein, Albery) who are cashing in on the commercial possibilities of it.

G. We do not at the Royal Court command a public for our policy –

it is either stars or 'hit reviews' which attract. This is the same situation as it was five years ago, except that what a star will appear in or what will get a hit review has changed.

The analysis demonstrates how much had changed in a few years, though whether Neville Blond understood it is doubtful. Devine's perspective goes back to pre-war theatre and he could see that there had been a revolution. The new five-year plan would now aim at what he calls 'reformation': 'The English Stage Company must maintain its essential function of leadership (at present it is coasting).' Devine wanted two new developments. The first was to be an arts centre 'where the cross-fertilisation of the theatre and other arts can be carried out, and a high level of instruction and experimentation can be achieved under reasonable conditions'. He felt that the Court with 'reconstruction and addition' would be the obvious site. The second was to be a popular theatre 'where the opening out of the drama from within and towards a larger public can take place'. The vision is a powerful one. The annual subsidy, he estimates, is 'at least £25,000 a year. The National Theatre will not provide such services to the theatre. And certainly no one else will'. There is no record of Blond's reaction and the plan, though never implemented, influenced subsequent policy, not least in the quest by some Court people for additional and/or alternative theatre space, an issue of perennial debate in the Company's history. On the same date as Devine's letter, the first leader in the *Sunday Times* for 26 March noted the Chancellor of the Exchequer's decision to increase state aid to the arts by nearly half a million pounds per annum, though at the same time Selwyn Lloyd refused to fund the building of the National Theatre.

The impetus for what Devine, at the top of this chapter, called the 'French season' in fact came from Lewenstein and for him it was not a season. Lewenstein had acquired the rights to Ionesco's *Jacques*, Sartre's *Altona*, and Genet's *The Blacks* and *The Balcony*, and his press release speaks of presenting the first three plays at the Court by invitation of the English Stage Company and in association with the Court management. *The Balcony* was to go straight into the West End in the autumn. Acquiring the rights and the actors was not easy for

Lewenstein. Peggy Ramsay, whose relationship as agent for and lover of Ionesco is a matter of record,[5] wrote to Lewenstein in August 1960 to say that Ionesco did not want *Jacques* done since it 'is not a good enough play'. Ionesco preferred Lewenstein to produce *The Bald Prima Donna*.[6] Lewenstein wrote to Ionesco to say that he had no definite plans but was looking for 'the right theatre'.[7] The deal with the Court was set up. Slight problems with the Lord Chamberlain ('For "in the lavatory with their knickers down" substitute "in their gymslips"') were resolved, but a furious row erupted in February between the Court and Lewenstein. The Court had taken to calling the three plays a season, raised seat prices and invited the French Ambassador. An enraged Lewenstein wrote on 9 February to say the term was for internal purposes only, that raising the prices was 'swindling the public' and that 'all three plays are an attack on the very things the French Ambassador stands for ... What on earth is happening to the Court? Both your proposals seem to be absolutely out of keeping with its purposes and public face.'

Jacques, for its twenty-eight performances, managed under 20 per cent. Devine wrote to Saint-Denis to say that it was 'a disaster. The critics slaughtered it and we lost a lot of money. The Sartre will probably do better.'[8] It did, at 80 per cent. Lewenstein had successfully wooed Diane Cilento to play Leni, but casting the play had had its difficulties. In casting Cilento, he went against Sartre's wishes. The latter favoured Betsy Blair who was not favoured by the play's star, Lawrence Harvey. Harvey's agent suggested that the star would withdraw if Blair was engaged. Harvey wanted Pamela Brown, and eventually withdrew by sending Lewenstein a cable which compensated the impresario to the tune of £10,000. The money was divided equally between Lewenstein's company and the Court. Harvey was replaced, successfully, by Kenneth Haigh.[9] Part of the point here bears out Devine's sense of the Court functioning as a try-out theatre for impresarios, as suggested in his letter to Blond of late March 1961. Lewenstein was casting these plays, especially their stars. As he developed the production of Genet's *The Blacks*, he wrote to Bertice Reading in New York to ask her to come over ('just what is your financial position? Probably you are broke as usual') and to Paul

Robeson to offer him a part.[10] Neither appeared in the play which managed 30 per cent at the box office. Of the three, only *Altona* transferred. By 13 June, losses on the 'season' amounted to nearly £14,000.

Devine had begun the year thinking actively about the development of both an arts centre and a bigger, popular theatre. By May, the opportunity seemed to be opening up. The arrival of the (now) Royal Shakespeare Company at the Aldwych and the Arts Theatre provided the London base that Anthony Quayle had looked for in the fifties. The competition had begun to arrive. It was in this context that a scheme developed for the amalgamation of the Court with the Old Vic under Devine's overall artistic direction with Robin Fox as General Administrator. This could come about if the Government went ahead with building the National Theatre and offered it to the Old Vic Company. The ESC Council was told of this in May at a meeting where no Minutes were taken. In June, Devine, Richardson, Blond and Fox met for lunch at a private location ('May I suggest that the Ivy is much too "theatre world" for such a meeting. The gossip set up by it would be tremendous!').[11] A working party was created, with Devine's caution, born of long experience with the Old Vic, in evidence: 'I don't think we want to show our hand too much too soon. Let's get them into the open.'[12] Devine wrote to Olivier on 10 August in reaction to Olivier's tentative suggestion of a closer liaison. Devine outlined his thinking:

> My position is really as follows: as I told you in Brighton I am
> convinced I have to find an *additional* larger theatre for the near
> future to house an expansion of this Company's work. To this
> end, the proposed merger with the Old Vic was mooted ... but
> the whole project was changed in aspect by the revival of the
> NT scheme.[13]

Devine was offered the post of Director of the Old Vic in October,[14] at a time when he was recovering from a nervous breakdown and was on three months' leave.[15] On 8 November with a persistence which hallmarks his life, Devine was urging Blond to seize the opportunity presented by the Old Vic plan:

The strength of our position is that the Vic is desperate to get *me* and I have said I won't go unless we can amalgamate ... The oldest theatre in the country comes to *us* for help and is prepared to swallow its pride and accept a link up with a very junior (but more famous today) organisation. The prestige to us is going to be tremendous.[16]

The scheme collapsed, partly because of financial crises both at the Old Vic and at the Court and partly because the developing plans for the National Theatre involving the Old Vic meant that the Vic was not now available. Devine's association with the Vic once again was inhibited by the emergence of the National.[17]

As the matter of the Old Vic continued throughout the year, the Court continued its work. By 31 May, *The Kitchen* and *Luther* were in rehearsal. The former in one sense dominated the year with eighty-six performances, achieving overall an impressive 60 per cent. If Devine was cool about Wesker's work, it certainly fared well at the Court and vindicated the pressures of the Assistants on Devine to put the play on. It may have helped that, as the Artistic Committee was told on 31 May, *The Kitchen* 'was extremely simple as it had no scenery, and only cooks' costumes'. *Luther* was more complex. Richardson wanted Albert Finney for the lead, but Finney was playing *Billy Liar* very successfully for Lewenstein. After *Billy Liar* and *Saturday Night and Sunday Morning*, Finney was a star. The delay put the production back to July, although Richardson had been ready during February. Instead he did *The Changeling*. A canny Lewenstein pointed out that *Billy Liar* was playing to over £6,000 per week and that to release him entitled Lewenstein to very favourable terms. He therefore demanded and got, much to Robin Fox's annoyance, a co-presentation and a 50 per cent investment right in any West End transfer. It is not difficult to see why Blond and Fox, for different reasons, were unhappy with Lewenstein. Devine considered that, although Lewenstein's terms were not against 'common theatrical practice ... it is unpleasant to be put in a cleft sick by anybody'.[18] *Luther* was a triumph, with Finney cited as best actor at the Paris Festival. Devine, playing the Vicar-General Staupitz, then embarked on the direction of the third and final play for the Court by Nigel Dennis.

August for the People was arguably Devine's least happy experience in the theatre. It began well enough. Devine wrote to Harewood late in 1960 to say that he had read the first act of the play and was pleased with it: 'Nigel is very keen that Rex Harrison should play the leading role.'[19] As soon as rehearsals began, it was clear that the author and leading man did not get on and the atmosphere degenerated rapidly. Harrison's own account of the play was that it had 'a marvellous first act, an unplayable second act'.[20] By 2 August, Harrison was complaining to Devine privately:

> it is quite obviously a waste of time to continue with dear Nigel Dennis present. He is completely a *novice* as far as the theatre is concerned ... We must have a free hand from now on to cut where we will ... That brings me to what it is about, 'a plea for individualism', but nobody will realise this unless we are allowed a free hand to say so. *Theatrically* ... This must be cleared up *otherwise I couldn't go on.*[21]

Despite poor reviews, the play succeeded financially until Harrison, having been offered the role of Caesar in the Burton–Taylor film of *Cleopatra*, left the production in mid-run. The Court and the author were compensated but only financially, and it is clear that the attack on Dennis and the latter's fury – he never spoke to Devine again – precipitated an already exhausted Devine's nervous breakdown. In part, his policy of recruiting novelists was damaged beyond repair; and a great friendship was gone. Harrison allows himself to have been 'over-hasty',[22] but for many at the Court the unpleasantness of the affair hastened Devine's end. Harrison was for some

> a monster. He was always going round saying that everybody's equal at the Court ... but he expected everybody to kowtow to him. The first play he did ... he wasn't quite so bad. *Platonov* was a bit out of his normal range so he was very glad to be helped. But the thing that really upset George was *August for the People*. To begin with he didn't want to play it as Nigel

> Dennis had written it because he said that's not what his public would want to come and see him in ... He made it very difficult for everybody concerned. The film company gave us about £10,000 for the release of the contract. But of course that was the end of the transfer to the West End and it absolutely broke Nigel Dennis's heart.[23]

Devine, astonishingly, wrote to Blond on 15 September to announce his going away for a rest and his proposal to ask Dennis 'to do some more work on the script'.

Devine actually stayed away from the Court on doctor's orders for three months, and Richardson took over a programme which included an Albee double bill, Chapman's *That's Us*, Gwyn Thomas's *The Keep* and Frisch's *The Fire Raisers*. As part of the Cambridge Arts Scheme, all ran in Cambridge for a week and transferred to the Court. The plays were directed by Gaskill, Dexter and Anderson. The Scheme, as with the earlier provincial repertory link, failed and was not repeated.

Towards the end of the year, protests arose, inevitably from Ronald Duncan and, to a lesser extent, Greville Poke, about the Artistic Committee. Duncan had eventually to be dissuaded from asking at the Annual General Meeting that the Artistic Committee be disbanded 'as it is now only a rubber stamp'. He was of course quite right. If the year had brought a kind of freedom to Devine's position, it had also exacted a heavy personal price. The following two years were not dissimilar, with notable exceptions.

On 25 October, Richardson wrote to Blond with details of the incoming programme. The first slot in January would either be *Man is Man* or *A Midsummer Night's Dream*. The Brecht play was frequently discussed at the Court but it was not until 1971 that it was finally directed by Gaskill. *The Dream* was scheduled to play for eight weeks. After the production, with a young cast, 'was given one of the most severe critical drubbings in the Court's history',[24] it came off after twenty-nine performances which averaged less than 23 per cent. According to Vanessa Redgrave, whose brother Corin and sister Lynn were in the production, the critics relished the attack: 'The critics

who only five years before had ridiculed the Royal Court for intro-
ducing the kitchen sink into drama were now equally incensed that
the home of the kitchen sink should be invaded by fairies and magic,
and lampooned the efforts of Tony and his young cast mercilessly.'[25]

Devine, now installed after his leave, found that things did not
change much. The imminent arrival of a new Arden play alarmed the
Council. *The Workhouse Donkey* had been turned down by the
Coventry Cathedral Festival as too large for the celebrations. Devine,
in a tongue-in-cheek letter to Harewood, asked him to read it because
'there seems to be a small conflict brewing up about the play in the
organisation'.[26] The plan was for Anderson to direct it in November.
Blond, in a memo to Devine of 5 April, carefully opined that 'Our
success with John Arden has not been all that could be desired' and
suggested a Sunday Night. Devine, almost cheerily, replied that Arden
'has been the most expensive dramatist we have promoted' (6 April). If
he kept faith, he also had to bend occasionally and the play found a
home in Chichester for the National Theatre, directed by Gaskill.

In April, Devine wrote a piece for the *Guardian*, called 'Court
account' (2 April). After producing carefully formulated statistics for
six years' work, Devine, rather wearily perhaps, defends his and Joan
Littlewood's work. Together, the two companies 'have done more to
enhance the reputation of British theatre abroad than any other
groups'. However, it is Devine's contention that the two companies
still do not get their just deserts:

> But no! It's the opera, the Old Vic, the Royal Shakespeare, the
> provinces that are in favour, because they are safe politically.
> Goodness knows, we at the Court have become infinitely more
> 'corrupt' than in our early passionate days. But we wanted to
> survive. So calculation has been added to conviction, and
> compromise abounds. The sharp point of our endeavour has
> been somewhat blunted ... On reading the letters of Shaw to
> Granville Barker about their struggles in this very building in
> which I write this, I realise that very little has changed in the
> past fifty years.

The conclusion to the piece highlights the paradox of Devine. He was offered the Court Directorship because he was in many ways establishment, certainly theatre establishment. The Old Vic experience taught him to work from the inside out. Yet he knows the dangers of seduction: 'I suppose in our minds we know that to be accepted completely by the middle, to be smiled upon by the top, is the first sweet kiss of death. So we carry on, flirting with death in order to live.'

The Keep, which had opened at the Court on 20 February, had transferred and finished its run at the Piccadilly on 21 April. Not thought of as quite a Court play, it nevertheless produced some vital funding. The Knack, considered a real Court play, had opened on 27 March and done well at a little under 50 per cent. The real success, however, was with Wesker's Chips with Everything, originally turned down by the Court, but presented in association with a commercial management (Bob Swash) and, with Tennessee Williams' Period of Adjustment, was the only financial success of the year.[27] The Wesker transferred to the Vaudeville on 13 June, having earlier satisfied the Lord Chamberlain on a few niceties ('for "wind from a duck's behind" substitute "wind from Mount Zion"') and, whatever his reservations, Devine would have been happy at the play's success. He would not, however, have been happy at the reaction to Osborne's double bill, Plays for England. The Sunday Times for 29 April obtained a copy of the play and in effect reviewed it before it was produced. The Court threatened legal action, which came to nothing, but in some ways the reaction typifies the mood of the Court during the year. The mood was not helped by a piece in the Daily Telegraph of 21 May by W. A. Darlington. Darlington suggested that the figures proved 'that the kind of new play generally put on at the Royal Court has little appeal to the general theatre-going public', precisely what the Court needed at this stage in its development. Two months later, the Financial Times carried a piece by Cuthbert Worsley on the rise of Stratford and Peter Hall. On 27 July Blond sent an angry letter to W. E. Williams of the Arts Council to complain about Hall's 'desire to snaffle the cream of the artistic profession ... I have yet to see anything brilliant about this young man, who does not appear to have an original thought, but is trying to get artistic directors in the shape of Peter Brook and

Michel Saint-Denis at £5,000 a year.' Williams replied on 30 July to agree that 'Peter Hall, of course, is an empire builder. He is spending the earth securing options on people, a fact which will make it extremely hard, in due course, to recruit a team for the National Theatre.' However, Williams's letter betrays his surprise that Devine had endorsed Hall's Aldwych venture and did not regard him as a competitor.

While *Plays for England* had managed 58 per cent and *Brecht on Brecht*, with a memorable visit from Lotte Lenya, had climbed to 64 per cent, the rest of the year's programme was indifferent financially. Neither of the remaining main bill shows, the English première of *Happy Days* and a double bill by Waterhouse and Hall of *The Sponge Room* and *Squat Betty*, did well. At least *Happy Days* maintained the connections between Beckett and the Court but even here there were difficulties. Devine and Beckett had been waiting for almost a year for Joan Plowright to become available to play Winnie. Devine had come out of *Brecht on Brecht* in early October to begin rehearsals for the Beckett because the scheduled director, Donald McWhinnie, had withdrawn. Plowright also withdrew because she was pregnant. Eventually Brenda Bruce was cast on the recommendation of John Dexter.[28] While *Happy Days* was running, 9 December saw the début of one of the major playwrights of the Court and of modern British theatre. Edward Bond's *The Pope's Wedding* played, ironically in view of how Bond came to regard Beckett, on the main stage with Winnie's mound becoming Alen's hut. Four days later, Devine commissioned another play from Bond. This was *Saved*.

On 4 November, Devine flew out for a one-month tour of Brazil for the British Council.[29] On his return, one element of his early 1962 plans was beginning to be discussed, that of the reconstruction of the building. This had formally surfaced at the Artistic Committee meeting of 13 November. The proposal was that the Court should leave Sloane Square for the six months of 1964 while rebuilding took place. However, Richardson said that it was hoped to secure a large theatre for a period of eighteen months from a date in 1963, including the six months for reconstruction, in order to present large-scale shows in conjunction with Lewenstein or another management.

Richardson proposed either Vanessa Redgrave in *The Seagull* and *St Joan of the Stockyards* or Finney in *Luther* and *Arturo Ui*. It was agreed to present 'big, moneymaking productions with stars' and to 'stockpile' new plays for the Court's re-opening. Thus the entire operation was to leave Sloane Square, as it was to nearly a quarter of a century later. It was an alternative way of Devine's securing his larger house but in the event only the months allotted to alterations to the Court came about. In the last section of a difficult year, Ashcroft wrote to Harewood about Devine:

> I cannot help feeling that he may have tried to come back to it all too soon ... it would be a very good thing if he took a sabbatical year and let the Court be run by a triumvirate – Gaskill, Dexter and Anderson – Tony being obviously too involved in other things ... It would rest and refresh him ... and I think it would be excellent for the other three to take the responsibility – how good it would be for the Court I don't know![30]

Ashcroft's idea never came to fruition though her foreboding proved entirely accurate.

These were lean times for the Court. Devine noted of 1963 that it was 'A thin year again, although we kept the new dramatists' flag flying'.[31] The reference is to Henry Livings's *Kelly's Eye* (which won the Britannica Award for Playwrights), Frank Hilton's *Day of the Prince* (from a Sunday Night in September 1962) and Barry Reckord's *Skyvers*. None of these made money. With 22.5 per cent, *Skyvers* did the best at the box office. Financial failure brought inevitable pressure from the Council. Devine pugnaciously defended the plays: 'All deserved better treatment than they got. Fortunately, *Luther* was doing fine in New York.'[32] And at last the club upstairs became available. Clement Freud wrote to his members to announce that his lease would run out in January 1963. He transferred his members to the newly opened Establishment Club in Greek Street: 'Dear Member, I have had your money, you have had my hair and my waistline ... goodbye'.

If the lack of good new plays was increasingly noticeable, it did not deter Devine from pursuing his grand objective, which had been developing during 1962. A memo on the Court Development Scheme went to the Calouste Gulbenkian Trust in January of 1963. The preamble argues for a studio to cater for the development of all kinds of theatre artists and 'the nucleus of a company of actors'; an arts centre; and the development of new audiences, 'especially the young'. The Court itself was to be completely reorganised to provide sixty extra seats, 'extensive new public space' and extra bars. The stage would have a wider proscenium 'and a more open and simplified method of presentation'. The studio theatre, of 120 seats, would be built behind the stage. The sweep and ambition of the scheme is visionary and contemporary. If put in place 'the Royal Court could be a day and night cultural centre in Sloane Square, take on a new lease of life and make, once more, a unique mark on British theatre'.

One aspect of the vision began on 17 February for ten weeks. The Court's Actors' Studio, directed by Gaskill, started in the newly built but not yet opened Jeannetta Cochrane Theatre in Kingsway. At this stage, Gaskill was invited to join Olivier and John Dexter to begin the National Theatre. Olivier had wanted Devine. Failing that, he wanted Devine's trainees. Gaskill's account of this emphasises the temptations. The Studio concentrated on improvisations of different kinds. Initially, it was comic improvisation; Claude Chagrin and mime; Keith Johnstone and Gaskill with masks; and Devine with comedians' tricks. The work produced a Sunday Night, 'First Results', on 28 April. The Studio became a vital part of the Court's life. On the other hand, the temptation for Gaskill was the lure of a genuine ensemble at the National: 'The idea of an ensemble haunted all our dreams'.[33] He was to return to it as Devine's successor.

Some of the more interesting plays were to be found amongst the Sunday Nights for much of the year. *Skyvers* began life as a Sunday Night on 7 April. *Spring Awakening*, damaged by the Lord Chamberlain's pencil, appeared on 21 April. And a piece by Vanessa Redgrave, based on her visit to Cuba after the Bay of Pigs débâcle, called *In the Interests of the State*, found a slot on 24 March. According to Redgrave, Devine was George V reviewing the British troops in Dublin; Robert Stephens was Byron denouncing Judge

Jeffreys; Redgrave delivered 'a complacent Christmas Day broadcast speech by Elizabeth II, which I counterpoint with radio reports of school children's demonstrations in Cyprus and the sounds of violence of the British troops in Kenya'.[34] As interesting, but as main-bill shows not yielding much cash, were *The Diary of a Madman*, put together from Gogol by Anderson and Richard Harris, and a translation by Diane Cilento of Pirandello's *Naked*.

Problems with the plan to rebuild the Court surfaced at the Management Committee meeting on 15 March when it was reported that Lord Cadogan had declined to extend the lease on the theatre, though 'Conscious of our desire and conscious of the importance of our work as a potential experimental branch of the National Theatre [*sic*] he expressed a desire to help us in every way practical'. It was therefore decided to proceed in stages. At the same time, a proposal was developing for a federation with the National Theatre. Devine felt the way to handle this was via the Court's Actors' Training Scheme, with Gaskill working six months for the Scheme and six for the National. Both the rebuilding and the federation were in one way part and parcel of the same progression. A 'new' Court, allied to a new National Theatre could work to everyone's advantage. By 19 April, the Management Committee was hearing that the Cadogan Estate had plans for developing an 'Island Site' within the next ten years. It was decided therefore to concentrate on the existing building, the lease for which expired in 1991. The building proposed at the rear of the Court now seemed unlikely. Tony Richardson said that 'he thought we ought to make full use of the top part of the theatre premises previously occupied by Mr Freud'. This of course did not happen until February 1969, when the Theatre Upstairs opened. The meeting then considered Scheme A and B by the architect, Elidir Davies. Scheme A provided for a more spacious foyer and additional bars. Scheme B would widen the auditorium area and have a single sweep of seats. Scheme A, which also included improved stage lighting, an adjustable forestage, a new and better-raked stalls floor and a new counterweight system, would cost £80,000. Scheme B, the bigger and closer to Devine's ideas, was not costed. The theatre would close on 1 November for the six months' work 'and it was decided that we should make arrangements to operate from a West End theatre during the period'. Devine wrote to Byam Shaw to say that 'We are going to redo our auditorium – not very fundamentally, I fear'.[35]

The federation, rather like the great plans for the rebuilding of the Court, never really got off the ground. The interests of the two theatres were separate. Devine was unhappy at the idea of his Court becoming the National's experimental annexe. Richardson was very suspicious of the whole affair. Writing to Blond, he felt it was all 'extremely vague. I suspect everyone concerned is as muddled as everyone else and that only when and if something more detailed and practical is worked out can one clearly take any position.' Although Olivier and Devine issued a joint memo of intent concerning the Studio training for actors from both theatres, finally the practicalities ensured the demise of the scheme.

On 12 September, Alec Guinness appeared at the Court for the first time in Ionesco's *Exit the King*, having played for a week at Newcastle and a week at the Edinburgh Festival. Business was very good (93 per cent box office) but the show ended on 2 November because of Guinness's other commitments. Devine began rehearsing Tennessee Williams's *The Milk Train Doesn't Stop Here Any More* in the first week of October. On 8 October he had what he described as 'a small heart attack'.[36] The show was cancelled. Devine was ordered to take three months' leave. Guinness wrote a note of sympathy: 'How beastly for you. Do hope you are feeling chirpier now and not bothering your white head with Court worries ... I took Ionesco to lunch last Saturday. He read *Plays and Players* instead of the menu and asked for a slice of Natasha Parry.'[37] Devine wrote to Saint-Denis, agreeing with this letter: 'What's the point of killing oneself for what amounts to very little!' Devine was struck by letters of sympathy he received from New York after an item about him appeared in the *New York Times*:

> Whereas London has been comparatively silent. I suppose they would like to see me out of the way. It's not that. It's just indifference. Even from the many people for whom one has worked to promote. Extraordinary. Except John Osborne, not

one dramatist, not *one* director (Tony excepted) has sent me a line of encouragement. Well, fuck them all, I say.[38]

Devine concluded the letter, saying 'There is no damage. Just a warning', and carried on working, albeit initially on a reduced level.

With the Court imminently going dark for the ESC (although other shows did appear[39]), Devine had some time to relax and think. But only briefly. On 2 November he reacted to a letter from Blond to say that the figure now for rebuilding was £140,000. Devine confessed himself 'rather shaken' by the news. By 14 November Devine sensed that Blond was contemplating abandoning the entire scheme and wrote to him:

> Suddenly we get a request for a programme in case we do not go ahead with the alterations! As you know the programme is set for the West End – staff have been dismissed – and nothing has been worked out for the immediate future. Surely it is not your intention to drop the whole idea and just carry on as before? Maybe we must study a modified scheme of a much less ambitious nature.

Devine from his letter is certain that Esdaile has unsettled Blond and wants his theatre back. Six days later, Devine presented a radically modified scheme in a Management Committee meeting. This involved, amongst other things, a new lighting box, a new stage floor, new counterweights, a new stalls floor and bar, and a newly decorated dress circle.[40]

Devine, once again, saw his plans go awry at the end of an enormously difficult year. At the same meeting, he asked for help, an assistant, and nominated Gaskill. Devine had shouldered the entire burden as usual, suffered a nervous breakdown, taken a little leave, worked again and had a heart attack. It was a poor reward for his achievement. He began 1964 still without what was now called a Co-Artistic Director. Gaskill eventually turned it down, as had Michael Elliott, who thought that when they met Devine appeared depressed: 'He had aimed at a kind of reform that would extend into the West End, but things in the theatre at large were much as ever; he felt he hadn't achieved what he wanted.'[41] The next suggestion was that Anthony Page be appointed Artistic Director, with Lindsay Anderson as his Associate, for one year from September 1964. The suggestion came from the two directors. Page had a firm offer from the Royal Shakespeare Company which required an answer by 19 January. Thus at an emergency Artistic Committee meeting on 15 January, the incoming directors proposed a policy which reflected the dearth of new plays and focused more on modern classics: 'Their policy envisages a fair proportion of small cast plays – a small nucleus of a company – and a return to our original policy, of some kind of simplified setting' (Doreen Dixon, General Manager, to Blond, 28 January). The shift in policy was made clear at the Management meeting of 25 February where it was stated that 'new plays will be presented only if they are deemed to be suitable for production and not solely because they happen to be new plays. This procedure would necessarily mean that there would be a number of revivals included in the programme.' This very clear snub was made the more unpalatable because it was Devine himself, in the absence of Page and Anderson, who presented the policy to the Committee. The implication of reckless presentation, regardless, of new work, must have been very difficult for Devine to accept. Harewood, absent from the meeting, queried strongly the wording of the policy shift, and insisted that a different form of words be found for any press release (to Poke, 19 March).

The Seagull opened the ESC's season at the Queen's and was rapturously received. Devine played Dorn in a company which included Ashcroft, Redgrave and Peter Finch. As Dorn, Devine was perceived by Court people to have in some way represented them all on stage, and also a lot of himself. As Lewenstein said of Dorn's speech after Konstantin's play in Act I, where Dorn says he likes the play: ' "There's something in it ..."', this was not just a play but our own lives upon the stage. All that scene had the same wonderful connection with George's life in the theatre'.[42] For Redgrave, 'George was Dr Dorn.'[43] For Richardson, 'it was the summing-up of the past ... in that it was the last time we – George, Jocelyn, Peggy and I – were together'.[44] As Devine wrote to Lewenstein about the opening of *The*

Seagull: 'Tony is now so high powered that anything like common sense seems out of place' (17 October 1963). *Saint Joan of the Stockyards* did not do well. Redgrave, who was very pregnant, collapsed during rehearsals, was replaced at very short notice by Siobhan McKenna, and the play was withdrawn after three weeks at a cost of £15,000.[45] The third play was to have been Michael Hastings's *The World's Baby* but it was felt not to be up to standard and was being rewritten.

Before the ESC returned to the Court to open on 9 September with *Inadmissible Evidence*, Page and Anderson had parted company. Anderson remembers it being about casting *Julius Caesar*, which opened on 26 November:

> after starting with the idea of a company, and Anthony being
> very keen on it and in fact persuading me to use an actress
> whom he had had in *Inadmissible Evidence* in *Julius Caesar*,
> when it came to the case of Daniel Massey, an ideal person to
> play Ben Travers [in *Cuckoo in the Nest*, which preceded
> *Caesar*], Anthony absolutely refused and insisted on using
> Nicol Williamson who wasn't particularly suited to playing
> farce. That left Dan with only one part to do and I thought that
> this was so indicative of a lack of a collaborative spirit that I
> said he ought to carry on and finish the season himself.[46]

Anderson quit, not for the first or last time. The press quickly picked up on the new régime. *Theatre World* noted 'a significant switch in emphasis ... to concentrate as much on rediscovery and re-interpretation of the classics as on new work'.[47]

The great success of *Inadmissible Evidence* was followed by *Cuckoo in the Nest*. Devine professed himself at the Management meeting of 19 October to be 'reasonably sanguine about its success', but he cannot have contemplated without some dismay what was happening to his theatre. Page had proposed that the Court operate a repertory scheme with a bill of plays hardly designed to do other than transfer. Thus *Inadmissible Evidence* could not be exploited immediately because some of its principal actors were contracted to appear in other plays of the season. The play in fact had to wait until March

1965. *Caesar*, in modern dress, opened on 26 November to mixed notices, and the year ended with a revival of *Waiting for Godot*.[48]

The year also saw Devine's resignation, which he put in a letter to Blond of 14 October. He wrote two days later to Poke that 'It is clear to me that I need a change, although I don't know what as yet.' The Devon contingent was quick to act. Blacksell wrote to Harewood to say that Devine 'has served us well, but in my opinion for too long'. He further opined that someone was needed 'who has an interest in music and dance as well as drama'.[49] Harewood replied quite sharply to say that Blacksell's ideas added 'unnecessary complications to the already difficult business of finding an artistic director ... the business of organising a theatre, choosing plays, and putting them on satisfactorily is beyond most people, but to add to that a positive interest in music and dance, and in the educational possibilities of theatre, is making the field so narrow as to be almost non-existent'. Undeterred, Blacksell suggested Robert Helpmann, Robert Shaw and Harewood himself.[50] Blacksell then circulated a memo on artistic policy which, among other things, said that Devine's advice on a successor should be sought 'but he should not be the kingmaker'. He again proposed Harewood or, if not, Poke. Blacksell's perception of what had developed at the Court is amply demonstrated by this last.

Meanwhile, the outgoing Artistic Director contemplated the year's work:

> A new season in a renewed theatre opens with a new
> tremendous Osborne – INADMISSIBLE EVIDENCE. New excitement.
> A young Artistic Director, ANTHONY PAGE (ex-Assistant
> Director) takes the helm while I am in the background,
> avuncular. This is as it should be. The NATIONAL THEATRE has
> five of our ex-Assistants. The ROYAL SHAKESPEARE is doing
> ENDGAME and is accused of being 'dirty'. Well! Well![51]

Devine's resignation was publicly announced by Blond at the annual lunch for critics at the Savoy. In his resignation speech, Devine spoke of his work:

> To say that this is an emotional occasion for me would be a

gross understatement. In a few months' time I shall be giving up a work which has engrossed me day in and day out, weekends and all, for ten years of my life. And sitting round this table there are many who have been through most of these ten years with me ... I am deeply tired. The weight of this edifice has driven me into the ground up to my neck, like poor Winnie in *Happy Days*. I should have passed the job on several years ago ... I am getting out just in time.

Devine reviewed the number and range of plays done at the Court, and paid his graceful tribute to the one writer without whom the Court would surely have died: 'The jewel in our crown – our line in the history books – among all these is Mr John Osborne'. The occasion, according to Lindsay Anderson, elicited no response among the assembled critics:

Nobody turned a hair. I was next to John Osborne and Jocelyn Herbert was on the other side of him and Tony Richardson was on the other side of the table. I was appalled by this and I could see that Jocelyn was very hurt by it. George of course just sat there and didn't say anything and I whispered across to Tony and to John, 'Go on, for God's sake, get up and say something.' And everybody was beginning to get up and drift off in a characteristically English way and I just got up and said something. I haven't the remotest idea what I said. I felt it had to be done. And afterwards Bill told me that he then and there decided he would take it on.[52]

Herbert says that Anderson 'off the top of his head made a most wonderful speech about George. It needed saying. Bill was so moved – sentimental old bugger – by the speech that he said he would come to the Court after all.'[53]

Devine wanted Gaskill above all others to take over: 'Bill was a chosen son of George ... though he was not at all the closest person to George', according to Harewood,[54] and Gaskill perhaps found the real reason:

I think one reason George wanted me to run the Court and

responded to me was because I was a teacher and I tapped into all that passion he had. Because I had taken up the mask work, he saw my response to all that excitement *he* had at the London Theatre Studio and the Vic School. There was no-one else, not Lindsay, not John, who were into teaching. George saw me as having some sense of the cultural tradition and he valued that above everything.[55]

The press floated names such as Anderson, Page, Tynan, Olivier, Brook. Jo Hodgkinson lunched Blond to discuss the succession, together with Harewood and Fox. Blond wrote to Blacksell on 19 January to say that he had asked Harewood to succeed. This was declined. Hodgkinson also declined because he had four years left to serve with the Arts Council. Blond did not suggest Poke 'because I do not feel I could agree with this'. He says further that the Artistic Committee was to meet that afternoon. Harewood's notes of the meeting record an assortment of names, including Iain Cuthbertson, Page, Piers Haggard, Frank Dunlop, Gaskill, Jim Haynes and Robin Midgely. Duncan, inevitably, argued against the selection method. Poke's notes of the meeting record that Duncan wanted the post advertised. Herbert was not very happy about Gaskill and preferred Page. Devine, however, wrote to Blond on the same day to stress the confidentiality regarding 'the possibility of Gaskill. May I *beg* you not to talk about this to anyone till we meet because if it got out, especially to Olivier, before Gaskill has talked to him, it would wreck everything.' Gaskill was duly appointed to become Artistic Director from September 1965. The *Bradford Telegraph and Argus* was ecstatic. The appointment 'is exhilarating news for the provinces. And it could be of exceptional benefit to Bradford' (4 February).

The main-stage productions which attracted attention for the remainder of Page's run were *Spring Awakening*, brought in from a Sunday Night of April 1963, *Meals on Wheels* and *A Patriot for Me*. There were also important Sunday Nights during the year. Peter Gill's first play at the Court, *The Sleepers' Den*, was performed on 28 February, and 8 August saw his début as a director of Lawrence's *A Collier's Friday Night*, the precursor of the celebrated Lawrence trilogy of 1968. David Cregan, an important Court writer, saw his first play, *Miniatures*, performed on 25 April and Michael Hastings's play, intended for the 1964 season at the Queen's, finally emerged on 29 August. Thomas Osborne's translation of *Spring Awakening* had been preceded by *Happy End* (lyrics by Brecht; book by Dorothy Lane; music by Kurt Weill) but, unlike the Brecht, Wedekind's story attracted the attention of the Lord Chamberlain. According to Johnstone,[56] the Chamberlain called for two scenes to be cut 'and gave two warnings about kissing between boys' – this for the Sunday Night show. A licence was issued for the 1963 production, but cuts were made, and 1965 saw the acceleration of the row between the Court and the censor. It is a measure of the Court's growing importance and fame that, whereas it could previously have been dismissed as a small, out-of-the-way venue, its reputation now attracted a far wider audience. Thus the Court showed the first ever public performance of *Spring Awakening* in Britain.

The difficulties with the Chamberlain were included in a speech Devine gave in Stratford at the annual birthday celebrations for Shakespeare. Invited to propose the toast to 'the drama' (which he promptly changed to 'the theatre'), Devine inveighed against 'the most undemocratic institution in our public life ... we must be freed from this antiquated absurdity'. He also suggested that the standard of theatre criticism must be raised: 'The life of a theatre critic is a dog's life. Who wants to be criticised by a dog?' Attending dignitaries and ambassadors would no doubt have been bemused by someone who opened his speech with: 'Mr Mayor, Your Excellencies, My Lord Bishop, My Lord, My Lord Mayor, Your Worships, Ladies and Gentlemen. I've never heard myself say that before. I don't suppose I ever will again. It was worth the train fare to hear myself say it.'

Meals on Wheels also attracted the censor's attention. A script submitted to the Chamberlain by the Bristol Old Vic on 15 June 1964 produced requests for alterations. No agreement resulted in the production being abandoned, although there were other reasons. Lewenstein, who had bought Charles Wood's play, reacted with amusement to the Chamberlain's demands: 'I think it is ridiculous that they should insist on the Duke of Windsor not being mentioned and I think we should fight this all the way before giving in. I can understand them being protective towards the Virgin Mary but not the Duke of Windsor.'[57] The play then went to the Court with Page attempting to move the Chamberlain over some proposed cuts in a letter of 3 April 1965 to Colonel Penn at the Chamberlain's office. On 23 April, the Chamberlain asked for a clean copy 'as they are completely out of their depth with all the amendments and alterations attached to the old one'. Early in May, the play received a licence and went on at the Court on 19 May, directed by John Osborne. During its run, the play was ' "inspected" by a representative of the Lord Chamberlain who noticed a number of deviations ... Lord Cobbold decided to take no action ... "Generally I agree with the *FT* critic that all this is such drivel as to be inoffensive and incapable of corrupting a rabbit." '[58]

He was not so lenient about *A Patriot for Me*. Devine had reported on 28 August 1964 that he had received the play and that it was too big for presentation at the Court. At the Management Committee meeting, Devine suggested it be offered to Finney for presentation in a series of plays in a large theatre. By 19 October, Richardson was offering to direct the play at the Court, though large and expensive. Osborne had offered to help financially. The biggest blow was that the Chamberlain was refusing a licence and the Court might have to turn itself into a theatre club in order to present the play to members only of the English Stage Society. The latter occasionally had its uses, but the notion of a club theatre was strongly antipathetical to Devine. It was, however, the only way, and the play began rehearsing with Maximilian Schell playing the lead on 24 May, after a succession of nervous British actors had refused it. The part of Baron von Epp, the drag queen hostess, had been written for Devine, whom Page made audition and wait while he saw other hopefuls.[59] Herbert records that Devine 'dressed in his office at the top of the building and used to sail through the secretary's room in his high heels and corsets smoking a cigar saying, "Excuse me, I'm just going to the Ladies." '[60] On 7 August, Devine, having completed his performance, had another heart attack, was taken to St George's Hospital, and on 13 August suffered a stroke. The left side of his body was paralysed. He was discharged in mid-October and confined to a wheelchair. He was fifty-four.

A week after his collapse after the performance, he wrote to Osborne: 'I can't help feeling I made a balls of it by collapsing last week, but I suppose I should not have gone on on Saturday night. But the thought of all the flap and the understudy in my costume and that packed house and one's innate vanity. Oh well, best love to you both from the Baron who went too far.'[61]

4   A socialist theatre, 1965–1969

I think it is a fact that isn't generally appreciated about the Court that there really
were, after George and Tony, two very distinct kinds of tradition at the Court. One
was Bill, together with Peter Gill. The other was Anthony and myself .
(Lindsay Anderson, interview with the author, 5 December 1984).

All of them seemed to me to be non-political animals. The Court had a name for
being a radical theatre but it was radical in a rather vague sort of way. It wasn't
radical in any sort of way that connects with political philosophy.
(Oscar Lewenstein, interview with the author, 14 December 1983)

Before he officially took over as Artistic Director, Gaskill produced on
26 March a position paper in which he reviewed the current state of
the theatre. Some important things had changed. These included:

1.   The emergence of the two large-scale permanent companies –
     The National Theatre and the Royal Shakespeare, playing in
     repertoire modern as well as classical plays.
2.   The decline of the West End Theatre as a home for straight
     plays.
3.   The death of weekly rep and the growth of two or three weekly
     rep companies and the raising of the standard of plays (though
     not necessarily of the performance) in the provinces'.

The theatre world had moved on since Devine began the venture, and
the Court needed to reassess its position. The danger was that of
innovator being overtaken. In particular, the question of 'classic plays'
was to recur. Gaskill's own view as to the Court's role in the new
scheme of things was that it should 'maintain itself as a theatre where
risks can be taken in a way that the larger companies cannot afford'.
There was, Gaskill argued, only one way of doing this which was as a
permanent company playing in repertoire: 'excited by two years with

a permanent company at the Old Vic, I took the Court back to its beginnings'.[1] He did this, as had Devine, via George Harewood, who wrote to Blond on 26 March to say that Gaskill 'wants to suggest a policy that is basically long term and should in the end in his view save us money – but it is long term, and may not pay off in the first year':

> He wants to do the plays in true repertory, that is to say with a choice of more than one play a week. This pattern has not only been made familiar to audiences recently at the Old Vic and the Aldwych, but it is also attractive to actors who thus avoid the monotony of eight repetitions a week. In this way we can avoid the ignominy and waste of money of 'dark' weeks, as we can never be caught without a play already rehearsed.

Gaskill's paper argued for the Court to do 'only contemporary work – whether revivals or new plays, with a small nucleus of actors under short term contract, either six months or a year ... I don't want the Court to become institutionalised, but I think it should have continuity of work to ensure the growth and development of all working in it.' Gaskill had seen playing in true repertory fail with Devine and, to a lesser extent, with Anthony Page in his 1964 season, but his experiences with the system at the National had a marked effect on him. It was also true that, with the advent of the RSC and the National, the audiences were rather more educated in their theatre-going than had been the case in 1956. Gaskill had to develop his own distinctive route, which would distinguish the Court from the others, and himself from Devine.

The Council was dubious, but acquiesced, given the persuasion of Harewood. Poke was 'very suspicious ... but a feeling that if you've got a new Artistic Director he should be given his head ... Bill wanted to have a go and ... our attitude was, OK, good luck to you and we'll see how it works. And it didn't'.[2] One of the spin-offs from the system was the creation of a group of like-minded actors 'who worked with enormous intensity. When it broke up, it had already created a pool of actors who were used over a number of years ... and that did give the Court an identity'.[3] Gaskill was perfectly realistic in his sense of a gamble being taken, but also in his conviction that 'the important thing is to start as strongly as you can. If you are going to be eroded by compromise, then let it happen, but it's really important to start with the clearest principles you can.'[4] In his convictions, he was supported strongly by Devine, who taught his successor the intricacies of budget making.[5]

Starting strongly also meant starting again, which in turn meant changes in personnel. Gaskill decided that his Associates would be Keith Johnstone and Iain Cuthbertson, then at the Citizens', Glasgow. Johnstone was already at the Court but had directed very little. Gaskill felt that in theory the combination of Johnstone – the 'unpaid conscience of the Court'[6] – and Cuthbertson – 'to stand for traditional and popular theatrical values'[7] – would broaden the base of the Court's work, but 'the combination was disastrous', since Cuthbertson was nervous about the Court and Johnstone was unhappy as a director.[8] But there was more to it than that. Gaskill had to make his own statement about the original Court ethos. Devine always had endorsed enthusiasm, as his Associates learnt. If that was there, Devine would go with it, even if, as with Wesker, the work was not particularly to his liking. The consequence of this was that in Devine's time the mix was catholic, and the commitment personal; not fundamentally ideological, not committed exclusively on a political basis, but the product of fervour. Gaskill expressed this later:

> when I was working there as an assistant we felt there were two kinds of Royal Court. [One] which used the same group of actors, which had tremendous loyalty to particular writers and their relationship with directors, and there was an alternative Royal Court which was always looking towards the West End and the stars, and I think that dichotomy was in the Court from the very beginning.[9]

In stating that the Court would try true repertory again; that there would be as a consequence no transfers; that there would be a resident company; and that the writers associated with the Court would be pre-eminent, Gaskill effectively discarded one of the 'Royal Courts', deliberately narrowed the focus and attempted to create what Devine himself had looked to build.

Discarding one strand of the former activity also involved former colleagues, particularly Anderson and Page. They were comprehensively 'elbowed'. The strand they represented was excluded and they never forgave Gaskill for it. Anderson recalls talking to Miriam Brickman, who had been Casting Director:

> and Bill announced to her that he was going to be a new broom and sweep clean. So when he brought in Keith . . . and he brought in Jane Howell and Cuthbertson, this really was Bill's replacement for us. So we were not just officially anything to do with the Court, but we were really out in the cold. It's rather characteristic of Bill to feel, well, to hell with all that old stuff. In getting rid of people like Anthony and myself, he was opting for a different kind of theatre.[10]

Gaskill added to Cuthbertson and Johnstone Jane Howell, John Gunter as resident designer and Helen Montagu as General Manager. Peter Gill was already resident and, together, it looked like a formidable team. However, without well-received plays, the team could be as good as it liked. True repertory depends totally on a group of productions which are well liked. It's possible to carry one problem by re-organising the others. It's not possible to go further. The plays which opened the first season were all by Court writers. Jellicoe's *Shelley*, the first play in the repertoire, opened on 18 October. Nineteen performances created 28 per cent at the box office and extremely hostile reviews. Simpson's *The Cresta Run* (26 per cent) was also savaged. The third play was *Saved* (3 November).

Saved was originally going to open Gaskill's reign at the Court. It was to be, and subsequently became, Gaskill's statement of intent. The play had arrived at the Court on 18 September 1964 but by April 1965 no decision had been reached and the Court's option on it lapsed. At this stage, the script was with Page. Doreen Dixon, the General Manager, apologised to Bond and let him know of Gaskill's intention to commission another play 'which I gather is a comedy' (5 April). Gaskill eventually got the script at the end of April and 'I remember reading it straight through and being absolutely convinced that it should be done and that I should direct it myself'.[11] Johnstone was originally slated to direct *Saved* and Gaskill the Simpson (since he had directed the others), but they swapped. Gaskill sent the play to Devine, who replied on 28 April, having marked the script up where he thought the Lord Chamberlain would object. The list demonstrates the process involved in obtaining a licence:

1. The intrinsic violence will automatically disturb the reader.
2. I have marked with pencil all the things I could spot that are likely to meet with objections. I may have missed some. It should be checked.
3. My advice is to cut out all the words we *know* will not be passed – such as bugger, arse, Christ, etc, *before* submission. To have them in creates immediate hostility. The problem is to *get the play on with a licence*: not to alter the L.C. I presume.
4. I suggest that Charles Wood's technique is a good one. Swallow pride and reinvent, even one's own swear words and phrases. Rewrite scenes, if necessary, to retain intrinsic rhythms etc rather than arguing over words or phrases which he will never yield on.
5. Cut out stage directions which suggest sexual situations. I have bracketed these.
6. I think you might get away with the stockings scene if you present it carefully, as I have indicated . . .
7. As for the baby, I don't think the scatological bits will get through under any circumstances. Worse kinds of violence may well be passed but references to shit and piss will never pass in my opinion . . .
    PS a few less bloodies would help – esp. Act II.[12]

The Chamberlain's office returned *Saved* to the Court on 30 July with a request for more than thirty cuts, including most of scenes 6 and 9. Neither Bond nor the Chamberlain would budge, the latter even after Gaskill and Cuthbertson had paid a visit on 3 August. On the same day, Gaskill wrote to Harewood to brief him. The letter also reveals that at one stage the Chamberlain was pondering an outright ban. Gaskill proposed, as had Devine with *A Patriot for Me*, to turn the Court into a club theatre in order to get the play on.

The play opened to a closed audience on 3 November to a storm of outrage, amidst which there was the occasional sympathetic review.[13] No one should underestimate the tension as opening night approached. Nothing like *Saved* had appeared on the modern stage. No one, especially the critics, were prepared for what happened. It followed that reaction was, inevitably, distorted, for very little in critical experience would have prepared them for such a piece. According to Richard Butler, a cast member (interview with the author, 7 January 1984):

> I remember the first night very well. Bill was white at the gills and we were all a bit edgy, more so than on an ordinary first night, and I remember him saying to us, 'Look, don't get upset if people protest from the front, if people walk out, be prepared for that', he said, almost visibly shaking ... It was a nailbiting time.

One audience member, however, recalls 'verbal interruption and abuse during the course of the play, and there *was* the odd physical punch-up in the foyers at the interval and afterwards'.[14]

A teach-in at the Court was held on 14 November, chaired by Tynan. The night before, Tynan had made television history by being the first person to say 'fuck' on television, a moment subtly defined by a *Daily Express* reporter as 'the bloodiest outrage I have ever known'. An internal Court memo of 19 November noted a number of reporters around 'interested in seeing Mr Tynan concerning his television appearance the previous night. I passed to them a message from Mr Tynan.' The nature of the message is unspecified. Gaskill's considered view was that 'We were back at the centre of things. The Lord Chamberlain was against us, the critics were against us, but our fellow-workers were with us.'[15]

The Chamberlain was certainly against. On 13 December police questioned Gaskill and Cuthbertson under caution. On 5 January 1966, Gaskill, Poke and Esdaile (Artistic Director, Company Honorary Secretary and Licensee) were summoned to appear on 13 January at Great Marlborough Street Magistrates Court, on a charge of presenting an unlicensed play contrary to Section 15 of the 1843 Theatres Act. The hearing was postponed to 14 February, but at a meeting with John Gower, the Court's Counsel, on 13 January, it became clear that the Chamberlain, perhaps vexed at the club idea being used, as with *A Patriot for Me*, to circumvent the licensing procedures, and, equally, conscious that the Court by now was rather more than a coterie art house, was taking concerted action. Gower's view was that the censor was 'gunning for the Royal Court as an avant-garde theatre ... It is an attack on the Royal Court and not on club theatres in general.' Thus it was that Devine's theatre reached a logical and inevitable confrontation with authority.

In the meantime, the repertory system was persisted with, even though there were ominous signs of a financial crisis. The revival of *Serjeant Musgrave's Dance*, attacked violently in October 1959, began on 9 December and was producing close to 50 per cent box office. Gaskill, however, given his repertory policy, displaced it for performances of both *Shelley* and *The Cresta Run*. By the year's end, the average was only 31 per cent of capacity. On the other hand, the end of the year saw the end of all mortgage and loan liabilities. Council, to its credit, maintained its backing of Gaskill's policy and even acceded to his request that Council members should not attend first nights. The one victim of the policy was the Studio which effectively ceased operations at the end of 1965. It could not survive, given the intense level of activity throughout the building.

The following year, 1966, opened with *A Chaste Maid in Cheapside*. During its run, George Devine died on 20 January. His successor spoke of him in a way of which he would surely have approved: 'Our sense of loss at his death is immeasurable, but there is no sudden stop, only a pause while we who worked with him – writers, directors, actors and designers – remember how much of our creative development we owed to him.'[16] Lindsay Anderson said simply that 'He was unique in his time.'[17] A grieving Margaret Harris wrote from Devine's house in answer to a phone call from Michel Saint-Denis to say that it was 'almost intolerable to think of George having to suffer all this pain, fear and the indignity of being so helpless. Thank God that Jocelyn is such a marvellous person.'[18] And

Saint-Denis himself suffered a stroke a few days later. Already ill, he heard of his friend's death:

> je suis parti pour l'Angleterre la mort dans l'âme et, lorsque je commençais à aller mieux, malgré certains troubles cardiaques, mon ami George Devine a eu une attaque compliquée contre laquelle il a lutté pendant cinq mois: il a été emporté cette année à fin janvier. Je l'ai enterré ... et quatre jours plus tard, j'ai été frappé à mon tour ... j'ai été paralysé du conté droit. Je vais mieux ... mais naturellement je n'ai plus la même vie et mon meilleur ami est parti.[19]

After the funeral on 25 January,[20] Devine's friends met for a memorial meeting at the Court on 18 February. They included Evans, Ashcroft, Plowright, Guinness, Anderson, Gaskill, Finney and Osborne. Osborne announced the launching of a memorial fund and spoke eloquently of his friend as not having 'an element of piety and he was in many ways an uncomfortable and astringent man [and] some of us loved him and respected him so much. He did set his face very strongly against success, and I don't mean in the crude, journalistic sense, but in success in all its forms of approval-hunting, trimming and hedging.' Perhaps a fitting comment on Devine's greatness is also a characteristically practical remark on his copy of the programme for Peter Gill's *The Sleepers' Den* produced on 28 February 1965. Devine wrote: 'Touch up back wall'.[21]

The first hearing of charges over *Saved* took place on 14 February, where it was alleged that members of the public had seen a performance without having to prove that they were club members. The hearing was adjourned until 7 March. The magistrate, Leo Gradwell, ruled that there was a case to answer, at which point John Gower called, in succession, Laurence Olivier, Lord Harewood and Norman Collins. According to Poke, Olivier was a little reluctant to go into the witness box but was persuaded and gave a fine performance – literally, since

> he'd learnt it. He'd written it all out and Patricia [Lawrence, Poke's wife] noticed that he kept taking out of his pocket a

piece of paper and was learning his lines. And he then went into the witness box and it was one of the most wonderful performances that she had ever listened to because it appeared to be thoughts coming into his head as he spoke to the magistrate. Donald Wolfit couldn't have done it better. And then, when it was all over, the magistrate said, 'That was absolutely fascinating, but totally irrelevant.'[22]

At the final hearing of the case on 1 April, Gradwell ruled that the Theatres Act had been contravened. The defendants were conditionally discharged, with fifty guineas costs. The issue was completely unresolved and the dividing line between a genuine theatre club and other forms of presentation effectively blurred. Far from being a test case, all it did was waste a good deal of time. What had, however, been publicly demonstrated was the activity of the Lord Chamberlain's office in the pre-censorship of plays.

The Court coalesced in defence of itself and the profession. The censor had united and focused the company and given it an objective: 'the whole atmosphere of everybody fighting together for what they believed in cemented friendships, cemented beliefs. It was a very remarkable period.'[23] The *Saved* case began the process which ultimately removed from the Chamberlain any jurisdiction over the theatre. It was to be enshrined in the Theatres Bill of 1968.[24]

The togetherness of the Court family was coming under pressure financially. By 31 March, the position was not irredeemable but there were warning signs, despite a large grant increase from the Arts Council. It rose to £85,000 for 1966–67.[25] The dream of true repertory was in real danger of fragmenting and Gaskill acknowledged that if matters did not improve, the Court would have to revert to straight runs from July. The losses amounted to some £45,000 over six months for true repertory. The straight run policy ensured that there was no deficit for the following three years.[26]

In April, the Company was ten years old and used the occasion to launch the George Devine Award, still thriving at the time of writing. Blond's speech pointed to the dearth of good new plays. According to Gaskill, the Court was still the only subsidised theatre which attacked the Establishment in any serious way.[27] There was a scathing rejoinder to this from Hilary Spurling who, three years later, was to be at the centre of an enormous row over critics. Spurling described the Court as 'Touchy, lugubrious, embattled, inflexible, middle-aged in outlook if not in years – aren't the company's attitudes precisely those of an establishment, and not so very different from the ones they attacked so gaily all those years ago?'[28] Ms Spurling's popularity with Court directors was thus permanently assured.

A week after the tenth birthday celebrations, Ronald Duncan resigned. In his letter to Blond of 12 April 1966, he accurately reflects on how out of sympathy and touch he had become with the Company and its policy: 'But I would emphasise that it is not the plays that we have produced that makes me wish to withdraw from the Company, but the plays we have not produced'. In telling George Harewood of his decision, Duncan remarks on the irony of being 'booted out of the English Opera Group and now the ESC'. He cannot have felt there was anything left he could do and the truth is that his influence was never particularly great, certainly not as great as the volume of his complaints. In Gaskill he found someone less likely to mince his words than Devine. Gaskill's reaction to two of Duncan's plays sent to him shows in his reply of 27 September 1965, where he declares himself 'deeply out of sympathy with both of them'. Duncan's place in the history of the ESC is that of unwitting kingmaker and thereafter frustrated observer from the sidelines.

One of Gaskill's more favoured authors, Harley Granville Barker, appeared as part of the celebrations. *The Voysey Inheritance* opened on 11 April and ran for fifty-five performances, alongside some performances of *Serjeant Musgrave's Dance* and a new Wesker, *Their Very Own and Golden City*. Gaskill's persisting with the Court's first discoveries as a policy was proving difficult. He 'liked the play less well than Arnold's earlier work ... My determination to be loyal to the original members of the writers' group had not been productive ... The ties that had bound us together sitting by Ann Piper's fire in the room by the river were no longer strong.'[29] The writer who came in unexpectedly was Christopher Hampton, whose *When Did You Last See My Mother?* opened on 5 June as a Sunday Night and transferred to the West End a month later.[30] Another was Heathcote Williams with *The Local Stigmatic* (27 March). Both Hampton and Williams were important in the Court later. So, too, were Howard Brenton and Joe Orton, who had to be content on this occasion to share a Sunday Night double bill on 21 August.

At an Artistic Committee meeting of 19 April, it was decided that the immediate programme would consist of revivals pending the acquisition of commissioned new work. There were also plans developing to utilise the club space for the presentation of new plays or new work. The Court had at this stage a series of possibilities but that was all. At the same meeting, it was minuted that Johnstone and Cuthbertson would leave. Thus, by mid-1966, playing in true repertory had gone and so, soon afterwards, had Gaskill's two Associates. His new Associate was Desmond O'Donovan, then at the National. This proved to be another mistake, which took a little time to rectify. Gaskill was also under close scrutiny by both the Arts Council and Neville Blond, a pressure to which he responded angrily. Writing to Poke on 3 May, he set out his stall unequivocally:

> I want to make one thing clear to the Management Committee. Although I am fully aware of the financial responsibilities involved in running this theatre and the absolute necessity to remain solvent at all costs, I don't think that our work should be judged by the amount of profit we make. I sometimes get the impression that Neville thinks this is a commercial enterprise. It ought to be clear by now that what we have to do is to survive by whatever means we can. The fact that George Devine left a profit on his last year is largely due to the increase in the Arts Council grant.

Gaskill was also right to feel that Blond was less happy about his programme so far than he had been with some of Devine's. The Arts Council, with an increase in total grant of approaching £2 million for 1966–67, was beginning to flex its muscles in a way that, later on, would enable its politicisation in the eighties to be a relatively easy matter. Poke had told Blond on 2 May that the Arts Council was

'wondering ... as to whether we have got sufficiently competent staff
to keep a firm and rigid hand on the expenditure'.

The straight run policy began with Cuthbertson's direction of
Ubu Roi, designed by David Hockney.[31] This managed 38 per cent,
better than David Cregan's *Three Men for Colverton*, which followed
(27 per cent). The next home-grown production was *Macbeth*, with
Alec Guinness and Simone Signoret. *Macbeth* reflected a change to
the straight run policy which the Management Committee had
accepted. Originally, the idea was to do eight plays for six weeks
each. Gaskill, however, after announcing to a subsequent meeting of
the Committee that he wanted to do four major productions of
masterpieces, running for eight weeks, and four productions of,
ideally, new plays, for four weeks each, swiftly briefed Harewood on
the same day, 20 May. His letter reflects his worry about the lack of
a regular audience: 'If a play like *Voysey* does not ring the bell we are
in real trouble.' Gaskill's analysis accepts the failure of a policy
which kept faith with the Court's senior writers. He also distin-
guishes between keeping faith and mounting productions for which
there is a real enthusiasm. It would, in his view now, be better 'to do
seriously those things which most stir one's blood'. Thus primed,
Harewood went to a joint meeting of the Management and Artistic
Committees. Misgivings were expressed, but the policy was accepted. There was concern that the Court was becoming indistin-
guishable from the other major companies, to which Gaskill
responded that, in effect, the Court's version of a classic should and
must be different.

Macbeth was different, and for many the production was one of
Gaskill's finest achievements. For others, it was a disaster which
centred on the difficulty Signoret, who had been suggested by Guinness, had with some of the blank verse. In many respects, the design
solutions by Christopher Morley, described in detail by Gaskill,[32] and
the direction of the play realised many of the Court's strong but
unstated priorities. The design subsequently became the model for
design work at the Royal Shakespeare Company.[33] Critical reaction
was violent and hostile and brought to a head the simmering row
between critics and the Court, which had existed from the early days.

This was not simply an argument about the production; it was an argument about the place of the Court in the hierarchy of modern theatre. Gaskill's concept of a 'Court' Shakespeare, commonly accepted now, set a challenge to preconceived ideas, to which most critics proved themselves unequal. The insulting quality of critical response upset Gaskill and his staff. In a few months, from *Saved* to *Macbeth*, Gaskill had received a critical drubbing. Five days after *Macbeth* opened, Gaskill, without clearing it at the Court, wrote both to reviewers and to editors, threatening to withdraw future invitations. Reactions were predictable. Gaskill went on holiday to Tunisia, but telephoned Poke on 30 October. Poke's notes of the call read: 'Bill phoned. Distressed. Felt he ought to come back. If he remained it would be said he was afraid to face critics. Said he had no idea when he wrote those letters it would create the storm it has. Asked what he should say in relation to the Company on tv'. Gaskill returned to appear on 'Look of the Week' to discuss the issue.

If Gaskill was felt to be naive by some, his writers backed him strongly. Ann Jellicoe wrote to Blond on 31 October to praise Gaskill's 'courageous and responsible stand ... it demonstrates his quality and is worthy of a man in his position'. David Cregan wrote in a similar vein on 1 November, and Edward Bond weighed in on 6 November to describe Gaskill as 'of irreplaceable assistance and encouragement to me as a writer'. This reaction came about because, in the absence of Blond in America, Esdaile was in charge, and had appeared to suggest he would call for Gaskill's resignation. He also criticised the production.[34] His comments provoked the letters from the writers and also a strong letter from Peggy Ashcroft for when Blond returned. She attacked Esdaile's 'gratuitous condemnation'. She had two further things to say: 'Firstly, that I think the production of *Macbeth*, though not flawless, is an achievement that the ESC can be very proud of; secondly, that it seems to have been largely forgotten in the press, and certainly by Mr Esdaile, that the theatre is playing to capacity, and, on the night I went, to an exceedingly responsive and attentive public.' Gaskill's public reaction to Esdaile's comments, reported in the *Evening News* for 31 October was: 'Mr Esdaile is just making trouble. I do not think he has a personal motive. He is a very warm-hearted but impulsive man.' Privately, however, the enmity remained and was to flare up again with Bond's *Early Morning*.

The fracas eventually subsided but Gaskill felt battered by the critics over *Saved* and then *Macbeth*. Reflecting on it, he could later see that the backing of Council from *Macbeth* onwards began to erode 'and gradually Neville started to turn against me'.[35] The difference was, in an important respect, temperamental. Devine 'had had many years previous experience of dealing with awkward personalities and George had a way of getting his own way. Bill wasn't that kind at all. He took up a point of view as a matter of principle and he stuck to it and it did lead to quite considerable animosity between himself and the chairman.'[36] From *Macbeth* onwards, Chairman and Artistic Director watched each other closely.

The rest of the year was taken up with a Sunday Night of Gill's *A Provincial Life* and a main-stage production of Soyinka's *The Lion and the Jewel*. This achieved nearly 50 per cent, one of the few plays from an original member of the Writers' Group to achieve respectable figures. Finances, largely because of *Macbeth*, were very healthy. Its box-office figures were surpassed only by *The Entertainer* and *Rhinoceros*. After Gill's version of Otway's *The Soldier's Fortune* came a revival of *Roots* as part of Jane Howell's schools project.[37] As the incoming programme formed and reformed – *Three Sisters* did not have opening dates, the Living Theatre was to be contacted, Bond's new play 'would almost certainly be banned' – *The Daughter-in-Law* appeared in the main bill and flagged up what in 1968 was to become one of the greatest of all Court successes.

If the programme looked attractive, and notwithstanding the success of *Macbeth*, Blond, under pressure from the Arts Council, was clearly unhappy. At a Management Committee meeting of 12 January, he asked the officials to withdraw. He then spoke to Gaskill and to the Committee to say that 'he was very dissatisfied with the management control of the theatre. Personally he felt he was responsible to the Arts Council for the effective utilisation of their grant.' It was agreed to review the matter in three months' time. Perhaps Blond, used to Devine's way of keeping in close contact, felt remote from the centre of the Court's world, since Gaskill briefed him only when he had to.

It's also true that the degree of autonomy won by Devine logically allowed his successor more freedom than was the case when the Company began operations. The issue of the theatre's management was a crucial one. Poke had discussed with Jo Hodgkinson of the Arts Council the idea of appointing an administrator. In his letter to Blond of 18 January, he reported that Helen Montagu's inexperience was the root of the problem: 'Obviously we must put it right because Jo was pretty critical about our artistic achievements since George's death. He thought the Schools Scheme a lot of flannel.' To which Blond replied (20 January) that 'When I discussed this with Jo the other day, he said, "Why wait three months?" I am inclined to agree with him.'

Gaskill, meanwhile, was talking to his ally, Harewood. He wrote on 7 February that 'We are in the same cleft stick that we always were: that is if we do Restoration comedies with reasonably well-known actors we are assured of a reasonable commercial success, and if we do a new play which is not by John Osborne we will almost inevitably fail'. Six days later, Gaskill reported on a Management meeting which Harewood was unable to attend. Bond's new play was discussed: 'from what I hear of it, I think it will cause something of a stir. This is not for publication but it does involve a lesbian affair between Victoria and Florence Nightingale – the latter disguises herself as John Brown in a kilt, which solves that particular mystery. This is unless Edward is pulling my leg.'

After a well-received *Three Sisters*, which opened on 18 April, Gaskill began a season of low-budget shows. These were plays by James Casey, David Storey and Donald Howarth. The surprise of the three was Storey's *The Restoration of Arnold Middleton* which eventually became Gaskill's first transfer, to the Criterion on 31 August. Storey was subsequently to become one of the major Court writers. Although the play was a critical success, a depressed Gaskill decided to leave the Court. David Storey recalls that Bill

actually told me after *Arnold* was over – he wrote me a letter in which he said he was going to resign. He was heartbroken, he said, because his tenure there had been a disaster and he couldn't stick it any more. Until *Arnold Middleton* came along, the audiences, together with the critical reception, made his work there totally valueless and he saw no point in going on.[38]

By 14 July, Gaskill had not absolutely decided but told Harewood he felt he would like another two years. His third season, after season two had 'marked time', 'must be a humdinger ... If I am careful I don't see why we can't risk a whole season of new plays and recent revivals.' Copied to Blond, this letter would certainly have made his eyes water, given that the new Bond 'will almost certainly fail, but in the best Royal Court tradition'. Gaskill also lists a new Cregan, two Osbornes, Wood's *Dingo*, a Lawrence trilogy, possibly a revival of *Look Back in Anger*, and Orton's new play. It is, as he says, 'an impressive list'. Harewood replied with enthusiasm on 17 July, urging Gaskill to stay. Meanwhile, Osborne was publicly lamenting the changes at the Court: 'Since George Devine died and the atmosphere changed at the Royal Court, I feel a lack of context in which to write. There's been no falling out. I admire Bill Gaskill very much. But it's not the theatre I knew. I was a very spoiled boy. It was my place, and it's my place no longer.'[39]

Osborne was right. Other influences were emerging. In August, by arrangement with Michael White, the Court presented a group of plays by the Open Theatre of New York, the first of a series of influential visits by American companies, whose work affected a number of important theatre workers. Among them was Max Stafford-Clark:

> These weren't really writers' theatres. The writers played quite
> a small part in that movement. But it was like a new language.
> Suddenly, music and movement seemed a part of what was
> important, electric and interesting, and that influenced me
> enormously. I think that the work I did after that absorbed
> those influences into the tradition I had already been working
> in, which had been based on the writer, so that one absorbed
> that lesson and applied it to the texts he worked with.[40]

America Hurrah! opened on 2 August with the intention of transferring to the Vaudeville, but the Lord Chamberlain indicated the possibility of a prosecution even if the Vaudeville was turned into a club theatre. As a consequence, the plays stayed at the Court and the Wood play, *Fill the Stage with Happy Hours*, due to follow *America Hurrah!*, went to the Vaudeville and the actors were paid Royal Court rather than West End rates.[41] The decisive battle with the censor was imminent.

In late 1967, the Arts Council published its 'Report on the Needs of the Subsidised Theatre in London'. The Report pays a good deal of attention to the Court under Devine which 'initiated something of a transformation of the British theatrical scene ... What was begun at Sloane Square was followed up and implemented by the achievements of the Royal Shakespeare Theatre and the National Theatre ... The provincial theatres, growing and strengthening in this period, became, in their programmes and outlook, more and more influenced by what was going on at the Royal Court.' While noting the difficulty of building a steady audience for the Court, the report asserts that 'The rest was triumphantly successful.' Following Devine, it goes on, was Bill Gaskill, 'in outlook and training, very much a Royal Court product', who had to face increased competition and a steady growth in the subsidised sector. The Report felt that the results under Gaskill were 'disappointing' and that the Court had not yet 'found its new role'. Its financial needs were assessed at approximately £100,000. The Report is a reasonable assessment but perhaps inclined to fall victim to the danger it itself warns against: 'It would, however, be easy to be dazzled by the successes of this Company in the Devine period'. Gaskill wrote to Blond on 17 October about the Report in a rather mild and reflective manner: 'In its policy of taking risks, not only on writers, but also on directors and actors, it must often fail and often be open to criticism, and its achievements will always seem to be in the past rather than the present.'

The present was very much with Gaskill as he wrote this letter. Since early in 1967, he had had the script of Bond's *Early Morning*, which was eventually announced as a club production for January 1968. The internal battles surfaced on 16 October when the Artistic Committee was told by the Management Committee to read the play. It refused to re-appropriate the executive function it had surrendered during Devine's time. The fear was to do with the nature of the legal decision in the *Saved* case, which had succeeded only in making a grey area greyer. On 8 November, the play was returned to the Court from the Lord Chamberlain's office with the single comment that 'his Lordship would not allow it'. Gaskill waited until 15 January 1968 to reply to Lt.-Col. J. F. D. Johnstone, MC, asking why the total ban had been imposed. Was it, he wondered, to do with 'the presentation of royalty, in this case Queen Victoria, as not wholly sympathetic?'. The delay in writing may have to do with the fact that on 1 November the government had dropped its bill to end theatre censorship because of pressure of business. That bill was replaced by a Private Member's Bill sponsored by George Strauss. Gaskill's absolute insistence on keeping faith with a Court writer meant that the production must go on. The Court's Council and the Arts Council feared that the Chamberlain, whose days were numbered, might have a final fling. Bond, writing to his American agent, Toby Cole, on 4 December, told her of the ban and referred to the pressure on Gaskill who would not withdraw the production, 'naturally'. On the same day, Robin Fox, as a member of the Arts Council's Drama Panel, wrote to Blond to say that the Panel privately admitted its inconsistency in allowing the Court to present three unlicensed plays but were now 'withholding agreement in relation to a fourth'. The Council decided that it 'could not give agreement but [it] was not saying "you must not do this play"'. However, Abercrombie, the Council's Secretary-General, rejected Blond's request to turn the Court into a club once again in a letter of 5 December. The Arts Council did not come out of all this well and Hodgkinson admitted as much at an extraordinary meeting of the Court's Council on 6 December.

This was a critical point in the evolution of the Court. Its Artistic Director spoke for a central belief in saying that he thought 'that when the Royal Court could not put on new plays and certainly not the most important new plays, then the ESC would cease to have any function'. Yet the business end of the Court was hostile to an irrecoverable degree, certainly as far as its Chairman was concerned. Not even a surplus to the end of September 1967, of £11,700, was sufficient balm. This moment also demonstrated the steady growth of power in the major funding body. From now on, the Arts Council would be a significant factor in the operation of any of the subsidised theatres. As the confrontation continued, Gaskill fell ill with pneumonia and a cobbled together *Twelfth Night* was put on.

Battle resumed with Gaskill telling the Artistic Committee on 20 February that the Chamberlain now would prosecute a run of *Early Morning* but would not move against Sunday performances. It was decided that if the Theatres Bill got through its second reading, then Sunday performances would go ahead. Gaskill felt that 'they tried to stop *Early Morning* being done, quite definitely. They being Neville and the Arts Council. The Arts Council was leaning very heavily on Neville to stop it.'[42] Alfred Esdaile, who had been frightened by the *Saved* case, wrote to Blond on 13 March, complaining of the play's 'obscenity and bad taste'. He objected as Licensee to its presentation, and his lawyers wrote on 21 March to say that 'he proposed to take steps to ensure that it did not take place'.

At a Management Committee meeting of 12 March, matters came to a head with a blistering attack on Gaskill by Blond who started the meeting 'with a list of my crimes, this over-spending being the worst, and demanded my resignation'.[43] Poke recalls taking Gaskill out to lunch before a Management meeting with Robin Fox 'with the sole object of trying to persuade him to be nicer to Neville. I don't think we succeeded.' At the meeting 'within seconds of each other, they both resigned ... And then both withdrew their resignations'.[44] Harewood saw clearly that Blond 'wanted Bill out. I didn't think he was right ... [tycoons] want in the end that their instinct prevails'.[45] As the pair of them resigned, 'Neville's secretary [Joan Taylor], who always used to come to the meetings, started to attack Bill on behalf of Neville. In the middle of it, Oscar interrupted her and said, "And when did you become a member of the Council?"'[46]

The Artistic Committee of 15 March reaffirmed its decision to put the play on as a Sunday Night, even though its costs were very high for such an occasion. The Minutes of the meeting were entirely rewritten by Harewood. The draft Minutes record Gaskill's state of mind more directly: 'Mr Gaskill said that at the last Management meeting he had felt dispirited, and he could not have abuse hurled at him again. He felt that some of the Committee were working against him, and he did not wish to stay if he had not the Council's confidence behind him.' The Artistic Committee by now lacked Peggy Ashcroft, who had resigned from it on 30 January. One of Devine's staunchest allies, she remained on the ESC Council, but according to Poke 'artistically she does not see eye to eye with Bill' (to Blond, 3 February). Many did not, but in fighting for *Early Morning* he was defending everything the Court stood for. Robin Fox was a staunch ally, as was Harewood, though he was not keen on the play.

Early Morning duly had its Sunday Night on 31 March in a production by an exhausted Gaskill celebrating the twelfth anniversary of the Company. Police questioned Gaskill and Esdaile on 2 April. There was threat of a prosecution. Esdaile as Licensee then banned a proposed second Sunday Night. It was replaced by a teach-in on censorship. But a second performance was given because of a brainwave by Poke to designate it 'a non-paying, private production and call it a dress-rehearsal'.[47] In one way, the day was saved. In another, all that was allowed of an extraordinary work was one Sunday Night and a private dress-rehearsal.

The Court was furious with Esdaile. Fox wrote to Blond, recalling both Esdaile's comments to the press about *Macbeth* and now this: 'Alfred behaved disgracefully over the matter of Gaskill and the unauthorised press release and has now done so again: he should be asked to resign and the licence should be transferred to you or Greville'. Gaskill wrote to Harewood to say that

> The situation with Alfred is intolerable, and will have to be resolved if I am to carry on working. I have had very strong support from Greville who has been really wonderful over the last few days, and from Robin and Oscar. We have to face the possibility that we cannot do Sunday Night productions in future, and if this were to happen it would be the end of the ESC. This is the last ditch stand and it has got to be fought by all of us united if Alfred is going to oppose it. He must go by whatever means.[48]

Another letter from Gaskill to Blond on 20 May designated Esdaile as 'the world's biggest liar', was construed as libellous, and quietly filed away.

This was one of many serious and deeply felt crises in the life of the Company. Blond wrote privately to Blacksell at this stage to chronicle Gaskill's sins ('He forgets he is an employee'), and stated bluntly that 'I want a new Artistic Director and an Administrator to run the theatre.'[49]

Amidst the crisis had developed one of the most successful series ever seen at the Court. Lawrence's three plays, directed by Gill, won great critical acclaim and occupied the gap between the time slot for *Early Morning* (January) and its eventual Sunday Night (March).[50] In contrast, May would see the new Osbornes, *Time Present* and *The Hotel in Amsterdam*. In between, Gaskill told the Artistic Committee that six short plays had been performed in the Club and more were proposed. These included *Red Cross* by Sam Shepard, who was to become virtually a Court house writer, and pieces were proposed by Jack Shepherd, Keith Johnstone and William Inge. Gaskill fought off a proposal by Esdaile that the Club be used 'for the purpose of providing club facilities for young accountants' (Management meeting, 19 April) and was obviously looking for ways of expanding the experimental wing of the work. However, Blond, by now unwell, told the 5 June Council of his persistent unhappiness about the theatre's management and the unauthorised expenditure on, for example, *Early Morning*. Blond cannot have been happy to hear a Gaskill proposal that the play be scheduled for an autumn production.

The Osbornes, strongly cast, achieved 75 per cent and 96 per cent. Both transferred. Both were regarded by Gaskill as 'West End plays . . . I personally didn't want to do them, but one of my associates, Anthony Page, said, "I want to do them." In fact, Oscar Lewenstein very much wanted to do them, and they both made money . . . from that money, the rest of the season was done. But if you do it too often, you are in trouble.'[51] The Osbornes were in fact anathema to Gaskill and he even discussed a co-production with Beaumont for the West End.[52] Osborne, according to Lewenstein, had by this time 'fallen out' with the Court but was persuaded to start the plays off there.[53] After that, new work by Antrobus, Hampton and Cregan inevitably fared less well, though Hampton became the first Resident Dramatist in London, funded by the Arts Council. Another revival of *Look Back in Anger*, directed by Anthony Page, attracted a review by Tynan which in turn produced an annoyed response from Page. This is in effect a view of the play thirteen years on from its première:

> I am sorry that you, as an early champion of *Look Back in Anger*, should either have missed the tone of my production, or else have been so anxious to make a journalistic point that you had to oversimplify it in terms of black and white.
>
> One of the factors in the play that I found most powerful is that Jimmy Porter, armed initially with the beliefs and articulacy of a fervent left-wing intellectual has become a man whose energies are absorbed into passionate conflict with his wife. The balance between his individual personality, his objective belief and the circumstances of his life is extremely complex, and can hardly be just summed up in two phrases relating to current affairs and then rounded off with 'Hence, no doubt, his frustrations'.
>
> I can't, of course, vouch for the performance you saw; but you have thoroughly misinterpreted the intentions of Victor Henry and myself ... Many young people who saw the production and Victor's performance found his problems and character far from pathetic or neurotically isolated.[54]

As an old play was being defended, a new one was being hotly debated. Michael McClure's play, *The Beard*, was offered to the Court by Michael White and Tony Richardson. It featured Jean Harlow and Billy the Kid arguing about celebrity and performing oral sex. The play thus arrived in the aftermath of the *Early Morning* affair, the liberation of the theatre from the attentions of the censor, and the ensuing worry about other forms of prosecution. Reactions to the play varied from Osborne, who thought it was 'rubbish' and was not prepared to go into the witness box or risk being fined for such a play; to Poke who found it obscene; to Harewood who was lukewarm. Gaskill wrote to Harewood on 15 July to say that he would not accept a decision 'which is based on the Committee's opinions of a play's merit ... I must have freedom in the choice of a play ... We have battled all these years against the censor and he is eventually going, *without ever actually having stopped a play reaching the stage*'. Gaskill insisted and got a clause about his artistic freedom added to his next contract. The show finally went on as a late-night after performances of *Look Back in Anger*.[55]

After the 17 July Artistic Committee meeting, Fox wrote at length to Harewood about the new legal dispensation and its implications:

> The passing of the Theatres Act will create great problems and I don't doubt, in the short term, will result in extravagances both of good and bad taste but, more importantly for the future, may induce attitudes in 'Management' of ultra-caution bred of the threat of criminal prosecution and the uncertainty of what constitutes 'guilt'.
>
> We have, I imagine, been the most intense, committed, free, relaxed, contradictory, constant, tawdry, glorious theatre to exist in memory. We have ... the chance to attract the best Artistic Director in England; or to keep him. We have and should have a great responsibility in considering the problem of his relationship to the theatre. If we, as the Artistic Committee, agreed that the Artistic Director be given contractual freedom, budget apart, we might not get this through the Council. If we didn't get it through, the result would probably be a swing against the present director of the Company ... If we don't try to get it through I believe we shall have failed to understand our past and will distort our future.[56]

There are few better instances of the extent to which the Court's first two Artistic Directors were shielded and fought for by Fox and Harewood.

Meanwhile, performances in the Club had become very popular and Gaskill proposed to expand the operation so that the Club could seat up to 150 people. It was not thought of as a second auditorium at this stage, but more as an outlet for young directors and writers, since the main bill was, at this point, committed to keeping the Court solvent. It was also Gaskill's reaction to the growth of small theatres in the spring and summer of 1968, freed now from the censor. Gaskill obviously felt something was developing of which the Court was not a leader. By 12 November, the space was named the Theatre Upstairs, with that complexity which so characterises the Court at its best. It was said that the name was suggested by Hodgkinson of the Arts Council. The Theatre Upstairs, directed by Nicholas Wright, opened on 24 February 1969 and, after a very shaky start, emerged as the first small second house in the UK.[57]

The other major event of early 1969 was the Bond trilogy of *Saved*, *Narrow Road to the Deep North* and *Early Morning*. The freeing of Bond's plays was the freeing of all plays, made possible by a theatre whose Artistic Directorate would not succumb to pressure, either internal or external. Bond and the Court existed in a symbiotic relationship for the years of the censor and nothing shows the determination of both better than this struggle. It was of an intensity both exhilarating and, subsequently, depressing. When the battle was won, the downswing in energy began. Gaskill, tired out from an exhausting three seasons, contemplated a rest. It was at this point that Lindsay Anderson, at Gaskill's invitation, returned to the Court to direct David Storey's second play for the Court, *In Celebration*. Anderson was to be significantly around the Court for the next half dozen years. And Gaskill felt that after the Bond season:

> the four years' work were justified. We'd got rid of the Lord
> Chamberlain. It's so difficult to imagine now, but it did loom
> enormously large over our lives. He had in a strange way given
> us a kind of *raison d'être*. There was a line through our work
> that, if nothing else, we were fighting the censor and, in
> particular, we were fighting the censor on behalf of Edward
> Bond. If the Court meant anything, his plays had to be done ...
> we did his plays and it was for me really as if something was
> over and I felt very empty and directionless.[58]

5   A humanist theatre, 1969–1975

I believe that the Court in the early seventies was primarily an aesthetic theatre,
not a political one. And the reason why it then lost the loyalty of so many writers
in the following years was because it finally refused to move into the field of
English politics, although it was presenting excellent political work about the
Third World. A direct confrontation finally occurred between those who wanted
the Court to be a socialist theatre and those who wanted it to be a humanist
theatre and, no question, the humanists won.

(David Hare, in Findlater, 142)

In 1969 Gaskill decided to take some leave to direct elsewhere. He
omitted to consult the Council. Part annoyed and part ready to see
Gaskill's leave become rather more permanent, Council rejected the
idea of Jane Howell standing in for Gaskill and took the opportunity to
bring Anthony Page in as a temporary replacement. He, in turn, as he
had in 1964, invited Lindsay Anderson to join him. As Jocelyn Herbert
tells it:

> I suddenly discovered ... that Bill was going away for six
> months abroad to do a show and I happened to see Robin and I
> asked did he know ... and he didn't. Nobody knew and he was
> leaving Jane Howell to look after it all. Robin and the Council
> thought this wasn't a good idea.[1]

There were Council people, including Blond, who had called for
Gaskill's resignation before this moment, and who clearly seized the
opportunity to modify the policy line then existing at the Court.

For Page and Anderson, particularly the latter, the resentment
at being shut out in 1965 made them determined that it was not going
to happen again. According to Anderson, 'Bill was told to get somebody of calibre, attested calibre, to take over the theatre. I know he
was asked to choose between Anthony Page and myself, and he chose

Page. And once again Tony rang me up and said would I go and do it with him and I said okay.'[2] Anderson and Page demanded that their return be part of a continuing and developing relationship with the Court: 'we're not going to come in and just do this, help you out for six months, and then be told to piss off, so let's work out exactly what this is going to consist of'.[3] Gaskill, somewhat naively, had 'never realised how much my old associates had resented not being asked back when I took over, as if they'd been cut out of the family firm ... Our relations in the old days under George had been cordial because we all had equal status. But I had been running the theatre autocratically for four years and found it difficult to share power.'[4]

Anderson clearly saw that a certain inertia dominated the Court's management and artistic structure. At an Artistic Committee meeting of 7 July, he resisted the immediate implementation of the triumvirate process, and also decided that the Committee itself had been reduced 'to a kind of impotence'. The Committee met again the following day. Harewood and others were worried that the arrangements simply would not work and insisted that a long-term solution be arrived at by the end of the year. Council had in one way reacted against Gaskill from *Early Morning* onwards and had quickly taken the opportunity to broaden the base of the Court's work, that is to bring together the two strands of the Court's work which had existed during Devine's time. A consequence, however, was the readmission of Anderson, whose idiosyncratic attitudes made it impossible to contemplate the future with much equanimity. From Anderson's point of view, here was the opportunity to rescue the Court. He also, however, was quite aware that the Court was filled with Gaskill's people, a group fused by the fight with the censor and entirely used to and happy with Gaskill's policy. The long-term effects of the reintroduction of Anderson split the Court into factions. The wedge driven into the theatre's sense of itself was to create powerful disharmonies through the seventies. Unwittingly, Gaskill himself was partly the author of this. The establishment of the Theatre Upstairs, always disliked by Anderson, who never worked there, enabled a split in the work to be easily arranged. It meant that a certain kind of work would find a home, but not on the main stage.

I opened the Theatre Upstairs, went away for six months, and when I came back they'd closed it. It was a bit like that because Lindsay didn't want the Theatre Upstairs. Lindsay wanted to go back to the old Sunday Nights. I think that things did change during that period, but there were a lot of very good productions. But I don't look back on it with any pleasure at all.[5]

Moreover, David Hare, then the Court's Resident Dramatist ('All resident dramatists in this period had their plays rejected; it became a feature of the job'[6]), says that Anderson and Page 'developed an attitude to new work which made the championship of new scripts so arduous and humiliating that it's a wonder people stuck their necks out at all'.[7] Nicholas Wright, himself later to cross swords with Anderson, notes that 'There was a strong split at that time; 1969 was the year when a quite coherent generation of playwrights began appearing, including David Hare, Howard Brenton and Snoo Wilson, and they were being staunchly resisted by the establishment of the Royal Court.'[8]

Ironically, the Court's house writers were particularly prolific at this stage in a way that some house writers were not when Gaskill tried to keep faith with them in 1965. The period saw three plays by David Storey in *The Contractor* (1969), *Home* (1970), and *The Changing Room* (1971), all directed by Anderson, all transferring to the West End. Hampton's *The Philanthropist* (1970) transferred, as did Osborne's *West of Suez* (1971). Bond's *Lear* did not. Whitehead's *Alpha Beta* went to the Apollo in 1972. Nearly all achieved box-office takings of 80–90 per cent. *Lear* took 45 per cent. It is therefore the case that the new generation of writers were kept away from the Court's main stage by a combination of Anderson's hostility and the work of the established writers. The loss to the Court was a whole generation of young artists. Whereas Gaskill could and did dislike the Osbornes of 1968, but used the money to finance the Bond season of 1969, that inevitable price to be paid operated less evidently during the time of the triumvirate. Anderson felt the triumvirate worked 'because it enabled Bill Gaskill to do the kind of plays which he thought highly of, and perhaps I didn't'.[9] Lewenstein saw it differently: 'They didn't work well together. The meetings were a constant battle and quarrel. I was the Chairman of the Artistic Committee at that time and tried to referee these battles. I don't think any of the Minutes can indicate how stormy they were. Usually it's the decisions you get into the Minutes rather than somebody calling another person a cunt.'[10]

On one matter, the three directors completely agreed. Divided by all manner of policy issues and by temperament, they all loathed the critics, an honourable tradition born with the beginnings of the Court under Devine. On 2 October 1969, a press release announced that facilities would be withdrawn from Hilary Spurling, the theatre critic of the *Spectator*. She was not barred, she was simply not invited to review Court productions. Although newspapers carried the press release on 3 October, the situation only began to escalate on 29 October when Anderson presented an account of the affair to the Management Committee. Mrs Spurling had, it was said, walked out of a performance Upstairs of Peter Gill's *Over Gardens Out* in August. The piece was not reviewed because Spurling apparently said, when telephoned, that she had not liked the piece. Anderson recalls the moment:

> I remember very well the occasion when Anthony and Bill and I
> were all in the office at the Court and we were very, very
> annoyed about Hilary Spurling's actions ... In order to get out
> she had to climb over people. Someone said, perhaps me, well,
> let's stop inviting her and everybody saying, jolly good thing,
> too, fuck her, and that's how we did it. Bill, Anthony and myself
> were totally committed to that idea.[11]

Anderson told his Committee that the editor of the *Spectator*, Nigel Lawson, had written to him 'rather like a summons from a headmaster to a fifth-former, who had not reported to him for cheeking Matron'.

The affair began to generate heat when it became clear that the triumvirate objected to most of Spurling's notices for Court productions and that the incident at Peter Gill's play was the trigger for the explosions, together with the fact that Lawson had contacted his friend, Arnold Goodman, at the Arts Council, to complain. On

7 November, the Arts Council (Goodman, Hugh Jenkins, Jo Hodgkinson) met Lewenstein, Fox, Anderson, Gaskill and Poke. The latter
was virtually a lone voice at the Court in opposing the action taken
against Spurling, both as a matter of principle and because the Court
had reaffirmed press rights over the *Macbeth* row:

> I saw it as an interference with the freedom of the press ... we
> were in receipt of public money and I was convinced the Arts
> Council would step in. I nearly resigned at the time and I was
> saved from resigning by the fact that Lord Goodman rang me up
> and said, don't ... I tried to become the honest broker because I
> was an ex-journalist. I volunteered to go and see Nigel Lawson
> but I got nowhere with him. He was very difficult.[12]

At its 7 November meeting, the Arts Council made its disapproval
clear. It was eventually agreed, according to Poke's notes, that
Goodman should inform Lawson that tickets would be sent to the
Spectator but not to Hilary Spurling, and that 'In the meantime we
must carry on according to the present accepted practices.' On the
same day, Paul Channon, MP, wrote to Poke from the House of
Commons to express his worry about the attitude of a theatre 'in
receipt of such large sums of public money' and indicating that he
might well put down a question in the House.

The Court split on the matter, when the broad backing of the
Management Committee, including an ailing Blond, was given to the
Artistic Directors, contrary to the decision over *Macbeth*. Poke
strongly objected. What was actually opening up here was the relationship of the Arts Council to its clients, in particular to the Court.
The issue rapidly became one of who controlled whom and to what
extent. At a Council meeting of 3 December, the policy of critical
freedom for the press was reaffirmed, 'while also expressing disapproval of any action by a critic which could disturb the actors or
audience'. Poke's private notes of the Council meeting, and subsequently, provide an insight as to the forces at work:

Nov 29 Saw Nigel Lawson.
Dec 1 Tea with Neville. Discussed meeting with Lawson.

> Agreed to recommend to our Council restoration of critics' facilities.
>
> Dec 2 Neville in interview with *Standard* said tickets would be restored to *Spectator*.
>
> Dec 3 Council meeting. After my statement of events, Anthony laid whole emphasis on Mrs Spurling's alleged misconduct. Bill Gaskill said: 'Let's be honest. That was purely incidental. The real reason we did not invite her was because of the dreadful notices she has written about our work.' This caused an uproar and brought a strong protest from Norman Collins. Long argument ensued and a statement was prepared which was approved by those of Council remaining. I said this statement would inevitably bring the question from the Press as to whether tickets were to be restored to the *Spectator* and the answer I was given was yes ...
> Anthony phoned me violently protesting at the decision of Council – threatened again Lindsay's resignation if decision was not changed. Reported all this to Jo [Hodgkinson] ...
> Neville said that Anthony, Lindsay and Helen wanted to see him at 8 that evening. Neville said he would refuse to see them unless the letter to the *Spectator* was sent. He asked me to phone Helen to say this. I tried and she was out.

It appears that Neville Blond was persuaded to sign a letter to *The Times* which contradicted Council's decision to restore facilities to the *Spectator*, independently of a now-furious Poke. As Poke put it in the same document, 'It is unfortunately true that the Artistic Directors cannot stand criticism and do not believe in the press's right to comment unless it is favourable ... The Arts Council have I think quite rightly tried to stop our Committee and Council from being led along this childish course by the Artistic Directors but alas they have not accepted Lord Goodman's advice and there is no knowing where this will lead to.'

Gaskill wrote to Harewood on 23 December about the Council decision and *The Times* letter in terms which demonstrated a real crisis in the Court's affairs:

> The Council meeting was a fiasco with Greville pushing a poor decision through while people were leaving for lunch and the letter we forced Neville to sign, though it had the approval of you, Peggy and Robin, was strictly speaking out of order. Since then, there had been considerable intrigue between Greville and Hugh Willatt [Arts Council], who wrote us a threatening letter, telling us what we had to do.

Gaskill sees the acute danger of 'an anarchic situation' for 'Neville is too old and too weak to control such situations ... The present situation would not have become so inflated or out of control with a strong chairman ... If he doesn't go – and soon – I predict that the organisation will collapse ... We do need someone to be tough with us, to resist us and to control the planning and expenditure.' Gaskill's sanity and sense of imminent collapse is also tied to his worries about Arts Council power. It 'increasingly tries to control our decisions – either through blackmail of poor Neville, intrigue with Greville or, I'm afraid, Goodman's diplomacy'. What had begun as a stand against poor critical practice had become a large issue of internal and external control. This particular matter continued and the Arts Council, at a Court Council meeting of 23 February 1970, stated that its 'relationship with the English Stage Company was seriously affected by this affair'. On 9 April, Blond reported the contents of a letter from the Arts Council to his own Council. The letter threatened the withdrawal of the grant for 1970–71 unless tickets were restored to Mrs Spurling. The Court by then had no option and gave in. Typically, Anderson dismissed the Council: 'it was a great chapter and a very sad failure because they were chicken in the end ... The row that blew up was a marvellous illustration of English hypocrisy and a kind of superstitious conservatism, in my opinion well worth a fight. We kept it going for a while.'[13]

The unity of the directors over Spurling did not, however, extend to much else. Gaskill had said that he would be returning to the Court at the beginning of February 1970 but that no programme could be set in motion until May. Anderson's contract ended in March and he had a film in mind. Page was rehearsing *Uncle Vanya*. There was no one to run the theatre. On 12 January, the Artistic Committee met to try to find a solution. This eventually consisted of Gaskill acting as Artistic Director and the other two as Associates. Anderson wanted acknowledged 'an element of instability of temperament' in the whole set up, and demonstrated it by referring to the Theatre Upstairs as 'the Gaskill'. On the same day, Harewood wrote to Blond, as Gaskill had urged in his letter of 23 December. Referring to the fact that Blond, some seven or eight months earlier, had talked to Harewood about stepping down, Harewood's letter lays out the situation: 'I believe we are at the moment in a tricky situation *vis-à-vis* the Arts Council and the *Spectator* affair, and that unless we act with some decisiveness, we shall not only look foolish in the eyes of the world but shall be facing a crisis of confidence inside the organisation.' In fact, Blond had only a few months to live, in which time he saw the company finances turn a deficit of £12,754 into a position in July where the finances were better than anticipated by £6,900.

By early 1970, the two strands of the Court's work were separating as between two auditoria. If the main stage housed established writers, Upstairs saw something of the new writers and for some at the Court was a useful repository of under-achieved or doubtful work, as had been the Sunday Nights to some extent in Devine's time:

> The Sunday Nights had died. They were a really important part of the work of that theatre and they were replaced by the Theatre Upstairs. As soon as you have two theatres like that in the same building, you do siphon off something and you do start to say, well, it's all right for the Theatre Upstairs, whereas in the early days at the Court, anything that was of any quality had to be shown in the main house.[14]

The creation of Upstairs allowed new work in, but only Upstairs. It freed the main bill for more of the same. It is unsurprising that Anderson quite liked the arrangement. It did not, of course, prevent him from expressing his views. Upstairs 'was always to me fringe and I've never approved of the alternative society ... a bit of a self-glorifying ghetto'.[15] The ghetto, however, produced in 1970 work by Brenton, Halliwell, Beckett, Heathcote Williams, Jellicoe, Hampton, Ionesco, Hare and Barker. That they were excluded from the main bill meant that they were not ultimately Court writers. Gaskill's vision in erecting a small auditorium, which set the model for other theatres, also effectively disinherited a generation of writers.

Neville Blond died on 4 August 1970 aged 74. Anderson nicely summed Blond up as far as the Court was concerned: 'a remarkable man in my view and although not sophisticated in the ways of art or the theatre, he had a very strong common sense, a very loyal attitude to the theatre, and a great sense of justice'.[16] Everyone at the Court testified to the toughness of mind which Blond exhibited about the theatre. Gaskill, at odds with Blond a good deal of the time, defined him as 'deeply emotional, vulgar and a bully but he forced one to define one's own values'.[17] Blond's death occasioned a rethink. Three new members joined the Council: Elaine Blond, John Montgomerie and Michael Codron. At its meeting of 1 September, the Council proceeded to discuss Blond's successor. Poke declined on the grounds that recent animosities over the Spurling affair meant he would not enjoy the confidence of the Artistic Directors. Harewood declined – too busy – but both Fox and Lewenstein were prepared to serve. Council dithered. The matter was resolved by a message that Fox and Lewenstein were prepared to act as Co-Chairmen. This was agreed for a two-year period. It is worth noting that both Osborne, writing to Lewenstein on 17 August, and Hugh Willatt for the Arts Council, on the same day, urged him to take the chair. At the same time, the position of Vice-Chairman, held by Alfred Esdaile, was abolished, given that there were now Co-Chairmen. Both Gaskill and Anderson saw this time as a watershed. For Anderson, and this became an often-repeated theme of his, Blond's death meant the weakening of the administrative structure of the Court:

And through all that period and after Neville I think the power of the Council waned, partly because it wasn't renewed, partly because people wanted to remain on the Council because it gave them something to do once a month.[18]

Gaskill brought in Peter Gill as an Associate to balance up the Artistic Directorate. Christopher Hampton was replaced by David Hare as Resident Dramatist, and the new Literary Manager was Jonathan Hales.

A major attempt to bring both auditoria together, that is to act upon the changes taking place outside the Court, was the *Come Together* festival, which opened on 21 October. Over twenty groups participated in a drastically reorganised Royal Court, occasioning the *Sunday Telegraph*'s comment on 18 October that the Court, 'dismayed by its run of commercial success ... was about to run an Underground festival so that the theatre could be empty and lose money again'. Though it is true that the festival managed only 31 per cent at the box office, it is more sadly true that little trace of it remained:

> That was a real kind of attempt to push something, not something of my own work but my response to what was happening in the theatre at large, something that we mustn't miss out on ... I thought it was extraordinary, an amazing three weeks. But it didn't actually feed anything into the theatre. I don't think it left much trace in the work that followed. It immediately reverted to being what it had been.[19]

The festival occasioned a row at the 2 December Council when Tony Richardson questioned whether it had been worth the effort, given that some of the productions were not 'worthy of the high standards of the English Stage Company'. It is hard to resist labelling some attitudes and comments at the Court during these days as reactionary and entrenched. Times were changing. George Harewood ceased to chair the Artistic Committee in favour of Lewenstein and became the first President of the Company.

The new year began with the death of Robin Fox, one of the unsung heroes of the Court since 1957. Like Harewood, Fox frequently defended the Artistic Directors and, via his close friendship with Neville Blond, and his charm, could usually resolve difficult moments, especially if it involved calming Blond down. With Fox gone, Lewenstein took sole responsibility as Chairman.

The Artistic Committee, another survivor from the earliest days and skilfully packed by Devine with his own people, was under threat since Anderson had queried its purpose back in July 1969. Since then, the Artistic Directors had met with Lewenstein in the chair. This arrangement now replaced the Artistic Committee and Jocelyn Herbert was co-opted.

As the Court reached its fifteenth birthday, the *Guardian* assessed its achievement and current status. It welcomed the second flowering of established Court writers and the function of Upstairs as 'a fine place for writers whose reputation is not as secure or even conceived'.[20] The definition of a booming Court, particularly the placing Upstairs of developing writers, is one that Anderson would approve of. Devine would not have approved of such siphoning off of the equivalent of Arden. If, outwardly, the Court flourished, privately there was a growing unease. Bond himself described the Court in September 1971 as 'an unobtainable ideal' for some countries: 'Yet how much, and how well – as writers and audience – do we use the Royal Court?'[21] An entirely relevant question for, as one reviewer noted when watching a performance in August of the new Osborne, *West of Suez*: 'When Sir Ralph Richardson makes his entrance ... the audience claps for several respectful moments. It seems all too fitting – the knowing star in a well-made hit by our leading dramatist. Who mentioned anger? Who whispers now of a theatre of dissent?'[22]

Such as there was came in the form of a round robin, dated 8 December, signed by twenty-three Court staff, including Casting Director Gillian Diamond, E. A. Whitehead, Jonathan Hales, Pam Brighton, Andy Phillips and Harriet Cruickshank. The petition voiced 'a growing concern at the number of Royal Court productions which appear in many respects to be designed for the West End. We feel that several unhealthy factors have appeared, and we wish to register our protest and concern:

1. The Royal Court should not be a try-out theatre for Shaftesbury Avenue.

2. Plays which do not transfer are not, therefore, failures.

3. It is intolerable that the planning, casting and mounting of plays at the Royal Court should be prejudiced and seriously affected by the requirements of transfers which, more and more, are set up long before the plays have opened at the Court.'

The petition was delivered while Storey's *The Changing Room* was preparing to transfer to the Globe.

This stood as a direct comment on most of the main-bill work of the time and, according to Pam Brighton, 'Lindsay's reaction was that we should all be sacked'.[23] Anderson inveighed against 'a perverted, puritanical feeling that success is dubious. What they're saying is that plays that *do* transfer are suspect. What the petition really showed was the damaging effect of subsidy.'[24] For once, Lewenstein is in accord with Anderson: 'their worries about it were connected with the disease of considering success as some sort of evil'.[25] Osborne weighed in with a letter of 31 January to Gillian Diamond, describing the petition as 'feeble, ill-written, ignorant, glib, arrogant, naive ... I think you should all get the boot for crassness and treachery. Fortunately, that is not in my gift.' A meeting was arranged for 27 January 1972:

> Oscar took the chair and I was there as secretary. The staff tried to argue their case, and Lindsay really lashed out at the staff over this petition and told them exactly what he thought of them ... and the whole thing collapsed.[26]

At the Council meeting held on the same day, Lewenstein reported that the meeting had been 'fairly short with an exchange of views about policy'. The problems did not go away, as Lewenstein and Poke and Anderson were to discover.

The 27 January Council, as well as reporting on the petition, proved to be momentous for the history of the Company, for it involved discussions to do with moves to larger theatres and it determined the next Artistic Director of the Court. The potential expansion schemes involved, on the one hand, a second auditorium in a new theatre building at Hammersmith, and, on the other, the Old Vic had expressed an interest in the Court occupying its premises once the National Theatre moved to its new building. Additionally, the Roundhouse could become available for six months in any given year. Council was put off Hammersmith primarily because the Arts Council appeared to back the Vic scheme. The decision was in favour of pursuing the Vic idea and it was to dominate Councils from this point until 1973.

The question of the Artistic Directorship was in one way already determined, for discussions with Oscar Lewenstein, as well as with the Artistic Directors, had been going on 'over the last few months'. Lewenstein was asked to make a statement to Council after which he withdrew. In turn, Gaskill, Page, Gill and Anderson had their say. The decision was to ask Lewenstein 'to assume artistic control as from 27 July'. The idea of Lewenstein had been growing for a while, especially since the Council thought Gaskill was going: 'Then Bill suddenly put in an application to say that he'd changed his mind.'[27] Gaskill had in fact written to Poke as Honorary Secretary on 24 January with his proposals. They included the formation 'of a small semi-permanent group of actors based in the Theatre Upstairs but capable of touring outside London. Fixed Seasons of experiments in the main bill downstairs – both of short runs of untried writers and work based on a company'. There were other proposals but to a weary Council the idea of returning in effect to true repertory was horrifying. Gaskill's cause was lost before he was interviewed. Lewenstein, on the other hand, 'came in with a very down to earth practical programme. I don't think he ever pretended that he was going to direct a play.'[28]

Poke's notes of the 27 January Council, and subsequently, reflect the desire of the Council to appoint Lewenstein. A telephone conversation with Richardson produces the note: 'Good idea ... Not ultimate authority in artistic matters ... not creative ... not to have final power'. What the Court thought it was getting in Lewenstein was a Director of the theatre, and not an Artistic Director. The notes show that Lewenstein was determined to gain what for him was the ultimate goal, that of directing policy at the Court. Although he 'dithered' over giving up everything else, it is also clear that 'if none of the others continued, he would carry on'. After he had left the room, Harewood referred to him as a 'Known quantity' who would exert a 'benign despotism' in the Court's affairs. Gaskill in his interview felt that 'this is a false crisis. Great success. Pity at this moment not to continue as at present'. Page spoke the truth about himself in asserting that he 'cannot direct and administrate at the same time'. Peter Gill, with little to lose, said boldly: 'Does not think an administrative person right to run a theatre ... Should be a director ... thinks it should be Bill'. Lindsay Anderson worried away: 'with Bill you never know. Always changing things ... Oscar would strengthen and give continuity ... Lindsay supported the idea of Oscar. Blackie [Blacksell] asked if Lindsay would give enthusiastic support if decision was made. He said yes. Probably true'. As a subsequent Artistic Director was to observe drily: 'Lindsay would have seen it [Lewenstein's appointment] as a bastion against [change]. He was the one who was most hostile to people getting in.'[29] And it is true that, having been instrumental in appointing Lewenstein, Anderson spent the next few years trying to get him out, as he was to do in the case of Lewenstein's successors, Robert Kidd and Nicholas Wright.

The 'humanists' won the day but as Pam Brighton put it 'something was so ruptured in the Court' when Gaskill went.[30] Harewood was asked to replace Lewenstein as Chairman but declined in order to run Sadler's Wells. Anderson, Page and Gill agreed to remain as Lewenstein's Associates. Gaskill declined to be an Associate and was replaced by Albert Finney. He appears to have felt that Lewenstein 'had been biding his time'.[31] His last production as Artistic Director was the British premiere of Mueller's *Big Wolf*, which followed *Veterans* and *Alpha Beta*. This was in many ways the end of a significant phase in the evolution of the Court. As Gaskill went, so did a number of his appointments, including the Casting Director, Gillian Diamond; the General Manager, Helen Montagu; the Chief Lighting Designer, Andy Phillips; and Pam Brighton, Schools Programme Director. The new Chairman was Greville Poke.

Lewenstein's three years as Artistic Director were tempestuous. As he puts it:

Although I had been associated with the Court for the past 16 years ... and knew the directors and other workers at the Royal Court, I had no idea just what taking on this job would mean in terms of stress, and how difficult I should find it to work in a more formal relationship with my colleagues there. Being the Chairman and trying to keep the peace between the various directors had not been easy, but compared to my new task it was a piece of cake.[32]

The problem was both to do with personality and status, as well as definitions of the post. For Jocelyn Herbert, Oscar 'wheedled his way in ... because they all argued so much, he thought it would be good if there was a kind of chairman to their debates and this was agreed to. And then Bill left and Oscar became Artistic Director, but it was never meant to be that way, but that's how it happened ... You always felt he'd got there by default. I know we all resented him. He wasn't one of us. He wasn't an artist.'[33]

Anderson, not for the first time, felt he had succeeded in manipulating affairs to match his sensibility:

I think that we tended to think that Oscar would be the Director of the theatre, employing a strong Artistic Committee. Oscar plainly thought otherwise and Oscar was determined to be the Artistic Director of the theatre and in our estimate this proved to be a mistake ... Oscar's ambitions overreached his capacity. He had it in his grasp to be the Manager of quite a strong Royal Court, but he wanted to have it, for him to be the Artistic Director.[34]

Nicholas Wright offers a subtle analysis of a man who began his theatre life as Esdaile's Manager and who at this stage in the Court's life had reached, for him, a pinnacle. Oscar

was on the wrong side of that Royal Court snobbery which is very hard to cross and which he had never crossed. I don't think anybody liked him really, or behaved as if they liked him. The truth about Oscar was that he was a very good, generous employer and he programmed the theatre very well. Some of the best shows I've seen at the Court were put on by Oscar, but he was always patronised at best and abused at worst by the Royal Court establishment. [It was] partly anti-Semitism, partly that he was linked with the commercial theatre. Oscar wasn't a Zionist, he was anti-Zionist. Blond was strong for Israel. You bet. Oscar was not a proper Jew and he was a communist. He was also an extremely manipulative man, and when he became AD, the thought that he should take on those artistic pretensions was pretty out of order.[35]

For someone without artistic temperament, Lewenstein's record as an impresario in the three years from July 1972 to July 1975 is impressive. As in the time of the triumvirate, the senior Court writers were very much in evidence on the main stage. Lewenstein aimed to extend the range of plays at the Court: 'I felt that in the period preceding me the plays of the Court had become less plays on public issues than had been the situation under Devine; the plays seemed to have narrowed in focus.'[36] The period saw plays by Wesker (programmed by Gaskill), Osborne, Bond,[37] Storey and Hampton, to which were added Beckett,[38] three plays by David Lan, all Upstairs; work by Abbensetts and Matura; by Edna O'Brien, Brian Friel, Howard Brenton and Snoo Wilson. Brenton's *Magnificence*,[39] a Gaskill commission, got on to the main stage, in the teeth of strong opposition from Anderson. *The Rocky Horror Show* opened in June 1973 and transferred to the Chelsea Classic, enjoying a cult all of its own. Important dramatists such as Robert Holman and Caryl Churchill[40] first appeared during Lewenstein's time and perhaps his finest moment came with the season in January 1974 of three of Athol Fugard's plays. His tenure of the post of Artistic Director ended with the Orton season of three plays in 1975.[41] A deficit of £40,000 was, however, carried into 1975.

Yet Lewenstein was, as far as the Court's establishment was concerned, a usurper, not to be compared with his two predecessors, Devine and Gaskill. Anderson felt this most keenly, given that he had thought that Lewenstein's role was to be one of taking the administrative burden on his shoulders, leaving Anderson and others to direct plays. And he began sniping early. A letter of 6 September 1972 from Anderson to Lewenstein, aside from stating that he only lasted to the interval of Wesker's *The Old Ones*, complains about the general state of the theatre, the poor decor and the dingy lights in the auditorium. Osborne weighed in with a letter to Poke of 16 November: 'I detect a very clear deterioration throughout the building itself, at every level, and this could be irreparably damaging.' Anderson decided to withdraw from the Artistic Committee for, as he told Poke in a letter of 21 January 1973, there is 'a continual abrasion between Oscar's determination to occupy (and, most important, *be seen to occupy*) the position of "Artistic Director", and his falling back (for security) on an Artistic Committee, to which he cannot bring himself to give any real authority'. It is ironic, given Devine's fight for artistic autonomy, to find one of his appointments complaining about similar actions by Lewenstein, who, according to the same letter 'had considered resigning from the Directorship when the National Theatre announced that its departure from the Old Vic would be postponed'. Lewenstein in fact announced to a Council meeting of 15 March that the postponement meant that the ESC could not move now to the Old Vic until July 1975. Warning lights began to flash when 'some members said that the policies to be pursued at the Old Vic were not clear to them'. Lewenstein undertook to prepare a policy paper which, if approved at the next Council, would go to the September meeting of the Arts Council.

The Old Vic had been offered to the ESC in November 1972, but the discussion between Lewenstein and Alfred Francis (for the Vic) had been going on from the beginning of the year. The ESC agreed to pursue the idea in March 1972. Lewenstein was in touch with Val May of the Bristol Old Vic to discuss a link when the ESC went to the Vic. He also set up the possibility of Frank Dunlop's Young Vic becoming more closely associated with the ESC, it being clear that when Peter Hall took the National into its new home he did not want to take the Young Vic. On 19 October, the Governors of the Old Vic approved the proposal, despite the fact that some Governors, as Poke told Blacksell on 13 November, 'do not want to see "kitchen sink" on the boards of the Old Vic'. Colin Benham, Chairman of the Governors, had never seen a show at the Court. As the news of the venture became public, some worries were expressed. Michael Billington, in the January 1973 *Plays and Players*, asked 'what business has a company devoted to new and often difficult work with a theatre seating 1,000 people? I suspect this could mean the end of everything Devine, Gaskill and others so tirelessly worked for.'

In June 1973 Council agreed Lewenstein's policy document for the scheme but dissent was apparent. Poke wrote to Caplan on 5 June to say that Richardson, in an 'extremely unpleasant meeting' was difficult 'and seemed hell bent on attacking Oscar ... In this, to a minor degree, he was supported by Jocelyn Herbert who in any case has never been particularly happy at the thought of going to the Old Vic'. At the meeting, to which David Storey was invited 'because he is probably the most vocal of the opponents', only Herbert voted against the scheme. Ashcroft and Michael White abstained.

Lewenstein envisaged that Finney and Scofield would become directors of the Old Vic and Anderson would run the Court. Finney had written to Poke on 6 June to say that 'the expansion is organic, overdue and an opportunity not to be missed'. However, in October, Anderson returned to the Court after completing his film, *If*. He very quickly made his feelings clear at an Artistic Committee meeting of 3 December. The scheme was 'unworkable'. The Vic would become an actors' theatre with Finney and Scofield and not a writers' theatre. The ESC 'should be concerned with retrenchment in the Royal Court ... making it run effectively and protecting it from the chill winds that were beginning to blow'. Storey and Page also complained of being 'railroaded'. Herbert felt the Vic would drain funds from the Court. The Committee voted six to one against taking the Old Vic. Lewenstein's grand scheme crashed and he remained bitter. The same meeting referred to 'an unpleasant scene between Lewenstein and Mr Anderson at the party given for Ann Jellicoe and the Court's writers'. The scale of the animosity between the two resulted in blows. As Nicholas Wright tells it, at a party Upstairs 'Lindsay accosted Oscar and I was there and he hit him, like, really hard, and Oscar tottered a bit and he was completely furious. It was round about that time that Lindsay decided that Oscar had to go. He called a meeting at Lois Sieff's house and he made a speech about how Oscar had to be got rid of. I will never forget the brilliantly theatrical throw-away inflection with which Lindsay said, "he's a communist of course".'[42] Poke turned up uninvited: 'it caused intense embarrass-ment all round and I sat there and listened ... It was just a hymn of hate.'[43] Herbert's view of the plan was that 'it was a scheme to enlarge Oscar's empire. Lindsay wasn't having any of that.'[44] And Anderson says 'it was a piece of plotting between Lewenstein and Finney ... there was this really unpleasant feeling that Oscar had been conniving with Albert essentially to get Albert to the Vic ... really scandalous ... It was like finding out that this was happening in the nick of time.'[45] Whether Anderson's view is correct is unclear. It is very clear, however, that, though there were murmurs of discontent about the scheme, it only became a full-scale assault on Lewenstein when Anderson returned. At its meeting on 8 January 1974, Council, appar-ently dominated by Anderson, recorded a majority in favour of dis-continuing negotiations.

The last word on the Vic scheme is also a comment on the state of play at the Court. Harewood, who was at the 8 January Council, wrote to Anderson on the same day to say that 'Every aspect of the Court has tended to run down ... the Council is a vast shambles and at my end of the table at that important meeting one had the feeling of being quite out of touch with a large number of people ... I think the leadership must in future be artistic as it is really chimerical to think it can ever normally come from the Chair.' The Council resisted suggestions that the present Associate Artistic Directors become members out of a concern with the Company's charitable status, though it seems rather more likely that Council did not welcome the idea in any sense. No action was therefore taken. The lack of action was interpreted in some quarters as a reactionary gesture by a beleaguered group with a weak Chairman. On 17 May, Jocelyn Herbert wrote to Poke to ask 'that the question of the future Artistic Director of the Royal Court should be put on the Agenda for the next meeting'. The letter looks to July 1975 when Lewenstein's three-year contract would be up. Moves were clearly being made in advance to replace him, since

Herbert wanted a sub-committee 'to really go into the question and seek out possible candidates'.

On 12 June Council was told that Lewenstein did not wish a further period as Artistic Director. Poke announced the result of his discussions with Lewenstein and their agreement that the post be offered to Anderson. Anderson, at the meeting, indicated his reluctance on the grounds that he was no administrator and felt the Company 'should take on a new look and break with the traditions of the past, both from an artistic and administrative point of view'. For someone of Anderson's beliefs, the notion of breaking with tradition is almost comic.[46] What Anderson did want, however, was a complete restructuring of the Council, together with its Chairman and its committees, and in this he was obviously correct. Council did carry on as if little had changed since Devine's time and, as a consequence, a wholesale rebellion was less than two years away. Anderson formally declined the post in a letter to Poke of 28 June. Lewenstein was unsurprised: 'He was happy to criticise others, but, when it came to it, not willing to accept the kind of responsibility being Artistic Director involved.'[47]

A sub-committee of Lois Sieff, Jocelyn Herbert, Oscar Lewenstein, Michael White and Lindsay Anderson was set up. An advertisement was placed and a questionnaire sent to applicants, earning the derision of *Plays and Players* (November), which hoped that the new regime would be 'sufficiently radical to ensure both a continuation of the fading prestige of the Royal Court as a home for the best new British writing and a clean break with the shadow of previous administrations'. Forty-nine applications were received, including those from Stuart Burge and Max Stafford-Clark, both of whom were to run the Court later. The Sub-Committee took advice where available and tabled a strong letter from Edward Bond to Poke on 8 November 1974. In it, Bond declares himself 'quite certain we should choose someone who has trained at the Court, or worked there long enough to have soaked in its atmosphere. I'm sure we don't need anyone from outside.'

Among the Court-trained people to apply were Robert Kidd and Nicholas Wright, both of whom began at the Court in Gaskill's time. The original suggestion, from Kidd, was that the two of them, plus Bill Bryden and Barry Hanson, should jointly apply. Bryden and Hanson, for different reasons, dropped out and Kidd then suggested that he and Nicholas Wright apply:

> It appealed to me because Robert had an extraordinarily good commercial track record, a very good feeling for shows running and transferring which in those days was very important economically ... my interest in those days was in the work of new writers which I'd been doing in the Theatre Upstairs ... I thought it a very good combination when he suggested it.[48]

Poke's notes on the interview with Kidd on 28 September support the idea: 'Bob told us that he would not mind if he did not direct plays at the Royal Court as his main interest was in running the theatre.'

It was Anderson who effectively appointed Kidd and Wright:

> Lindsay really organised and browbeat the election committee ... When we had those interviews, no matter who we saw, and we saw some incredibly prestigious and able people, Lindsay, as soon as they'd gone, went into battle and squashed every suggestion. He went on and on and on. The same thing happened when it went to the Council. And then of course he disappeared.[49]

Jocelyn Herbert

> kept trying to persuade Lindsay to do it but he wouldn't. Kidd and Wright applied and I was dead against them. Max applied. Lindsay wanted to have these two and he thought he would be the *eminence grise* and they'd do all the work. He swung it, of course. I always thought it was a terrible mistake ... I know he felt with Max, God knows what would have happened. Max was never a socialist but he wrote a rather good paper. I was quite for him in a way.[50]

Council met to discuss the proposal that Kidd and Wright be jointly appointed. Peggy Ashcroft, unable to attend the meeting, gave her support in a letter to Poke: 'it seems to me the right way to follow the tradition of the Court directors for the Court, and yet bringing it in line with the present generation'. Anderson lobbied Harewood on 27 November to send a letter of support for the two to Poke as Chairman. The entire selection committee, except Lewenstein, who reserved the right to oppose it at Council, voted for the two. In the same letter, Anderson tells Harewood that he has persuaded Norman Collins to send his support to Poke. Harewood duly wrote on the same day. At the 2 December Council, the proposal was accepted, as was the suggestion by Herbert that Anderson be appointed to Council.

Lewenstein's tenure ended in July 1975 but perhaps one of his most striking moments was a letter he sent to *The Times* for 15 October 1974. Signed by fourteen Artistic Directors, the letter expressed strong concern at the danger of the new, three-auditorium National Theatre draining the profession of both resources and skilled workers. There was a threat to the remainder of the subsidised theatre at the time of financial stringency, and the letter attested that the National was tempting technicians with salary offers beyond the capacity of other theatres. 'The implications of this are unhealthy.' Hall professed himself 'terribly hurt about it, although pretending not to be'. When the two met, the same evening, 'I blew. I called him a shit and a creep.'[51] It is something of an irony that Lewenstein, the impresario, attacked Hall for sucking the life blood of the subsidised theatre. It is also the case that the Court, which under Devine began the changes in the modern British theatre which enabled the subsidised theatre to flourish, should, during the period of 1969 to 1975, have given so much succour to the commercial sector.

6 Changing places, 1975–1979

When he started, Devine did not fully know what he was doing, and ever since
then the Court has not accepted the responsibilities that go with being the sort of
place it claims it wants to be – even though these responsibilities are now clearer
... What now happens to the Court depends entirely on what decisions it makes in
this matter. If it became what it should be, then, yes, the state might try to shut it
down – and it might then find new friends. If it tries to avoid its true
responsibilities ... well then, yes, it might amble on. But it will not be the home of
the New Theatre.

(Edward Bond, in Findlater, 124)

Having placed Kidd and Wright as Artistic Directors of the Court,
Anderson, in between attempting to replace Poke as Chairman with
Hugh Cudlipp, clearly felt he effectively controlled artistic policy. He
was mistaken. Kidd and Wright rejected Anderson's proposal for a
revival of *The Seagull* with Paul Scofield, and he was told that the
opening programme was already fixed. According to Nicholas Wright,
Anderson's support for them did not last long:

> it didn't last any time at all. It lasted up to the horrible meeting
> before we even started, really, where Lindsay was just talking
> about shows that he wanted to do at the Court, which horrified
> me. One was *The Seagull* with Scofield; another was *Hamlet*
> with Frank Grimes. I thought it would be an absolute joke if you
> appoint two young guys and then you do this kind of stuff ... He
> was absolutely furious and he became a sworn enemy, mostly
> because he obviously thought that [we'd] got the job anyway
> under his wing and would repay him by letting him do his
> productions. From that moment the whole thing became very
> unpleasant. The price of Lindsay's support was unaffordable.[1]

Anderson, in a letter to Hugh Cudlipp, described the rejection as 'precipitate and rash', using it as a prime example of the 'administrative malaise at the Court'.[2] Once crossed, Anderson did not forget. He instanced the Kidd–Wright reign at the Court as a perfect example of the danger of artistic autonomy: 'nobody must discuss anything and nobody did discuss anything and I would have to say that the result of that in the end was catastrophe. When nobody would question the right of Kidd and Wright to put on plays which were not generally liked or approved, the result was practically to bankrupt the theatre, with the impotant liberals saying, well, after all they are the Artistic Directors. To me that's bullshit.'[3]

As a result of his plans failing, Anderson resigned from the Artistic Committee, which had been selected by Kidd and Wright, and declined the offer of a place on the Council. He set out his account of the events in a confidential letter to Council of 30 May. His version of the story is lucid and no doubt represented his truthful sense of being misreported and misjudged. However, it is very difficult to avoid the belief that he expected to be able to have a free hand with Kidd and Wright. In so doing, he would have perpetuated his definitions of the Court, something he clearly felt, wrongly, was going to be the case with his support of Lewenstein. It is also odd for him not to have weighed the fact that both Kidd and Wright were Gaskill's appointments. Kidd had been appointed an Assistant Director in 1967; Wright had been Gaskill's Casting Director, an Assistant Director in 1968 and the first Director of the Theatre Upstairs in 1969. They were hardly likely to be susceptible to notions of revivals, even by Anderson. He was wrong about them, as he was about Lewenstein. He was not wrong about the weakening hold of Council. It is a gross irony that the very weakness he so vehemently castigated allowed him such power. The Court paid a high price for its Council's love affair with Lindsay Anderson, not simply because he was wrong but because he favoured resigning as a virtual methodology as opposed to staying and fighting.

The proposed programme by Kidd and Wright was very impressive. There were new plays by David Hare, Howard Barker, Edward Bond and Christopher Hampton; important work by Samuel Beckett; the latest David Storey; and Richard O'Brien's follow-up to *The Rocky Horror Show*. However, by 8 April, Council was being warned of a serious financial problem in the shape of a £40,000 deficit at the end of March 1975. By July, the figure was £47,000. The Arts Council had firmly indicated that the 1975/76 grant would not be increased. The Artistic Directors were therefore told to present a programme costing no more than £140,000. Poke, in the Minutes, opined that it was 'bad luck that the Artistic Directors should be taking over at such a time of crisis'. Almost unnoticed at the meeting was the report of the death of Alfred Esdaile.

Guestimates for the first four plays in the season (by Hare, Bond, Barker and Hampton) were rejected by the 22 April Council. Kidd and Wright, faced with a gap of £90,000 between the theatre's needs and the Arts Council grant, argued the case, financially not artistically, for the temporary closure of the Theatre Upstairs, a measure saving £40,000 in a full financial year. If the case for closing Upstairs was essentially financial, it was also true that costs Downstairs were known at this stage to be high, particularly with regard to Bond's play, *The Fool*, and that therefore there was in fact an element of artistic choice. *The Fool* cost £18,650, played to 53 per cent of financial capacity, and lost £20,000. Wright said later: 'What it came down to, was *The Fool* or the Theatre Upstairs.'[4] Osborne weighed in with a comment on the memorandum to Council by Kidd and Wright about closure with the, for him, remarkable assertion that the closure indicated a policy of being 'an adjunct of Shaftesbury Avenue, and a mere launching pad for West End management who like to use this theatre for personal conveniences'. Osborne's letter of 21 May also lambasts the Council:

> If some of the rich, perhaps even millionaires, and influential people on the Council were to chip in or work for a living instead of indulging themselves in the luxury of committee do-goodery and dubious charities, we would not be going around with a begging bowl to the Arts Council and the Government after what is generally acknowledged ... to be the creation and now probable end of a unique chapter of achievement in English creative history ... P.S. Perhaps the boys at the end of *If were* right. Bang!

153

A combination of a daunting economic climate nationally, the growing reluctance of West End managers to take risks and the tight budgeting of the Arts Council made for a situation in which thriving financially became imperative. It also made a nervous Council reject the importing of John Morris's play, *Tulloch*, from Edinburgh's Royal Lyceum, principally because of a hostile review by Harold Hobson. This occasioned a strong protest by the Artistic Committee at the interference of Council in an artistic matter. In this context, with the exception of Hare's *Teeth 'n' Smiles*, and Hampton's *Treats*, both of which transferred and made a little money, other Court productions, both critically and financially, fared poorly. Bond's *The Fool* was the most expensive show mounted at the Court and brought a sharp reprimand from Anthony Field, Finance Director of the Arts Council, in a letter of 26 January 1976 to Jon Catty, the Court's Company Secretary and Accountant. Field professed himself 'appalled' at the £11,000 overspend on the play and warned Catty that the next set of estimates needed to be scrupulously careful. Field advanced £10,000 against the incoming Arts Council grant, but the threat of action is clear in the letter. Kidd and Wright in one way were upholding the Court tradition of presenting new work. In a time of economic crisis, the money-givers assume disproportionate power. The last nine months of 1976 saw average takings of approximately 35 per cent, as opposed to a norm of 55 per cent.[5] However, productions did include Beckett's own direction of *Waiting for Godot* from the Schiller Theatre, Berlin; a revival of *Endgame*; a Beckett triple bill; and two powerful Joint Stock pieces, *Yesterday's News* and Churchill's *Light Shining in Buckinghamshire*.[6]

Internally, the life of the Court was tense. Jon Catty resigned late in 1976. This was ostensibly to do with a row about holiday pay for Simone Reynolds, the Court's Casting Director. It actually, for Catty, went rather deeper. At an emergency meeting of the Management Committee on 25 August, Catty was emphatic that the holiday pay issue 'was only the tip of an iceberg'. It was 'symptomatic of bad management which was costing the Court money'. Catty's criticisms related to the General Manager, brought in by Lewenstein, Anne Jenkins, and to the Artistic Directors' handling of personnel. His chief complaint was massive overspending on budget and 'general lack of financial control'. On 12 September, Catty produced a document which painted a picture of sloppy processes in a period of acute pressure. Although the document was inevitably to do with finance rather than aesthetics, it was sufficient to concern the Council. In a letter to Poke of 13 October, Lord Sainsbury expressed the worries of a number of Council members 'about the organisational structure of the English Stage Company and the relationship between the Management Committee, the Artistic Committee and the Council'. A crisis was looming, not at all helped by the growing friction between the two Artistic Directors, and

> as a result, we looked inwardly and adopted a rather combative stance toward everyone else. The joint creature we had created really lacked the generosity which was necessary. We were both inexperienced in running a large theatre, but, more important, we weren't very good at creating the kind of atmosphere in which it is very easy for people to give advice.[7]

Wright put it another way in 1996:

> A lot of people were fuck-all help. Bill had the grace afterwards to say, well, you didn't get much advice, did you, meaning himself, that he hadn't really bothered. His behaviour was angelic if you compare it with Lindsay's or with Oscar's. Oscar clearly marked himself out as hostile. He was completely unhelpful ... Jocelyn was very supportive. She was critical of all sorts of things but she behaved absolutely impeccably.[8]

In November, Wright attempted to resolve the problem by proposing himself as Artistic Director with Kidd as his Associate. Kidd supported the idea. This was discussed at a Management Committee meeting on 2 December, as were the names of replacements, including Stuart Burge, Giles Havergal and Richard Eyre. Before anything was decided, the Arts Council intervened. At an emergency Management Committee meeting on 8 December, the results of a meeting with Anthony Field of the Arts Council were graphically expressed. The Court would get only a 10 per cent increase in grant

155

and must also substantially reduce its deficit. On the same day, Council accepted the Arts Council's proposals. Also on the same day, Robert Kidd resigned, having previously indicated to Poke that he would unless the Court Council stood firm. In his formal letter of resignation to Poke, of 10 January 1977, he cannot hide his anger at what had happened:

> It was then made plain, verbally and subsequently by letter to you, that unless we cleared this deficit by 30 June (pigs might fly) we should 'pay off outstanding creditors as at that date out of balance of available subsidy and then *cease operation . . .*' – in mid-summer! In other words go dark in a very real sense involving, as I see it, the probable sacking of the permanent staff . . . The Management Committee met and took that decision to decide by 1 May to 'reassess' what the position would be at the end of June.

According to Kidd, the Committee then regrouped as the Council and accepted the decision. It had 'under your chairmanship . . . complacently, hurriedly and most crassly sold the Royal Court down the river'. The letter was circulated to all staff. Since the contracts of both Artistic Directors were linked, one resignation involved another. Peter Hall noted with initial *schadenfreude*, hastily corrected, an encounter with Lindsay Anderson: 'He told me the Royal Court is in terrible danger – Nicholas Wright and Robert Kidd are leaving and somehow he's got to help. There was that awful pleasure in the air at the ill-fortune of others. Well, it could be coming to me over the National.'[9] For many Council members, there was a sigh of relief at Kidd's resignation. Elaine Blond, elected President in succession to Lord Harewood, who had resigned in May 1976, talked of Kidd accusing the Council of 'defiling the unique reputation of the Royal Court. Before storming out, he called for my resignation as President.'[10]

But, for Kidd, the Court was rather more than, as Elaine Blond once called it, 'Neville's folly'. His Co-Artistic Director generously and, it would appear, accurately, characterises Kidd's motivation:

He came from an extraordinary poor working class Scots family
and there was an incredibly pugnacious drive in the direction of
success and fame ... In an argument to get his own way, I've
never come across anybody so uncompromising [who would]
fight his corner so ferociously.[11]

According to Wright, Kidd did not resign over the Arts Council grant:

I think he resigned out of a huge sense of disappointment that
he hadn't achieved what he wanted to, his enormous ambitions
for a theatre that he adored. He loved the Court, had had the
time of his life there, had worshipped certain figures there like
John Osborne and Bill certainly. Bill had been so incredibly good
to him ... It was his whole life and the fact that our joint
running of the theatre had been so unhappy and that it was
thought not to be successful was devastating. There was in his
relationship with the Royal Court an element of class war
raging.[12]

In November 1976, Poke had quietly set up a sub-committee
with the task of finding a new Artistic Director. He wrote to the group
on 4 January 1977 to say that Giles Havergal of the Citizens' Theatre,
Glasgow, was very interested after Poke had explained the situation
'without mentioning Stuart Burge's name'. By 10 January, Poke noted
privately: 'Meeting with Hugh [Willatt] and Stuart. Latter to think
about it'. The link between Willatt and Burge was that Willatt had
been instrumental both in the creation of the new Nottingham Playhouse in 1963 and the installation of Burge in 1970 as a replacement
for John Neville, the departing Artistic Director. Neville left amidst
considerable acrimony. It was left to Burge to restore the good fortunes
of the Playhouse which he did spectacularly over the two years. Burge
also arranged the succession in 1973 of Richard Eyre to Nottingham.
He was therefore known as a troubleshooter, quite apart from his
distinguished record as a director.[13]

The difficulty at this stage was that Burge was poised to run
the National's Cottesloe auditorium. As Jocelyn Herbert recalls: 'I
saw Stuart and we had lunch. The funny thing about him was that

he'd always loved the Court and never been let in. He talked very well and he was prepared not to go to the National. There was something about him that I liked. So I did support him.'[14] Burge's version of this was that he 'was among people in the undergrowth prowling around outside, waiting to get in for many years'.[15] Pressure was applied to Peter Hall to release Burge: 'The argument is that unless I do, the Court may close forever. It's good old-fashioned blackmail and very upsetting, even though I know it's over-stated. Stuart is torn. He says it's his duty to go to the Court, although he recognises that emotionally he wants to come to us and is committed'.[16] Which is odd, since, according to Willatt the day before, 'Hugh tells me Stuart cannot get PH to agree and has regretfully come to conclusion that providing PH agrees to his terms now ... he feels he must accept PH. At same time feels he is making a mistake'.[17]

Meanwhile, Poke had to face staff at the Court and external calls for his replacement. Poke's notes of a staff meeting on 14 January record reactions with some bewilderment: 'Not very satisfactory. Resented they had not been kept in picture ... Seemed to want to argue about everything. Seemed to support [Kidd's] view that Arts Council should have given us more money. Friendly lot all the same'. On the day before, Anderson had written to the Arts Council to state that 'the resignation of the Chairman and of at least half the members of the Council would be an essential pre-requisite to the healthy revival of the fortunes of the Royal Court'. In this, Anderson for once was supported by Court staff.

On the same day, Burge told Willatt that 'he had taken the wrong job'. Poke's notes record his telephone conversation with Burge, who made it very clear that he 'Did not want to follow policy of safe revivals. I agreed but suggested interesting revivals not out of keeping with us. He said he did not want to supervise the death of the Royal Court.' Burge makes plain the basis of his taking the Court and he was the first outsider to do so, notwithstanding the fact that he had known George Devine well and worked at the Old Vic Theatre School. Hall's anger at the events is clear: 'But now he has decided he must go to the Court. So I have released him. And I am in a mess. Spoke to Hugh Willatt at lunchtime, who thanked me for being public-spirited about Burge. Public-spirited be damned. I have had to bow to the inevitable and it's upset me very much.'[18] It is possible that Burge's decision was to do with who ran what: 'Peter was running the theatre and when the Royal Court came to me, I probably, foolishly, thought, "Oh well, that's more my cup of tea, to run a small theatre like that, rather than being involved in that huge organisation".'[19]

Pressure on the Council and the Chairman to resign mounted as part of an attempt to effect a clean sweep with Burge's appointment. Jocelyn Herbert circulated a letter to Council asking for signatures in support of Poke's resignation. Poke noted that 'Jocelyn is the voice of Lindsay.' Her letter referred to 'talented people' who would not work under Poke. Poke, at an Artistic Committee meeting of 19 January, insisted that no one talk individually to the press and that everyone should try to 'Correct feeling that Stuart had been appointed by old fuddy duddies (*sic*). Get directors and well known actors to say how delighted they are'. Writers began to add their voices. Steven Berkoff generously offered himself in a telegram of 19 January ('Is England's best'). Howard Brenton was one of the generation of writers effectively excluded in the early seventies and sent this on 21 January to the Council:

> As many of us see it, the theatre that George Devine and John Osborne made with courage and hope has sold its birthright. The one independent and, at its best, rebel stage in England of any size, has pawned itself to the Arts Council, even by all reports, to the extent of allowing that government agency to dictate its choice of Artistic Director. This disgrace is not because of the indifferent programme of the last year. That is only a symptom.
>
> The truth of the matter is that steadily, through the 70s, and now totally, the Royal Court has lost the trust and the respect of a whole generation of playwrights. I beg you, grasp that harsh fact and act upon it. Close down the English Stage Company to let a new Royal Court form. Give a decent burial to the old successes, failures and traditions preserving only one thing – independence. For there is no real future for new writers in the

theatres to which they have been blown by the ill-wind from the Royal Court ... The playwrights and the public need an independent and rebel Royal Court in the 1980s.

David Hare, a day later, reinforced Brenton's anger:

the Council has no real idea of how deep the disaffection of writers with the Court is. It is not a question of small scale adjustments to the constitution of the Council: it is a question of replacing it. I also think it is idiotic to appoint an Artistic Director at a time when the Council commands no support among artists. It would be tragic if the last act of a dying Council were to commit the Court to a particular artistic director; and it would be unfair on whoever is to succeed you ... this is an important moment to consult writers, directors and theatre staff about what *kind* of Royal Court we all want in the future. It is only after that kind of discussion that a new director should be appointed.

To appoint a director without having the grace to consult those who actually do the theatre's work will just sow the seeds of more and worse trouble in the future.

Edward Bond also wrote at length on 21 January in an attempt to have the matter fully discussed. He argued that 'The time for a radical change in the membership of the Council has come ... The Council must have more writers, designers and directors as active, attending members, and backstage and front of house ought also to be represented on it ... At the moment the Arts Council is squeezing the Court by the throat and lecturing it for not breathing deeply.'

In fact, Council had demonstrated its inability to understand by already appointing Burge, even though a formal announcement was not made until later. Council's meeting on 24 January confirmed the appointment, with Osborne and Lewenstein voting against it. IIt took effect from 1 February. At the same meeting, Council debated the future of the Company. Poke's draft notes for the Chairman's Report (edited for the official Minutes) contain a strong attack on the press in general and Lindsay Anderson in particular who, Poke maintains, when it became apparent that Kidd and Wright would not allow him to dictate the choice of play 'departed in a huff'. At the meeting, Poke and others offered their resignations but it was decided that a sub-committee, chaired by Hugh Willatt, be set up to look at 'the structure and activities of the Company'. The group was to try to report back within two months. Something had happened, but not a lot; just a sub-committee. Poke's notes of the meeting record a good deal of indecision, amidst which Jocelyn Herbert urged the need for Council to look at itself 'for a change'. She felt that 'writers and workers in the theatre should be part of the structure. We are thinking in terms of 1956 ... Jocelyn feels appointment of Burge good because it takes us away from incestuous situation. Hopes SB will bring back the talent'. After the meeting, Herbert sent a memorandum to the Council to denounce the meeting:

> If anyone doubted the need for the Council to have a new look at itself – that meeting must have convinced them. The lack of any understanding or even interest in the opinions of the people who actually work in the theatre or write plays for it ... and instead the Council's obsession with saving face and avoiding any clear and honest statement at all costs was, to put it bluntly, nauseating.

She resigned. Although she regarded Poke as a weak Chairman, she wrote to him on 27 January to say that 'It must have been hell for you this last two weeks – with all the shit flying around. If it is any help I do assure you that the shit is aimed at the organisation and, although as Chairman a lot of it has fallen on your shoulders, there is no personal odium intended. Indeed, everyone who knows you regards you with affection and respect.'

While Willatt's Committee, consisting of John Montgomerie (Council), Richard Findlater (writer and critic) and Ian Kellgren, an Assistant Director at the Court, began its deliberations, past and present Court workers began theirs. Burge managed to avoid being tainted in the way Council had, partly because his conviction that the financial crisis which so alarmed the Council and the Arts Council 'was hugely inflated by the press ... a large proportion of the Council was old and nervous, and also number of them had been replaced'.[20] Burge felt that the Arts Council 'were behaving pretty unreasonably, I thought'.[21] Such a view would ally him with the Court staff, as would his suggesting a series of workers' meetings to debate the future. The meetings 'were to try and find, by a lot of discussion, whether there was some other way of running it'.[22]

One of the first meetings of staff was on 28 January to discuss a proposal by Lewenstein, following Bond, that 'the future of the Company shall be in the hands of all those who work or have worked for the Company' (letter to Poke, 24 January). The staff passed this proposal by a majority of nineteen.[23] On 24 February, eighteen writers debated the issues. A motion to change the name of the English Stage Company was passed by eleven to three. Another suggestion of moving from the Court was upheld, as was the idea of the workers running the theatre. Ted Whitehead, Howard Brenton and Caryl Churchill were elected to meet Willatt's group. On 25 February, nineteen directors met, ranging from Anderson to Stafford-Clark. This time the proposal to do with the workers was passed 'with a small majority, but with a large number of abstentions', so that the proposal did not go forward. The actors needed three meetings on 28 February, 20 March and 3 April to agree to workers' control which would effectively run the entire operation. Twenty-seven past and present permanent staff met on 1 March. No motions were proposed. Finally, there was a meeting on 15 March, which included Jon Catty, Helen Montagu and Gillian Diamond. This meeting rejected the idea of a collective and detailed a suggested Board of Management to replace the Council. The last word in the series came on 21 March in a paper by Nicholas Wright, who had been asked to stay on for six months as Burge's Associate Director. Speaking from hard experience, Wright makes it clear that the job of the Artistic Director is

> to produce a programme of plays each of which satisfies at least one of the following requirements:
>
> (a) It takes £1,000 per week more that the 55 per cent budgeted for (£1,000 equals 17 per cent of the house).
> (b) It is unusually cheap: a two-hander, say, with one simple set.

(c) Half the costs are borne by a commercial management and/or the play transfers to the West End, where it makes a profit.

(d) The production started somewhere else and can be brought in without any production costs to speak of.

He points out that requirement (c) 'is harder and rarer than it once was, because the West End is now more conservative than in past years, and managers play a more cautious game'. Wright's point is that unless the Arts Council grant goes up, the Court runs the risk '*either* of electing to present a programme so safe that all sense of identity is lost *or* of running up a new deficit, which will probably amount to £50,000'.

Wright's document is both sane and realistic. He knows that the Court has reached a watershed, that the moment is to be seized and that the Court is now 'artistically, a new organisation. Most of the writers and directors of the last decade are now dispersed, working in other theatres or in the United States. Few of the staff have been here more than four or five years ... In other words the past suggests that the Court has much to gain by exploiting the freedom from the past it now enjoys; and a similar approach, applied to the management structure would express absolutely the Court's best qualities.' The document was included as part of the Willatt report which was considered by Council on 26 September, together with a minority report by Ian Kellgren, who broadly represented the view of Court staff and writers as to a workers' Council. There was a good deal of heated debate at the meeting, centrally to do with the suggestion of an elected rather than invited membership of Council. Oscar Lewenstein, perhaps showing more of his old experience of his Glasgow Unity days, failed in his bid for a co-operative and resigned. His ties were cut after twenty-one years with the ESC. The meeting also received a letter of resignation from Peggy Ashcroft: 'it is time, as one of the "old brigade", I stepped down. I think it essential that, whoever forms the new council, it should be people who have *time, energy* and *new ideas*' (to Poke, 18 September).

Council offered to resign, but agreed to continue until a new Council could be formed, now with three staff representatives, but in

THE ROYAL COURT AND THE MODERN STAGE

reality not much had changed. As Findlater notes: 'the underlying pressures remained – intensified by the growing pressures of the time – beyond the scope of the Willatt committee'.[24] The problems were to surface again in the eighties.

Burge abandoned the idea of an Artistic Committee 'almost as soon as I was there. It was time wasting. No decisions were ever come to, and although individually the people were very useful to talk to, you could talk to them anyway.'[25] He appointed as his Associates Jonathan Miller and Max Stafford-Clark. Miller was someone Burge knew from his Nottingham days – 'I mean, Jonathan can't say no to anything and I did suggest he become Associate Director and he said, yes, and that's about the last we heard of him'.[26] With Stafford-Clark, 'I knew about him and I'd seen one or two productions of his':

> the main thing was Joint Stock and that was really where I knew him. And I just thought he was a very likely Associate Director ... I think the first thing you have to do when you become an Artistic Director is seek out your successor. I thought he would be a candidate ... I tried to get him to come as co-director but the board wouldn't have him ... to leave it to the board to choose the new director is a bit irresponsible actually. Because how can a board know who to appoint?[27]

A further appointment and an innovation was to have a full-time Literary Manager, who was not, at that stage, a writer. Rob Ritchie

> was recommended by Trevor [Griffiths] – I think mainly because he'd majored in Trevor. It was an absolute godsend. I thought he was wonderful. He was very objective and efficient and had tastes that I went along with. But then of course when I appointed Max as Associate Director they got on well and Max kept him on.[28]

This team bore out Wright's assertion of the newness of the Court's operation artistically. It also became very clear that Burge was extremely astute at managing the Court's affairs, notwithstanding the predilection of older Court figures for lamenting the present. Osborne, for example, begged Arnold Goodman to find a good Chairman and get rid of the 'dim amateurs and muddlers on the Council'.[29] When that did not work, he wrote to Hugh Willatt on 12 September to demand the resignation of most of the Council ('My fishmonger in Edenbridge High Street had more sense of theatre . . .'); the replacement of Poke; the scrapping of the Theatre Upstairs and the 'Youth Theatre. Merely an outlet for third rate talents'.

Initially, Burge had little money to play with. He imported a number of productions by, amongst others, Soho Poly, 7:84 Scotland, Tyneside Theatre Company, the Abbey Theatre, Birmingham Repertory Theatre, and Pirate Jenny. He cut costs wherever he could and he judged the financial possibilities of Mary O'Malley's *Once A Catholic* very precisely. The play had been commissioned by Nicholas Wright and Ann Jellicoe and was programmed for production by the previous Artistic Directors. No commercial management was interested in a co-production. When it was a hit at the Court (88 per cent at the box office), 'we were in a very strong bargaining position and were able to auction it so that we could get a very good deal for it. Subsequently, it helped enormously to pay off debts, and it still provides an income.'[30] As Burge remarked, the play when he arrived 'was really all ready to do. I've never understood why it hadn't been done actually. Not that it was really a Royal Court play, but it would have got them out of the deficit.'[31] The play, together with a special one-off grant of £20,000 from the Arts Council and 'one or two lucky breaks',[32] wiped the deficit out within two years of Burge's appointment.

Talk of finance tended to mask the fact that Burge and Stafford-Clark were developing a policy of new work as central to their thinking. Shepard's *Curse of the Starving Class* had its world premiere in April 1977, directed at Shepard's request by Nancy Meckler. Burge thought it 'quite the most worthwhile play amongst those I had read in recent months' (letter to Council, 3 October 1977). Barker's *Fair Slaughter* followed in the main house, while Upstairs saw Michael Hastings's *For the West* and David Lan's *The Winter Dancers*. Writers such as Robert Holman, Alan Brown, Heathcote Williams, Ron Hutchinson, and Lenka Janiurek were all produced Upstairs. Nigel Williams's *Class Enemy* transferred from Upstairs to the main bill in

April 1978, after Burge had turned down an earlier play by him, *WC/PC*.[33] Robert Wilson's *I was Sitting on my Patio ...* , a two-hander, was, according to Burge, 'deeply pretentious but very stylish ... the design was tremendous, and I knew it would attract a sort of okay audience'.[34] A revival of *Inadmissible Evidence*, directed by Osborne and starring Nicol Williamson was a great success. Burge wanted to see it done 'because I thought it was John's best play ... I wasn't going to direct it because Nicol was going to do what he liked anyway, and I thought it was best that John should direct it, who was desperate to do it'.[35] Stafford-Clark's production of Babe's *Prayer for my daughter* followed the Osborne, then came Alan Brown's *Wheelchair Willie*, which was, in part, to do with Burge's sense of the purpose of the Court *vis-à-vis* new work. The play was directed by Stafford-Clark, of whom Burge was 'very supportive. I think "proper" is the right word. He has always had a proper idea of what role the Royal Court should be fulfilling.'[36] For Burge, Alan Brown was a

> very sweet, gentle, smiling man, and he had written this play of
> such degradation as I've never seen or read in my life. It was real
> horror about a boy in a wheelchair and this terrible mother ...
> the effect of the play was extraordinary and it was the strongest
> thing, I think, that had ever been seen at that time about
> poverty in English cities.[37]

Stafford-Clark, responding to staff unease about the play, notes in his diary that the play will 'disturb, upset and anger. It is likely to get hostile notices and it is likely that it will play to poor houses.'[38] He talked to Court staff about the play, giving his reasons for doing it: 'And that was a rallying point. Once they'd heard that, they were absolutely OK.' Stafford-Clark felt that he had at that moment gained a commitment from the staff to the play and to himself.[39]

After David Edgar's *Mary Barnes* had transferred from Birmingham, saving the Court any production costs, Burge revived Ravenscroft's *The London Cuckolds*. Churchill's *Cloud Nine* came from Joint Stock, to be followed by Martin Sherman's *Bent*, a play about a gay relationship in a concentration camp. With Ian McKellen in the cast, the play was 'a candidate for outside finances. We there-

fore only had to give it house room and bear the running costs.'⁴⁰
Burge is dismissive of the piece: 'It was one of those plays you do
when you're short of money ... I don't think it's the greatest play in
the world but anyway it was sensational. McKellen and Tom Bell
were wonderful.'⁴¹ After *Bent*, 'we needed something to fill the house
... [Beckett] had long been promised from way back. He said that he
wanted to do *Happy Days* with Billie [Whitelaw].'⁴² The main bill for
the year concluded with Leigh Jackson's *Reggae Britannia*, Nicholas
Wright's *The Gorky Brigade* and Lan's *Sergeant Ola and His Followers*.

By this time, Burge had taken leave for up to six months to
direct a television version of *Sons and Lovers*. Having effectively put
his artistic successor in place, Burge had tried to appoint Poke's
successor as Chairman of the Company. The Council had begun to
search in the autumn of 1977 and the name which recurred was that
of Sir Hugh Carleton Greene who had recently left the post of
Director-General at the BBC. Greene eventually declined the invitation in a letter to Poke of 14 March 1978. He gave as the reason the
judgement of a throat specialist that his commitments should be
reduced and that he should spend four months each year in a warm
climate. For Burge, Greene was

> Anti-establishment but very influential. But he came to one
> Council meeting and I remember it being very acrimonious and
> he was completely bewildered by the whole thing. And then he
> wrote to me and said he didn't think he would be able to do it.⁴³

The Council meeting Greene attended was rearranged in order to fit in
with Greene's schedule. It took place on 14 March, the same day as
his letter to Poke. Greene opted for a more tranquil life than that of
controlling the ESC Council, and he recommended Howard Newby
who left the post of Managing Director, BBC Radio, in May 1978. He
became Chairman of the ESC in July 1978.

By December 1979, it was apparent that Stuart Burge, who had
never intended to stay at the Court for long, was not returning.
Stafford-Clark was asked to continue running the Court until the end
of 1980. The original arrangement, spelled out at the meetings in late

1979, was that Burge would return in the spring of the following year 'and release Mr. Stafford-Clark to work with Joint Stock'. The Court therefore faced the prospect of not having an Artistic Director. Jocelyn Herbert's recollection of the time is that

> Max said he didn't want to take it on and so I told John [Dexter] this and he said do you think they'd have me back? . . . Unfortunately, John told Bill [Gaskill]. Bill told Max who immediately applied. Perhaps he just didn't want one of those old boys back. Max got signatories from all the people at the Court saying they wanted him to stay. John just withdrew.[44]

Dexter noted on 19 May: 'Been approached about taking over Royal Court', and on 23 May: 'Talked to JH who will talk to Greville Poke and then . . .'.[45] Stafford-Clark's Diary entry for 28 June reads: 'News about Dexter wanting the job . . . first reaction is one of shock and enormous disappointment. On the other hand I haven't declared myself up to now and disappointment alternates with relief. I guess I will fight all the same.'

The selection committee, consisting of Newby, Poke, Herbert, Hare and Gaskill, met at Poke's house. According to Gaskill,

> we had to choose between Max and Dexter . . . but there was no question but that Max was a much better idea than John. Jocelyn, of course, was very strongly for Dexter but because David and I were so positive, it went to Max.[46]

Greville Poke's version is that the committee meeting

> was a disgraceful thing. I never thought that Howard Newby was the kind of Chairman that the ESC should have and the way he behaved over John Dexter was just unbelievable . . . we took a vote and the majority were in favour of Dexter by just one vote. So Newby said, 'I think we're all agreed it ought to be Max. Besides, it will be less trouble.'[47]

It was to be the first of a number of encounters between Stafford-Clark and selection committees, but the symbolism between old and new Court is resonant. Because there were now elected staff representatives on Council, an invitation was issued by them to Dexter to meet the staff and discuss his plans for the Court. The invitation was not taken up. Dexter wrote to Osborne, after the dust had settled, to say: 'I too think I might have infused some life into the building, but there you are. The workers voted against us.'[48] He subsequently referred to the invitation as emanating from 'the Chair-person of the Royal Court Workers' Committee'. Dexter withdrew and Stafford-Clark was appointed for two years from April 1981.

Greville Poke told the story of the appointment process in a letter to Osborne of 13 October 1980, which included as its final paragraph:

> Before I finish this letter there is one factor I should mention to you which horrified me. At the meeting [of Council] were a number of younger people who said they knew nothing about John Dexter's work. They had heard of him of course.

Osborne replied on 17 October: 'How depressing it all is, especially about the Young Turks knowing nothing of Dexter. But it figures'. It did indeed figure as the Court entered the eighties under its new Artistic Director.

7   Theatre in a cold climate, 1980–1986

"I don't know if I want to be the director of a theatre, but if I do, it would be the
Court", he says. "Why?" "Because what else is there?"
(Victoria Radin, 'Max at the Court', *Observer*, 21 October 1979)

On 1 January 1980, Stafford-Clark wrote in his Diary: 'Lesson from
Devine biography is one of continuity: how to develop the beliefs and
roots we've started from. In my case, how to utilise the Traverse
Workshop, Joint Stock and use that background for the Royal Court'.[1]
As Stafford-Clark tried to steer the Court through the eighties, he
faced circumstances quite unlike his predecessors in their intensity
and duration. This was not simply a matter of finance, critical though
that was. It was also to do, in a less easily definable way, with the
temper of the times. If the problems of the seventies were largely
internal, the eighties saw a furious assault on most forms of art from
external forces. Managing the well-being of a theatre like the Court
over the decade involved strategic skills as well as aesthetic abilities.
Stafford-Clark kept the Court together in a very difficult situation. In
so doing, he attracted hostility as well as admiration, animosity as
well as respect.

Unable to resist the obvious and neat, assorted critics reviewed
the decade past. Nightingale loftily found that 'Sometimes one felt
benumbed with worthy boredom, notably at that social research unit
which continues to call itself the Royal Court.'[2] Hiley worried that
the Court's position was one of vulnerability. It was a theatre with
massive overheads and compared with the Bush its costs were high.
The Arts Council had, a few years earlier, considered, albeit hypothe-
tically, the closure of a theatre which used to be 'a living symbol of
the English theatre's seriousness, a communal repository for the
profession's self-respect'. Stafford-Clark 'inherits a solvent organisation without an aesthetic heart'.[3] The inevitable tirade from Osborne

about the Court's decline and fall[4] produced a rebuke from the Court's Chairman, Howard Newby, pointing out that Osborne as a Council member was criticising himself. And at the same time, the Arts Council was asking difficult questions. Stafford-Clark's Diary notes of the 3 March Council have Dennis Andrews of the Arts Council suggesting that the 'RC is an expensive way of subsidising new drama. Obviously it's much cheaper to sponsor new plays in smaller theatres.'

A central problem was that the Court for a long time had not existed as the sole outlet for new writing. The talent was thinly spread, but the critical expectation was always one of continuous high-grade programming. Bill Gaskill, whose *protégé* Stafford-Clark was, put the dilemma clearly: 'there is never a situation in which you have six plays that you desperately want to do, that you believe are well crafted and mean something. You are lucky if you have one.'[5] And Stafford-Clark objectively analysed his early situation at the Court:

> I came to the Court as a free-lance director and as a director
> working for Joint Stock, where I had to commit myself to only
> three plays a year, but that is not difficult; one can give total
> passion and commitment to that. But to give one's total passion
> and commitment to eight plays downstairs plus another eight
> upstairs, plus the Young Writers' Festival, plus other aspects of
> the operation, becomes more difficult.[6]

Devine had nurtured his writers via the Writers' Group and other means. A modern variant of this was the creation in 1979 of the Young Writers' Group. The suggestion came from Nicholas Wright, who became the Group's first tutor, to be followed by Caryl Churchill, and other important writers. The showing of such work had continued patchily since Devine and in the face of some opposition who felt either that it diverted the Court from its central purpose or that it was a waste of time. There are those who still feel this, but there is no doubt that the work of Jane Howell, who ran the scheme from 1966 to 1970, followed by Pam Brighton (1970–72), Joan Mills (1972–76), Gerald Chapman (1976–80), David Sulkin (1980–88), and Dominic

Tickell (1988–97), provided both a vital link with a younger generation and, on occasion, a source of new writing.[7] A Young Writers'
Festival began in 1975 and one of its most notable plays came in the
1980 series. This was Andrea Dunbar's *The Arbor*, which appeared in
the main bill on 24 June 1980.

The Arbor arrived at the Court via BBC Radio Leeds. After
Stafford-Clark read it

> I went up to see Andrea and she was, at that point, in a refuge in
> Keighley and I saw her in a social worker's home in Haworth ...
> And she had never been in a play and she was quite shut off, not
> very giving ... And then she came down and saw rehearsals and
> she had never been in a rehearsal before, and of course, what she
> was writing were real events that had happened to her. The
> autobiographical events in the play were absolutely clear to her.
> And she would say: 'No, he was sitting down when he said that.
> No, he didn't laugh then, he laughed at the other line. He
> laughed then.' So she was writing her life, and her gift, her ear
> for dialogue and also for the humour of the situation, was just
> exquisite, quite extraordinary.[8]

Preceding *The Arbor* in the main bill was Richard Eyre's
production of *Hamlet*, both an artistic and financial success.[9] Michael
Coveney, who was to clash regularly with Stafford-Clark during the
eighties, used the occasion to blame the 'fringe' for its refusal to
engage with the classical tradition. Stafford-Clark was taken to task
for rejecting the classics and being 'proud of the fact that he has not
been seen at a West End show for seven years', together with other
accusations.[10] However woolly and provocative the piece was, it
nevertheless signalled in one sense that a new theatrical phase was
beginning. The 'fringe' was now to be attacked for not being mainstream. Younger directors were to be rebuked for not directing classics
or running the National. A backlash had begun, which the Arts
Council did nothing to control. Meanwhile, Stafford-Clark looked for
a policy and a means of satisfying some of the Court's critics. His
Diary for 24 July articulates the problem:

Umbrella for season: permanent company. Plays Upstairs, cast in tandem: own kind of idea and vision for the future rather than just stumbling on. Easy to be pragmatic and just do the next 'best' play we have Downstairs. A workshop? Are there more people like Andrea and G. F. Newman outside the main, as it were, artistic pool who should be sought out?

Six months in as Artistic Director, Stafford-Clark referred again to Wardle's biography of George Devine. His reaction, in his Diary for 27 July, is instructive:

> What surprised me was how little had changed in 25 years. Basically the same philosophy inspired the policy decisions and the same difficulties lead to similar compromises ... over the last 25 years, the RC has constructed its own mythology in a manner unrivalled by other contemporary British theatre. It is a mythology that transforms the past into a golden age and makes the present hard to live with ... The challenge which the Court provides is that it is the only organisation whose main objective is mounting new work in a major proscenium theatre.

One possibility for new work was to go to a writer and ask. Edward Bond had accepted a commission. Stafford-Clark's draft letter to Bond of 14 August in his Diary responds to Bond's conditions, including Bond's request to direct the play himself but, should that not be the case, Stafford-Clark resists the notion that a director should be chosen by Bond: 'That seems an abandonment of responsibility. In practice I have no intention of imposing a director or composer upon you.' The play was *Restoration*, which appeared on 21 July 1981.

Towards the end of 1980, Stafford-Clark reviewed his first year and the year ahead:

> Apart from the launch of *The Arbor* and *Hamlet's* good fortune, not much has been achieved. *A Short Sharp Shock* [Brenton and Howard's attack on Thatcher] didn't make it critically but above all there are no good new plays ahead and none from major playwrights on the horizon. Stephen Lowe's *Glasshouses* and Kilroy's *The Seagull* are the only two probabilities and the

25th anniversary year looks bleak in terms of major revivals . . . and we aren't funding the next generation. (Diary, 3 September 1980)

Nevertheless, the 1980–1981 season, as Stafford-Clark reported to the Council on 12 May, was the fifth best year in the Company's history for the percentage of seats sold. The success of *Hamlet* was a key factor and to some extent masked underlying financial problems. *The Seagull*'s run was extended to 6 June 1981, followed by a joint production with Oxford Playhouse of Barker's *No End of Blame*; Bond's *Restoration* was scheduled to begin on 21 July. *The Seagull* taught Stafford-Clark a lesson about classic writing:

> Bill Gaskill said, 'It's all very well, but if you must do classics, then you must direct them yourself.' And I didn't really understand what that meant, but I do now . . . we must measure new writing against the best every so often. It must never be the main drive of the Court's work, but to do a classic occasionally is a wonderful measuring point.[11]

Meanwhile, the noises coming from the Arts Council were ominous. At the end of 1980 the Arts Council's Drama Panel decided to investigate the Court's cost-efficiency. The Panel clearly wanted to know whether the funding of the Court for new work was justified, given that it could be done more cheaply elsewhere. The Arts Council had in 1980 cut the grants of forty-one companies. This change of policy in the context of the worst national recession since the Second World War caused considerable anxiety in the arts generally. It was not to be resolved for some time since the Government delayed its declaration of grant to the Arts Council.[12] The ESC Council heard on 14 July that the figures were not available but there could be a reduction in real terms. Theatres should therefore prepare for 'standstill' subsidy. An action committee was formed to monitor the progress of the Arts Council assessment.

If directing *The Seagull* had indicated to Stafford-Clark the usefulness of a classic, *Restoration*, which opened on 21 July, indicated how quickly relationships between writer and producer could fracture. The play, originally commissioned by the Royal Shakespeare Company, 'is an example of a production where we refused to be hemmed in by the financial restraints ... So we go ahead and commit to doing the play because no one else will do it. And it had a big cast, with musicians, which was very expensive for the Court.'[13] A confusion arose as to which of Bond's new plays was the one commissioned by the Court. Stafford-Clark believed it to be *Summer*, which he proposed to include with Bond's 1962 play, *The Pope's Wedding*. On 12 November 1980, a Diary entry reads: 'Edward would like Yvonne Bryceland to be in *Summer*. Would prefer *Summer* to be at the RC'. Stafford-Clark undertook to try to provide funds for a Court post for Bond. *Summer* actually went to the National and Stafford-Clark wrote to Bond's agent, Peggy Ramsay, on 8 March to say that he was 'obviously sorry that the Court won't be doing *Summer* but pleased that Edward has a home for it and the actress he wants. I look forward to talking to him about *Restoration*.'[14] Unfortunately, the relationship between the two deteriorated. Bond complained at having only the normal four weeks' rehearsal; Stafford-Clark blenched at the size of the budget and the knock-on effect across the financial year. The play achieved 66 per cent at the box office and the costs were supported by sponsorship. Camel Cigarettes put up £15,000 for the production to Bond's great displeasure. The Court admitted to 'pure pragmatism' and a general cynicism. Camel apparently liked the idea of sponsoring a musical.[15]

As if that were not enough, the general air at the Court was one of disenchantment. Stafford-Clark's Diary for 27 August notes that it is 'falling apart with internal bickering. I think we all feel a bit tired, frazzled and overworked. Lots of people are leaving. It needs a renewal of commitment all round.' Stephen Lowe's *Tibetan Inroads*, directed by Gaskill, opened in late September and fared poorly in financial terms. On the other hand, a critic like Wardle, noting the arguments of the Arts Council as to the expensiveness of the Court and the strike rate of new work, could still conclude that if the Court were to go 'we shall be losing the single most important organ in the body of the British theatre'.[16] That new plays were becoming more difficult to obtain is shown in a draft letter from Stafford-Clark to David Hare,

27 September, urging him to allow the Court to do *A Map of the World*. As opposed to the National, 'the Court needs it more; like, what's the point in running a theatre committed to new work if the new plays you are most passionate about don't get put on there'. Hare was at pains to defend the theatre at that time, but the Court did not get his play.[17] It did get Hanif Kureishi's *Borderline*, a co-production with Joint Stock, which finished its run on 28 November.[18]

The year ended more hopefully. On 7 December Council heard that the overall increase to the Arts Council had been 8 per cent. It was understood that the report of the Arts Council had been favourable. However, it was established that a deficit of between £30,000 and £50,000 would be carried into the next financial year. In prospect was G. F. Newman's *Operation Bad Apple*, a co-production with the Sheffield Crucible for eight weeks from 4 February, followed by a revival of Paul Kember's *Not Quite Jerusalem* for twelve weeks. Upstairs would see nothing from 9 January until the new financial year. The Young Writers' Festival would not happen in March, but go to an extended slot in October. A number of shows awaited a slot, including *Salonika* by Louise Page, Terry Johnson's *Insignificance*, Andrea Dunbar's *Rita, Sue and Bob Too*, Robert Holman's *Other Worlds* and Beckett's *Ohio Impromptu*. Works by Churchill and Snoo Wilson were close to completion.

The new year began with a row over Newman's *Operation Bad Apple*. The play had been commissioned by Stafford-Clark in 1980. Newman remembers the context: 'I went to the Royal Court and talked to them about it, and they said, "That's great. Does Mrs Thatcher come up out of the stage?" I said that wasn't the sort of stuff I did ... The Court remained enthusiastic and commissioned a play.'[19] Newby's reaction as Chairman was to ask for a report from a criminal lawyer, Anthony Burton, as to where the Court stood in relation to Operation Countryman, which enquiries resulted in the trial of five police officers at the Old Bailey on 1 February. Newman's play dealt with corruption in the Metropolitan Police Force, and the link between the play and the trial had been made in *The Times* 'diary' for 20 January. Before Council met to discuss this on 27 January, an informal meeting with Burton was set up on 25 January, largely because of a letter from the Attorney-General to Stafford-Clark, copy to Newby, about *The Times* piece and the play. A not very subtle hint of the possibility of an action for contempt of court, and perhaps libel, was sufficient to alarm Howard Newby. Stafford-Clark noted in his Diary at the end of the meeting that 'Howard is clearly backing out.'

The Council of 27 January, with Newman in attendance, was stormy. Legal opinion was ambiguous. The discussion centred around the prospect , as Newby saw it, of legal action. As others – Newman, Gaskill, Ritchie and Burge among them – saw it, the Attorney-General's letter constituted a threat of censorship. Burge said 'there was no clear issue ... we should go ahead. It was up to "them" to stop us.'[20] Newby was all for writing to the Attorney-General and submitting the script. Newman left the meeting for another appointment. Stafford-Clark said 'he would withdraw if the play was sent to the Attorney-General. Mr Newby said Mr Stafford-Clark must not hold a pistol to his head. Mr Gaskill said that we must send the letter and go ahead with the play.' Incredibly, a frightened Newby then asserted 'that he could overrule a decision taken by the Council and he might do so'. The Minutes blandly record that 'Those present at the meeting disagreed with this statement.' One result of this was a staff petition of no confidence in Newby and a call for his resignation. A second extraordinary meeting took place on 3 February, at which Newby apologised and hastily retracted his threat to overrule a decision of Council. The Old Bailey trial had begun and as Burge expressed it: 'Bill and I had to reassure [Newby] that the Attorney-General was bluffing. He couldn't possibly have us for contempt of court because the trial had started, the jury were locked in the hotel. They couldn't come to the Court.' At the meeting, Stafford-Clark said that 'The voice of the play was important and to feel half-hearted about it was very wrong. We must stand firm in the position this theatre has always taken.' With one dissenting voice, the decision to go ahead was taken. According to Stafford-Clark:

> The key turning point in that meeting was that Gordon
> Newman was allowed to be there, and that was a tactical error
> on the part of those who wished the play to be withdrawn.

Because once the writer is there, then he's an authority, an artist that everybody in a way defers to. He pulled the artist's card out and said, 'This is the play I've written. This is what I believe happened. This is what I want on.' And people like Bill ... You know, in the end, you are trained at the Court that it's a writers' theatre, and the writer is the authority and people deferred to that. It was a rallying point for those who championed the play.[21]

The absolute affirmation of one of the Court's central principles was to be severely tested five years later in the case of *Perdition*. Council of 15 February heard that the Attorney-General was not proceeding against the play 'so everything had ended happily'. Apart, that is, for an upset Isador Caplan, whose firm had acted as the Court's solicitors since its inception, because the Court had consulted Anthony Burton and not him. He was reassured of his importance.

Operation Bad Apple did very good business, but the incoming Arts Council grant showed an increase of only 6.8 per cent which, given inflation, was virtually a cut. Stafford-Clark explained this to a meeting of the Royal Court Theatre Society on 16 February, which was held in a theatre that was dark. The money had run out. Ironically, good new plays were now available. Four were waiting to be done Upstairs, and a complete year's programme was available Downstairs if and when money was forthcoming. Despite the situation, Stafford-Clark could still enter in his Diary for 2 June: 'I believe whatever we haven't done and whatever mistakes we've made, however many changes of staff there's been ... that we are beginning to find our voice'.

That voice was more the voice of the theatre workers than it was the voice of the Council. One of Stuart Burge's innovations was the reforming of the old Management Committee into an Executive Committee, chaired by the Artistic Director. The main members were staff heads of department. Two members of the Council sat on the Executive: 'And one was able to choose the two members of the Board that actually were competent to make comments ... We arranged the meetings to occur two weeks after each production so that the budget for the previous production could be checked and the budget for the next production could be proposed; it was a more streamlined system.'[22] Stafford-Clark 'inherited a Court where, not only Joint Stock, but also the meeting that Stuart had held with different people, had made essential some form of consultative management'.[23] Looking back, Stafford-Clark was amazed to discover

> how much in 1981 we had flirted with the idea of some form of
> co-operation at the Court. There were meetings ... talking
> about whether or not the salaries should be equal ... And we
> flirted with the idea of lists of the theatre management being
> alphabetical rather than hierarchical, how we went with some
> form of co-operative management.[24]

One such meeting felt, on 29 June, that 'eventually all decisions to do with the running of the theatre should be the responsibility of the entire staff', thus echoing precisely the sentiments of Bond, Lewenstein and the majority of the staff at Burge's meetings in the early months of 1977. Stafford-Clark also held staff outings to Brighton in 1981 and 1982, and subsequently to Leeds Castle. At the Grand in Brighton: 'Everybody had a day out at the seaside. But it was interspersed with me talking about the artistic programme for the coming year. Talking also about – and I think this is one lesson I did bring across from Joint Stock – what plays cost. So there were a series of seminars at which staff were told about budgeting.'[25]

The programme itself over the period reflects the volatile nature of the activity. Griffiths's *Oi for England* and Page's *Salonika* played to capacity Upstairs, and Johnson's *Insignificance* had fared well in the main bill. Byrne's *The Slab Boys Trilogy* was about to appear in the main bill until 18 December. Holman's *Other Worlds* was moved into 1983. The Court went dark for two weeks over Christmas and New Year. A projected deficit of around £20,000 was forecast by the end of the financial year, but the programme was unclear. *Other Worlds*, it was known, 'would necessarily be expensive but [Stafford-Clark] attached great importance to it' (Council, 6 September 1982). It remained, however, unscheduled.

By 21 October, an important innovation was presented to the

Executive Committee. It was announced that negotiations were proceeding with Joe Papp of the Public Theater, New York, to exchange productions. The Court would take Churchill's *Top Girls* to open in New York on 21 December; New York would bring a play by Thomas Babe. *Top Girls* would then return to the Court for seven weeks.[26] Though it is the case that Court productions going to New York made no money because of the costs of transferring them, Stafford-Clark was 'able to stage them for another season and do very well with them as "New York hits"'.[27] Financial necessity was quickly becoming dominant. The projected £20,000 deficit at the end of the financial year was only turned into a profit of some £17,000 by moving *Other Worlds* into the next financial year and replacing it with Barker's *Victory*, a co-production with Joint Stock. By 1 December, Stafford-Clark could not risk bad box office: 'the famous phrase, "the right to fail", could only be risked on plays with four actors and one set' (Report to Council). However, the Young Writers' Festival, in October, in both theatres, attracted a good deal of praise with work by Dunbar and Lenka Janiurek. David Sulkin's report to Council on 6 December was concerned with innovatory work 'carried out with young black women', and worried that to the outside world the festival 'was perceived as a rather worthy event ... There is no doubt that the Festival has nationwide attention [but] It will be some years until we attempt another such event in the Main Theatre'.

In January 1983, Stafford-Clark reviewed the state of play at the Court. Chronic underfunding, in common with other theatres, was 'hitting us very hard at the moment – simply in terms of the amount of work we can undertake and the amount of writers we can service as a theatre ... theatres concerned with new drama are particularly vulnerable'.[28] Such theatres are also vulnerable to criticism of one kind or other. Coveney thought that 'While the Court had a very fine year in 1982, I do feel that the net is not cast wide enough, that the clamour raised on its stage is not sufficiently varied in hue and cry.'[29] This was a recurring problem to do with the means whereby Court successes were exploited, to the advantage of both the theatre and the writer. The West End as a resource had virtually ceased. On the other hand, keeping a Court success on stage too long logically meant that other new writers were barred. It could be seen as a variant of the situation in the early seventies, when the main bill was dominated by the Court's senior house writers, to the exclusion of everyone else. The equation between new writing and 'new' new writing was one to be juggled each year. However, there was staff disquiet over some long runs and, while Stafford-Clark notes in his Diary for 6 March: 'I think it's probably best to have a sleeping Council who don't interfere much', he also later recalled on 21 May 1984 'the disquiet that led to the founding of the management meeting over the length of the run for *Not Quite Jerusalem*'. The play had run for a total of nineteen weeks. As a result, at a staff meeting on 12 May 1983, Rob Ritchie presented a discussion paper, which was a proposal for a Management Committee. The proposal was clearly an attempt to include all personnel in the process of decision-making and to accept responsibility for the overall running of the theatre. It would meet weekly and effectively liaise with other meetings at the Court. The proposal, slightly modified, was accepted. A further modification was added on 5 September, when it was agreed that an Executive Management meeting should be held every five weeks to enable selected Council members to attend. The process of workers' control appeared to be virtually complete, and was to be a huge bone of contention when Matthew Evans took over as Chairman in 1984.

In June, as Margaret Thatcher was re-elected, Council was told that *Top Girls* had played to 90 per cent after its New York run. However, *Other Worlds* had played to 13 per cent, and occasioned a powerful response by Ritchie 'to one of the worst critical receptions any new play has received at the Court in recent years'.[30] Although attacking critics 'is like calling the Queen Mother a nazi', Ritchie's point is to do with critical laziness, thus echoing the cries of Court staff from George Devine onwards. The piece was written before the General Election, but it accurately predicts some consequences: 'If the opinion polls are accurate, we shall all be living in a one party state intent on a one way trip to the 19th century. So far, the arts have not featured prominently in the party campaigns ... [but] Clearly, five more years of Thatcherism will accelerate structural change within the theatre economy'.

During the year of the General Election, Brenton's *The Genius* (originally titled *Galileo's Goose*) achieved 51 per cent at the box office, Churchill's *Fen* 56 per cent, and *Falkland Sound* (Upstairs) reached 88 per cent. Sarah Daniels' *Masterpieces* and *The Devil's Gateway* also appeared Upstairs and further extended, whether by accident or design, the remarkable flowering of female writers, a feature of the Court's work during this period. The Court kept going, but Stafford-Clark had to report to the 12 September Council that 'Seven commissioned plays were all rather disappointing and all needed work.' There was a predicted deficit of £9,000, but the figure for the same time last year had been £40,000. *Top Girls* had significantly reduced that, but no comparable show was available this time round. Given the present level of subsidy, only a season from April to December 1984 could be planned 'with the last three months of the financial year hand to mouth'. By December, incoming costs had made the figure escalate to over £37,000. The figure reduced to £10,000 after Alan Brown's *Panic*, scheduled for Upstairs, was, like *Other Worlds*, removed to the next financial year. This continuous ducking and diving obviously affected morale. Worse followed. The Arts Council wrote to Newby, as it did to some of its other 'clients', on 11 November, to announce a review both of itself and also of its funding policies. The process was to lead to its document, *The Glory of the Garden*, in 1984. For now, 'clients' were asked to react seriously to the questions in a context which recognises that funding levels were unlikely to rise significantly. Among the answers required were reactions both to a 25 per cent subsidy increase and a 25 per cent decrease. The answers were required by 30 December. The context of this was a general fear that the Government planned to dismantle the Greater London Council and the Metropolitan County Councils, a move which could see the collapse of locally funded arts organisations. The argument about the Court which developed in 1984 was what kind of theatre it was, that is a local or a national resource, or both. No one in the arts world believed that money spent by the Metropolitan authorities would effectively be replaced by a combination of Borough Council and Arts Council funds. This was a Government which in the previous July had cut public spending by £500 million. Initial incredulity was quietly replaced by a realisation that, within a very short space of time, a number of companies could cease to exist. The Court, which had already been characterised by the Arts Council as a very expensive producer of new work, went into 1984 with appropriate foreboding.[31]

The projected deficit of £10,000 dropped in January 1984 to less than £7,500 when *Masterpieces* produced £4,500 more than estimated. Programming was proving more difficult in circumstances where no announcement had been made about funding, but when Rob Ritchie reported to the Executive Management Committee on 24 January, the bill consisted of visiting companies, once Hastings's *Tom and Viv* had finished. Joint Stock would present Sue Townsend's *The Great Celestial Cow*; Open Hearted Enterprises were to do Terry Johnson's *Cries from the Mammal House*; the Opera Factory would play Tippett's *The Knot Garden* and *La Calisto*; and the Women's Playhouse Trust would, it was hoped, bring Aphra Behn's *The Lucky Chance*. 'The rest of the programming for the Main Stage remains speculative.' The same meeting saw the launch of a campaign to save the Greater London Council.

The funding position was lucidly summarised by Philip Hedley, Artistic Director of the Theatre Royal, Stratford East. Writing in the *Stage* on 5 January, he notes that the Government White Paper, 'Streamlining the Cities', indicated special protection for the National, the RSC and Manchester's Royal Exchange while leaving the rest to 'the charity of their local councils', who were in turn to be rate-capped. According to Hedley, 'Those of a suspicious mind might imagine that the government has deliberately attempted to remove the influential boards of the three chosen theatres from the growing chorus of protest at its actions.' At the same time, the Government accepted the main recommendations of the Priestley Report on the RSC and the Royal Opera House, wiped out their deficits and considerably increased their grants. The Court, like other important theatres, was excluded from the protected group and would therefore have to fight for its existence. The grant for 1984–85 was an across-the-board increase of 2.9 per cent, barely one half of the rate of inflation. The Court added its signature to that of seventeen other

London theatres in a letter to the *Stage* of 9 February, protesting at Government policy. The Arts Council itself, together with the Independent Theatre Council, pointed out the potential disaster of leaving theatres to the discretionary decisions of individual councils.

Rumours began to circulate of the Court being first on a list of closures. Nicholas de Jongh's piece in the *Guardian* for 17 March suggested the imminent withdrawal of grant and noted that it was the Council itself at the Arts Council which decides, chaired by Sir William Rees-Mogg, and that Council did not have to listen to its Drama Panel. It was also suggested that the rumour was deliberately started, so that when Rees-Mogg actually revealed what he was doing, there would be relief that it was not quite so draconian as had been believed.[32] David Hare arrived at the Court to help orchestrate the Court's defence. For a month, he, Ritchie and Stafford-Clark ran in effect a tightly focused campaign office. The *Guardian* piece provoked an instant response by letter from the profession. Eight members of the Council's own Drama Panel wrote to describe the strategy as 'irresponsible and dangerous ... undemocratically introduced ... a species of blackmail ... It is not about "new money"; it is about robbing Peter to pay Paul.' Protests against the closure of the Court came from fifty-five members of the RSC, from Olivier – drafted by Hare (19 March) – from Hall, Hands and Nunn (*The Times*, 20 March), from Brenton (22 March: 'Why is the Arts Council bent on destroying one of the world's greatest theatres just as it is in the midstream of a splendid revival?'). Lord Goodman, Chairman of the Arts Council from 1965 to 1972, told the *Guardian* (24 March) that the Court 'At a relatively moderate cost ... does what the National Theatre does not do'. Thirteen regional theatre directors deplored the suggestion that the regions should benefit from the closing of the Court (27 March). Gielgud weighed in on the same issue. There were many more. It was an astonishing display of solidarity, even by those who stood to gain. Even if it was an artful strategy, the response it provoked must have made the Council pause. Replying to a letter from David Hare, Rees-Mogg recognised 'the strong feeling of loyalty and admiration which the English Stage Company has generated. The Council will be reconsidering the position tomorrow and will be well aware of the support that the Company has.'[33] He should have been. His own Drama Panel notes: 'we were told by the Chairman of the Drama Panel that the Council proposed to withdraw subsidy from the Royal Court. The panel rejected that proposal unanimously. If anyone got that proposal "superbly wrong" it was those Council members who devised it.'[34] Unsurprisingly, the Court's local borough, the Royal Borough of Kensington and Chelsea, had made it plain in March that it would not shoulder the cost of the Court and it was clearly being realistic.[35]

While the massive changes announced in *The Glory of the Garden* were being assimilated and responded to,[36] the Court was trying to develop its programme for the season and deal with internal change. After serving as its General Manager for eleven and a half years, Anne Jenkins was to leave on 13 April. She was succeeded by Jo Beddoe. Rob Ritchie was to leave his job of Literary Manager at the beginning of July, as was Gilly Poole, his Literary Assistant. Mike Bradwell was appointed as Associate Director and Simon Curtis suggested at an Executive Committee meeting of 17 April that Council needed new members 'in order to fight the forthcoming battles'. The programme after *The Lucky Chance* looked to consist of an Irish season, followed by a proposed season of weekly repertory and one new production after Christmas 1984. Upstairs might have to close. *Tom and Viv* could well go to New York and then run again at the Court.

A major change at the Court was the offer of resignation by its Chairman. At the 11 June Council meeting, Newby 'stressed the need to strengthen the Council to better equip it for the ensuing fight'. A sub-committee met to discuss the matter of a successor. The Council of 9 July reduced a list, which included John Mortimer and Matthew Evans, to two to be approached. They were Richard Hoggart and Sir Denis Forman, the latter to be contacted first. At its meeting of 10 September, it was reported that neither were able to accept the offer. Council moved on to approach John Mortimer. Should that response be negative, Newby would approach Matthew Evans. Mortimer turned the job down. A Council member, Derek Granger, together with Stuart Burge, put up Lord Hutchinson, but by then Newby had contacted Evans, who took over as Chairman at the age of forty-three, at the Annual General Meeting of the ESC on 3 December.[37]

At the end of the year, Stafford-Clark reported to Council on 3 December that Hutchinson's *Rat in the Skull* and Newman's *An Honourable Trade* were the sole shows to be produced by the ESC. The Hutchinson play, together with Peter Cox's *Up to the Sun and Down to the Centre*, which opened Upstairs on 10 September, constituted an Irish season of two complementary plays.[38] *An Honourable Trade* was the occasion of Matthew Evans's first visit as Chairman designate. It was not an auspicious occasion:

> I think I was over-defensive ... And he thought [the play] was not very good. And his wife didn't like it. I remember defending the play rather over vigorously ... because it was the first play he'd seen I was rather over-loyal and I was aware after that that his disdain for the management and my dismissal of his opinion, had got us off on a wrong foot that we never really recovered from.[39]

According to Evans, Stafford-Clark invited his frank and honest opinion and Evans said, '"Max, I thought it was absolutely terrible, and obvious and naive, for the following eight reasons". And he went berserk. He got very, very upset and it was clear to me that he didn't want the discourse ... I just felt there was a siege mentality there.'[40] From that moment, before Evans took over, there was a powerful animosity between two extremely strong-willed figures, which was to last until Evans stepped down.

The end of the year saw two plays by Edward Bond in the main bill. His 1962 play, *The Pope's Wedding*, opened on 23 November, directed by Stafford-Clark. *Saved*, from 1965, opened on 15 December, directed by Danny Boyle. The last encounter between Bond and Stafford-Clark, over *Restoration* in 1981, had been bruising. So was this. Bond objected strongly to the production of *Saved*, less so to *The Pope's Wedding*.[41]

It would be unsurprising if Evans's phrase, 'siege mentality' did not have a truth about it, and even internally, there was anxiety about the role of the Management Committee. A special Management

Committee meeting of 23 October, concerned about lack of atten-dance, noted: 'There was felt to be an indifference which might be attributed to a feeling that the important decisions were in reality made elsewhere.' Running a theatre in the mid-eighties was not an easy option. For example, there were mutterings about the quality of the New York exchange. Stafford-Clark's Diary for 21 May notes: 'I make it clear we cannot veto play or director and that any co-produc-tion or exchange involves us in compromising our taste.' And to round off a stressful year, Lindsay Anderson met up with Matthew Evans to discuss the Court. Anderson sent Evans, on 5 December, earlier documents relating to the Court, including old brochures, Ronald Duncan's 1960 complaints against Devine, Anderson's letter to Hugh Cudlipp and the 1971 staff petition. His letter concludes: 'I hope I've not bored you with all this material. Of course the social and historical and artistic situation today is vastly different from what it was when the English Stage Company started operations. The old "Royal Court" is part of history now, but it would be a heart-warming miracle if the old body could be re-animated.' Evans's recollection of the meeting was that he 'got on tremendously well with him. He is a 120 per cent octane troublemaker. He's a great guy. He sent me some papers on the Court ... and some letters saying what a complete cunt Max was.'[42] Evans's reply to Anderson set the tone for 1985: 'I decided as the best tactic to go in hard at once before I get sucked into alliances and the politics of the place myself, and what I will probably do is to ... present a paper to the Council in March at my first meeting.'[43]

After the Bond season, *Tom and Viv* returned on 22 March from New York. This was to be followed by Robert Holman's *The Overgrown Path*, and the return of *Rat in the Skull*, which would go to New York before opening at the Court on 28 June. The London International Festival of Theatre, and Wallace Shawn's *Aunt Dan and Lemon* made up the rest of the short-term programme Downstairs. Upstairs would show Stephen Wakelam's *Deadlines*, a co-production with Joint Stock, to be followed by a series of readings, including Gems's *Susan's Breasts*, Marchant's *The Attractions*, Rudet's *The Basin* and Wertenbaker's *The Grace of Mary Traverse*. Jonathan Gems's play, together with Wertenbaker's, received full productions, the former Upstairs in May, the latter Downstairs in November. A full programme could not, however, disguise the underlying strains. Rob Ritchie noted that the Bond season had retained a company of ten playing in repertory and had 'put more actors on the Court's main stage than had been there all year ... If the theatre wanted to revive David Storey's rugby club drama, *The Changing Room*, they would have to persuade the author to switch the action to when the players had gone home.'[44] Council did hear on 1 April the good news that Joe Papp had offered $50,000 dollars annually if the Court could provide matching funding, and set about so doing.

Early in the new year, Matthew Evans launched his attempt to reorganise the Court's administrative structure. At an Executive Committee meeting of 8 January he 'asked for clarification on the difference between the Executive and ordinary Management meetings'. He wrote to Jo Beddoe and Stafford-Clark on 18 January to give notice of a discussion paper and to ask the same question about committee structure. He subsequently wrote to David Hare, giving his view that the 'whole thing is a bit of a shambles from top to bottom'.[45] Evans felt that the Council was too big, rather backward-looking, and should have some people shunted off to become Vice-Presidents. Hare had written to Evans about the board's composition on 25 February:

> I was originally brought on to the board in order to protect Max at a time when there was an attempt by John Dexter's admirers for him to take over. As Max had only been in the job for a year, this was felt to be unfair. So I was brought in simply as a vote.
>
> My only achievement on the Council was to do a lot of the work last year when he was threatened by the Arts Council. Howard Newby took a very relaxed and unrealistic attitude to the seriousness of the Arts Council's intentions, and so I stepped in, or else the theatre would have gone under.[46]

Evans's paper went to Hare and defined his role as 'somebody trying to work within and extend *The Glory of the Garden*, pushing Gowrie as well as the Arts Council'.[47] Hare's reply suggested to Evans that he 'drag the Royal Court back into the mainstream and replace the siege mentality ... As long as Max is working there, then you see on the stage the best work with actors that is done anywhere in London. But the representational and promotional side is absolutely dire. It is worse sold and worse marketed than any theatre in London.'[48]

The instinct of Evans was to attempt to claw back some of the power which had steadily been appropriated by staff. At two Council discussions, of 11 March and 1 April, the role of the Council itself was debated and its relationship with other committees. Essentially, the discussions were a re-run of the debates in the mid-seventies, which resulted in the Willatt report to the Council. The Chairman eventually argued that the Executive Committee was not in fact executive and a new structure was proposed 'comprising staff and Council members'. He pushed through by the 10 June Council a new form of Executive Management Committee, in which staff would be represented by function. Staff expressed serious concern that the ordinary management meeting was being eroded. This was ostensibly met by an elected member of that committee joining the Executive, which, on a six-month trial, would consist of the Artistic Director, the Deputy Director, the General Manager, and the Financial Administrator, together with Evans's selection of Council members.

The conflict between Stafford-Clark and Evans was to do with the relationship of Artistic Director to Chief Executive. Lacking any real personal warmth, the relationship was essentially a power struggle. Whereas, for George Devine, the argument had been about artistic autonomy, the temper of the eighties was much more to allow artistic autonomy only within reason. The latter increasingly was translated as what was financially feasible, what could be done within constraints. There is no doubt that Stafford-Clark's sense of democracy was also a sense of control, but it is very difficult to see what other route was feasible. If the Court was not fundamentally about the new writing and thus posited artistic control above all else, what then was its purpose? Stafford-Clark's Diary for 15 March admits the position:

Of course we are paranoid, entrenched, defensive, suspicious ... We're overworked, over crowded and underpaid. The path is clear. We'll end up with one Artistic Director, one General Manager and a Youth Opportunities person. The attempt to perpetuate standards and the staff that maintain those standards will have failed.

Looking back, Stafford-Clark felt 'it's easy to see in retrospect that the styles of management were on a collision course ... the bottom line was that our beliefs were incompatible ... I think both of us tried'.[49] Evans's view is that the Court 'was run by Max as a fiefdom and if you didn't agree with Max, forget it. He had neutralised the board. He's a clever chap, Max. There's no question about that ... what Max wanted was a neutral castrated board and not a heavily interventionist Chairman who had some idea of where things should go.'[50]

The Arts Council began the year by informing the Court of 'stand-still' funding and it became obvious that its gamble of devolving funds to the regions against the fantasy of additional Government funding was primarily that. The Court for 1985–86 received £503,500 from the Arts Council, and the Arts Council received a strong letter from Stafford-Clark. He wrote to the Drama Director, Dickon Reed, on 16 February, to point out that the Court's productivity in the last ten years had halved. It now stood at four plays for Upstairs and four on the main stage. The Court sought an immediate meeting with the Arts Council to ask why it had been kept at a 'stand-still' when other London theatres received small increases. The attack on the Court was also visited on all the theatres. A furious Peter Hall used the *Evening Standard*'s Awards ceremony at the end of January to attack both Gowrie, the Arts Minister, and the Arts Council. Hall threatened cuts of his own and the closure of the Cottesloe. Stafford-Clark called a meeting of eleven London theatres at the Court on 12 February. The meeting felt that the Arts Council activity 'was the beginning of a move by the government to eliminate arts subsidy, to privatise the arts and to divide arts organisations in the process'. Gowrie was reported in the *Stage* two days later as saying that 'Arts spending isn't a wow with the general British public.' And Rees-Mogg's view was that subsidy 'can weaken the sinews of self-help', as reported in the

Stage for 14 March. The cycle of accusation and counter-accusation was proving nothing and building a climate of cold anger and, on the part of the Arts Council, desperation. When Gowrie said that Hall was talking 'irresponsible rubbish' (*Stage*, 14 March) and suggested the real culprits were not the Government but the Metropolitan councils, there was obviously a complete impasse (*Stage*, 27 June). The Arts Council had been politicised throughout. The best to be said of it was that it had been comprehensibly deceived by the Government; the worst that it had been a willing collaborator. The Council belatedly attacked the inadequacy of Government provision to make up for the loss of subsidy when the Metropolitan councils were abolished, but a more realistic figure was, it said, nearer forty rather than the sixteen million offered.

Gowrie quit as Arts Minister in September, inviting the derision of a beleaguered profession when he gave as a reason that 'living in central London is not possible on £1,500 per month (net)'.[51] He was replaced by Richard Luce, one of the Foreign Office officials who resigned with Lord Carrington at the beginning of the Falklands crisis. The Court, in the centre of the battle, put its case graphically. Holman's *The Overgrown Path*, with some excellent reviews, was likely to achieve only 25 per cent. Stafford-Clark gave this to a 10 June Council as a prime example 'of how the theatre could no longer afford to champion a writer like Holman'. At the same meeting, the question of Stafford-Clark's contract, which would expire in March 1986, was discussed, with the Artistic Director asking for five years, including a sabbatical year. Stafford-Clark said in the meeting that he did not view the Court as a 'stepping-stone to a larger ambition. He wished to be at the Royal Court and he saw much that he wanted to achieve and felt willing and able to undertake it'. The discussion was a lengthy one and held over. Evans privately 'thought it would be in the interests of the Court to get rid of Max. I told this to Max ... I think what we were all afraid of was that the Court was just a sort of fragile entity and that if we really went to war with Max the whole thing might collapse.'[52] It was, however, agreed at the first meeting of the new Executive Committee, that the Council wished to renew the contract, subject to further discussions. The meeting also heard that Ann Pennington had been appointed as a part-time fundraiser. The post was to be a crucial one. By the time of Council for 13 January 1986, Stafford-Clark was able to reveal a fundraising figure of £45,389. A gala performance of *Torch Song Trilogy* had raised £20,000; £5,000 came from the Rayne Foundation; and a further £20,000 came from direct personal donations. The Artistic Director struck a prophetic note at the difficulties henceforth involved in approaching the same people year after year.

As the end of 1985 approached, Greville Poke, the longest serving member of the Court, stepped down from the Vice-Chairmanship and was succeeded by Anthony Burton. The Executive heard on 5 December of the death of the Court's President, Elaine Blond. The last link with the Blonds had gone. The Arts Council informed its 'clients' that it could no longer guarantee its twelve months' notice of 'withdrawal or significant reduction of funds'.[53] And a play called *Perdition* was said to have been withdrawn by its author, Jim Allen, because he was not offered a production in the main bill. The 9 December Management Committee meeting was told of the possibility of a rehearsed reading for February 1986. The play had been at the Court since August.

It had been a difficult and depressing year. In his report to Council on 13 January 1986, Stafford-Clark described 'the dilemma of how to survive without a serious erosion of purpose at the start of the year'. The ability of the Court to sustain writers had become sharply diminished. The programme ahead included Gaskill's production of Barker's *Women Beware Women*; Martin Sheen would play in Kramer's *The Normal Heart*, and Alan Bennett's *Kafka's Dick* was scheduled. Upstairs would see a programme of three plays by Northern writers. 'North' would include Terry Heaton's *Short Change*, *Road* by Jim Cartwright, and Andrea Dunbar's *Shirley*. On 14 February, however, Evans was told by the Arts Council that 'standstill' funding or a tiny increase was probably all that would be on offer.[54] But Stafford-Clark was able to tell Council on 14 April, which was the last time the ESC held a meeting in St Michael House (Marks and Spencer), that *Women Beware Women* had been a success both artistically and financially (67 per cent). A gala performance of *The Normal Heart* had raised £9,300 for the Court and £10,000 for AIDS

research. A surplus overall of £55,000 had been reached to meet Joe
Papp's challenge, and $10,000 had been received. It was anticipated
that Larry Kramer's play would make a surplus of £20,000. The
advance for the play had been £25,000, five times the usual. Using a
star, as of old, paid off. It transferred to the Albery, opening on 20 May
for eleven weeks.[55] The Bennett would now open in the autumn. Its
original slot would be filled by Kilroy's *Double Cross* on tour, after
which Cartwright's *Road* would be brought down from Upstairs. This
would be given as a promenade performance, with seats removed from
the auditorium.

On 9 May, the Royal Court Young People's Theatre (YPT)
formally opened its new base at 309 Portobello Road, North Kensington. Its team consisted of four full-time staff and a part-time
writer in residence. The search for premises had been going on for five
years. As it took over its new base, the YPT in its current form
celebrated its tenth birthday under its director, Elyse Dodgson. The
work for young people has endured, often against considerable odds,
to form an important aspect of the Court's work. However, by 20
October, Dodgson was reporting to Council that the new studio had
real problems with extensive damp to the point of walls crumbling
and the drains being sub-standard. To balance this, the thirteenth
Rank Xerox/Young Writers' Festival was under way Upstairs and
Hanif Kureishi was the writer in residence. This was all put to the
Council of 29 October. It was also at this meeting that the production
of Allen's *Perdition* was first queried. Evans's notes record that

ME reported a phone conversation with Lord Weidenfeld who
was concerned about the production of *Perdition* by Jim Allen
... Sonia Melchett [a member of Council] said she had been
approached by Lord Weidenfeld. ME asked that an outline of the
play be given. MSC described the play and said that we had
commissioned a report detailing inaccuracies etc. which have
been shown to Jim Allen who has become an expert in the field
himself. It will be provocative but serious. MSC felt he had been
responsible at every stage. Simon Curtis said that we would not
have programmed it without believing in it. ME said that if

MSC and SC believed in the play and it was historically as correct as possible, and since the rumours going around seemed to be based on no real knowledge of the play, the criticisms should be resisted by Council.

The play was to give rise to the worst crisis in the Court's history.

At the same meeting, Stafford-Clark reviewed the previous three months. *Road* had been enormously successful. Karim Alrawi's *A Colder Climate* had only made 13 per cent. Anne Devlin's *Ourselves Alone*, a co-production with Liverpool Playhouse had played to 40 per cent before a tour of Northern Ireland and the Dublin Festival. *Kafka's Dick* was currently playing to 87 per cent. Readings Upstairs included Winsome Pinnock's *A Hero's Welcome* and Debbie Eisenberg's *Pastoral*. There had been a September workshop on Churchill's *Serious Money*, and Sarah Daniels' *Byrthrite* began Upstairs in October. Ahead lay *Perdition* and *The Emperor*, developed from Kapuscinski's novel by Michael Hastings and Jonathan Miller.

After a good deal of negotiation, Max Stafford-Clark's contract as Artistic Director was renewed for three years from April 1986.

8   Holding on, 1987–1993

I can't disguise from you the fact that the position of this theatre has changed. We are supposed to be the spear-head; but how do you keep sharpening the spear?

(Devine, in Wardle, 235)

By their sales returns shall ye know them.

(Brenton, *Guardian*, 29 November 1990)

The first Council of 1987 was held on 12 January. It was given the good news that Bennett's *Kafka's Dick* had played to 81 per cent and achieved a surplus of around £40,000. The play did not transfer but Stafford-Clark indicated that 'long runs of this nature can clearly counter under-funding and are likely to be a feature of future programming'. The Court needed one big hit each season in order to survive and cushion those projects which it was important to do, but which did not do well at the box office. For example, a Joint Stock production of *A Mouthful of Birds* had only achieved 29 per cent. Ahead was Churchill's *Serious Money* and Dusty Hughes' *Jenkin's Ear*. Upstairs would see *Perdition* and *The Emperor*.

However, *Perdition* never appeared at the Court. It was withdrawn by Stafford-Clark on 20 January, two days before it was to receive its first performance. The circumstances which led to the decision, taken by the Artistic Director alone and not the Court's Council, constitute a quite extraordinary story, the details of which brought to a head the simmering resentment of some Court people against Stafford-Clark. Jim Allen's first stage play, according to Stafford-Clark, was commissioned by the Court at the suggestion of Michael Hastings, the Court's Literary Manager. The play was, 'on the particular subject of the behaviour of Hungarian Jews in 1944'.[1] The themes of the play were that the deportation of Jews from Hungary in the last months of the Second World War was only made possible by the co-operation of Jewish leaders, in particular a Zionist group led by a Rudolf Kastner. This action, the play alleges, was to do with the Zionist doctrine of Nazi collaboration in pursuit of the creation of a Jewish homeland. When the play arrived in August 1985, the Court commissioned a report from David Cesarani, then at the University of Leeds. He wrote to Hastings on 28 November to say that he respected 'the serious historical research which has given rise to a large body of material on the subjects dealt with. However, the play offends against canons of historical scrupulosity and it contains some rather nasty attacks on Jews and Judaism which it would be hard for most Jews, and many non-Jews, to accept.' According to Cesarani, the play deals with historical events and questions which are 'part of a legitimate, on-going debate [about] the behaviour of the Jewish Councils in Nazi-occupied Europe, the contact between Zionists and the Nazi regime, "blood and soil" Zionism, Zionist attitudes towards Jewish refugees'. Given that the form of the play is that of a trial, the Court took a silk's advice as to the accuracy of the proceedings in the play. This was dated 26 August 1985. Hastings produced an account of the play, dated 12 September, which concluded:

> this play is a fictionalised interpretation of a notorious trial
> which the author has used to his own political purposes, and
> those are not purposes of firing up ancient anti-Semitism, but
> they do provide a subtext acutely aimed at discrediting
> Zionism, and thus this fictional account must be honestly
> declared right from the start.

An anonymous report from the Institute of Jewish Affairs condemned the play as one-sided in its attack on Zionism.

It is clear that the impending difficulties the play might cause were being vigorously flagged up in the second half of 1985, but it's equally clear that most of those at the Court, including the Artistic Director, for whatever reason, failed to appreciate them. Stafford-Clark recalls that the reports arrived, 'And I didn't read them. I didn't think this was going to be enormously difficult. But I had no idea of the furore that would follow. And I suppose I should have done.'[2]

The decision was taken to produce the play Upstairs. Copies of the text were sent in advance to the press. The play's director, Ken Loach, subsequently believed this to be a manoeuvre to expose the play, although he had agreed to it. Stafford-Clark was, as he says, 'naive in thinking that sending out the script would defuse any argument. And, of course, it didn't defuse it. It did the reverse. And that was really the situation at the point when the play went into rehearsal.'[3] The result of the publicity was pressure. Matthew Evans was clear that a powerful lobby was forming.

> There was a lot of intimidatory stuff going on. I was called to a meeting with Lord Goodman and out of the woodwork came Lord Rayne and they sat me down and Lord Goodman, a great exponent of free speech who I had admired, said, 'You cannot do this play. It is inaccurate. It is an insult to the Jewish community.' He started to cry ... What I was reconciled to, as were the rest of the Council, was putting on a bad play that was going to cause all sorts of difficulties with the Jewish community. But that's what the Court is all about.[4]

A recipient of the script was David Nathan, the theatre critic of the *Jewish Chronicle*, who passed it to Dr Stephen Roth, Director of the Institute of Jewish Affairs. On 13 January Roth met with Stafford-Clark, Ken Loach and Joe Beddoe to ask for a statement to be put in the programme to the effect that *Perdition* was a work of fiction. Ken Loach felt that a conspiracy to ban the work was developing and that Stafford-Clark was part of it.

As the storm grew, so did Stafford-Clark's sense that he was in great difficulties. He had not been tuned into the progress of the play and he had not informed his Council of the potential problem. The press began to build a huge controversy. Typical of the reaction was David Rose's *Guardian* piece of 14 January 1987, entitled 'Rewriting the Holocaust', producing precisely the reaction predicted by Cesarani. Six days before the play was withdrawn, the piece quotes Evans, in the true Court tradition, as saying, 'As Chairman I'm very much in favour of putting it on.' On 16 January, Stafford-Clark's Diary quotes Evans saying that the 'Israeli Govt. will make representations and the Israeli Ambassador is involved.' The Diary records that Sonia

Melchett had asked Evans and others, including Stafford-Clark, to a meeting to listen to the respected historian, Martin Gilbert, on the same day. On 18 January, another meeting was held at Sonia Melchett's house, at which Lord Weidenfeld was a guest. Stafford-Clark was not there. It was at that meeting that a full extraordinary Meeting of Council was set for 20 January, two days before the play's opening night.

Council met for four hours. Stuart Burge, unable to be present, sent a letter suggesting it was 'particularly suitable that the Court, which has for so long been indebted to prominent Jewish families, should mount something as contentious as this seems to be'. Council was unhappy that the Artistic Director had not made the reports on the play available. However, if it was the case that Stafford-Clark was slow to realise the implications of the piece, it was also true that Council would not normally want to see chapter and verse with regard to a particular play. This Council meeting was one that Stafford-Clark has 're-played in my head and edited the dialogue of several times, many, many times since ... the Council were hostile to me with the exception of Bill [Gaskill] and Caryl [Churchill]. Nobody said it was an anti-Semitic play ... At the same time the Council meeting was reported in full on the front page of the *Daily Telegraph* the following morning. Someone on the Council leaked the whole debate.'[5]

The crucial points of the meeting came from Gaskill who 'felt that we must not evade the issue. The Council has to stand behind Mr Stafford-Clark and Mr Stafford-Clark has to stand behind the play.' Gaskill asked the Artistic Director 'if he went along with the anti-Zionist stance', and gave his view that 'not to do the play would be dishonourable to the Court'. This was the critical moment. However the question and opinion were framed, and recalling the affirmation over *Operation Bad Apple* as to the centrality of the writer, Stafford-Clark was in the impossible position, to a large extent of his own making, of being invited to endorse the great tradition of the Court's commitment to the writer via a play he did not rate highly. His Diary notes on the same day: '8.00 Decision to withdraw play taken'. On returning to the Court after the meeting, Stafford-Clark told Evans and Anthony Burton of his decision, which they supported. As he said later, 'I think it was both the wrong decision to do the play and the wrong decision to withdraw the play, but I don't think there were any right decisions that were available at that point.'[6]

The issue would not go away for several months since the withdrawing of the play was construed by many as censorship. Stafford-Clark told Loach of his decision on the same evening and faced the actors the following morning. His Diary entry of 21 January records that it was 'The worst twenty-four hours of my life'. It was to last rather longer than that as the newspapers developed the story. Burge's view was that 'I don't think it's Max's fault altogether. I think Matthew Evans should have said, "No, you can't cancel it." Because if they had done that, there would have been protests and then in three weeks the whole thing would have been forgotten. But because of what he did, it went on for months ... everybody thought that the Council had stopped Max doing it, and that's not true'.[7]

Council met again on 9 February. Stafford-Clark was present for the first part of the meeting, after which he attended a reception at Downing Street. Before the meeting, he had seen the first run-through of *Serious Money*. One of the issues raised was to do with the press release Stafford-Clark wrote in which the use of 'we' rather than 'I' implied Council backing. He admitted he should not have done that. Stafford-Clark rehearsed the events leading to the decision to withdraw the play. Some Council members felt that their treatment by their Artistic Director was both contemptuous and inept. After Stafford-Clark left the meeting, Evans threw the discussion open. There was animosity from some but also support from Caryl Churchill and Simon Curtis. Evans reviewed his difficult relationship with Stafford-Clark. The meeting, in effect, was using *Perdition* as a starting point for a discussion of Stafford-Clark's running of the theatre. Gaskill, responding to the suggestion that Stafford-Clark was indifferent to the Council, reflected that he, when Artistic Director, had never been indifferent to Council. He had 'hated their guts'.[8] But he had Blond to face and the current Artistic Director 'needed someone to stand up to him'. This implicit criticism clearly stung Evans, who argued that he had done precisely that. Evans asked if Stafford-Clark should be asked to resign, but the general feeling of the meeting was against this. The

Council agreed that the Artistic Director's contract 'is finally over in April 1989' and a group was set up to find a replacement.[9] The relationship between Evans and Stafford-Clark would not have been improved had Stafford-Clark known that the source for an *Observer* piece a few days later, which appeared libellous, was his Chairman.[10]

On 18 February, Ken Loach published in the *Guardian* an 'Open letter to the Council of the Royal Court', a powerful attack on the Court's betrayal of its own history because of the withdrawal of the play. Stafford-Clark replied, again in the *Guardian*, 13 March. The reply was drafted by Stafford-Clark and worked on by Evans and Burton. Evans wrote to his Council on 3 March to say that it had been decided to proceed in this way for, if Evans had replied, 'an article by me telling the real story would be divisive'. In his piece, Stafford-Clark called what he had done 'Without doubt the hardest decision I have ever had to take'. The Theatre Writers' Union wrote to Evans on 15 March to say that 'there was deep concern that the Court, of all theatres, should have taken such a step'. The Court was invited to 'make an informative statement enabling writers to understand the Court's position'.

One consequence of the resolutions of the 9 February Council was the resignation of Jocelyn Herbert, Jane Rayne and Bill Gaskill. Herbert wrote to Evans to say that she had decided to resign before the Council meeting and 'nothing that transpired and the final decision to let bygones be bygones and continue as before made me want to change my mind'. The Court was 'no longer the same theatre that I had loved and worked for for so long'.[11] She was persuaded to stay by Evans in order to help find a new Artistic Director: 'as I do anticipate – even at this stage – some reluctance on Max's part to let go of the reins'.[12] Jane Rayne, Chair of the Fundraising Committee, gave profes- sional and family reasons for resigning, but as a member of Council she had been at the 9 February meeting.[13] On 18 March, Gaskill wrote to Evans that he had decided to resign: 'I think Max was wrong to withdraw *Perdition* and we were wrong to support his decision. The controversial nature of the play demands that it should be given a hearing, at the Court of all theatres, and to prevent this is a form of censorship. However we may choose to gloss it, we did yield to pressure and I want to disassociate myself from that.'[14] Evans worked hard to dissuade Gaskill, pointing out that it was Gaskill's questions to Stafford-Clark at the 20 January meeting which were decisive, and suggesting that Gaskill's resignation would seriously damage the Court. Gaskill would not budge and advised Evans to 'be tough'.[15] Simon Curtis wrote an upset letter to Gaskill, confirming that 'it was *your* words at that extraordinary meeting that had such a significant impact. Of all the Council members you are the person Max most respects.'[16] And Stafford-Clark himself wrote to Gaskill to say: 'I can think of no colleague or friend whose approval I value more or whose disapproval causes me more dismay.'[17] One of the saddest and most damaging moments in the history of the Court closed with the destruction of a close friendship.

The relationship between Council and the Executive Committee, together with the Artistic Director, was the subject of an Executive Committee meeting of 28 March. The Minutes record a discussion about communication being improved and how the Council had suffered in the past from lack of leadership. Various improvements were agreed. Stafford-Clark recorded in his Diary that 'Their anger is unbelievable. I just don't see what I can have done to provoke it in quite this way . . . So this is their revenge.' The Executive was clearly capitalising on the fall-out from *Perdition* to re-assert its function. By 13 April, Stafford-Clark was able to report to Council that *The Emperor* had sold out five weeks in advance. *Serious Money* was playing to capacity. *Road* had had a full house on tour. Churchill's play transferred to Wyndham's on 15 July, and added urgency to the debate as to whether to transfer or revive hit shows. Stafford-Clark and Curtis were congratulated for the work currently at the Court. The meeting also discussed an issue which was to occupy the coming period, about regional as opposed to national theatres. It was vital that the Court be seen as a national resource, as Stafford-Clark argued. The question of sponsorship and its implications began to bear in on the debate. Two performances of *Serious Money* had been sold out to individual companies. Caryl Churchill was reported to be opposed to speeches from the stage at the buy-out evenings encouraging future sponsorship. This eventually became a resigning issue for Churchill and reflected the funding pressures on companies such as the Court. Exploitation of successes, the increasing reliance on other than public funding, the erosion of resources for development work – all combined to create an uneasy climate.

By 11 July, Stafford-Clark, according to his Diary, had decided to quit the Court in eighteen months' time, create a new company and nurture new writers. He would have been interested in a letter from the Arts Council's Jean Bullwinkle to Evans about the succession. The letter suggests that the decision to replace Stafford-Clark be confirmed and, given the present success at the Court, 'there might be just as much danger at the present time of a reversal of the decision on a somewhat euphoric basis ... the Council might be persuaded that a change would not be helpful'.[18] On 2 October, Stafford-Clark was 'resolved to make a further bid for the RC and will write letter indicating that I intend to reapply' (Diary). The November Council insisted that a record of the discussion about the job of Artistic Director, held on 13 July, be circulated to Council members. Evans had attempted to block its circulation. After the November Council, Stafford-Clark drafted in his Diary for 14 November a letter of intent to Evans. The meeting had been informed of the death from AIDS of Gerald Chapman, former Director of the Court's Young People's Scheme. It also heard about the last three main-house shows. The first had been George Wolfe's *The Colored Museum* from New York (82 per cent). The piece had transferred for four weeks to the Duke of York's. *The Emperor* translated less well from Upstairs. The third was Sam Shepard's *A Lie of the Mind*, which was very well received and would run to 19 December. The early part of 1988 would begin with a season of visitors Downstairs. *Serious Money* was re-rehearsing with a new cast for Wyndham's, while the original cast went to New York. A Churchill play, not for the first time, was keeping the Court's head above water.

The centenary year of the Royal Court began with a discussion of fundraising, and ended with the Arts Minister again disappointing the subsidised theatre. The Court's new fundraiser, Tom Petzal, planned a Centenary Appeal launch to raise £800,000. He told Council on 18 January that the competition for funds 'was so intense that he was keen to accept whatever money the Appeal was offered'. There could, however, 'be no question of artistic compromise to suit a sponsor'. The Arts Council representative referred at the meeting to the allocation from Whitehall of £5 million for 'incentive funding'. This was to be a merit award for improvements in marketing, box office returns and sponsorship, as detailed in the *Stage* for 12 November 1987. The Arts Council explained its thinking about a three-year funding programme and the Incentive Funding schemes in a letter of 14 March. It requested a three-year plan from the Court and invited an application for Incentive Funding. Most of this depended on 'the level of income you will earn from the private sector'. The Arts Council also expected 'at worst' an accumulated break-even figure at 31 March 1991. The Incentive Funding Scheme was of course competitive.[19] The Court submitted an application and planned to increase revenue at the end of the three-year period by £300,000. The Arts Council rejected the application but invited resubmission the following year. Despite the Arts Council's attempts to sell this as good for the profession, no one seriously believed it in other than monetarist ideological terms. The privatising of the theatres was underway.

The January Council heard that Manfred Karge's *Man to Man* from the Traverse was doing excellent business and would be followed by Heggie's *A Wholly Healthy Glasgow* from Manchester, and then a three-way production with Leicester Haymarket and the Wrestling School of Barker's *The Last Supper*. A Brenton season was planned, and plans for a pair of plays, consisting of Farquhar's *The Recruiting Officer* and an adaptation of Keneally's novel, *The Playmaker (Our Country's Good)*, were also developing.

The first meeting of the Search Committee to find the new Artistic Director was held on 25 February. Stafford-Clark knew very well of Evans's determination to get rid of him. The Arts Council were 'not at all happy with the idea of me as Chairman writing to people, sending them the advertisement and inviting them to apply. They say that I mustn't do this.'[20] As is the Court's way, everyone had a view. Bond wrote to Evans on 7 May to urge a change. Bill Gaskill replied to a letter from Evans saying 'I thought he'd been there long enough and it was time we got someone new. For some reason, a copy of this, by some awful secretarial mishap, was sent to Max and the fat was really in the fire.'[21] Stafford-Clark's entry in his Diary for 17 May is 'Interview went well. They were charming. If I don't get it, it will be my own fault. I did.' Evans's view is that 'We had a fresh look and Max was the best candidate on the day.'[22] The contract was renewed for three years from April 1989.[23]

Council decided that as a body it 'was valuable in times of crisis', but that otherwise it needed to meet only twice each year, with the Executive Committee meeting every six weeks. At its 11 July meeting, it received news of sponsorship efforts from Petzal and from the new Chairman of the Appeal Committee, Gordon Taylor. There was a projected variance of £48,000 for the year, including a fund-raising shortfall of £22,000. If, however, the Centenary Appeal (patron Laurence Olivier) reached its goal of £95,000 towards revenue costs, there would be a £12,000 surplus. Part of the problem for the year was the financial failure of the main-bill Howard Brenton season. *Greenland*'s best figures were 36 per cent and the critical reaction to it was poor. Stafford-Clark hoped for better than 50 per cent from either *The Recruiting Officer* or *Our Country's Good*. He warned that 'a debate about the future of the Royal Court cannot be long postponed. It seems unlikely that we can continue to operate for much longer in the manner we have for 32 years. Our funding is no longer sufficient.'

Stafford-Clark's gloom in his presentations to Council was partly tactical, a way of preparing Council for the worst situation, and a means of pressuring Council into responding. For the current financial year, the Court received a 2 per cent increase on the previous year.[24] This meant that every aspect of the Court's life was under pressure. In her report (30 October) for the Young People's Theatre, Elyse Dodgson saw staff funding having to be reduced by 25 per cent and the future of this aspect of the Court's work was not secure. The end of the year seemed to confirm the worries. Rees-Mogg of the Arts Council introduced the three-year planning document at a conference in October. From 1989 to 1991, the Council would effectively divest itself of its traditional buffer role and devolve much of its financial and administrative responsibilities to the regions, the private sector and the theatres themselves.[25] Although the Arts Council received a

15 per cent increase in grant over the three years, much of it was earmarked for touring projects, international contacts, alternative funding and 'management improvements'. Moreover, inflation levels for the year had risen from 4.5 per cent to almost 6 per cent. Some theatres could be forgiven for wondering how much worse the picture could become in 1989.

The funding of the Court involved large outlays for the staffing of the building. The overheads had been queried before by the Arts Council and Stafford-Clark noted in his Diary for 11 January that the Court was 'becoming marginalised. We no longer have the facility to compete with the Manchester Exchange or the National Theatre Studio, or even as far as Upstairs is concerned with an imaginatively run pub theatre. We are being pushed closer and closer to a cliff edge of viability.' His report to the 16 January Council indicated that since there had been no big financial hit in 1988–89, the Court faced a deficit, but also had a strong list of plays waiting, including Churchill's *Icecream*, Ian Dury's musical, *Apples*, and plays by Iain Heggie and Robert Holman. The net result of the deficit was that Upstairs was closed for six months from April. This was at a time when the Arts Council Appraisal Team had visited the Court. Letters went from Stafford-Clark to Sir Brian Rix, Chairman of the Arts Council Drama Panel on 10 February and 2 March. The increase in grant of 1.5 per cent meant, as Graham Cowley, Jo Beddoe's successor as General Manager, put it, that the picture 'continues to appear bleak'.

A slight quiver of anxiety arose from the proposed platform performances before *Icecream* of a piece by Brenton and Tariq Ali. *A Mullah's Night Out* was discussed by the Court. The title was thought to be inflammatory, given that the play was a response to the *Fatwa* hanging over Salman Rushdie for his novel, *The Satanic Verses*. Concern was of two kinds. Firstly, there arose a question of supporting the play once a decision was made, and Council heard on 20 March that support was near total. Secondly, *Iranian Nights*, as it was re-named, made Richard Pulford, a Council member, feel that the Court might have to have permanent security staff. He asked if the Court was insured against terrorist attack.[26] It was. The play went on with Rushdie's approval, and no terrorist attacks.

On 1 April, Peter Palumbo replaced Rees-Mogg as Chairman of the Arts Council. He endeared himself to everyone by announcing that he would not tolerate 'temperamental' or 'prima donna-ish' behaviour within the arts world in his resolve to create a national structure for the arts.[27] By September the Arts Council had drafted contingency plans in the event of the Government deciding that the arts, like everything else, should suffer inflation and its consequences as best they could.[28] On the same day, the *Guardian* reported that at least forty companies could lose their grants, in order to divert funds to protect the Royal Opera and Royal Ballet, English National Opera, the RSC and NT, plus some regional companies and orchestras. The Arts Council, having duly obeyed its political masters in all things, had a mere 1.8 per cent to pass on, against an inflation rate of 7.5 per cent. Inevitably, the Court, 'the National Theatre of new writing', faced the axe yet again, it would appear. Nicholas de Jongh in the *Guardian* for 15 September said boldly that, minus its grant, it would become an ordinary commercial theatre. This, despite the fact that the Arts Council Appraisal Report recommended additional subsidy and national status for the Court.

It is the case that those days of cyclical deprivation of funding or esteem for the arts had a profoundly depressing effect across the board. It was impossible to create a policy, let alone a consistent view, when a place like the Court appeared to lurch from one financial blow to another. That it produced such high-quality work during this period is extraordinary. That the Chairman and the Artistic Director survived each other is equally astonishing. A piece, described by Stafford-Clark in his Diary for 9 June as 'a malicious spiteful ambush' moved even Matthew Evans to apologise for his comments in the article. He could 'only blame myself for trusting a journalist who let me down . . . I'm sorry about my contribution to that.'[29] At the same time, Tom Petzal was leaving the fundraising struggle and was critical of the lack of effort made by influential Court people to make personal approaches. The Financial Administrator, Stephen Morris, was leaving, principally because such figures could command considerably higher salaries elsewhere. David Kleeman left the Council and the Executive, and Gordon Taylor, Chairman of the Olivier Appeal, acted unilaterally in writing on 22 June and 24 July to Peter Palumbo to complain about management style at the Court. He further suggested that no increase in funding should be forthcoming until there was a massive shake-up. Taylor also implied that Evans 'agrees in principle' with his views. Evans's response on 19 August 1989 was to ask for Taylor's resignation. It's an instructive moment. Evans himself had thought that the organisation of the Court, when he arrived in 1984, was ramshackle but, as the disciples of monetarism invaded the theatre, Evans found himself, to his credit, defending a theatre to which he believed he had brought some order.

The Arts Council Appraisal Report was presented to Council on 23 October. It would form the basis of the Arts Council's attitude towards the Court for the next five years. The Court was now held in 'very high regard' and the Arts Council accepted the recommendations in principle. The central recommendation was 'that ways be found to increase the level of public subsidy available to the Company. Without this, the Team believes that there is a danger that this vital resource for new writing may disappear.' It looked as if, finally, the Arts Council was beginning to comprehend the uniqueness of the Court. Stafford-Clark's report at the same meeting characterised the year as one 'when the Royal Court raised most money for its own productions and, at the same time, produced the smallest number of plays in its history'. The successes of the year were Wertenbaker's *Our Country's Good* and Farquhar's *The Recruiting Officer* which attracted 'glowing notices' in Australia and Canada, played to over 60 per cent box office, and were to transfer to the Garrick on 29 November. On the other hand, Ian Dury's musical, *Apples*, designed to make the Court a good deal of cash, didn't. Dury had written two songs for Caryl Churchill's *Serious Money*, and *Apples* came from this. In June Graham Cowley was looking for investors for the Court run and 'subsequently in the West End'. The history of the Court contains examples of shows mounted for their financial capacities. None worked. Stafford-Clark's Diary for 10 October reads: 'I think we're in deep trouble with *Apples*. I think we'll be slaughtered by the critics.' The notices were poor, despite opening to a large advance. A rough estimate at the time was that it would play to 40–45 per cent, cost £40,000 above budget and all investors would lose out.

If *Apples* was driven by the times, the issue of sponsorship was likewise a reflection of the prevailing circumstances. Stafford-Clark announced sponsorship from Barclays Bank of half a million pounds over three years to commission and produce a Festival of Independent Theatre. Caryl Churchill 'objected strongly ... She felt that the acceptance of the need for private funding had gone too far. She also wondered why there had been no discussion of the issue by Council.' It appears that Churchill's was a lone voice at this Council meeting. She left immediately after this item, and then resigned in a letter to Evans of 3 November. At the Council of 10 July, she had, with Jocelyn Herbert, advocated the complete withdrawal from commercial sponsorship, and was increasingly troubled at the theatrical expansion of such funding. A report prepared for Council by Cowley indicates both that discussions with the bank via the agents, Kallaway, had been going on since June, and that Churchill, in a phone call to Cowley on 24 August, had talked of resigning. In her letter, Churchill objected that the scheme had been launched without Council discussion. The letter is powerful and passionate and reflects what had happened to the arts in the eighties:

> I can understand and respect the view that what matters is to keep the work going and so the theatre should take whatever money it can get. But I can't share it. I feel that my plays are saying one thing and the theatre something else. It is a serious problem and not just for me, because if the theatres are making a political statement by their acceptance of this government it's very hard for anyone who doesn't agree with that to work in them with any spirit. There's been a lot of talk in the building about 'the times' as if they were a force of nature – we are part of them just as much as the government, the city, and business interests, and our opposition can be part of them. It's been put to me that under this government the theatre can't survive without embracing sponsorship and all that goes with it but I question what it is that's surviving. I think we and others will

look back at this time with astonishment at what we went along with.[30]

In his reply of 6 November, it is clear that for Evans the main issue, as before, is lack of communication between the Artistic Director and the Council: 'I despair that after all the problems over the years, the communication is still so bad.'[31]

The special meeting of the Council to discuss sponsorship took place on 3 November. Before the discussion, Matthew Evans announced that he wished to retire but would stay on until a new Chairman was found. Council, after a long debate, voted to continue to accept sponsorship by fourteen votes to four. The commitment to Barclays New Stages was affirmed eleven to three votes. Caryl Churchill declined to withdraw her resignation and the meeting also heard of the resignations of David Hare and Derek Granger. Henni Gestetner followed in December. The Court, if survival was the main game, as opposed to resisting, felt unable to resist sponsorship. It was the size of the problem which upset some. When, in 1958, Schweppes sponsored Jellicoe's *The Sport of My Mad Mother* to the tune of £1,000, and Oxo promised a similar amount, there was not the insidious growth of business interests within the arts. Devine certainly did not object to sponsorship. However, Devine did not face Stafford-Clark's problems. The latter kept the Court afloat during his tenure, a fact which some might regard as exceptional. As he took his staff to an away-day at Leeds Castle on 18 December to discuss the Court's response to the Arts Council Appraisal Report, he could at least reflect that his meeting with Peter Palumbo at the Arts Council had produced a strong indication of an increase in grant for the incoming year.

The grant increase for 1990–91 was £60,000 above the standard increase of 6.5 per cent. It was welcomed but it was also pointed out that to achieve the production levels asked for by the Arts Council Appraisal would require, at an average net cost of £25,000 for each of six productions, an increase in subsidy of £150,000. As its General Manager pointed out in his response to the Arts Council (15 March), the Court had been run without a deficit for eight years. But 1989–90 saw the theatre unable to maintain the minimum level requested of four shows in each theatre. The Court's status as the centre of new writing was recognised. It did not, however, receive the necessary funding to develop further.

The new Chairman was John Mortimer, who was invited by Evans after Council had voted unanimously on 20 March. Evans, somewhat tongue-in-cheek, told Mortimer that the workload 'is somewhere in the region of two hours a week. My general view is that it is not an arduous job. It's fun and it's interesting.'[32] John Mortimer became Chairman in June. Two hours a week proved to be something of an underestimation.

The programme for the early part of the year began with Howard Barker's *Seven Lears*, a Wrestling School production in association with the Leicester Haymarket and the Sheffield Crucible. Following Clare McIntyre's *My Heart's a Suitcase* (Upstairs 1989), her new play, *Low Level Panic*, was her first on the main stage. Sarah Daniels followed with *Beside Herself*, a co-production with the Women's Playhouse Trust. *Beside Herself* was directed by Jules Wright, the new Deputy Director. Upstairs re-opened in May with a two-month programme of documentary work, dialogue and debate, under the umbrella title *Maydays*. It began with a revival of *Falkland Sound*, paired with Hugh Stoddard's *Gibraltar Strait*, and subsequently there was a four-week series of eighteen commissioned dialogues and arguments. Though Stafford-Clark told the Executive Committee on 23 April that six of the eighteen had been delivered 'and the mix looked interesting', the general reaction was not strong. Stafford-Clark's Diary for 16 June felt that the season 'has been rightly dismissed by the public. The pieces are insufficiently challenging.'

John Mortimer chaired his first meeting of the Executive on 25 June. One of his first actions was to undertake to write to the Drama Director of the Arts Council, Ian Brown. Brown had become concerned that the Court had rejected a recommendation of his Appraisal team that staff should not be full members of the Executive but simply in attendance. The Executive unanimously reiterated its commitment to full staff members. The Arts Council was not allowed its way in everything. Mortimer, interestingly, asked David Hare for 'some ideas about the Royal Court ... I'd love to know what you think'.[33] He was soon to find that the apparent largesse of the Arts Council and its recognition of the Court's uniqueness did not prevent the Arts Minister devising a scheme to devolve most of the clients of the Arts Council to the Regional Arts Associations. For the Court, the idea spelled disaster, given its relationship with local authorities and the Greater London Arts Board. The matter was developing before Mortimer took over. Secretary-General Anthony Everitt wrote to Mortimer on 27 September to say that the delegation would take place over 1992–94. Mortimer replied to Palumbo himself the following day to protest. Stuart Burge wrote a strong letter to the *Guardian*, 2 October, to suggest that the Arts Council 'by bucking its responsibility to provide a lifeline for daring programming ... will send these companies down the slippery slope to conformism and dependence upon funding bodies that, under pressure of capped poll taxes, will insist on a repertoire of popular classics and reproductions of West End successes'.[34] Representatives of the Court, the Bush, Hampstead Theatre Club and the Soho Poly met the Arts Council. Their appeal was rejected, but the devolution process was delayed. In fact, it was not until 1993 that the matter was resolved, when the Chairman reported to his Council on 3 February that the National, the RSC, touring companies and the Court were to be the only theatres to be retained as clients by the Arts Council.

Visitors to the Court in 1990 included the Dublin Gate's *Three Sisters*, which opened on 19 July, followed by Churchill's *Mad Forest* from the Central School. Visitors Upstairs included Soho Theatre Company's *Killing the Cat* by David Spencer, and then Holman's *Rafts and Dreams*. Gay Sweatshop ran Byrony Lavery's *Kitchen Matters* for a week, succeeded by Martin Crimp's *No One Sees the Video*. Home-grown shows were Marlane Meyer's *Etta Jenks* and Sharman Macdonald's *All Things Nice*. Neither of these was a massive success, but Stafford-Clark's production of *Etta Jenks* was felt to be one of his 'finest ever'.[35] The decade ended with the resignation of Margaret Thatcher as Prime Minister. Howard Brenton reflected on 'the banal desolation of what happened in our country in the eighties' and hoped that in 'keeping our feet in Thatcherism's philistine hurricane there is the possibility of a new counter culture. The fun palace may yet be built.'[36]

The new year saw a revival of one of the Court's great successes. *Top Girls*, in a co-production with the BBC, opened on 10 April 1991. The Barclays New Stages Festival opened on 17 June, showing four dance and performance art companies. In July the link with Joe Papp's Public Theater produced George Wolfe's musical play, *Spunk*. Budgeted for 70 per cent, it only managed 25 per cent. After *Spunk* came Wertenbaker's *Three Birds Alighting on a Field* (78 per cent). Upstairs, black writers were in evidence. Fred D'Aguiar's *A Jamaican Airman Foresees his Death* and Winsome Pinnock's *Talking in Tongues* produced new commissions for both writers. In June, Jude Kelly's production of *Getting Attention* was brought in from the West Yorkshire Playhouse. In July, Ariel Dorfman's *Death and the Maiden*, with Juliet Stevenson and Bill Patterson, was a success.[37] It transferred Downstairs at the beginning of November. The Dorfman was preceded by *The New World Order*, a sketch by Pinter. It was Pinter's first appearance in Sloane Square since 1960.

In many ways, the major event in 1991 at the Court was the appointment of the Artistic Director, since Stafford-Clark's contract expired at the end of March 1992. He applied again. Figures associated with the Court made clear their astonishment. Matthew Evans insisted that, on being re-appointed in 1989, Stafford-Clark had agreed that he would go in 1992.[38] Stafford-Clark himself drafted a letter to Mortimer of 12 May in his Diary to the effect that 'it may seem stubborn and wilful to seek a further term of office when I have been at the Court for nearly twelve years. It is also true that I am fifty. I don't believe either of these are crippling limitations or indeed that relevant. The sole issue is who is best equipped to lead the Court through the next few years ... My intention is to re-apply for my post but if either you or the Council advise me that this will not serve the Court's best interests I would be happy to withdraw/reconsider.' Mortimer wrote to Burge at about the same time to say that staff members of the Council 'in varying degrees, support Max'. Mortimer also says that he has spoken to Howard Davies who agreed to lunch on 3 June at the Garrick 'and wear a tie for the occasion'. Mortimer was 'concerned that we don't lose Max and get someone less able to run the theatre, although I'm also conscious of the general feeling in favour of a change'.

The job was advertised on 22 July. By 8 September, the *Observer* was speculating, as were others, on the likely candidates. For Coveney, the strong contenders were Simon Curtis, who had left the Court for the BBC, and Lindsay Posner, then in charge of Upstairs and the enthusiastic promoter of *Death and the Maiden*.[39] Coveney's hostility to Stafford-Clark could not, however, disguise the fact that very few young directors had any particular association with new work. One name not mentioned by Coveney was that of the Artistic Director of the Gate, Stephen Daldry. That he applied was partly to do with Jocelyn Herbert:

> I used to go to the Gate quite a lot and I rather liked what
> Stephen was doing there and Lindsay [Anderson] and I went
> together quite often ... and I asked Stephen if he would be
> interested if I put his name forward ... and he said yes, he would
> be.[40]

According to Daldry, Herbert

> came to me on her own to the Gate and asked me whether I
> would like to run the Royal Court ... I did go round later to
> Jocelyn's house and talked it through with her and Lindsay.
> Lindsay became quite important to me, not just within that
> process of appointment, but subsequent to that. I did spend
> quite a lot of time with him. It's a generational thing. They're
> my grandparents, for want of a better way of looking at it. And
> Max had reacted against the parents and rejected them, so the
> grandparents were feeling anxious and fed up that the child
> wasn't including them. I went back to the grandparents.[41]

It was common knowledge that Herbert did not like Stafford-Clark. Gaskill 'could never quite understand why she was so bitter about Max ... He was never invited to be on the George Devine Awards Committee, which is amazing for the Artistic Director of the Royal Court. I don't know whether at some point he'd said something about the past.'[42] Stafford-Clark's view was that 'there was certainly an animus against me from Jocelyn but whether that was because I wasn't a member of the family I don't know. Bill said, "You've never had the papal laying on of hands from her. You've never had your succession blessed." And that was true.'[43]

The animosity is partly explained by an exchange of letters early in 1998, when Stafford-Clark wrote to Herbert to ask to be considered for the George Devine Award Selection Committee (28 January). Herbert's reply (4 February) made it clear that her reservations

> were not to do with your own productions, many of which I admired very much, but to do with the feeling that you engendered of animosity towards all that had gone before in George's time, and your attitude to most of the writers and directors who had worked there showed an insensitive misunderstanding of what those ten years had meant to so many people. To be suddenly not welcome in the building which had been central to their work and to their lives was a very traumatic experience for many of them.

Stafford-Clark's reply of 23 March suggested that

> respect is a two way street. Many of the seminal figures at the Court were, or at least seemed to be, implacably hostile to writers and directors of my generation ... I didn't feel lack of respect so much as downright suspicion at the perceived hostility of the great figures from the past, including at times yourself.

Herbert was determined that Stafford-Clark should go and was angry that he had been allowed to re-apply: 'I thought John Mortimer's behaviour was appalling about this. He let Max re-apply instead of saying no ... Not only that, but John Mortimer put on this Selection Committee [people] who were all Max supporters. It was already too big. So Max came and gave an interview and everybody said, marvellous. The next person to come in was Stephen, full of ideas and excitement.'[44] And Burge, who was on the Committee, recalls 'attending all these interviews of all the other people who, quite frankly, had much more likely qualifications as far as new work is concerned. But when Stephen came in there was absolutely no question in my mind . . . he was extremely convincing, very bright and you really felt it was what we wanted'.[45]

Interviews had begun on 16 September. By 19 October, there was a decision to re-interview Stephen Daldry, Jenny Killick and Paul Unwin. The *Guardian* for 11 October suggested that the Committee was deadlocked and that some form of compromise was likely with Stafford-Clark working in tandem with either Daldry or Killick. On 18 October, Mortimer set up meetings between Stafford-Clark and Daldry and then Killick. Daldry and Stafford-Clark met on 23 October, on which occasion Stafford-Clark suggested that he direct Upstairs and Daldry Downstairs: 'He obviously found the conversation embarrassing and peculiar. Well, so it is' (Diary). Others were joining in the growing criticism of what appeared from the outside to be vacillation by Mortimer and the Committee. As if on cue, Lindsay Anderson called the Court 'craven' and demanded resignations.[46] The *Guardian* for 31 October reported that Daldry was withdrawing. This report was in fact Daldry's doing:

> Once I'd understood the political game playing I thought I'd just do the same. If this is going to be played this way in the newspapers, I'll start ringing up the newspapers if they all are. It was horrible for John [Mortimer] primarily but I thought this is a playpen. I'll get in the playpen and start throwing a bit of sand about and see what happens. So I didn't withdraw to John. I just told the papers.[47]

Nicholas de Jongh asserted that the Committee, after a great deal of havering, chose Daldry but with the proviso that Daldry and Stafford-Clark work together for an overlapping period. The issue then became the duration of the overlap with Daldry back in contention. The *Observer* for 3 November announced Daldry's appointment. Stafford-Clark's Diary reads: 'Ah well. He's certainly behaved fine and good luck to him. I think perhaps I should start my own company.' By Monday, the Diary reads: 'No. Today it's all rather different. Harriet

[Cruickshank] and Stuart [Burge] and Anthony [Burton] and John [Mortimer] attempt to broker a deal whereby I remain AD for nine months and then pass it on to Stephen Daldry. I respond no deal. I want parity. I'll do it for eighteen months and then become his associate for eighteen months, or I'll do it jointly with him for three years ... He has certainly gripped their imagination.' Daldry's argument with the brokering group was that 'an eighteen month crossover was too long and I wanted a year. The conditions, which took some negotiation, were a veto on programming and I had to earn the same as Max.'[48]

The Selection Committee met for the last time on 8 November. At one point, Jocelyn Herbert thought that Stafford-Clark was about to triumph and 'I had to make the most impassioned speeches about how the theatre had been started to do new plays but it didn't mean you had to do every bloody new play that came along.'[49] The decision was made that Stephen Daldry be appointed Artistic Director Designate and Max Stafford-Clark Artistic Director, from 1 April 1992 to 30 September 1993. On 1 October 1993, Daldry would become Artistic Director for two years, with Stafford-Clark as his Associate.

Unsurprisingly, not everyone was happy with the outcome. Jane Rayne, a Council member, had written to Mortimer on 6 November to complain that Council remained 'unaware of the selection process'. On 8 November, as the names were announced, she wrote again to complain about the secrecy and also about the length of time Stafford-Clark would remain at the Court, at the lack of courage apparent in not appointing Daldry alone, and at the selection process itself. She alleged that some applicants were not considered in detail and some on the original short list were not told why they failed to get on to the final short list, and that the Court's good name had been damaged. Externally, there was the inevitable attack by Michael Coveney: 'Daldry has no experience of running either a large-scale new writing policy or a large theatre budget; and the feeling has grown within and without the Court that Stafford-Clark has outstayed his welcome.'[50]

As the dust settled on what Stafford-Clark calls in his Diary entry for 27 December 'the second battle of Sloane Square', it revealed

the Arts Council still complaining about the low number of productions. A meeting on 25 November rehearsed the issue in the new
jargon. The Court was a 'strategic resource' and the job was one of
'enabling' writers (Diary). The meeting was reported to the Executive
on 16 December. The Arts Council wanted some account of Daldry's
role in the artistic programming and objected, once again, to the size
of the Court's Council. *Plus ça change* ... On 21 January, the Executive Committee discussed the Arts Council's demands and accepted
ten productions each year as a target, which had in fact been reached
in 1991–92. The Court's 'flexible programming policy ... had saved
the ESC from deficit for most of the past ten years' and the nature of
the policy was to be explained in detail to the Arts Council. At the
same time, the Council was re-structured so as to have a maximum of
thirteen members, together with a President, two Vice-Presidents and
an Advisory Council. The President was to be Greville Poke, the
longest serving member of the Court, having begun as Honorary
Secretary in 1954.

The new year (1992) began with the Abbey Theatre's revival of
Friel's *Faith Healer*, which was a success, followed by Ron Hutchin-
son's *Pygmies in the Ruins*, a disappointment financially. Brenton's
Berlin Bertie gave way to John Guare's New York hit, *Six Degrees of
Separation*, directed by Phyllida Lloyd. John Byrne's *Colquhoun and
Macbryde* was preceded by April de Angelis's *Hush* (her first on the
main stage). After that, there was a ten-week run of Wertenbaker's
Three Birds Alighting on a Field. A noticeable début Upstairs was
Adam Pernak's *Killers* under the banner of the Young Writers' Fes-
tival. The productions director of the Festival, Ian Rickson, was to be
Daldry's successor as Artistic Director. The year was also noticeable
for Stafford-Clark's absence from the Court for part of March and
April. He was in Stratford to direct Richard Brome's *A Jovial Crew*,
and it was inevitable that he reflected on what he would do now and
where he would go next. His Diary for 12 April has: 'As for the Royal
Court absence makes the heart grow absent.' It was in April that John
Major led his party to another victory in the General Election. Writing
to David Hare on 21 May, Stafford-Clark said he was 'shocked by the
election. Cynicism always shocks me ... The prospect of permanent

opposition is chilling.'[51] On 24 May, he records in his Diary: 'Working with Stephen is enjoyable ... but unless I'm able to come to some arrangement with Stephen/Royal Court about a company, I will have to approach the Arts Council and start my own. As of last week I have a name: Out of Joint.'

Stafford-Clark's swan-song production as Artistic Director was *King Lear* early in 1993. His Court career effectively began in 1980 with Richard Eyre's production of *Hamlet*, and Stafford-Clark returned to another classic, as he had with *The Recruiting Officer* and *The Seagull*. The moment occasioned a rash of retrospective articles.[52] Ahead lay *The Treatment* by Martin Crimp, *Oleanna* by David Mamet and *Hysteria* by Terry Johnson. The Crimp play, *The Treatment*, together with Mamet's *Oleanna* and Anna Devere Smith's *Fires in the Mirror* would, with Howard Korder's *Search and Destroy*, form part of an American season.

Stafford-Clark's last Council meeting was on 23 August. According to the Minutes, he reviewed the recent past and felt that 'not only the choices of plays but their commercial exploitation had been very productive. Financial resources had been built up which gave the theatre more options. The only pity was that so many Americans had been the ones most successful. He stressed what he felt was the Royal Court's primary aim, which was to discover and nurture writers and bring their work to the widest public'. Whatever is said about Stafford-Clark's reign as the longest-serving Artistic Director of the English Stage Company to date, there can be no doubt that he achieved that objective, and that he can lay a large claim to be the most distinguished director of new work that the British theatre still has. During his time at the Court, a formidable list of plays appeared, including *The Arbor, Rita, Sue and Bob too, Insignificance, Top Girls, Victory, Tom and Viv, Falkland Sound, Rat in the Skull, Aunt Dan and Lemon, Serious Money, The Emperor, Road, Our Country's Good, My Heart's a Suitcase, Death and the Maiden* and *Three Birds Alighting on a Field*. In a hard and bitter decade, Stafford-Clark kept the Court alive. It is difficult to think of anyone else who could have done it.

Afterword

This crumbling ramshackle building has the status of a myth. It holds the
fingerprints of the greatest writers and actors of our age. One said to me that if you
squeeze the bricks, blood would come out.

(Stephen Daldry, 'Omnibus: Royal Court diaries', BBC1, 25 October 1996)

Daldry viewed his partnership with Stafford-Clark as a fertile one: 'it
combined the two different areas of taste that were working together.
And Max educated me in lots of ways ... the age gap was a huge
advantage because Max could take me on as a pupil in a sense'.[1]
Stafford-Clark's view was that in 'the eighteen months we worked
together, not only, contrary to all predictions, did we not quarrel but
we made a very firm friendship ... And, at the end of it, there was a
£300,000 surplus'.[2] Daldry's policy as Artistic Director, however,
consciously diverged from Stafford-Clark's. He took as a model his
reading of Devine's methods of running a theatre:

> I changed the organisation of the theatre away from Max
> towards what I thought George had done. George had run it
> with his Associates ... to make sure there was never any single
> dominance of taste. George got himself surrounded by people
> who had often contradictory tastes to his own, but whom he
> trusted. Max had run it much more singularly. He would play to
> the extent of his own taste but what he tended to do ... was to
> get people to work within his own parameters of taste. What I
> thought I'd do was set up a series of satellites who actually had
> much more freedom not just in producing but also
> commissioning.[3]

Daldry's sense of the Court's tradition, combined with a
certain irreverence for aspects of it, is, in one way, no more radical
than any of the theatre's Artistic Directors. Each phase of the Court's

life necessarily reinvents the tradition. When it does not, as was the case in the early seventies, the Court becomes backward-looking to no creative purpose. Daldry's view of Devine as a facilitator enabled him to do what he really wanted: 'I've always wanted to run a building. I've never wanted to direct more than two or three plays a year. I find them so exhausting.'[4] And it is the case that his time at the Court as Artistic Director was less taken up with directing than it was with fundraising and enabling a new generation of artists to find a voice and a place. However, Daldry made his directing début on the main stage on 22 February with Wesker's *The Kitchen*, first performed as a Sunday Night in September 1959. The theatre floor was lifted to the level of the circle with new seats at the back of the stage to create a theatre in the round.[5] For Jocelyn Herbert, 'It was just amazing. Completely unnecessary as far as I could see ... The whole thing's gone full circle, let's face it'.[6] The success of *The Kitchen* led to a discussion at the Council meeting of 1 March 1994 and it was reported that negotiations were ongoing with Howard Panter of Duke of York's Theatre (Holdings) Ltd to present seasons of Royal Court classics at the Duke of York's. These would complement seasons of new work at the Court itself. The first season was initially to have been Friel's *The Faith Healer*, Lawrence's *The Daughter-in-Law* and Shaw's *John Bull's Other Island*.

A main plank in Daldry's artistic policy was one of expansion. Announcing his first full season as the Court's Artistic Director, he listed four productions Upstairs and four Downstairs, thus doubling the programme and more than doubling the budget. As he put it in the *Observer* of 3 July 1994: 'It's important to expand when you feel threatened ... There's a huge exuberance of new writing around and I don't mean the old Royal Court plays with a bit about the state of England in the middle of Act II.'[7] The season was to include Jonathan Harvey's *Babies*, *The Editing Process* by Meredith Oakes and the return of Stafford-Clark's Out of Joint Company with Stephen Jeffreys' *The Libertine* and Etherege's *The Man of Mode*. Upstairs would see Joe Penhall's *Some Voices*; the Young Writers' Festival; *Peaches* by Nick Grosso; and Judy Upton's *Ashes and Sand*. Extra funding would come from the Jerwood Foundation and the Audrey Skirball-Kenis

Foundation. The season Upstairs was to be produced in association with the National Theatre Studio, which would save some rehearsal costs. The Young Writers' Festival, 'Coming on Strong', featured Rebecca Prichard's *Essex Girls* and Michael Wynne's *The Knocky*, both of them significant débuts by young writers. In the same piece, Daldry points out that the theatre building itself was falling down: he is 'hoping for £2 or £3 million from the Millennium Fund'.

The increase in output caused some tension. Daldry and Graham Cowley took all the Court's permanent staff on retreat near Tunbridge on 14 June. The main concerns, as reported to Council on 30 June, were a great increase in workload, ineffective internal communication, and a confusion over decision making. As a consequence, it was decided to formalise departmental hierarchies into teams which would then link in turn with the Monday morning Script Meeting (described by Daldry as 'the heart of the theatre'); the Planning Group; the Heads of Department Meeting; and the meeting of Senior Management. The report nowhere mentions the Court's Council. The distance from the days when George Devine was not even consulted about policy seems immense.

During 1994, two of the Court's greatest figures died, Lindsay Anderson on 30 August and John Osborne on 24 December. A memorial evening was organised for Anderson by his great friend, Jocelyn Herbert, at the Court on 20 November. Osborne's widow, Helen, turned down a similar event for Osborne: 'I honestly don't think (and I *know* John would have hated it) that an evening at the Court is a good idea. He loved that theatre with a passion, but it was a passion spent many years ago, and it pained him to even walk past the building.'[8]

The following year opened with a fierce controversy and ended with the Court in possession of a £15.8 million pound grant from the Arts Council's share of National Lottery money. The year also saw the decision of the Company to rehouse itself in two West End theatres, while the refurbishments to the Sloane Square building were carried out. In one year, Daldry and his colleagues accomplished what for Devine remained a dream.

The controversy concerned *Blasted* by Sarah Kane, a work and a writer subjected to attacks comparable to those mounted against

Edward Bond for *Saved* in 1965. *Blasted* was directed by one of
Daldry's Associates, James Macdonald. It opened Upstairs on 17
January as part of the season sponsored by the Jerwood Foundation.
Daldry reported to the 30 January Council that the *Daily Express*
'continued to hound Sarah Kane'. He had asked several senior writers
to see the play. Edward Bond's piece (*Guardian*, 28 January) powerfully defended the play: 'The humanity of *Blasted* moved me. I worry
for those too busy or so lost that they cannot see its humanity. And as
a playwright, I am moved by the craft and control of such a young
writer . . . this is the most important play on in London'.

Applying for Lottery money was an extension of process which
had developed at the Court over several years. Graham Cowley
locates its beginning in the Olivier appeal:

> Because we'd had the Olivier appeal which was focused on the
> building, we had a kind of continuing examination of what we
> needed. Basically, I was plundering every new funding scheme
> that came along. It all started because of the Arts Council
> Incentive Funding Scheme. The process of arriving at that had
> given us a group of people who were discussing issues about the
> building . . . there was a forum which met every now and again.
> We were geared up to lottery thinking before the Lottery was
> even thought of. When Stephen arrived, he became focused on
> what the stage could do. When Stephen started to join these
> conversations, the whole emphasis shifted and we started to
> think in a much more radical way.[9]

Daldry's version of this is that the meetings were called 'Pork Chops'
since at this stage 'it was like flying pigs. Then the Lottery came in
and we went up a stage . . . we really started going for it. It was driven
primarily by the production department, not from an administrator or
even the Artistic Director's vanity.'[10]

The movement towards a Lottery bid had been discussed at
Council on 10 January 1994. The deadline was 31 March 1995. At the
Council of 6 March (Graham Cowley's last as General Manager, and
Vikki Heywood's first as his successor), it was announced that of the
six architectural firms invited to apply for the design portfolio,

Haworth Tompkins had been chosen. The interviews had revealed architects 'who turned out to be either experienced and somewhat traditional in feel, or young and with the potential for new and exciting ideas'. Steve Tomkins's experience of theatre work was limited, but his ideas caught Daldry's imagination. At this stage the ideas existed only as a feasibility study and in the form of a white cardboard model. The 6 March Council voiced some concern about the effect of the Court's closing for the alterations. Daldry at this stage felt it probable that the work would go on 'either in several theatres at once, or more likely, [we would] create a temporary home in one theatre'. He indicated that the earlier idea of a season of Royal Court classics at the Duke of York's was once more a possibility. The original reasons for the season were: to broaden the canvas by showing a new generation of theatregoers both 'present and past successes; to generate income'; and 'the perceived need to re-invent the West End'. These reasons were now added to an urgent need to find a new home. The Duke of York's would, Daldry hoped, house the Court's main house programme for the duration. At this stage, there is no obvious discussion of the fate of Upstairs.

The Lottery application was submitted on time. It asked for £14 million pounds with a target of £4 million to raise. On 21 September, the grant announcement was made. It was more than was asked for but with more partnership money to find. In 1964 George Devine had proposed a radical change in his theatre. He looked for a new auditorium with a single sweep of seats, a widening of the proscenium and the abolition of the 'hierarchy of stalls and circle'.[11] The scheme collapsed for want of funds. As his biographer remarks of the compromise plans: 'No shred remained of the original dream. There would be virtually no change to the existing building; but it would be in less danger of falling down, and the price could be met without any windfall of fairy gold.'[12] Over thirty years later, the fairy gold had arrived.

Daldry began a lengthy consultation process and a series of inspections of other theatres both in the UK and elsewhere. Perhaps the most significant meeting occurred on 23 November 1995 when he brought together former Court artists – directors, and designers of the calibre of Herbert, Bryden, Dudley, Gaskill, Gill and Stafford-Clark. Gaskill for one was deeply impressed:

> the way he treats the oldies is very nice. He has a kind of flair
> ... a kind of generosity and panache in the presentation of work
> ... we were all there, all the people who were surviving. There
> was a real sense of caring about the future of the building.
> Stephen's sense of doing that was very, very shrewd, a real
> awareness of the value of traditions. The building is not going to
> be changed very much ... it gives the particular value of an old
> fashioned theatre to new work and if you make it into a bare
> box, it's just one of many bare boxes.[13]

At the meeting, Gaskill said that he had always liked the Court because 'the plays were seen as being measurable against the greater work of the past'.[14] Before the meeting, Daldry had found Devine's 1964 plans for the Court 'to make it into one single raked auditorium and I'd looked quite carefully at what he'd tried to do and I disagreed fundamentally with the thesis but that's an historical disagreement. It's not with George, it's with the idea of democratic seating.'[15] Daldry's early instinct was to rip all of the stage area out. The stage was the issue, not the auditorium. The meeting changed his mind: 'Bill shifted everything in that meeting.'[16] Stafford-Clark's Diary records that 'Bill says the plays were given weight by the classic nature of the auditorium.' Reflecting on the meeting later, Daldry commented: 'What emerged, and I totally concur with, is to retain it as a Victorian playhouse.'[17] The changes were therefore ones of maintaining the essential Court. Crucially, apart from stage improvements, seating capacity would remain the same at 400 seats. The only reason to increase the seating would be economic, 'but the advantage of 400 seats for the Royal Court in terms of its overall mission to do new work is that it doesn't expose a play to the vagaries of an economic situation where you have to start filling 600 or 700 seats; there's a danger that if you increase capacity, it determines a conservatism within the programme'.[18]

The placing of the work Upstairs was solved by Daldry's signing a lease with Duke of York's Theatre (Holdings) Ltd, who, early in December, acquired the Ambassadors Theatre. The lease, for two years, was signed in advance of the Royal Borough of Kensington and Chelsea granting permission for the alterations to the Court. The Ambassadors was extensively redesigned by William Dudley with the lower part closed off and the creation of a new, more intimate auditorium based around the circle. The Court thus achieved something not done before except as a temporary measure: it created a presence in the West End. The Duke of York's became the Royal Court Theatre Downstairs; the Ambassadors the Royal Court Theatre Upstairs. For Daldry, it was an essential step, if occasioned by the accident of the Lottery: 'We need to be seen to be taking risks in the heart of the commercial sector, and originating work in the middle of town rather than just transferring work into it.'[19] During its history, there were many attempts to move the Company from Sloane Square. They all failed. As Gaskill saw it, 'There was always a very reactionary opposition to the move. Everyone was finally a bit scared of the move and of course Stephen is not. So amazing to take over two theatres in the West End. It's got a kind of splendour about it ... it will mean that the Court will have an identity apart from the building, which it's never quite had.'[20]

At the same time as the proposals developed for the Lottery bid, the life of the Court continued. Daldry reported that he had many new plays waiting for production to an appreciative Council in January. Most of the Upstairs writers were being commissioned and a scheme of attachments to the theatre had begun for new writers. The first were Rebecca Prichard and Michael Wynne. The latter's *The Knocky* had become a noted success. The March Council heard that Judith Johnson's *Uganda* was about to open Upstairs, and Phyllis Nagy's *The Strip* had opened Downstairs to mixed notices. There had been readings of Jez Butterworth's *Mojo* and Joe Penhall's *Pale Horse*. *The Strip* actually only achieved 20 per cent against a budget of 45 per cent. The commitment to new work on the main stage carried its risks. Sam Shepard's *Simpatico* was doing good business in April and May. The Barclay's New Stages Festival was to run on the main stage, followed by Jez Butterworth's *Mojo*, directed by Daldry's other Associate, Ian Rickson. Between the Festival and *Mojo*, Eddie Izzard would improvise a two-week show. Daldry told Council on 1 May that Izzard would bring a younger audience to the Court. After *Mojo*, Sebastian Barry's *The Steward of Christendom*, from Out of Joint, would return. In the autumn, the Court's classics season at the Duke of York's showed Ron Hutchinson's *Rat in the Skull*, followed by Terry Johnson's *Hysteria* and, finally, David Storey's *The Changing Room*. In many respects, 1995 was an extraordinary year in the Court's history. Howard Panter, of Duke of York's Theatre (Holdings) Ltd, accurately caught the principal reason. Daldry 'has a "can do" attitude. He brings in a lot of confidence. It's the appropriate response to the men in grey suits. The Court has produced more work in the last year than ever before. Its output against a backdrop of cuts and the recession has been Keynesian to a fault!'[21]

The following year, 1996, was the year in which the English Stage Company left Sloane Square and moved into the West End. In its fortieth year of continuous production, the English Stage Company saw a powerful group of productions, including Nick Grosso's *Sweetheart*, Fugard's *Valley Song*, the Druid Theatre, Galway's production of Martin McDonagh's *The Beauty Queen of Leenane*, Nigel Williams's *Harry and Me*, Clare McIntyre's *The Thickness of Skin*, *Mules* by Winsome Pinnock, Marina Carr's *Portia Coughlan* and Sebastian Barry's *The Steward of Christendom* from Out of Joint. During this period, Daldry was regarded by some as the natural successor to Richard Eyre at the National and at the same time rumoured to be Cameron Mackintosh's choice of director for *Mary Poppins*.[22] He was perhaps more preoccupied with the decision by the London Boroughs Grants Committee to withdraw its grant of £37,000 to the Theatre Upstairs at the beginning of the financial year. The decision meant that the Committee had reneged on a four-year deal that was supposed to conclude in March 1997.

The last main stage production before the move was Howard Korder's *The Lights*, directed by Rickson. It completed four decades of work by the Company. The audience, seated on the stage, watched at the end of each performance actors attacking the back wall with billhooks. The final performance was advertised at the equivalent of 1956 prices (75p) and was sold out within fifteen minutes of the box office opening. At a party on 28 September, Jocelyn Herbert revealed that 'the young people in the office' had sent out invitations to both Devine and Richardson.[23] It was reported to the 14 October Council that the party 'went exceptionally well. All costs were covered, and there were no complaints from the neighbours'.

In May 1997, Daldry decided, after six and a half years as Artistic Director, that he would leave when his contract expired in September. After three days of interviews in August, Daldry was succeeded by Ian Rickson. In fact, Daldry stayed on as Director of the Royal Court, with a contract which would run until the Company returned to Sloane Square. Daldry is properly obsessive about the refurbishment of the old building:

> We've been involved with every detail: from taps and water supply to the price of concrete. We've done it because then you can adapt and change as it develops. We're not going to arrive after five years, like they did at the Barbican, and ask why it's all underground, with this horrible strip lighting.[24]

George Devine would have absolutely endorsed that.

The Company's return to Sloane Square, originally set for September 1998, finally came about a year later. The delay was occasioned by difficulties with the building work and by the near-insuperable problem of raising the matching funding required as a condition of the Lottery grant. In February 1998, Daldry's view was a sanguine one. It was, he felt, 'highly unlikely, after a bit of argy-bargy, that a £25 million project ain't gonna happen for a few million.[25] By November, the Court had squeezed a further £2.5 million from the Arts Council, whose Chairman, Gerry Robinson, had, quite coincidentally, sat on the Court's own governing body. The total awarded thus rose to some £18 million, which left the Court to find £7 million in matching funding. It had raised £4 million. Discussions with the Cadogan Estate earlier in 1998 had fallen through because of the strings attached. The deadline for achieving the target was April 1999. Failure would mean liquidation.

The Court, throughout its history, has struggled with the consequences of being broke. And if, on occasion, the cry of despair has been a little louder than was warranted, it has always been true that the Court regularly lived on the edge of financial disaster. Its first Chairman never understood that a theatre such as the Court was not an ordinary business. The last twenty years has seen an insistence by the moneygivers that the Court and comparable theatres behave like ordinary businesses. This distorted logic has meant that many companies have been forced to look to the private sector for sponsorship. And even the private sector has limits to its self-seeking generosity. Donor fatigue by this stage was a fact of life. Finding a source to help with the matching funding was proving almost impossible.

In November, the *Stage* reported a rumour that the Jerwood Foundation, already involved with the work of the Court, was to supply the remaining £3 million. The rumour also suggested the idea that the Court be renamed (5 November). By 25 November, the *Guardian* carried the story of the Queen vetoing a proposal that the theatre be renamed the 'Jerwood Royal Court Theatre' on the grounds that there could not be another name in front of 'Royal'. More seriously, the writers were revolting at the very idea of a takeover and that the writers' theatre should become the 'Royal Court Jerwood Theatre'. Caryl Churchill's view was that to 'have a sponsor's name on a building is the start of a very slippery slope'.[26] And David Hare found it 'an absurdity and an abomination. The idea that a theatre that has a radical tradition, stretching back beyond the ESC, to Shaw and Granville Barker at the start of the century, should be renamed is preposterous.'[27] A delegation of writers was rebuffed in its suggestion that one of the two new auditoria be named after Jerwood. To the frequently voiced concern about sponsors calling tunes, Daldry and Rickson pointed out that corporate sponsors were thin on the ground and at least Jerwood was a charitable foundation.

On 3 December, the *Guardian* reported the deed done. The words 'Royal Court Theatre' were still to be on the façade, but above a neon sign would say 'The Jerwood Theatres at the Royal Court'. Inside there was to be the 'Jerwood Theatre Upstairs' and the 'Jerwood Theatre Downstairs'. In the *Independent* for 3 December, Peter Hall asserted that 'The Royal Court isn't the Jerwood theatre. It has a hundred years of history and Jerwood are buying those one hundred years for £3 million.' As if to aggravate sensitivies, Jerwood's Chairman, Alan Grieve, stated in *The Times* for 3 December that he occasionally read scripts as part of his current association with the Court. It was, he said, not a question of vetoing work, but perhaps suggesting when 'more work was needed … We ask to read scripts from time to time. I see no reason why that should upset writers.' It was the notion that he was unable to see why writers should be upset which upset them. Grieve, no doubt under a deal of pressure, retracted the comment in full. Two days later in the same newspaper, the Court's Chairman, John Mortimer, was emphatic in his assertion that the agreement with Jerwood carried a legally binding clause about non-interference. Mortimer defended the decision: 'this is the age we live in. Like it or dislike it, we have got to live in it. [Those decrying the deal] are living in a dream world if they think the arts are so valued that you can shame the government into coming to your rescue'.

The Court has always accepted some form of sponsorship, from the £1,000 offered by Schweppes to Devine, to private donations raised by Neville Blond, to the unwitting sponsorship of Bond's *Restoration* by Camel cigarettes. Sponsorship increased in the eighties, via, for example, Barclays Bank. The difference was that the Court somehow, and often shakily, managed to keep its distance from its benefactors. If it is somehow to remain the theatre of Shaw, of Granville Barker, Devine, Gaskill and their successors, it will need to find new and ingenious ways of reasserting its radical tradition.

Notes

Introduction: abortive schemes, 1951–1954

1   Wardle, 57–88.

2   *Ibid.*, 96–142; John Elsom and Nicholas Tomalin, *The history of the National Theatre* (Cape, 1978), 99–101.

3   Michael Billington, *Peggy Ashcroft* (John Murray, 1988), 136.

4   *Ibid.*

5   Interview with the author, 21 March 1995.

6   Interview with the author, 18 October 1995.

7   Typescript, 1–2 (JH).

8   Typescript, single sheet, n.d. (JH).

9   Letter to Laurence Olivier, 29 July 1951.

10   See the author's 'George Devine's visit to Edward Gordon Craig', *Theatre Notebook* 51 (1997), 14–23.

11   Interview, 21 March 1995.

12   Typescript of an interview with Alan Brien, a version of which was published in the *Sunday Telegraph*, 12 September 1965.

13   Herbert, interview, 21 March 1995.

14   Typescript of interview with Alan Brien. Tony Richardson's account of this is in his *Long distance runner: a memoir* (Faber, 1993), 59–62.

15   Richardson, *Long distance runner*, 59.

16   Esdaile beat off a bid for the theatre from The John Lewis Partnership, whose founder, Spedan Lewis, had tried to buy the Court in 1943, but was deterred by his surveyor's report of bomb damage. The Partnership was to be involved in the unfolding history of the Court until very recently (see the author's, 'Patronage and the arts: The John Lewis Partnership and the Royal Court Theatre', *Theatre Notebook* 53 (1999), 48–56).

17   See Desmond MacCarthy, *The Court Theatre 1904–1907* (1967).

18   Interview, 21 March 1995.

19 Some of these details are from Lewenstein, 2–7. Lewenstein indicates that the Court ran as a club at that stage because Esdaile had not done the work necessary to gain a public licence from the London County Council.

20 Devine to Hutchinson, 15 March 1953.

21 These papers are all in the possession of JH.

22 Typescript (JH).

23 Richardson to Goodman, 20 March 1953; Devine to Selfridges, 20 March 1953 (JH); Openheimer to Devine, 24, 31 March 1953; Rowntree to Devine, 29 March 1953; Hulton Press to Devine, 30 March 1953 (JH); T. R. Grieve to Devine, 8 April 1953; Hugh Beaumont to Devine, 1 April 1953.

24 Devine to O. B. Miller, 6 May 1953.

25 Lousada to Devine, 25 March and 24 July 1953.

26 See note 16, above, and Roberts, 'Patronage and the arts'.

27 Thorndike to Devine, n.d. Tony Richardson asserts that the revue (Laurier Lister's *Airs on a Shoestring*) was chosen by him and Devine 'to keep the Court warm' (*Long distance runner*, 63). This is not so. Wardle repeats the error, 162–3.

28 A young David Frost tells of making the Royal Court Club and the Blue Angel in Berkeley Street his prime targets for cabaret engagements. One night, Frost apologised for being late with the excuse that no tube train had run from Regent's Park to Sloane Square for more than half an hour. 'Immediately Clement looked intrigued. "Do tell me", he said, "what is it like down there?" What elegance, I thought.' (David Frost, *An autobiography. Part one – from congregations to audiences* (Harper Collins, 1993), 37).

29 Devine to Esdaile, 12 May 1953.

30 Williams to Devine, 27 April 1953.

31 Parker to Devine, 18 June 1953.

32 Clark to Devine, 12 May 1953.

33 Typescript of interview with Alan Brien.

34 Anthony Quayle, *A time to speak* (Sphere, 1992), 467–8. Quayle turned to Peter Hall as an alternative to Devine. There are differing accounts of this. In one, Hall is asked by Quayle and Byam Shaw if he would leave the Arts Theatre to direct modern plays for Stratford at its new London venue, the Royal Court (Stephen Fay, *Power play: the life and times of Peter Hall* (Coronet, 1995), 110–11).

35 Williams to Devine, 19 October 1954.

36 Devine to Saint-Denis, 14 April 1954.

37 Quayle, *A time to speak*.

38 Public Record Office, Misc. Papers, 1953/37,EL4/86. The Royal Court Scheme is included with these papers.

39   W. E. Williams, 'Economic and social aspects of the Theatre'; the Shute lectures, University of Liverpool, 1953. Public Record Office, Misc. Papers, 1953/36,EL4/86. The pioneering book on this subject is Richard Findlater, *The unholy trade* (Victor Gollancz, 1952).

40   W. E. Williams, 'Working party on the "theatre grid". A personal impression'. Arts Council of Great Britain, Council Paper 344, February 1954, Public Record Office, EL4/58.

41   Whiting to Devine, 23 August 1953. Whiting was somewhat less enthusiastic about the Court's work by 1959. See 'At ease in a bright red tie', in his *The art of the dramatist* (London Magazine Editions, 1970), 149–54.

42   Gielgud to Devine, 30 March 1954.

43   Devine to Saint-Denis, 14 April 1954.

44   Bill Williams tried intermittently throughout 1954 to keep interest going in Devine's scheme. He wrote to Devine on 14 September, to suggest that he talk to 'Binkie' Beaumont about the plan since 'I still cherish the notion of an experimental theatre on the lines you sketched in your Memorandum'. On 19 October, Williams wrote again to Devine to say 'I re-opened the business with you again last month [and] I only rehearse these matters, dear George, lest you should feel that my heart has at any time waned towards our project. It remains as keen as it ever was.'

1 Coincidences, 1954–1956

1   Blacksell to Harewood, 4 January 1954.

2   Lewenstein to Duncan, 14 April 1954.

3   Typescript of an interview with Alan Brien, a version of which was published in the *Sunday Telegraph*, 12 September 1965.

4   Lewenstein to Duncan, 14 April 1954. It was the eventual production of these two plays as a double bill at the Court by Devine, 15 May 1956, in a truncated form, which added to the growing animosity of Duncan towards Devine.

5   Lewenstein to Duncan, 29 April 1954.

6   *Ibid.*, 19 May 1954.

7   *Ibid.*, 2 June 1954.

8   *Ibid.*, 13 July 1954.

9   *Ibid.*, 16, 21 July 1954. Greville Poke, the new name here, had stepped down from editing *Everybodys*, and was in Devon with his wife, Patricia. Duncan had written articles for his magazine. Poke, at a loose end, sold £150 worth of advertising space for the Festival (Blacksell to Harewood, 15 June 1954). As Poke later put it: 'I had no idea it was going to lead to all this' (interview with the author, 9 March 1994).

10 Fry to Duncan, 25 July 1954.

11 Harewood to Duncan, 8 August 1954.

12 Wardle, 163.

13 Caplan to Harewood, 11 November 1954.

14 Interview with Harewood, 5 August 1993; Lewenstein to Poke, 25 September 1962.

15 'Dealing with divas : an intimate portrait of Lord Harewood', *Sunday Times*, 2 September 1962.

16 Poke to Duncan, 22 September 1962. Duncan's own account of this period is from the soured viewpoint of one who, in Court language, had been comprehensively 'elbowed' by Devine from the Court. In *How to make enemies. A second volume of autobiography* (Hart-Davis, 1968), 370ff., his assertion that he immediately called the venture by its eventual name (371) is incorrect. However, his remark that he tried to rent the Court in the summer of 1953, and that that was how he first met Lewenstein (371), though unsubstantiated, rings true.

17 Blond to Caplan, 22 December 1954. Esdaile eventually came down to £50,000.

18 'Man of the theatre', *Sunday Times*, 5 December 1954. Ten thousand copies of this were printed and inserted in the brochure which announced the launch of the Company, issued July 1955.

19 Lewenstein, 13–14.

20 Duncan to Devine, 21 January 1955.

21 Duncan, *How to make enemies*, 378.

22 Interview with the author, 5 August 1993. In his *The tongs and the bones: the memoirs of Lord Harewood* (Weidenfeld and Nicolson, 1981), Harewood refers to Devine as 'something of a legend in the theatre, content to maintain a low profile but possessed of extraordinary determination. He was perhaps ruthless in that he was quite prepared to "use" a company that had Ronnie Duncan as a key figure, even though he disliked the kind of play Ronnie wrote' (178).

23 Anthony Lousada to Devine, 10 January 1955.

24 Devine, 'Thoughts on the construction of a new theatre', 7 January 1955 (JH).

25 'First reactions of Margaret Harris', 8 January 1955 (JH).

26 'Tony Richardson's comments', 18 January 1955 (JH).

27 Devine, 'Notes on the Kingsway', 23 January 1955 (JH).

28 Duncan to Devine, 25 January 1955.

29 Radio Newsreel, BBC Light Programme, edition no. 2613, 21 January 1955.

30 Blond to Esdaile, 9 February 1955.

31 Blond to Devine, 19 February 1955.

32　Devine had come across Hodgkinson in 1946 when trying to drum up support for a regional network of youth theatre as part of the Old Vic Expansion Scheme. He noted in a diary he kept that Hodgkinson was a 'rather hearty Northerner but predisposed to be helpful ... one caution with him – doubtful if his theatrical standards are worth much' (Diary, 27 January 1946).

33　Blond to Caplan, 10 February 1955.

34　Harewood to Devine, 21 February 1955 (GH). The Arts Council 'could not help a feeling of disappointment that you were not to be the man who would get that institution into a first class position in the English theatre world' (Jo Hodgkinson to Devine, 7 March 1955).

35　Devine to Blond, 26 February 1955. The Council of 21 February had in fact authorised a maximum figure of £2,000. Devine never received a decent salary while at the Court.

36　Interview with the author, 9 March 1994.

37　Piper had been approached in November 1954 to produce a design but 'I'm going off to paint landscapes in Wales' (Piper to Poke, 17 November 1954).

38　Duncan to Whiting, 11 March 1955; Duncan to Ustinov, 11 March 1955.

39　Devine to Blond, 4 and 5 May 1955.

40　John Osborne, *A better class of person. An autobiography, 1929–1956* (Faber, 1981), 264.

41　Harewood to Blond, 27 May 1955.

42　See Wardle, 150–4; Michael Billington, *Peggy Ashcroft* (John Murray, 1988), 157–9; Audrey Williamson, *Contemporary theatre* (Rockliffe, 1956), 122–3. The tour opened on 6 June at Brighton; thence to Vienna, Zurich, The Hague, Amsterdam, Rotterdam; then a London season, followed by a provincial tour from 24 October to 21 November, and finally three weeks at Stratford. Apart from the exhaustion, Devine was effectively absent for a good deal of the second half of the year.

43　Interview with the author, 9 March 1994.

44　*Ibid*. Esdaile had sold the Kingsway by October.

45　Devine, notes on telephone conversation, 4 April 1955 (JH).

46　Typescript of interview with Brien.

47　Osborne, *A better class*, 275ff.

48　Lewenstein, 28.

49　Dennis to Devine, 5 September 1955.

50　Lehmann to Devine, 30 August 1955.

51　Devine, 'The stage of the Royal Court', 8 September 1955 (JH). Wardle, 169–70, relates how Devine and Ashcroft met Brecht and Helene Weigel while on the Stratford tour, at which point Brecht gave permission for the Court to give *The Good Woman of Setzuan*, with Ashcroft in the lead.

52 'Objects of the company and their fulfilment' (JH).

53 Devine in fact got Harewood to act as intermediary and to 'sell' the idea to Duncan (Harewood to Duncan, 30 November 1955).

54 Brecht to Lewenstein, 8 December 1955.

55 Devine to Brecht, 22 December 1955. Devine wrote again to Auden on 23 January 1956, again apparently without success. Osborne did not go to Berlin.

56 The importance of the Manager had been emphasised when Devine met Craig in 1951: 'Get your own manager and let them work for *you* and no-one else ... Get a business manager who is devoted to you and who will be ready to die for you and your work.' In Philip Roberts, 'George Devine's visit to Edward Gordon Craig', *Theatre Notebook* 51 (1997), 14–23. The Assistant Artistic Director was, of course, Richardson, whose contract was issued on 8 February 1956.

57 Dennis to Devine, 19 January 1956.

58 *Ibid.*, 21 February 1956.

59 Devine to Welles, n.d. (JH). Welles did not accept the offer but he did direct Olivier in *Rhinoceros* at the Court in 1960.

60 Byam Shaw to Devine, 17 February 1956.

61 Roberts, 'George Devine's visit to Edward Gordon Craig'.

62 Wardle, 173.

63 'Percy' Harris, interview with the author, 18 October 1995.

64 Interview with the author, 21 March 1995.

65 Wardle, 171.

66 Clare Jeffery, interviewed by the author, 28 September 1995.

67 Devine, 'The stage of the Royal Court'. The surround and the general renovation of the Court are well described in Wardle, 172–3.

68 'Percy' Harris, interview with the author, 18 October 1995. Clare Jeffery called the surround 'a kind of philosophy of design and could have worked extremely well ...' (interview, 28 September 1995). See also Michael Mullin, *Design by Motley* (University of Delaware Press: Associated London Presses, 1996), 126–7.

69 Conversation with the author, 27 August 1997.

70 Interview, 18 October 1995.

71 Interview, 28 September 1995.

2 The struggle for control, 1956–1960

1 The initial plays 'were known by the author's name because we were a writers' theatre. So we had the Wilson, we had the Miller, we had the

Osborne, and then there was a slight sort of worry when we had the Osborne Two. We stopped it because nobody could get Sir Laurence to talk about an Osborne Two; so it came to an end with *The Entertainer'*. Michael Hallifax (the Court's Stage Director), in Doty and Harbin, 50.

2 Beaumont to Devine, 18 April 1956.

3 Dennis to Richardson, n.d.; Wardle, 179.

4 Wardle, 179.

5 Devine to Miller, 11 April 1956.

6 R. L. Stevens to Devine, 5 May 1956 (JH).

7 Spender to Devine, 18 April 1956.

8 George Harewood, *The tongs and the bones: the memoirs of Lord Harewood* (Weidenfeld and Nicolson, 1981), 178–9.

9 Geoffrey Wansell, *Terence Rattigan* (Fourth Estate, 1995), 270.

10 Rattigan to Devine, 9 May 1956. Devine's reply was to ask Rattigan for Marilyn Monroe's address.

11 The phrase, 'angry young man' was not original. Leslie Paul's book, *Angry young man* was published in 1951, and related specifically to political disillusionment (Michael Pickering, letter to the *Observer*, 27 October 1991). The television excerpt was arranged by Cecil Tennant of the BBC, to whom Blond had written. Tennant's letter to Blond of 26 September also says that 'We cannot do very much as we have a family audience to think of.' Wardle, 185, is incorrect when he refers to 'a five minute' extract.

12 Michael Hallifax in Doty and Harbin, 38.

13 Paul Jackman, Edith Callum, Steven Baddeley and Betsy Lewis to the Court, 19 June 1956.

14 Wardle, 182–3. Indeed, Devine sent Duncan 'a note of good wishes' on 15 May.

15 Lewenstein, interview with the author, 14 December 1983.

16 Harewood, interview with the author, 11 September 1984. In his book (*The tongs and the bones*), Harewood notes the pressure exerted on Devine in this regard: 'it was not long before Neville's first reaction to every programme we presented was, "Which of these pieces you're offering me is going to transfer and make us some brass?" George didn't really like that' (180).

17 Lewenstein, 28.

18 See Chapter 1, and Wardle, 183–4.

19 2 November 1955. Unless otherwise indicated, all of the subsequent references involving *The Good Woman of Setzuan* are to documents in HRHRC.

20 Tina Morduch to Devine, 10 August 1956.

21 A good account of Ashcroft in the Brecht is in Michael Billington's *Peggy Ashcroft* (John Murray, 1988), 164–8.

22 *Long distance runner: a memoir* (Faber, 1993), 83.

23 Lehmann to Devine, 24 August 1956.

24 'The Royal Court', typescript of interview with Alan Brien, September 1965.

25 Wardle, 188–9, offers a good account of the production.

26 Interview with the author, 18 October 1995.

27 'The London Theatre Season', in Harold Hobson (ed.), *International theatre annual* no. 1 (John Calder, 1956), 13, 15.

28 Audrey Williamson, *Contemporary theatre* (Rockcliffe, 1956), 186.

29 Typescript of interview with Brien.

30 McCullers to Richardson, 11 January 1957.

31 *Long distance runner*, 34.

32 James Knowlson, *Damned to fame: the life of Samuel Beckett* (Bloomsbury, 1996), 433ff.

33 Typescript of interview with Brien. See also Gordon Bolar, 'The Sunday night productions without decor at the Royal Court Theatre, 1957–1975', unpublished Ph.D. dissertation submitted to Louisiana State University, 1984. The Sunday Nights began on 26 May with Charles Robinson's *The Correspondence Course*.

34 Interview with the author, 22 October 1996.

35 *Ibid.*

36 Interview with the author, 21 March 1995.

37 Harewood, *The tongs and the bones*, 180.

38 Lewenstein, 33. Richardson's account of the production is in his autobiography, *Long distance runner*, 84ff.

39 Wardle, 214.

40 Devine, 'Autobiography. Part one. Chapter one. The beginnings', n.d. Unpublished (JH).

41 Devine described the Giraudoux as 'a rather safe bet' in a letter to Mary Hutchinson, 27 December 1956. She had introduced him to Beckett, for which he thanks her in his letter.

42 Herbert describes the process in Cathy Courtney (ed.), *Jocelyn Herbert. A theatre workbook* (Art Books International, 1993), 21. This important book offers a comprehensive account of Herbert's work and its massive influence on the Court, and elsewhere.

43 2 May 1957 (RDA). Dennis wrote to both Devine and Richardson to report progress and the letters (in HRHRC) reveal the extent to which the two Artistic Directors shaped the emerging play.

44 Faulkner's play was a success but not with Devine or 'Percy' Harris, its designer. Devine labelled it 'that terrible play – the only play we have

ever done that I really disliked' ('The Royal Court', typescript of interview with Alan Brien), and 'Percy' Harris 'simply *hated* the play. I can't
bear it!' (Michael Mullin, *Design by Motley*, University of Delaware
Press: Associated London Presses, 1996, 131–2).

45   *Lysistrata*, which transferred to the Duke of York's in the following
February, attracted predictable responses. The *Daily Sketch* for 30
December felt the play was entirely suitable for the Court, 'a theatre
with limited seating capacity', but not for elsewhere. The review carries
the title, 'This dirt must not spread'.

46   Gaskill's own account of this is in his *A sense of direction. Life at the
Royal Court* (Faber, 1988), 26ff.

47   *Nearly* everyone. Poke wrote to Devine on 12 October 1957 to say that
'the operative words are Sport and Mad ... I must say that I did not
understand it at all.'

48   Doty and Harbin, 36. See also Gaskill, *A sense of direction*, 32ff., and
Courtney, *Jocelyn Herbert*, 25.

49   See Gaskill, *A sense of direction*, 35ff.; Doty and Harbin, 4; Ann Jellicoe,
'The Writers' Group', in Findlater, 52–6; Keith Johnstone, *Impro. Improvisation and the theatre* (Faber, 1979), 25ff.

50   See the *Daily Express*, 10 March 1958; Michael White, *Empty seats*
(Hamish Hamilton, 1984), 22.

51   Guinness to Devine, 11 March 1958.

52   *A view of the English stage* (Methuen, 1984), 218–20.

53   'Renaissance at the Royal Court', *Theatre Arts*, May 1958.

54   Typescript of interview with Brien, September 1965.

55   Arden to Devine, 6 May and 3 July 1958.

56   Arden to the Council, 5 September 1958.

57   It was probably true. Robert Stephens records that Lawson, revered as
an actor by other actors, would drink large whiskies with beer chasers
'*before* the show', *Knight errant: memoirs of a vagabond actor* (Hodder
and Stoughton, 1995), 159–60.

58   Wardle, 20ff. See also Courtney, *Jocelyn Herbert*, 27–8, and Knowlson,
Damned to fame, 448ff.

59   Anderson, 'Glory days', *Plays and Players*, May 1986.

60   *A sense of direction*, 37–8. See also Wole Soyinka, *Ibadan. The Penkelemes years* (Methuen, 1994), 26–7.

61   Eric White, *The Arts Council of Great Britain* (Davis-Poynter, 1975),
107.

62   Peter Hall to Devine, 3 May 1959.

63   Typescript of interview with Brien, September 1965.

64   Anderson to Devine, n.d; Devine to Anderson, n.d., but Easter 1959.

65   Gaskill, interview with the author, 22 October 1996.

66 Interview with the author, 9 March 1994.

67 Harewood to Poke, 3 July 1959 (JH).

68 O'Casey to Devine, 19 March 1959. The Archbishop of Dublin had opposed the inclusion in the Dublin Theatre Festival of an adaptation of *Ulysses* and O'Casey's *The Drums of Father Ned*. Beckett, who was to have allowed his work to be shown at the Festival, withdrew them in sympathy with O'Casey (see Knowlson, *Damned to fame*, 447–8).

69 O'Casey to Devine, 22 July 1959. See also Wardle, 218–19.

70 Wesker's own account of this is in his *As much as I dare: an autobiography: 1932–1959* (Century, 1994), 561ff.

71 See Anderson, 'Glory days'; Albert Hunt, 'Serjeant Musgrave and the critics', *Encore*, vol. 7 no. 1, January–February 1960. With her celebrated design for this play and for *The Kitchen* and *Roots*, Jocelyn Herbert became, rightly, a designer of international importance. See Courtney, *Jocelyn Herbert*, 32–43.

72 Fox to Harewood, 23 December 1959; Harewood to Fox, 30 December 1959.

73 Much of the correspondence is in Lewenstein's papers (BTM).

74 Interview with the author, 22 October 1996. Michael Billington, in his *The life and work of Harold Pinter* (Faber, 1997), 74–5, notes that Pinter understudied at the Court for a time.

75 A fuller account of the documents involved are in the author's *The Royal Court theatre 1965–1972* (Routledge, 1986), 4–7.

76 See Gaskill, *A sense of direction*, 42. See also Gaskill's 'Comic masks and *The Happy Haven*', *Encore*, vol. 7 no. 6, November–December 1960.

77 Roy Moseley, *Rex Harrison. The first biography* (New English Library, 1987), 206. See also Wardle, 220ff.

78 All of these references are in Devine's papers (JH).

79 Devine to Poke, Fox, Duncan and Ashcroft, 19 October 1960 (JH).

80 Caryl Churchill, 'Not ordinary, not safe', *The Twentieth Century*, vol. 168, November 1960, 443–51.

3 Conflict and competition, 1961–1965

1 Devine, 'The diary of a madman', *The Ambassador*, no. 11, 1964, 215–17.

2 Wardle maintains that the scheme involved a 'regional circuit following the French decentralisation pattern' (236ff.). The original memorandum suggests a rather more self-concerned motive was more accurate.

3 'The right to fail', *The Twentieth Century*, vol. 169, February 1961, 128ff.

4 Jocelyn Herbert, interview with the author, 21 March 1995. See also

Cathy Courtney (ed.), *Jocelyn Herbert. A theatre workbook* (Art Books International, 1993), 44.

5   Colin Chambers, *Peggy. The life of Margaret Ramsay, play agent* (Nick Hern Books, 1997), 63 and *passim*.

6   Ramsay to Lewenstein, 2 August 1960.

7   17 August 1960.

8   Devine to Saint-Denis, 17 April 1961.

9   Lewenstein to Diane Cilento, 19 December 1960; James Woolf to Lewenstein, 12 January 1961; Lawrence Harvey to Lewenstein, 18 January 1961; Harvey, cable to Lewenstein, 16 February 1961; Lewenstein to Robin Fox, 17 February 1961.

10   Lewenstein to Bertice Reading, 12 January 1961; to Paul Robeson, 16 February 1961.

11   Devine to Blond, 22 June 1961.

12   *Ibid.*, 25 June 1961.

13   Devine to Olivier, 10 August 1961.

14   George Chamberlain to Devine, 31 October 1961.

15   Wardle, 232.

16   Devine to Blond, 8 November 1961.

17   John, Lord Wilmot to Devine, 8 January 1962.

18   Lewenstein to the ESC, 23 December 1960 (BTM); Devine to Blond, 11 January 1961; Frank Evans's notes 'Not for inclusion in minutes', Management Meeting, 6 February 1961.

19   Devine to Harewood, 2 November 1960.

20   Rex Harrison, *Rex: an autobiography* (Coronet, 1974), 158. See also Roy Moseley, *Rex Harrison. The first biography* (New English Library, 1987), 211–12.

21   Harrison to Devine, 2 August 1961. Wardle, 228–32, gives a detailed account of the affair; Osborne gives an emotional, aggrieved one in *Almost a gentleman. An autobiography. Volume two: 1955–1966* (Faber, 1991), 196–7.

22   Harrison, *Rex*, 159.

23   Greville Poke, interview with the author, 9 March 1994.

24   Findlater, 74.

25   Vanessa Redgrave, *An autobiography* (Hutchinson, 1991), 103. She also says that Devine organised a Sunday Night performance of *Twelfth Night* (18 February) 'to cheer them up and take their minds off the bad notices' (*ibid.*). Devine explained in a letter to Bernard Levin, who complained at not being invited, that it was 'an exercise for the members of *The Dream* cast, who were naturally very shaken by their experience ... I was anxious that it should be a family affair' (19 February 1962).

26 Devine to Harewood, 8 March 1962. Osborne pays tribute to Blond's 'bemused loyalty to George ... although he still blenched at the whispered name of "Arden". I had grown very fond of him as each renewed blow from the front-of-house returns diminished his dreams of a knighthood' (*Almost a gentleman*, 172).

27 Findlater, 81; n.4, 51. A good discussion of *Period of Adjustment* was broadcast by the BBC Home Service on 24 June 1962.

28 James Knowlson, *Damned to fame: the life of Samuel Beckett* (Bloomsbury, 1996), 498ff. Devine had sent the script of *Happy Days* to his friend, Mary Hutchinson, on 11 July 1961. See also Courtney, *Jocelyn Herbert*, 53–4.

29 See the author's *The Royal Court theatre, 1965–1972* (Routledge, 1986), 11–12; Wardle, 239–41.

30 Peggy Ashcroft to Harewood, 6 September 1962.

31 'The diary of a madman'.

32 *Ibid.*

33 Findlater, 70. Findlater, 69, asserts that Devine planned to eliminate the proscenium arch in his plans. The memorandum uses the phrase 'a wider proscenium'. See also Wardle, 252–3; William Gaskill, *A sense of direction. Life at the Royal Court* (Faber, 1988), 54–5. A report on the first year of the Studio was circulated in August 1964.

34 Redgrave, *An autobiography*, 111–12. The show does not appear in Findlater's otherwise invaluable listings of Court productions.

35 Devine to Byam Shaw, 21 April 1963.

36 'The diary of a madman'.

37 Guinness to Devine, 14 October 1963.

38 Devine to Saint-Denis, 24 October 1963.

39 Minster Productions Ltd., presented *The Gentle Avalanche* from 12 November. It closed on 16 November, to be replaced by a Spur Productions Ltd./Bernard Delfont Ltd. presentation of *The Ginger Man*. A farce, *Monsieur Blaise*, opened in February, and transferred to the Phoenix. It was followed by *Spoon River*, which was withdrawn on 14 March. The Court then closed.

40 Findlater, 70; Wardle, 255–6.

41 Wardle, 257–8. Gaskill says that at the time he was 'too involved with what I felt was going to be the socialist ensemble of my dreams' (*A sense of direction*, 60).

42 Findlater, 164–5; Wardle, 258–9.

43 Redgrave, *An autobiography*, 116; Michael Billington, *Peggy Ashcroft* (John Murray, 1988), 209–11; Osborne, *Almost a gentleman*, 243–4.

44 *Long distance runner: a memoir* (Faber, 1993), 150–54. Richardson also sees *The Seagull* as announcing 'the end of the Court' (154). For

Herbert's design for *The Seagull* and the subsequent production of *Saint Joan of the Stockyards*, see Courtney, *Jocelyn Herbert*, 59–71.

45 The production saw Richardson, for all his rejection of Copeau, using masks when it became clear that the singers he had engaged could not act. Ironically, his last Court production thus utilised the very tradition he had inveighed against (see Courtney, *Jocelyn Herbert*, 66–71).

46 Interview with the author, 5 December 1984.

47 *Theatre World*, vol. 60, September 1964.

48 Knowlson, *Damned to fame*, 526–7.

49 Blacksell to Harewood, 25 November 1964.

50 Harewood to Blacksell, 7 December 1964; Blacksell to Harewood, 10 December 1964; Blacksell to Duncan, 18 January 1965; Blacksell to Poke, 18 January 1965; Blacksell to Harewood, 18 January 1965.

51 'The diary of a madman'.

52 Interview with the author, 5 December 1984.

53 Interview with the author, 21 March 1995. For Gaskill's account of the lunch, see *A sense of direction*, 60–61; for Osborne's, see *Almost a gentleman*, 247.

54 Interview with the author, 11 September 1984.

55 Interview with the author, 22 October 1996.

56 John Johnstone, *The Lord Chamberlain's blue pencil* (Hodder and Stoughton, 1990), 176–7. In an interview with J. W. Lambert, the then Lord Chamberlain, Lord Cobbold, supported the use of club theatres on the grounds that they 'give selected and interested audiences a chance to see experimental work ... my predecessors and I have never wished to interfere with genuine theatre clubs'. He also remarks presciently that if theatres use clubs to evade the Chamberlain's jurisdiction, then he 'would feel it his duty to challenge the arrangement and to test the law in the courts' (*Sunday Times*, 11 April 1965). He did just that with *Saved* later in the year.

57 Lewenstein to Charles Wood, 3 July 1964.

58 Johnstone, *The Lord Chamberlain's blue pencil*, 176–7. See Wardle, 270–1. See also Osborne, *Almost a gentleman*, 250ff.

59 Wardle, 272–7, gives a good account of this, as does Nicholas de Jongh in *Not in front of the audience. Homosexuality on stage* (Routledge, 1992), 90, 105–19. See also Johnstone, *The Lord Chamberlain's blue pencil*, 205–9. Osborne put up £7,000 towards the production costs; see *Almost a gentleman*, 251.

60 See Courtney, *Jocelyn Herbert*, 75.

61 From Osborne's unpublished speech at a Memorial Meeting for Devine, Royal Court, 18 February 1966.

4 A socialist theatre, 1965–1969

1 Gaskill, 'Glorious riches spring from talents in turmoil', *The Times*, 13 January 1986.

2 Interview with the author, 18 September 1984.

3 Gaskill, interview with the author, 13 December 1983.

4 *Ibid.*

5 William Gaskill, *A sense of direction. Life at the Royal Court* (Faber, 1988), 63. Gaskill's own account of his years as Artistic Director of the Court begins with Chapter 8. See also the present author's *The Royal Court Theatre, 1965–1972* (Routledge, 1986). Parts of Chapters 4 and 5 draw from this account.

6 Gaskill, interview, 13 December 1983.

7 Gaskill, *A sense of direction*, 65.

8 *Ibid.*

9 Interview, 13 December 1983.

10 Interview with the author, 5 December 1984.

11 Roberts, *The Royal Court Theatre*, 29.

12 *Ibid.*, 30.

13 They included Bryden, *New Statesman*, 12 November 1965; Brien, *Sunday Telegraph*, 7 November 1965; Marriott, *The Stage*, 11 November 1965; and Gilliatt, *Observer*, 7 and 14 November 1965. A selection of reviews and comments can be found in the author's *Bond on file* (Methuen, 1985).

14 Roberts, *The Royal Court Theatre*, 40.

15 'Glorious riches'.

16 'Man for the future', *Plays and Players*, March 1966.

17 *Tribune*, 28 January 1966. Anderson, in a letter to the author of 2 May 1984, wrote that Devine was 'quite selfless and absolutely without jealousy of the talents he nourished. George really respected and loved talent and was enough of his own man never to feel threatened by it.'

18 From a Xerox kindly supplied to me by Jane Baldwin.

19 To Valentine Tessier, 'hiver [winter] 1967'.

20 See Wardle, 280; John Osborne, *Almost a gentleman. An autobiography. Volume two: 1955–1966* (Faber, 1991), 265–8; Gaskill, *A sense of direction*, 71–4.

21 Other tributes to Devine include those of Tony Richardson, *Long distance runner: a memoir* (Faber, 1993), 184–6. Wole Soyinka wrote from Lagos on 25 February 1966 to offer his condolences. He apologises for his late reply because of the 'political circumstances in which I found myself for the last few months of last year'.

22 Interview 9 March 1994.

23 Poke, interview, 18 September 1984.

24 See *Hansard* for 17 February 1966; 8 March 1966; and the *Joint committee on censorship of the theatre. A report*, 26 October 1966 (HMSO, 1967).

25 Instrumental in overall rises in the Arts Council grant was the first Minister for Arts, Jennie Lee. Between 1964 and 1965, Labour's first year in office, and Jennie Lee's last budget of 1970–71, the grant rose from £3.2 million to £9.4 million (Patricia Hollis, *Jennie Lee: a life* (Oxford University Press, 1997), 288.

26 Findlater, 91.

27 *The Times*, 6 April 1966.

28 'Angry middle age', *Spectator*, 15 April 1966.

29 Gaskill, *A sense of direction*, 74.

30 *Ibid.*, 126–7. See also Roberts, *The Royal Court Theatre*, 46; Colin Chambers, *Peggy. The life of Margaret Ramsay, play agent* (Nick Hern Books, 1997), 245ff.

31 For Gaskill's account of this, see *A sense of direction*, 75, and Doty and Harbin, 191.

32 See *A sense of direction*, 76–81; see also Roberts, *The Royal Court Theatre*, 51–6.

33 Findlater, 96.

34 A few critics praised the production: see the *Times Educational Supplement* (25 November); Hobson, *Sunday Times* (23 October); Marriott, *The Stage* (27 October). See also Simone Signoret, *Nostalgia isn't what it used to be* (Panther Books, 1979), 370–6.

35 Interview, 13 December 1983.

36 Poke, interview, 18 September 1984.

37 See Roberts, *The Royal Court Theatre*, 57–8.

38 Interview with David Storey and Lindsay Anderson, 29 April 1985. See also Storey, 'Working with Lindsay', in Findlater, 110ff.

39 *Sunday Times*, 16 July 1967.

40 Doty and Harbin, 76; Gaskill, *A sense of direction*, 95.

41 Michael White, *Empty seats* (Hamish Hamilton, 1984), 91–5; Peter Ansorge, *Disrupting the spectacle: five years of experimental and fringe theatre in Britain* (Pitman, 1975), 22ff.

42 Interview, 13 December 1983.

43 Gaskill, *A sense of direction*, 99–100.

44 Poke, interview, 18 September 1984.

45 Interview with the author, 11 September 1984.

46 Poke, interview with the author, 3 February 1995.

47 *Ibid.*

48 Gaskill to Harewood, 9 April 1968 (GH).

49 For Gaskill's own account of this, see *A sense of direction*, 95ff.; Roberts, *The Royal Court Theatre*, 62ff.

50 See Gaskill, *A sense of direction*, 102–5; Roberts, *The Royal Court Theatre*, 69–82.

51 *A sense of direction*, 71.

52 *Ibid.*, 106.

53 Lewenstein, 123–4.

54 Page to Tynan, 24 February 1969.

55 Gaskill, *A sense of direction*, 116.

56 Fox to Harewood, 14 August 1968.

57 See Gaskill, *A sense of direction*, 108–9; Roberts, *The Royal Court Theatre*, 89–92.

58 Interview, 13 December 1983.

5 A humanist theatre, 1969–1975

1 Interview with the author, 21 March 1995.

2 Interview with the author, 5 December 1984.

3 *Ibid.*

4 *A sense of direction. Life at the Royal Court* (Faber, 1988), 107–8.

5 Gaskill, interview with the author, 22 October 1996.

6 Findlater, 141.

7 *Ibid.*

8 Doty and Harbin, 100.

9 Interview, 5 December 1984.

10 Interview with the author, 14 December 1983.

11 Interview, 5 December 1984.

12 Interview with the author, 18 September 1984.

13 Interview, 5 December 1984.

14 Gaskill, interview with the author, 13 December 1983.

15 Interview, 5 December 1984.

16 *Ibid.*

17 *A sense of direction*, 100.

18 Interview, 5 December 1984.

19 Gaskill, interview, 13 December 1983. A more detailed account of *Come Together* may be found in the present author's *The Royal Court Theatre, 1965–1972* (Routledge, 1986), 128–9.

20 Nicholas de Jongh, 'Court in the act', *Guardian*, 5 April 1971.

21 'The writer's theatre', issued with the programme of his *Lear*, which opened at the Court on 29 September.

22 Mary Holland, *Plays and Players*, October 1971.

23 Interview with the author, 13 December 1983.

24   Interview, 5 December 1984.

25   Interview, 14 December 1983.

26   Poke, interview with the author, 18 September 1984.

27   *Ibid.*

28   Poke, interview with the author, 3 February 1995.

29   Max Stafford-Clark, interview with the author, 13 December 1996.

30   Interview, 23 December 1983.

31   *A sense of direction*, 130. Early in 1973, Lewenstein brought Pam Brighton and Max Stafford-Clark in as Resident Directors. They were paid £25 per week.

32   Lewenstein, 147.

33   Interview, 21 March 1995.

34   Interview, 5 December 1984.

35   Interview with the author, 3 October 1996. Lewenstein, however, earned the gratitude of both Fugard and Matura for his support and help. See Findlater, 156–63.

36   Doty and Harbin, 13.

37   For Bond's plays, see Gaskill, *A sense of direction*, 124–5; Malcolm Hay and Philip Roberts, *Bond: a study of his plays* (Methuen, 1980), Chapters 6 and 8.

38   For Beckett, see James Knowlson, *Damned to fame: the life of Samuel Beckett* (Bloomsbury, 1996), 588ff.; Billie Whitelaw, *Billie Whitelaw . . . Who he? An autobiography* (Hodder and Stoughton, 1995), 116ff.; Cathy Courtney (ed.), *Jocelyn Herbert. A theatre workbook* (Art Books International, 1993), 87–91.

39   See Roberts, *The Royal Court Theatre*, Chapter 8.

40   See Colin Chambers, *Peggy. The life of Margaret Ramsay, play agent* (Nick Hern Books, 1997), 267ff.

41   Lewenstein, 147ff.

42   Interview with the author, 3 October 1996.

43   Poke, interview, 18 September 1984. Lois Sieff was a member of Council. For Lewenstein's version of the Upstairs incident, see Lewenstein, 170–1.

44   Interview, 21 March 1995.

45   Interview, 5 December 1984.

46   Gaskill's view of this is that 'Lindsay's whole life was a kind of archive' (interview, 22 October 1996).

47   Lewenstein, 173.

48   Wright, interview, 3 October 1996.

49   Poke, interview, 3 February 1995.

50   Interview, 21 March 1995.

51   John Goodwin (ed.), *Peter Hall's diaries: the story of a dramatic battle* (Hamish Hamilton, 1983), 121–5.

6 Changing places, 1975–1979

1   Interview with the author, 3 October 1996.
2   Anderson to Cudlipp, 27 March 1975. Anderson, together with two
      Council members, Lois Sieff and Norman Collins, tried to oust Poke
      from the Chairmanship of the Court and replace him with Cudlipp.
      Poke did not budge.
3   Interview with the author, 5 December 1984.
4   Quoted in Albert Hunt, 'Upstairs or Downstairs', *New Society*, 5
      February 1976. See, in addition, Clive Goodwin, 'Lament for the
      Theatre Upstairs', *Plays and Players*, August 1975.
5   Findlater, 173.
6   For the Beckett productions, see James Knowlson, *Damned to fame: the
      life of Samuel Beckett* (Bloomsbury, 1996), 615ff. For Beckett's *Foot-
      falls*, see also Cathy Courtney (ed.), *Jocelyn Herbert. A Theatre Work-
      book* (Art Books International, 1993), 92, and Billie Whitelaw, *Billie
      Whitelaw ... Who he? An autobiography* (Hodder and Stoughton, 1995),
      143–7. For Joint Stock, see Rob Ritchie (ed.), *The Joint Stock book: the
      making of a theatre collective* (Methuen, 1987), *passim*.
7   Nicholas Wright, in Doty and Harbin, 62.
8   Interview, 3 October 1996.
9   John Goodwin (ed.), *Peter Hall's diaries: the story of a dramatic battle*
      (Hamish Hamilton, 1983), 273 (13 December 1976).
10   Elaine Blond, *Marks of distinction* (Vallentine, Mitchell, 1988), 169.
11   Interview, 3 October 1996.
12   *Ibid.* Robert Kidd died on 15 July 1980 of pancreatic cancer.
13   See *The Observer*, 14 November 1993; *Plays and Players*, June 1969.
14   Interview with the author, 21 March 1995.
15   Doty and Harbin, 63. Burge's production of Wedekind's *Lulu* had played
      at the Court in December 1970.
16   Goodwin, *Peter Hall's diaries*, 280.
17   Poke, private notes for 10–15 January 1977.
18   Goodwin, *Peter Hall's diaries*, 281 (18, 19 January 1977).
19   Interview with the author, 9 July 1996.
20   Doty and Harbin, 63.
21   Interview, 9 July 1996.
22   *Ibid.*
23   I am grateful to Stuart Burge for a copy of this and subsequent accounts
      of the workers' meetings.
24   Findlater, 176.
25   Interview, 9 July 1996.
26   *Ibid.*

27   *Ibid.* Stafford-Clark notes in his Diary for 3 May: 'Job at RC commences'. I am grateful to Max Stafford-Clark for allowing me access to his Diaries.

28   *Ibid.* At the time of his appointment, Ritchie was reading for a Ph.D. on Griffiths at the University of Sheffield.

29   Osborne to Goodman, 13 July 1977.

30   Doty and Harbin, 134. *Once A Catholic* opened on 10 August and transferred to Wyndham's on 4 October.

31   Stuart Burge, interview with the author, 14 August 1996.

32   Doty and Harbin, 65.

33   Williams' account of the Court is in Findlater, 187–8.

34   Interview, 14 August 1996. Peter Hall saw it on 7 June 1978 and thought it was 'bullshit: aestheticism run riot' (Goodwin, *Peter Hall's diaries*, 357).

35   Interview, 14 August 1996.

36   Max Stafford-Clark, interview with the author, 13 December 1996.

37   Interview, 14 August 1996.

38   Stafford-Clark, Diary entry for 7 October 1978.

39   Interview, 13 December 1996.

40   Burge, letter to the author, 17 July 1996.

41   Interview, 14 August 1996. See also Nicholas de Jongh, *Not in front of the audience. Homosexuality on stage* (Routledge, 1992), 148–56.

42   *Ibid.* Billie Whitelaw's account of a not altogether trouble-free production is in her autobiography, *Billie Whitelaw ... Who he?* 148ff. See also Knowlson, *Damned to fame*, 657–9; Courtney, *Jocelyn Herbert*, 55.

43   Interview, 9 July 1996.

44   Interview, 21 March 1995.

45   John Dexter, *The honourable beast. A posthumous autobiography* (Nick Hern Books, 1993), 168.

46   Interview with the author, 22 October 1996.

47   Interview with the author, 3 February 1995.

48   Dexter, *The honourable beast*, 246. Dexter to Osborne, 5 November 1980.

7 Theatre in a cold climate, 1980–1986

1   The reference is to Wardle.

2   Benedict Nightingale, 'Less faith in concrete', *New Statesman*, 4 January 1980.

3   Jim Hiley, 'The Court case', *Time Out*, 8–14 February 1980.

4   'Why I am angry today', *Sunday Telegraph*, 10 February 1980. The piece drew a sharp letter in response from Stafford-Clark on 17 February.

5 Doty and Harbin, 70.

6 *Ibid.*

7 For an account of the evolution of this, see Findlater, 189–94; Gerald Chapman, 'Education and the Royal Court', *Plays and Players*, May 1978; Heather Neill, 'King's Road to Glasgow', *Times Educational Supplement*, 17 March 1978.

8 Interview with the author, 13 December 1996. See also Ann McFerran's interview with Dunbar, *Time Out*, 20–26 June 1980. Andrea Dunbar died of a brain haemorrhage when she was 29.

9 Eyre's account of the production is in his *Utopia and other places* (Vintage, 1994), 155–6.

10 *Observer*, 4 May 1980.

11 Doty and Harbin, 77.

12 For a discussion of the position to do with finance in 1980–81, see Doty and Harbin, 120ff. The conference, on which the book is based, was held from 7 to 10 October 1981, and the anxiety of some Court participants at this time shows forcefully.

13 Rob Ritchie, in Doty and Harbin, 141.

14 Stafford-Clark, draft in Diary.

15 Doty and Harbin, 119. Bond's feelings about his relationship with the Court and Stafford-Clark are available in his *Letters*, selected and edited by Ian Stuart (Harwood Academic Publishers); vol. 1 (1994), 143–4, 147–51; vol. 2 (1995), 89–90; vol. 3 (1996), 129–30.

16 'Why the Court must prevail', *The Times*, 21 September 1981.

17 Hare, 'Green room', *Plays and Players*, October 1981.

18 An account of the play is in Doty and Harbin, 23–4.

19 'Forum on political theatre', W. H. Smith/RSC Youth Festival, Stratford, 23 October 1982.

20 Interview with the author, 14 August 1996.

21 Interview, 13 December 1996.

22 Stuart Burge, in Doty and Harbin, 130.

23 Interview, 13 December 1996.

24 *Ibid.*

25 *Ibid.*

26 Doty and Harbin, 22–3.

27 *Ibid.*

28 *Plays and Players*, January 1983.

29 Michael Coveney, *Plays and Players*, March 1983.

30 *Plays and Players*, August 1983.

31 For an account of the effects of Thatcherism on the theatre of the eighties generally, see John Bull, *Stage right: crisis and recovery in British contemporary mainstream theatre* (Macmillan, 1994), 14ff.

32   See Sheridan Morley, *Plays and Players*, May 1984, and Stafford-Clark, 'Folk memories in Sloane Square', *The Times*, 1 September 1984.

33   Rees-Mogg to Hare, 27 March 1984.

34   Letter from the Arts Council Drama Panel, *Stage*, 3 May 1984, in response to a piece by Luke Rittner of the Arts Council, *Sunday Times*, 8 April 1984.

35   *Stage*, 5 April 1984.

36   See, for example, Graham Watkins, ' "Art grows where seed is sown"- a reply to *The Glory of the Garden*', *Stage*, 17 May 1984, and 'Bragg attacks *The Glory of the Garden*', *Stage*, 21 June 1984.

37   See Michael Geare, 'Behind the face of Faber', *Author*, Spring 1984.

38   See 'Ulster comes to Sloane Square', *Plays*, September 1984, and Rob Ritchie, 'Derry notebook', *Platform*, no. 5, Spring 1983.

39   Stafford-Clark, interview, 13 December 1996.

40   Interview with the author, 16 January 1997.

41   Bond, *Letters*, vol. 1, 147–51; vol. 3, 129–36.

42   Interview, 16 January 1997. Stafford-Clark's view of Evans uses the same epithet.

43   Evans to Anderson, 13 December 1985.

44   'Not quite a revolution', *Plays*, January 1985.

45   To David Hare, 28 February 1985.

46   To Matthew Evans, 25 February 1985.

47   To David Hare, 4 March 1985.

48   To Matthew Evans, n.d. (ME).

49   Interview, 13 December 1996.

50   Interview, 16 January 1997.

51   Editorial, *Plays and Players*, October 1985. For an attempted defence of Arts Council policy, see Dickon Reed, 'How glorious is the garden?', *Plays and Players*, July 1985. Peter Hall's impassioned defence of the profession is in: *Plays*, April; *Plays and Players*, April; and the *Stage*, 16 May, 1985. Jeremy Jehu produced two powerful and critical analyses of the Arts Council in the *Stage*, 14 March and 2 May 1985.

52   Evans, interview, 16 January 1997.

53   Luke Rittner, Secretary-General, Arts Council, to Evans, 9 October 1985.

54   Jean Bullwinkle, Acting Drama Officer, Arts Council, to Evans, 14 February 1986. In the event, the Court received an increase of 9.2 per cent.

55   See Nicholas de Jongh, *Not in front of the audience. Homosexuality on stage* (Routledge, 1992), 18off. *The Normal Heart* was the Court's first transfer since *Bent* in 1979.

8 Holding on, 1987–1993

1   Interview with the author, 13 December 1996.

2   *Ibid.*

3   *Ibid.*

4   Interview with the author, 16 January 1997.

5   Interview, 13 December 1996.

6   *Ibid.*

7   Interview with the author, 14 August 1996.

8   Longhand notes of Council meeting of 9 February 1997, taken by Jo Beddoe (ME).

9   *Ibid.*

10   Peter Hillmore as 'Pendennis', *Observer*, 15 February 1987. Hillmore wrote to Evans on 15 April to say 'It is a very noble gesture of yours to "own up" if necessary – but I forbid it. If I refuse to name my source I refuse to let them name themselves'.

11   Herbert to Evans, 10 February 1987.

12   Evans to Herbert, 19 March 1987 (ME). She agreed to remain in a letter to Evans of 31 March.

13   Rayne to Evans, 18 February 1987.

14   Gaskill to Evans, 28 March 1987 (ME).

15   Evans to Gaskill, 7 April 1987; Gaskill to Evans, 12 April 1987.

16   Curtis to Gaskill, 21 April 1987.

17   Stafford-Clark to Gaskill, 23 April 1987.

18   Jean Bullwinkle to Evans, 17 June 1987.

19   Luke Rittner to Evans, 14 March 1988.

20   Evans to Search Committee (Burton, Kureishi, Cruickshank, Burge, Granger and Hare), 21 March 1988 (ME). Caryl Churchill's name was subsequently added, together with a staff representative.

21   Interview with the author, 22 October 1996.

22   Interview, 16 January 1997.

23   Council was told on 19 May of forty-five applicants, of whom eleven had been shortlisted. *GQ Magazine* published in March 1992 a piece by Suzie Mackenzie, 'Intrigue at Court'. The article carried allegations by Evans against Stafford-Clark. *GQ* settled an action for libel out of court for £10,000.

24   See 'Poised for change', *Plays International*, August 1988, and '100 years of beating the establishment', *Stage*, 22 September 1988.

25   Report in the *Stage*, 27 October 1988.

26   Pulford to Evans, 16 March 1989. The evolution of the play is described by Brenton in the *Guardian*, 15 April 1989.

27   *Stage*, 30 March 1989.

28   *Daily Telegraph*, 14 September 1989.

29   The piece, 'Court in the crossfire' by Bryan Appleyard, appeared in the *Sunday Times Magazine*, 4 June 1989. Evans's letter to Stafford-Clark is dated 9 June 1989 (ME).

30   Churchill to Evans, 3 November 1989.

31   Evans to Churchill, 6 November 1989.

32   Evans to Mortimer, 20 March 1989.

33   Mortimer to Hare, 13 July 1990.

34   See also the *Independent*, 23 October 1990.

35   Jane Edwardes, 'A quiet year in Sloane Square', *Plays International*, February 1991.

36   'The art of survival', *Guardian*, 29 November 1990.

37   See the *Guardian*, 6 September 1995, for an article by Christine Eccles on the progress of the play.

38   *Evening Standard*, 2 May 1991.

39   See Eccles, *Guardian*, 6 September 1995. The *Observer* piece appeared on 8 September 1991.

40   Interview with the author, 21 March 1995.

41   Interview with the author, 4 February 1998.

42   Gaskill, interview, 22 October 1996.

43   Stafford-Clark, interview, 13 December 1996.

44   Herbert, interview, 21 March 1995.

45   Interview with the author, 9 July 1996.

46   *Evening Standard*, 22 October 1991.

47   Interview, 4 February 1998.

48   *Ibid.*

49   Interview, 21 March 1995.

50   *Observer*, 10 November 1991. For a later account of the selection process, see Mackenzie, 'Intrigue at Court'.

51   Stafford-Clark to Hare, 21 May 1992.

52   See Claire Armitstead, *Guardian*, 8 January 1993; Michael Coveney, *Observer*, 10 January 1993; Peter Roberts, *Plays International*, January 1993.

Afterword

1   Interview with the author, 4 February 1998.

2   Interview with the author, 7 March 1997.

3   Interview, 4 February 1998.

4   *Guardian*, 28 February 1994.

5   See *Plays International*, April 1994.

6   Interview with the author, 21 March 1995.
7   *Observer*, 3 July 1994.
8   Helen Osborne to Stuart Burge, 16 January 1995. Almost unnoticed was the death on 17 January 1995 of Isador Caplan, the ESC's solicitor at its inception.
9   Interview with the author, 4 February 1998.
10   Interview, 4 February 1998.
11   Wardle, 247.
12   *Ibid.*, 255.
13   Interview with the author, 22 October 1996.
14   *Omnibus: Royal Court Diaries*, BBC1, 25 October 1996.
15   Interview, 4 February 1998.
16   *Ibid.*
17   *Plays International*, October 1996.
18   *Ibid.* See also the *Observer*, 24 September 1995.
19   *Plays International*, October 1996.
20   Interview, 22 October 1996.
21   *Plays International*, February 1996.
22   See Michael Coveney, *Observer*, 7 January 1996, and the *Stage*, 14 March 1996, respectively.
23   *Independent*, 2 October 1996.
24   *Guardian*, 14 May 1997.
25   Interview, 4 February 1998.
26   *Guardian*, 25 November 1998.
27   *Ibid.*

Select bibliography

Primary sources

Privately held papers of: J. E. Blacksell; Neville Blond; George Devine; Earl of Harewood; Greville Poke.

Institutional archives: Ronald Duncan (University of Plymouth); Oscar Lewenstein (British Theatre Museum); The John Lewis Partnership papers (Stevenage); the Harry Ransom Humanities Research Center, University of Texas at Austin.

English Stage Company

Minutes of committees, 26 Oct. 1954–9 Dec. 1997.

Memorandum and Articles of Association of the English Stage Society Ltd., incorporated 16 Oct. 1954.

Aims and objects, 6 drafts, 1 Nov. 1955–April 1956.

'Memoranda on the Royal Court Theatre Studio', Feb. 1963–Aug. 1964 and Aug. 1964– Sept. 1965.

Taped interviews with the author

Lindsay Anderson, 5 Dec. 1984.

Lindsay Anderson and David Storey, 29 April 1985.

Pam Brighton, 13 Dec. 1983.

Stuart Burge, 9 July and 14 Aug. 1996.

Richard Butler, 7 Jan. 1984.

Graham Cowley, 4 Feb. 1998.

Stephen Daldry, 4 Feb. 1998.

Matthew Evans, 16 Jan. 1997.

William Gaskill, 13 Dec. 1983 and 22 Oct. 1996.

Earl of Harewood, 11 Sept. 1984 and 5 Aug. 1993.

Margaret Harris, 18 Oct. 1995.

Jocelyn Herbert, 21 March 1995.

Clare Jeffery, 28 Sept. 1995.

Oscar Lewenstein, 14 Dec. 1983.

Greville Poke, 18 Sept. 1984, 9 March 1994 and 3 Feb. 1995.

Max Stafford-Clark, 21 Feb. 1985, 13 Dec. 1996 and 7 March 1997.

Nicholas Wright, 3 Oct. 1996.

Letters

Mike Alfreds to Max Stafford-Clark, 1 Dec. 1985 (SB).

Lindsay Anderson to: Greville Poke, Nov. 1959, 21 Jan. 1973, 28 June 1974 (GP); George Devine, Easter 1959 (4 letters), 21 June, 8 Oct., 25 Nov. and 8 Dec. 1960 (JH); John Blatchley, 25 Nov. 1960 (JH); Earl of Harewood, 1 Dec. 1960 and 27 Nov. 1974 (GH); Oscar Lewenstein, 6 Sept. 1972 (BTM); Hugh Cudlipp, 27 March 1975 (LA); Philip Roberts, 2 May 1984 (PR); Matthew Evans, 5 Dec. 1984 (ME).

John Arden to: Tony Richardson, 6 May 1958 (JH); George Devine, 6 May, 3 and 31 July, 5 Sept. 1958 (HRHRC); Court Council, 5 Sept. 1958 (JEB).

Peggy Ashcroft to: Neville Blond, 3 Jan. 1957, 12 Dec. 1958 (GP); Robin Fox, 18 July 1958 (GP); Greville Poke, Feb. 1960 (GP); Earl of Harewood, 6 Sept. 1962 (GH).

Basil Ashmore to Neville Blond, 11 Feb. 1955 (GP).

Assistant Comptroller, Lord Chamberlain's Office, to Miriam Brickman, 2 May 1957 (GP).

Frith Banbury to George Devine, 3 Aug. 1950 (JH).

Hugh Beaumont to George Devine, 1 April 1953 and 18 April 1956 (JH).

Eric Bentley to George Devine, 17 Aug. 1956 (JH).

Eric Bessborough (Viscount Duncannon) to Neville Blond, 26 April 1956 (GP).

J. E. Blacksell to: Earl of Harewood, 4 Jan. and 15 June 1954 (GH), 25 Nov. 1964 (RDA), 10 Dec. 1964, 18 Jan. 1965 (JEB); Caryl Jenner, 14 Oct. and 15 Nov. 1954 (JEB); Ronald Duncan, 18 Jan. 1965 (JEB); Greville Poke, 18 Jan. 1965 (JEB).

SELECT BIBLIOGRAPHY

John Blatchley to George Devine, 19 Aug., 19 and 23 Nov. 1960 (JH).

Neville Blond to: Isador Caplan, 22 Dec. 1954, 10 Feb. 1955 (GP); Greville Poke, 23 Feb. 1955, 24 April and 20 Dec. 1956, 16 July 1957, 6 Jan. 1960, 20 Jan. 1967 (GP); Earl of Harewood, 2 June and 23 Nov. 1955 (GH); Cecil Madden, 7 July 1955 (GP); O. B. Miller, 19 Jan. and 3 Feb. 1956 (JLP); Reginald Kennedy-Cox, 19 Jan. and 5 Nov. 1956 (GP); George Devine, 9 Feb. 1955, 25 Jan. 1956 and 5 April 1962 (JH); Benjamin Britten, 30 Jan. 1956 (GP); Eric Bessborough, 18 July 1956 (GP); Michael Hallifax, 6 Dec. 1956 (GP); Jo Hodgkinson, 28 Dec. 1956 (GP); J. E. Blacksell, 24 Jan. 1958 (JEB); Harry Cookson, 12 Jan. 1960; Bill Williams, 27 July 1962 (GP).

Claire Bloom to George Devine, 17 Aug. 1960 (JH).

Edward Bond to: Neville Blond, 6 Nov. 1966 (GP); Toby Cole, 4 Dec. 1967 (PR); Greville Poke, 8 Nov. 1974 (GP); ESC Council, 21 Jan. 1977 (GP); Matthew Evans, 7 May 1988 (ME).

Bertolt Brecht to: George Devine, 2 Nov. 1955, 24 July and 17 Dec. 1956 (HRHRC); Oscar Lewenstein, 8 and 17 Dec. 1955 (BTM).

Howard Brenton to ESC Council, 21 Jan. 1977 (GP).

Benjamin Britten to: George Devine, 27 March 1956 (GP); Neville Blond, early 1956 (GP).

Peter Brook to Oscar Lewenstein, 24 Jan. 1959 (BTM).

Ivor Brown to Greville Poke, 16 Aug. and 14 Sept. 1955 (GP).

Elaine Brunner to Earl of Harewood, 30 Oct. 1954 (GH).

Jean Bullwinkle to Matthew Evans, 14 Feb. 1986, 17 June 1987 (ME).

Stuart Burge to: ESC Council, 3 Oct. 1977, 20 Jan. 1987 (GP); Philip Roberts, 17 July 1996 (PR).

Glen Byam Shaw to George Devine, 17 and 21 Feb., 31 March, 7, 12 and 20 April, 25 June, 10, 15 and 26 July, 10 Aug. 1956 (JH).

Denis Cannan to George Devine, 31 Jan. 1957 (JH).

Isador Caplan to Earl of Harewood and Greville Poke, 11 Nov. 1954 (GH).

David Cesarani to Michael Hastings, 28 Nov. 1985 (ME).

George Chamberlain to George Devine, 31 Oct. 1961 (JH).

Paul Channon to Greville Poke, 7 Nov. 1969 (GP).

Caryl Churchill to Matthew Evans, 3 Nov. 1989 (ME).

Kenneth Clark to George Devine, 12 May and 17 June 1953 (JH).

Harry Cookson to: Oscar Lewenstein, 9 Oct. 1958, 6 Jan. 1959 (BTM); Neville Blond, 2 and 16 Jan. 1960 (GP).

Hugh Cottrell to Greville Poke, 28 Nov. 1955 (GP).

Edward Gordon Craig to George Devine, 24 March 1956 (JH).

David Cregan to Neville Blond, 1 Nov. 1966 (GP).

Simon Curtis to William Gaskill, 21 April 1987 (WG).

Nigel Dennis to: George Devine, 5 Sept. 1955, 19 Jan. and 21 Feb. 1956 (HRHRC); Tony Richardson, early 1956 (HRHRC).

David Deutsch to Neville Blond, 22 April 1958 (GP).

George Devine to: Michel Saint-Denis, 3 Oct. 1943, 10 June 1945, 14 April 1954, 24 Jan. 1957, 17 April 1961, 24 Oct. 1963 (JH); Laurence Olivier, 29 July 1951, 9 Jan. 1959, 10 Aug. 1961 (JH); Mary Hutchinson, 15 March 1953, 27 Dec. 1956 (HRHRC), 7 Jan. 1957, 11 July 1961; Sebastian Earl, 20 March 1953 (JH); O. B. Miller, 23, 30 April and 6 May 1953, 28 Dec. 1955, 11 April 1956 (JH); Alfred Esdaile, 12 May 1953 (JH); Ronald Duncan, 23 Jan. 1955 (RDA), 15 May 1956 (HRHRC), 22 Dec. 1959 (JH); Nigel Dennis, early 1955 (JH); Neville Blond, 26 Feb., 4 and 5 May 1955 (JH), 30 July 1956, 2 Jan., 8 Aug., 3 Oct., 11 Nov. 1958, 14 Jan., 13 Feb., 11 May 1959, 12 Jan. and 27 Sept. 1960, 11 Jan., 22 and 25 June, 8 Nov. 1961, 6 April 1962, 14 Oct. 1964 (GP); Ella Winter, 8 Dec. 1955 (HRHRC); Bertolt Brecht, 10 and 22 Dec. 1955 (HRHRC); Roger Stevens, 27 Dec. 1955 (JH); Reginald Kennedy-Cox, 29 Dec. 1955, 30 Jan. 1956 (JH); W. H. Auden, 23 Jan. 1956 (JH); Greville Poke, 28 Feb. 1956, 10 and 24 Oct. 1958, 2 Nov. 1959, 16 Oct. 1964 (JH); George Fearon, March and 25 Oct. 1956 (GP); Arthur Miller, 11 April 1956 (GP); J. E. Blacksell, 5 July 1956 (JH); Orson Welles, early 1956 (JH); Terence Rattigan, May 1956 (JH); Royce Ryton, 1 June 1956 (JH); Eric Bentley, 26 July, 17, 21 Aug. and 12 Nov. 1956 (HRHRC); Elisabeth Hauptmann-Dessau, 5 July and 1 Oct. 1956 (HRHRC); Helene Weigel, 4 Nov. 1956 (HRHRC); the Berliner Ensemble, 4 Nov. 1956 (HRHRC); John Osborne, 4 Oct. 1957, 15 and 24 Oct. 1958, 23 Feb. 1960 (JH); Alec Guinness, 24 March 1958 (JH); John Gielgud, 24 Nov. 1958, 9 Jan. 1959 (JH); William Gaskill, 24 Oct. 1958, 28 April 1965 (JH); Tony Richardson, 9 Jan. and 21 May 1959 (JH);

Anthony Page, 16 June 1959 (JH); Harry Cookson, 12 Jan. 1960 (GP); Lindsay Anderson, Anthony Page and William Gaskill, 19 Feb. 1960 (JH); Arnold Wesker, 23 Feb. 1960 (JH); Lindsay Anderson, Easter 1959 (JH); Bertrand Russell, 16 Oct. 1960 (JH); Earl of Harewood, 2 Nov. 1960 (GP), 8 March 1962 (GH); Bernard Levin, 19 Feb. 1962 (GP); Glen Byam Shaw, 21 April 1963 (JH); Oscar Lewenstein, 17 Oct. 1963 (JH); 'Open letter to the Brazilian theatre', 1963 (PR).

John Dexter to John Osborne, 5 Nov. 1980 (GP).

Doreen Dixon to: Neville Blond, 28 Jan. 1964 (GP); Edward Bond, 5 April 1965 (PR).

Ronald Duncan to: Neville Blond, 19 Nov. 1954 (GP); George Devine, 21 and 25 Jan. 1955 (JH); John Whiting, 11 March 1955 (RDA); Peter Ustinov, 11 March 1955 (RDA); Greville Poke, 24 July 1958 (GP).

Tom Eastwood to Earl of Harewood, 9 June 1956 (GH).

T. S. Eliot to Countess of Harewood, 13 May 1954 (GH).

Alfred Esdaile to Neville Blond, 26 April and 12 Nov. 1956 (GP).

Matthew Evans to: Jo Beddoe and Max Stafford-Clark, 18 Jan. 1985 (ME); David Hare, 28 Feb. (HRHRC) and 4 March 1985 (ME); Lindsay Anderson, 13 Dec. 1985 (ME); ESC Council, 3 March 1987 (SB); William Gaskill, 7 April 1987 (WG); John Mortimer, 20 March 1989 (ME); Gordon Taylor, 10 Aug. 1989 (ME); Caryl Churchill, 6 Nov. 1989 (ME).

Anthony Everitt to John Mortimer, 27 Sept. 1990 (SB).

George Fearon to: Greville Poke, 1 March and 5 Oct. 1955, 26 Oct. 1956 (GP); George Devine, 12 March and 14 Nov. 1956 (JH).

Anthony Field to Jon Catty, 26 Jan. 1976 (GP).

Albert Finney to Greville Poke, 6 June 1973 (GP).

Robin Fox to: Earl of Harewood, 23 Dec. 1959, 14 Aug. 1968 (GH); Neville Blond, 4 Dec. 1967 (GP).

Lovat Fraser to George Devine, 1 Oct. 1951 (JH).

Clement Freud to: Greville Poke, 14 Jan. 1956 (GP); members of the Royal Court Theatre Club, 10 June 1959 (GP).

Christopher Fry to Ronald Duncan, 25 July 1954 (HRHRC).

William Gaskill to Earl of Harewood, 3 Aug. 1965, 7 Feb., 20 May, 14 July 1967, 9 and 15 April 1968 23 Dec. 1969 (GH); Ronald Duncan, 27

Sept. 1965 (RDA); Greville Poke, 3 May 1966 (GP); Neville Blond, 17 Oct. 1967 (GP); Lt.-Col. J. F. D. Johnstone, 15 Jan. 1968 (GP); Matthew Evans, 18 and 28 March, 12 April 1987 (WG).

John Gielgud to George Devine, 30 March 1954, 13 and 27 July 1956 (JH).

Clive Goodwin to George Devine, 20 Jan. 1959 (JH).

Frank Granville Barker to George Fearon, 5 Nov. 1956 (GP).

Hugh Carlton Greene to Greville Poke, 14 March 1978 (GP).

T. R. Grieve to George Devine, 8 April 1953 (JH).

Alec Guinness to George Devine, 11 March 1958, 14 Oct. 1963 (JH).

Peter Hall to George Devine, 3 May 1959 (JH).

Michael Hallifax to: Michael Balcon, 10 Nov. 1956 (GP); Neville Blond, 4 and 8 Dec. 1956 (GP).

David Hare to: ESC Council, 22 Jan. 1977 (GP); Matthew Evans, 25 Feb. 1985 (ME).

Earl of Harewood to: Ronald Duncan, 8 Aug. 1954 (HRHRC), 30 Nov. 1955, 27 Nov. 1956 (RDA); Dr Rennert, 19 Nov. 1954 (GP); George Devine, 21 Feb. 1955 (GH); Neville Blond, 12 and 27 May 1955, 8 Oct. 1958, 2 Feb. 1959, 26 March 1965, 23 Dec. 1969, 12 Jan. 1970 (GP); Greville Poke, 15 July 1955, 15 and 19 Nov. 1956 (GP); Tom Eastwood, 14 and 24 June 1956 (GP); Tony Richardson, 22 Oct. 1956 (GP); Robin Fox, 30 Dec. 1959 (GH); J. E. Blacksell, 7 Dec. 1964 (JEB); William Gaskill, 17 July 1967 (GH); Lindsay Anderson, 8 Jan. 1974 (LA).

Countess of Harewood to HRH the Princess Margaret, 12 March 1959 (GH).

Margaret Harris to Michel Saint-Denis, Jan. 1966 (JB).

Rex Harrison to George Devine, 2 Aug. 1961 (JH).

Lawrence Harvey to Oscar Lewenstein, 18 Jan. and (cable) 16 Feb. 1961 (BTM).

Michael Hastings to: Earl of Harewood, March 1960 (GH); Greville Poke, 19 May 1960 (GP); Neville Blond, 10 July 1960 (GP); George Devine, 29 Aug. 1960 (JH).

Elisabeth Hauptmann-Dessau to: Oscar Lewenstein, 29 Nov. 1955 (BTM); George Devine, 2 Feb., 3, 24 July and 25 Sept. 1956 (JH).

Jocelyn Herbert to: ESC Council, 24 Jan. 1977 (GP); Greville Poke, 17

May 1974, 27 Jan. 1977 (GP); Matthew Evans, 10 Feb. and 31 March 1987 (ME); Max Stafford-Clark, 4 Feb. 1998 (MSC).

Peter Hillmore to Matthew Evans, 15 April 1987 (ME).

J. L. Hodgkinson to: Greville Poke, 9 Feb. 1955, 1 June 1956 (GP); George Devine, 7 March 1955 (JH); Neville Blond, 4 Oct. 1956 (GP).

Elizabeth Jane Howard to George Devine, 4 Aug. 1956 (JH).

George Hume to George Devine, 15 Oct. 1951 (JH).

Mary Hutchinson to George Devine, 22 Nov. 1959 (JH).

Paul Jackman *et al.*, Letter to the Court, 19 June 1956 (JH).

Barry Jackson to Earl of Harewood, 1 March 1955 (GH).

Ann Jellicoe to Neville Blond, 31 Oct. 1966 (GP).

Caryl Jenner to J. E. Blacksell, 27 Oct., 7 Nov. and 21 Dec. 1957 (PR).

Reginald Kennedy-Cox to: Greville Poke, 3 March, 2 Aug., 30 Nov. 1955, 22 Jan. 1956 (GP); Neville Blond, 10 May, 5 Dec. 1955 (GP); 22 Jan. 1956 (GP).

Max Kester to Oscar Lewenstein, 1 Oct. 1954, 14 Feb. 1955 (BTM).

Robert Kidd to Greville Poke, 10 Jan. 1977 (GP).

John Lehmann to George Devine, 30 Aug. 1955, 24 Aug. 1956 (HRHRC).

Vivien Leigh to Neville Blond, 22 July 1959 (GP).

Vivien Leigh, Noël Coward, Laurence Olivier, telegram to Neville Blond, 29 July 1959 (GP).

Oscar Lewenstein to: Ronald Duncan, 14 and 29 April, 19 May, 2 June, 13, 16 and 21 July 1954 (RDA); Jan van Loewen, 22 July and 8 Sept. 1954, 22 June 1955 (BTM); Mark Blitzstein, 11 Aug. 1954 (BTM); Ruth Berlau, 14 Aug. 1954 (BTM); Helen Harvey, 10 Sept. 1954 (BTM); Greville Poke, 8 April 1955, 25 Sept. 1962, 24 Jan. 1977 (GP); Neville Blond, 29 July 1955, 12 and 21 April, 25 and 27 June, 18 and 27 July 1956, 4 March 1957 (GP); Bertolt Brecht, 25 Nov. and 13 Dec. 1955, 7 Feb. 1956 (BTM); Elisabeth Hauptmann-Dessau, 5 Dec. 1955, 7 Feb. 1956 (BTM); John Willett, 22 May and 24 Aug. 1956 (BTM); Audrey Wood, 3 Nov. 1956 (BTM); Michael Hallifax, 15 Nov. 1956 (GP); Jean-Paul Sartre, 25 Jan. 1957 (BTM); Cecil Tennant, 7 May 1957 (BTM); Harry Cookson, 13 Oct. 1958 (BTM); Albert Finney, 21 Nov. 1959 (BTM); Peggy Ramsay, 2 Dec. 1959 (BTM); Lindsay Anderson, 10 Dec. 1959 (BTM); Zero Mostel, 18 Feb. 1960 (BTM); Laurence Olivier, 18

Feb. 1960 (BTM); Eugene Ionesco, 17 Aug. 1960 (BTM); Diane Cilento, 19 Dec. 1960 (BTM); Bertice Reading, 12 Jan. 1961 (BTM); Paul Robeson, 16 Feb. 1961 (BTM); Robin Fox, 17 Feb. 1961 (BTM); Charles Wood, 3 July 1964 (BTM).

Spedan Lewis to: Alec Guinness, 7 Oct. 1939 (JLP); Sybil Thorndike, 30 April and 4 May 1953, 11 June 1956 (JLP).

Laurier Lister to Neville Blond, 4 Aug. 1955 (GP).

Christopher Logue to Oscar Lewenstein, 15 June 1959 (BTM).

Anthony Lousada to George Devine, 16 Feb., 25 March and 24 July 1953, 10 Jan. 1955 (JH).

Carson McCullers to Tony Richardson, 11 Jan. 1957 (HRHRC).

Colin MacInnes to George Devine, 16 June 1959 (JH).

Cecil Madden to Neville Blond, 11 July 1955, 26 Sept. 1956 (GP).

HRH the Princess Margaret to Countess of Harewood, 23 March 1959 (GH).

M.C.A. (England) Ltd. to Oscar Lewenstein, 25 April 1956 (BTM).

O. B. Miller to: George Devine, 21, 29 April and 5 May 1953, 19 Dec. 1955, 16 Jan. and 14 June 1956 (JH); Sybil Thorndike, 29 April 1953 (JLP); Greville Poke, 4 May 1956 (GP); Neville Blond, 14 June 1956 (GP).

Tanya Moiseiwitsch to Sam Wanamaker, 28 Nov. 1955 (HRHRC).

Henry Moore to George Devine, 29 Nov. 1952 (JH).

Tina Morduch to: George Devine, 10 Aug. 1956 (JH); Robin Day, 18 April 1958 (GP).

John Mortimer to: David Hare, 13 July 1990 (HRHRC); Peter Palumbo, 28 Sept. 1990 (SB); Stuart Burge, April 1991 (SB).

Allardyce Nicoll to George Devine, 10 Aug. 1953 (JH).

Sean O'Casey to George Devine, 19 March and 22 July 1959 (HRHRC).

Duncan Openheimer to George Devine, 24 and 31 March 1953 (JH).

Helen Osborne to Stuart Burge, 16 Jan. 1995 (SB).

John Osborne to: Greville Poke, 24 Feb. 1957 (GP); George Devine, 17 Oct. 1958 (JH); Hugh Willatt, 17 Aug. 1970, 12 Sept. 1977 (GP); Oscar Lewenstein, 17 Aug. 1970 (BTM); Gillian Diamond, 31 Jan. 1971 (HRHRC); ESC Council, 21 May 1975 (HRHRC); Lord Goodman, 13 July 1977 (HRHRC).

Anthony Page to: George Devine, Spring 1959, three letters *c.* June 1960

(HRHRC); Colonel Penn (Lord Chamberlain's office), 3 April 1965 (BTM); Kenneth Tynan, 24 Feb. 1969 (HRHRC).

Thane Parker to George Devine, 18 June 1953 (JH).

John Piper to Greville Poke, 17 Nov. 1954, 13 March 1955 (GP).

Greville Poke to: John Piper, 3 Nov. 1954, 11 Feb. 1955 (GP); Neville Blond, 6 June, 30 July, 22 Sept., 24 Oct., 23 Nov. and 31 Dec. 1955, 26 Sept., 16 Oct. and 8 Nov. 1957, 30 Sept. 1958, 2 May 1966, 18 Jan. 1967 (GP); Alfred Esdaile, 1 July, 30 Aug. and 30 Nov. 1955, 21 Jan. and 7 April 1956 (GP); Donald Wolfit, 23 July 1955 (GP); Isadore Kerman, 9 and 13 Aug. 1955 (GP); Ronald Duncan, 31 Dec. 1955, 28 March 1956, 22 Sept. 1962 (GP); John Minton, 7 June 1956 (GP); Isador Caplan, 13 Dec. 1956 (GP); John Osborne, 22 Feb. 1957, 13 Oct. 1980 (GP); George Devine, 12 Oct. 1957 (GP); Oscar Lewenstein, 5 Jan. 1960 (GP); J. E. Blacksell, 13 Nov. 1972 (GP); Earl of Harewood, 18 June 1973 (GP).

Richard Pulford to Matthew Evans, 16 March 1989 (ME).

Peggy Ramsay to: Oscar Lewenstein, 17 March, 28 Sept. and 28 Oct. 1959, 8, 23 Feb. and 2 Aug. 1960 (BTM); George Devine, 12 Dec. 1960 (JH).

Terence Rattigan to George Devine, 9 May 1956 (JH).

Jane Rayne to: Matthew Evans, 18 Feb. 1987 (ME); John Mortimer, 6 and 8 Nov. 1991 (SB).

William Rees-Mogg to David Hare, 27 March 1984 (HRHRC).

Tony Richardson to: Lord Goodman, 20 March 1953 (JH); Ronald Searle, 15 March 1956 (JH); Eric Bentley, 4 July 1956 (JH); Earl of Harewood, 7 Sept. 1956 (GH); Greville Poke, 11 Sept. 1956 (GP); Neville Blond, 17 Dec. 1956 (GP); Carson McCullers, 2 Jan. 1957 (GP).

Luke Rittner to Matthew Evans, 9 Oct. 1985, 14 March 1988 (ME).

James Roose-Evans to George Devine, 7 Jan. 1960 (JH).

Jean Rowntree to George Devine, 29 March 1953 (JH).

Bertrand Russell to George Devine, 25 Sept. 1960 (JH).

Lord Sainsbury to Greville Poke, 13 Oct. 1975 (GP).

Ronald Searle to Tony Richardson, 14 March 1956 (JH).

Michel Saint-Denis to Valentine Tessier, Winter 1967 (JB).

Society of West End Managers to Greville Poke, 12 March 1956 (GP).

Wole Soyinka to Greville Poke, 25 Feb. 1966 (GP).

Stephen Spender to George Devine, 18 April 1956 (JH).

Max Stafford-Clark to: Peggy Ramsay, 8 March 1981 (MSC); Dickon Reed, 16 Feb. 1985 (SB); William Gaskill, 23 April 1987 (WG); Brian Rix, 10 Feb. and 2 March 1989 (SB); John Mortimer, 12 May 1991 (SB); David Hare, 21 May 1992 (HRHRC); Jocelyn Herbert, 23 March 1998 (MSC).

Strand Electric Company to George Devine, 16 Dec. 1955 (JH).

Gordon Taylor to Peter Palumbo, 22 June and 24 July 1989 (SB).

Cecil Tennant to Neville Blond, 26 Sept. 1956 (GP).

Theatre Writers' Union to Matthew Evans, 15 March 1987 (ME).

Gwyn Thomas to George Devine, 9 April 1959 (JH).

Sybil Thorndike to: George Devine, 14 and 30 April 1953, 27 July 1956 (JH); Spedan Lewis, 2 and 5 May 1953 (JLP).

Mark Turner to George Devine, 21 Sept. 1953, 27 March 1956 (JH).

Jan van Loewen to: Max Kester, 6 Oct. 1954 (BTM); Oscar Lewenstein, 22 June 1955 (BTM).

Margery Vosper to Oscar Lewenstein, 7 and 10 Sept. 1955 (BTM).

Sam Wanamaker to: Neville Blond, 4 Oct. 1955 (GP); Bertolt Brecht, 20 Dec. 1955 (JH); Lotte Lenya, 21 Dec. 1955 (JH); Greville Poke, 3 July 1957 (GP); Oscar Lewenstein, 6 Dec. 1957 (BTM).

John Whiting to George Devine, 23 Aug. 1953 (JH).

Oliver Wilkinson to Philip Roberts, 5 and 26 Aug. 1995 (PR).

John Willett to Oscar Lewenstein, 10 April and 22 Aug. 1956 (BTM).

W. E. Williams to: George Devine, 10 Nov. 1952, 27 April and 21 Oct. 1953, 14 Sept. and 19 Oct. 1954 (JH); Neville Blond, 17 Jan. and 31 July 1956, 7 Feb. 1957, 30 July 1962 (GP).

Henry Williamson to Countess of Harewood, 16 April 1954 (GH).

John Wilmot to George Devine, 8 Jan. 1962 (JH).

Colin Wilson to Ronald Duncan, 28 Sept., 4, 14 and 24 Oct. 1957 (RDA).

Donald Wolfit to Greville Poke, 18 and 27 July 1955 (GP).

James Woolf to Oscar Lewenstein, 12 Jan. 1961 (BTM).

Other primary documents

'A theatre "grid"', The Arts Council of Great Britain, 16 July 1953, Public Record Office, Misc. Papers, 1953/37, EL4/86.

Arts Council of Great Britain, Minutes of a Council Meeting, 17 Nov.
1953, Public Record Office, EL4/57.

Report of the Arts Council appraisal team, Arts Council, Aug. 1989.

Bolar, Gordon, 'The Sunday night productions without decor at the
Royal Court Theatre, 1957–1975', unpublished Ph.D. dissertation submitted to Louisiana State University, 1984.

Bond, Edward, *The Writer's Theatre*, issued with the programme of his
Lear, 29 Sept. 1971.

British Transport Commission, Lease dated 15 Jan. 1953 between the
Commission and First Investa Securities Ltd.

Cadogan, Lease dated 23 May 1952 between Cadogan Estates Company
and First Investa Securities Ltd.

Devine, George, 'The Old Vic and its development towards the British
National Theatre', British Council lecture, n.d.

'Modern English methods of theatre training', British Council
lecture, n.d.

'Problems of modern play production', British Council lecture,
Oct. 1948.

'Royal Court Theatre scheme', 4 drafts. Draft 1 dated 16 March,
draft 4 dated 13 Aug. 1953.

'Memo on organisation and finance. Prepared for The John Lewis
Partnership', 12 April 1953.

'First notes on new theatre', 6 Jan. 1955; 'Thoughts on the
construction of a new theatre', 7 Jan. 1955; 'Further
notes', 8 Jan. 1955; 'Percy's first reactions', 8 Jan. 1955;
'Additional thoughts by Margaret Harris', 15 Jan. 1955;
'Tony Richardson's comments', 18 Jan. 1955; 'Notes on
the Kingsway', 23 Jan. 1955; 'Further details on the new
stage', 15 Feb. 1955.

'Technical requirements by the English Stage Company to
achieve the kind of stage desired', n.d.

'The stage of the Royal Court', 8 Sept. 1955.

'Notes on stage lighting at the Royal Court', 8 Dec. 1955.

'Objects of the company and their fulfilment', Nov. 1955.

'Autobiography. Part one. Chapter one. The beginnings', n.d.

'How it all started', n.d.

'Memorandum on artistic policy – aims and objects', 13 May 1960.

'The Royal Court', ts. of interview with Alan Brien, Sept. 1965 (JH). Version printed in *Sunday Telegraph*, 12 Sept. 1965.

Duncan, Ronald, 'Notes on the artistic policy of the English Stage Company', 1 March 1960.

John Lewis Partnership, 'Founder to Chairman', Memo. 39434, 24 Nov. 1955.

Chairman to Legal Adviser, Memo. 745, 2 March 1956.

Legal Adviser to Chairman, Memo. 3266, 5 June 1956.

'Memorandum on a proposed company sponsored by Mr Saint-Denis', Oct. 1938.

Osborne, John, Speech at the Memorial meeting for George Devine, Royal Court, 18 Feb. 1966.

Radio Newsreel, BBC Light Programme, Edition no. 2613, 21 Jan. 1955.

Taw and Torridge Festival, Minutes of the fourth meeting, 24 Oct. 1953; first Council meeting, 5 Dec. 1953.

Williams, W. E. 'Working party on the "theatre grid". A personal impression', Arts Council of Great Britain, Council paper 344, Feb. 1954, Public Record Office, EL4/58.

Secondary sources

Place of publication is London unless otherwise stated.

Allsop, Kenneth, 'Poezzing at the Court', *Spectator*, 1 May 1959.

Anderson, Lindsay, 'Vital theatre?', *Encore*, vol. 4, no. 2, Nov.–Dec. 1957.

'Glory days', *Plays and Players*, May 1986.

Ansorge, Peter, *Disrupting the spectacle: five years of experimental and fringe theatre in Britain* (Pitman, 1975).

Appleyard, Bryan, 'Court in the crossfire', *Sunday Times Magazine*, 4 June 1989.

Arden, John *et al.*, 'Court theatre dispute', Letter to *The Times*, 15 March 1960.

(and 86 other writers), Letter to the *Guardian*, 21 Nov. 1994.

Armitstead, Claire, 'Knackered', *Guardian*, 14 May 1997.

Arts Council of Great Britain, 'Report on the Needs of the Subsidised Theatre in London', 1967.

Bannister, Winifred, 'Opening of the Belgrade Theatre', *Theatre World*, May 1958.

Benedict, David, 'Interview with Sarah Kane', *Independent on Sunday*, 22 Jan. 1995.

'Bertolt Brecht: an iconoclast in the theatre', *Times Literary Supplement*, 9 March 1956.

'Beyond the ironing board', *Plays and Players*, May 1986.

Billington, Michael, *Peggy Ashcroft* (John Murray, 1988).

   One night stands: a critic's view of British theatre from 1971 to 1991 (Nick Hern Books, 1993).

   The life and work of Harold Pinter (Faber, 1997).

Blond, Elaine, *Marks of distinction* (Vallentine, Mitchell, 1988).

Bond, Edward, *Letters*, selected and edited by Ian Stuart, Harwood Academic Publishers, vol.1 (1994); vol. 2 (1995); vol. 3 (1996).

   'A blast at our smug theatre', *Guardian*, 28 Jan. 1995.

Brown, Ivor, 'Theatre and life', *Observer*, 13 May 1945.

   Theatre 1954–5 (Max Reinhardt, 1955).

Brenton, Howard, Letter to the *Guardian*, 22 March 1984.

   'The art of survival', *Guardian*, 29 Nov. 1990.

Browne, Terry, *Playwrights' theatre: the English Stage Company at the Royal Court* (Pitman, 1975).

Brustein, Robert, 'Repertory fever', *Harper's Magazine*, Dec. 1960.

Bull, John, *New British political dramatists* (Macmillan, 3rd edn., 1991).

   Stage right: crisis and recovery in British contemporary mainstream theatre (Macmillan, 1994).

Burge, Stuart, Letter to the *Guardian*, 2 Oct. 1990.

Caine, Michael, *His autobiography: what's it all about?* (Arrow, 1993).

Callow, Simon, *Being an actor* (Methuen, 1984).

'Call to big business to support the arts', *Coventry Evening Telegraph*, 2 March 1955.

'Censor's whim', *Evening Standard*, 11 Feb. 1958.

Chambers, Colin, *Peggy. The life of Margaret Ramsay, play agent* (Nick Hern Books, 1997).

Chambers, Peter, 'Dame Peggy cuts a rug', *Evening Standard*, 3 April
  1958.
'Change of policy at Court theatre', *The Times*, 7 Feb. 1956.
Chapman, Gerald, 'Education and the Royal Court', *Plays and Players*,
  May 1978.
Churchill, Caryl, 'Not ordinary, not safe', *The Twentieth Century*,
  vol. 168, Nov. 1960.
Conway, Harold, 'This dirt must not spread', *Daily Sketch*, 30 Dec.
  1957.
Courtney, Cathy (ed.), *Jocelyn Herbert. A theatre workbook* (Art Books
  International, 1993).
Coveney, Michael, 'Court in the act', *Plays and Players*, May 1986.
Craig, Sandy (ed.), *Dreams and deconstructions: alternative theatre in
  Britain* (Ambergate: Amber Lane Press, 1980).
Croft, Giles, 'Interview with Stephen Daldry', *Royal National Theatre
  Platform Papers*, no. 3, 1993.
Daldry, Stephen, 'Writing the future', *Guardian*, 7 Sept. 1994.
  'Royal Court moves', *Plays International*, Oct. 1996.
Darlington, W. A., 'Unwelcome at Court', *Daily Telegraph*, 16 Feb.
  1959.
Darlow, Michael and Hodson, Gillian, *Terence Rattigan: the man and
  his work* (Quartet Books, 1979).
Daubeny, Peter, *My world of theatre* (Cape, 1971).
De Jongh, Nicholas, 'Court in the act', *Guardian*, 5 April 1971.
  Not in front of the audience. Homosexuality on stage (Rou-
    tledge, 1992).
Devine, George, 'Lighting and the Modern Theatre', *New Theatre*, 5, 1
  (1948), 18–19.
  'Theatre research: the story of an important new society',
    Theatre World, Jan. 1949.
  'Training for the theatre', in Ivor Brown, *Theatre 1954–5* (Max
    Reinhardt, 1955), 126–30.
  'The Berliner Ensemble', *Encore*, vol. 3, no. 2, Easter 1956.
  'Look and learn', *Amateur Stage*, June 1956, 36–7.
  'The Royal Court theatre: phase one', in Harold Hobson (ed.),
    International Theatre Annual, vol. 2 (John Calder, 1957).

'Renaissance at the Royal Court', *Theatre Arts*, May 1958.

Letter to the *Observer*, 6 July 1958.

'Vital theatre', *Encore*, vol. 6, no. 2, March–April 1959.

'Contemporary godfather', *Plays and Players*, Feb. 1961.

'The right to fail', *The Twentieth Century*, vol. 169, Feb. 1961, 128ff.

'Court account', *Guardian*, 2 April 1962.

'The diary of a madman', *The Ambassador*, no. 11, 1964, 215–17.

Dexter, John, 'Chips and Devotion', *Plays and Players*, Dec. 1962.

> *The honourable beast. A posthumous autobiography* (Nick Hern Books, 1993).

Doty, Gresdna A., and Harbin, Billy J. (eds.), *Inside the Royal Court Theatre, 1956– 1981. Artists talk* (Baton Rouge: Louisiana University Press, 1990).

'Drama workshop – the Royal Court re-lives great days', *Montreal Star*, 31 March 1956.

Duncan, Ronald, 'Dealing with divas: an intimate portrait of Lord Harewood', *Sunday Times*, 2 Sept. 1962.

> *How to make enemies. A second volume of autobiography* (Hart-Davis, 1968).

Eccles, Christine, 'Court in the act of creation', *Guardian*, 6 Sept. 1995.

> 'Interview with Harold Pinter', *Plays International*, Feb. 1996.

Edwardes, Jane, 'A quiet year in Sloane Square', *Plays International*, Feb. 1991.

Elsom, John and Tomalin, Nicholas, *The history of the National Theatre* (Cape, 1978).

English Stage Company, *A record of two years' work* (1958); *English Stage Company, 1958–1959* (1959); *Ten years at the Royal Court, 1956/66* (1966); *Royal Court, 1970* (1970); *The Royal Court Theatre, 1888–1988* (1989).

'English Stage Company needs more support', *Stage*, 5 July 1956.

'Enter the second wave', *Times Literary Supplement*, 29 July 1965.

Eyre, Richard, *Utopia and other places* (Vintage, 1994).

Fay, Stephen, *Power play: the life and times of Peter Hall* (Coronet, 1995).

Findlater, Richard, *The unholy trade* (Victor Gollancz, 2nd edn., 1952).
  'No time for tragedy', *The Twentieth Century*, vol. 161, Jan.
    1957, 56–66.
  The future of the theatre, Fabian tract, no. 317 (Fabian Society,
    1959).
  'The shrinking theatre', *The Twentieth Century*, vol. 165, May
    1959, 493–500.
  'Plays and politics', *The Twentieth Century*, vol. 168, Sept. 1960,
    235–48.
  (ed.) *At the Royal Court. 25 years of the English Stage Company*
    (Ambergate: Amber Lane Press, 1981).
Forsyth, James, *Tyrone Guthrie* (Hamish Hamilton, 1986).
'Forum on political theatre', W. H. Smith/Royal Shakespeare Company
  Youth Festival pamphlet, 23 Oct. 1982.
Fox, Angela, *Slightly foxed by my theatrical family* (Collins, 1986).
Freedland, Michael, *Peter O'Toole* (W. H. Allen, 1983).
Frost, David, *An autobiography. Part one – from congregations to
  audiences* (Harper Collins, 1993).
Gaskill, William, 'Comic masks and *The Happy Haven*', *Encore*, vol. 7,
  no. 6, Nov.–Dec. 1960.
  'Man for the future', *Plays and Players*, March 1966.
  'Glorious riches spring from talents in turmoil', *The Times*, 13
    Jan. 1986.
  A sense of direction. Life at the Royal Court (Faber, 1988).
The Gazette (John Lewis Partnership, 5 Oct. 1985).
Geare, Michael, 'Behind the face of Faber', *Author*, Spring 1984.
Gielgud, John, *An actor and his time* (Pan, 1996).
  Letter to the *Guardian*, 27 March 1984.
Gilliatt, Penelope (ed.), 'Vital theatre: a discussion', *Encore*, vol. 6, no. 2,
  March–April 1959.
Goodwin, Clive, 'Lament for the Theatre Upstairs', *Plays and Players*,
  Aug. 1975.
Goodwin, John (ed.), *Peter Hall's diaries: the story of a dramatic battle*
  (Hamish Hamilton, 1983).
Goring, Edward, 'Kitchen sink theatre revolt', *Evening Standard*, 11
  March 1960.

Gritten, David, 'Advertisements for myself', *Sunday Telegraph*, 3 Nov. 1996.

Guthrie, Tyrone, *A life in the theatre* (Hamish Hamilton, 1961).

Hale, Lionel, *The Old Vic 1949–50* (Evans Brothers, 1950).

Hall, Peter, Terry Hands and Trevor Nunn, Letter to the *Guardian*, 19 March 1984.

Hansard, 17 Feb., 8 March 1966.

Hanson, Barry, 'Royal Court diary', *Plays and Players*, April 1968.

Hare, David, 'Green room', *Plays and Players*, Oct. 1981.

'Labour is betraying the arts', *Daily Telegraph*, 6 Dec. 1997.

Harewood, George, Earl of, *The tongs and the bones: the memoirs of Lord Harewood* (Weidenfeld and Nicolson, 1981).

Harrison, Rex, *Rex: an autobiography* (Coronet, 1974).

Hastings, Michael, *Three political plays* (Penguin, 1990).

Hay, Malcolm and Roberts, Philip, *Edward Bond: a companion to the plays* (Theatre Quarterly publications, 1978).

Bond: a study of his plays (Methuen, 1980).

Hiley, Jim, 'The Court case', *Time Out*, 8–14 Feb. 1980.

Hobson, Harold (ed.), *International theatre annual* no. 1 (John Calder, 1956); no. 2 (Calder, 1957).

Hollis, Patricia, *Jennie Lee: a life* (Oxford University Press, 1997).

Hunt, Albert, '*Serjeant Musgrave* and the critics', *Encore*, vol. 7, no. 1, Jan.–Feb. 1960.

'Upstairs or downstairs', *New Society*, 5 Feb. 1976.

'In Focus. George Hulme: profession – playwright', *Jury: a magazine of film and theatre criticism*, issue 6, 14 Feb. 1966.

Jellicoe, Ann, *Some unconscious influences in the theatre*. The Judith Wilson lecture, Cambridge, 10 March 1967 (Cambridge University Press, 1967).

Johns, Eric, 'Oldest actress in the business', *Theatre World*, Jan. 1959.

'Glen Byam Shaw's new year', *Theatre World*, Jan. 1960.

Johnstone, John, Interview, *Sunday Times*, 11 April 1965.

The Lord Chamberlain's blue pencil (Hodder and Stoughton, 1990).

Johnstone, Keith, *Impro. Improvisation and the theatre*, with an Introduction by Irving Wardle (Faber, 1979).

Joint Committee on Censorship of the Theatre. A report (HMSO, 1967).

Kelly, Jude, 'Pause for original thought', *Guardian*, 23 Nov. 1994.

Keown, Eric, 'At the rehearsal', *Punch*, 3 Oct. 1956.

Kissel, Howard, *David Merrick: the abominable showman* (Applause, 1993).

Knowlson, James, *Damned to fame: the life of Samuel Beckett* (Bloomsbury, 1996).

Lambert, J. W., 'The London theatre season', in Harold Hobson (ed.), *International theatre annual*, no. 1 (Calder, 1956).

Landstone, Charles, *Off-stage. A personal record of the first twelve years of state sponsored drama in Great Britain* (Elek, 1963).

Lesser, Wendy, *A director calls: Stephen Daldry and the theatre* (Faber, 1997).

Lessing, Doris, *Walking in the shade: volume two of my autobiography, 1949–1962* (Harper Collins, 1997).

Lewenstein, Oscar, *Kicking against the pricks: a theatre producer looks back* (Nick Hern Books, 1994).

   et al., Letter to the *The Times*, 15 Oct. 1974.

Lewis, Roger, *The real life of Laurence Olivier* (Century, 1996).

Littlewood, Joan, *Joan's book. Joan Littlewood's peculiar history as she tells it* (Methuen, 1994).

Loach, Ken, 'Open letter to the Council of the Royal Court', *Guardian*, 18 Feb. 1987.

McCrindle, J. F. (ed.), *Behind the scenes: theatre and film interviews from the* Transatlantic Review (Pitman, 1971).

Macdonald, James, 'Blasting back at the critics', *Observer*, 22 Jan. 1995.

McFerran, Ann, 'Interview with Andrea Dunbar', *Time Out*, 20–26 June 1980.

McGrath, John, 'Some other mechanism', *Encore*, vol. 6, no. 4, July–Aug. 1960.

Mackenzie, Suzie, 'Intrigue at Court', *GQ Magazine*, March 1992.

McMillan, Joyce, *The Traverse theatre story, 1963–88* (Methuen, 1988).

'Man of the theatre', *Sunday Times*, 5 Dec. 1954 (George Devine).

Marowitz, Charles, 'State of play', *Tulane Drama Review*, vol. 11, no. 2. Winter, 1966.

Marriott, R. B., 'No crisis now, but there may be unless . . .', *Stage*, 30 June 1960.

Maschler, Tom (ed.), *Declaration* (MacGibbon and Kee, 1957).

Matthews, H. G., '*Volpone* – final production of the Stratford season', *Theatre World*, Aug. 1952.

Milne, Tom, 'And the time of the great taking over: an interview with William Gaskill', *Encore*, vol. 9, no. 4, July-Aug. 1962.

'Modern plays in repertory: the Court venture', *The Times*, 2 April 1956.

Morgan, Geoffrey (ed.), *Contemporary Theatre: a selection of reviews 1966–67* (London Magazine Editions, 1968).

Morley, Sheridan, *Sybil Thorndike: a life in the theatre* (Weidenfeld and Nicolson, 1977).

Moseley, Roy, *Rex Harrison. The first biography* (New English Library, 1987).

Muller, Robert, 'The man who raised the curtain on life', *Daily Mail*, 24 Oct. 1960.

Mullin, Michael, *Design by Motley* (University of Delaware Press: Associated London Presses, 1996).

'The National Theatre', *The Times*, 29 Jan. 1946.

'Need playwrights go slumming for success?', *The Tatler*, 18 March 1959.

Neill, Heather, 'King's Road to Glasgow', *The Times Educational Supplement*, 17 March 1978.

'New Hope for Playwrights', *The Times*, 31 March 1956.

Nightingale, Benedict, 'Less faith in concrete', *New Statesman*, 4 Jan. 1980.

'North Devon festival of the arts', *The Times*, 22 April 1953. See also 14 July 1953.

'Now in theatre', *Manchester Evening News*, Nov. 1955.

O'Connor, Gary, *Ralph Richardson: an actor's life* (Hodder and Stoughton, 1986).

    The secret woman. A life of Peggy Ashcroft (Weidenfeld and Nicolson, 1997).

'Old Vic theatre plan', *The Times*, 15 April 1946.

Olivier, Laurence, *On acting* (Weidenfeld and Nicolson, 1986).

Osborne, John, 'Why I am angry today', *Sunday Telegraph*, 10 Feb. 1980.
> *A better class of person. An autobiography, 1929–1956* (Faber, 1981).
> *Almost a gentleman. An autobiography. Volume two: 1955–1966* (Faber, 1991).
> *Damn you, England* (Faber, 1994).

'Out and about: wit and whimsy at the Royal Court Theatre', *The Twentieth Century*, vol. 163, June 1958.

Pawley, Martin, 'Tunnelling under the sacred turf', *Observer*, 24 Sept. 1995.

Pearson, Kenneth, 'Atticus among the angels of the theatre', *Sunday Times*, 17 July 1960.

Pendennis, 'Hot on Broadway', *Observer*, 23 March 1958.

Pocock, Tom, 'Plenty of customers – but getting choosy', *Evening Standard*, 21 June 1960.

'Putting the drama in touch with contemporary life: two years of the English Stage Company', *The Times*, 19 March 1958.

Quayle, Anthony, *A time to speak*. (Sphere, 1992). With Preface by Dame Peggy Ashcroft.

Radin, Victoria, 'Max at the Court', *Observer*, 21 Oct. 1979.

Redgrave, Vanessa, Interview with Clive Goodwin, in Hal Burton (ed.), *Acting in the Sixties* (BBC Publications, 1970).
> *An autobiography* (Hutchinson, 1991).

Reed, Dickon, 'How glorious is the garden?', *Plays and Players*, July 1985.

'Resignation of three directors', *The Times*, 10 May 1951 and *passim* to 18 July 1952.

Richardson, Tony, *Long distance runner: A memoir* (Faber, 1993).

Ripley, John, *Julius Caesar on stage in England and America, 1599–1973* (Cambridge University Press, 1980).

Ritchie, Harry, *Success stories: literature and the media in England, 1950–59* (Faber, 1988).

Ritchie, Rob, 'Derry notebook', *Platform*, no. 5, Spring 1983.
> 'Not quite a revolution', *Plays*, Jan. 1985.
> *The Joint Stock book: the making of a theatre collective* (Methuen, 1987).

Roberts, Peter, *The Old Vic story. A nation's theatre 1818–1976* (W. H. Allen, 1976).

    The best of Plays and Players. vol. 1: 1953–1968. vol. 2: 1969–1983 (Methuen, 1988 and 1989).

Roberts, Philip, *Bond on file* (Methuen, 1985).

    The Royal Court Theatre, 1965–1972 (Routledge, 1986).

    'George Devine, Tony Richardson and Stratford', *Studies in Theatre Production*, 12 Dec. 1995, 125–32.

    'George Devine's visit to Edward Gordon Craig', *Theatre Notebook*, 51, 1997, 14–23.

    'The letters of George Devine to Michel Saint-Denis, 1939–1945', *Theatre Notebook*, 52, 1998, 161–171.

    'Patronage and the arts: The John Lewis Partnership and the Royal Court Theatre', *Theatre Notebook*, 53, 1999, 48–56.

Roberts, Rachel, *No bells on Sunday: the journals of Rachel Roberts, edited with A documentary biography by Alexander Walker* (Sphere, 1984).

Rogoff, Gordon, 'Richard's himself again: journey to an actors' theatre', *Tulane Drama Review*, vol. 11, no. 2, Winter, 1966.

Rose, David, 'Rewriting the Holocaust', *Guardian*, 14 Jan. 1987.

Rowell, George, *The Old Vic theatre: a history* (Cambridge University Press, 1993).

'Royal Court Theatre to reopen: a memorable history', *The Times*, 16 Jan. 1952. Also 26 Jan., 22 March, 3 June, 3 July, 6 Aug.

Signoret, Simone, *Nostalgia isn't what it used to be* (Panther Books, 1979).

Soyinka, Wole, *Ibadan. The Penkelemes years* (Methuen, 1994).

Spurling, Hilary, 'Angry middle age', *Spectator*, 15 April 1966.

Stafford-Clark, Max, 'Folk memories in Sloane Square', *The Times*, 1 Sept. 1984.

    Letters to George (Nick Hern Books, 1989).

Stephens, Robert with Coveney, Michael, *Knight errant: memoirs of a vagabond actor* (Hodder and Stoughton, 1995).

Taylor, John Russell, 'Ten years of the English Stage Company', *Tulane Drama Review*, vol. 11, no. 2, Winter 1966.

Taylor, Paul, 'A last look back (in awe, not anger)', *Independent*, 21 Oct. 1996.

Thompson, Lawrence, 'Can this man save the British theatre?', *News Chronicle*, 3 Oct. 1957.

To stage or not to stage: the case of Perdition (Britain/Israel Public Affairs Committee, March 1987).

Tredger, Victor, 'Sex play leaflet raid', *Daily Sketch*, 5 March 1958.

Trial Run. The Royal Court magazine for schools, Spring issue, 1963.

Tschudin, Marcus, *A writer's theatre. George Devine and the English Stage Company at the Royal Court, 1956–1965* (Berne: European University Papers, 1973).

Tushingham, David, 'Interview with Stephen Daldry', *Live 1* (Methuen, 1994).

Tynan, Kathleen, *Kenneth Tynan, letters* (Weidenfeld and Nicolson, 1994).

Tynan, Kenneth, 'The Court revolution', *Observer*, 6 April 1958.

'Court on trial', *Observer*, 26 Oct. 1958.

'The angry young movement', in his *Curtains* (Longman, 1961), 191ff.

Tynan right and left (Longman, 1967).

The sound of two hands clapping (Cape, 1975).

A view of the English stage (Methuen, 1984).

Wansell, Geoffrey, *Terence Rattigan* (Fourth Estate, 1995).

Wapshott, Nicholas, *Rex Harrison. A biography* (Chatto and Windus, 1991).

Wardle, Irving, 'Interview with William Gaskill', *Gambit*, vol. 5, no. 17, 1970.

The theatres of George Devine (Cape, 1978).

'Why the Court must prevail', *The Times*, 21 Sept. 1981.

Watkins, Graham, ' "Art grows where seed is sown" – a reply to the *The Glory of the Garden*', *Stage*, 17 May 1984.

Wesker, Arnold, *As much as I dare: an autobiography, 1932–1959* (Century, 1994).

'Whispers from the wings', *Theatre World*, June, Sept., Dec. 1953; April 1956.

White, Eric W., *The Arts Council of Great Britain* (Davis-Poynter, 1975).

White, Michael, *Empty seats* (Hamish Hamilton, 1984).

Whitelaw, Billie, *Billie Whitelaw ... Who he? An autobiography* (Hodder and Stoughton, 1995).

Whiting, John, 'At ease in a bright red tie', in his *The art of the dramatist* (London Magazine Editions, 1970), 149–54.

Williams, Harcourt, *Old Vic saga* (Winchester Publictions, 1949).

Williams, Raymond, 'Drama and the left', *Encore*, vol. 6, no. 2, March–April 1959.

Williams, W. E., 'Economic and social aspects of the theatre', the Shute Lectures, University of Liverpool, Lent term 1953. Public Record Office, Misc. Papers, 1953/36, EL4/86. Reprinted in *The Adelphi*, Third Quarter, 1953.

Williamson, Audrey, 'The Byam Shaws', *Theatre World*, Aug. 1946.
Contemporary theatre (Rockcliff, 1956).

Wiseman, Thomas, 'Elstree captures *Look Back in Anger*', *Evening Standard*, 28 April 1958.
'Unlikely recruit for the rebels – Rattigan', *Evening Standard*, 11 March 1960.

Witts, Richard, *Artist unknown. An alternative history of the Arts Council* (Little, Brown, 1998).

Worsley, T. C., 'The Sweet Smell', *New Statesman*, 21 Feb. 1959.

Wright, Nicholas, 'Interview with Jocelyn Herbert', *Royal National Theatre Platform Papers*, no. 4, 1993.

Index

Abbensetts, Michael, 144
Abbey Theatre, Dublin, 165, 217
Abercrombie, Nigel, 122
Actors' Studio, 93
Actors' Training Scheme, 94
Albee, Edward, 88
Albery Theatre, 193
Aldwych Theatre, 85, 91, 106
Allen, Jim, 192–4, 195–201
    Perdition, 178, 192–4, 195–201
Allsop, Kenneth, 69
Alrawi, Karim, 194
    A Colder Climate, 194
Ambassadors Theatre, 225
American Hurrah!, 120–1
Anderson, Lindsay, xix, 59, 62, 68,
    69–70, 71, 72, 73, 75, 77–8, 79, 88,
    89, 92, 97–8, 100–1, 105, 108,
    111–12, 128, 129–30, 131–2,
    132–5, 136–8, 139–40, 142,
    143–50, 155, 156, 158–60, 162,
    187, 213, 215, 221, 243 n.17, 246
    n.46, 247 n.2
Andrews, Dennis, 171
Anouilh, Jean, 59
    The Rehearsal, 59
Anstey, Paul, 32
Antrobus, John, 126
Apollo Theatre, 131
Arden, John, 57, 62, 63, 65, 72–3,
    76–7, 89, 139

The Happy Haven, 76–7
Live Like Pigs, 62, 65–6, 68
Serjeant Musgrave's Dance, 72–3,
    111, 114
The Waters of Babylon, 62
The Workhouse Donkey, 89
Arts Council, 4, 8, 11–15, 27, 38, 56,
    73–4, 90–1, 113, 115–16, 118–19,
    121–3, 132–5, 141, 145, 153–7,
    159–63, 165, 170–1, 172, 174–6,
    178, 182–5, 188, 190–2, 203–7,
    209–11, 217, 221, 227, 234 n.34
    Arts Council Drama Panel, 184–5
Arts Theatre Club, 64, 85
Ashcroft, Peggy, 2, 23, 39, 41, 52–3, 60,
    68, 73, 92, 97, 112, 117, 124, 135,
    146, 149–50, 163
Aspern Papers, The, 52
Assistant Artistic Directors, 56, 71, 86
Associate Directors, 71
Attorney-General, 177–8
Auden, W. H., 39
Audrey Skirball-Kenis Foundation,
    220–1

Babe, Thomas, 166, 180
    Prayer for my Daughter, 166
Badel, Alan, 18–19
Bagnold, Edith, 51
Baker, Frank, 8
Barber, John, 48, 51

Barbican Theatre, 227
Barclays New Stages, 208–9
    Barclays New Stages Festival, 212, 225
Barker, Howard, 137, 152–3, 165, 174, 180, 192, 203, 210
    Fair Slaughter, 165
    The Last Supper, 203
    No End of Blame, 174
    Seven Lears, 210
    Victory, 180, 218
    Women Beware Women, 192
Barry, Sebastian, 226
    The Steward of Christendom, 226
Beaumont, Hugh 'Binkie', 45, 48, 65, 125
Beckett, Samuel, 37, 49, 56, 58–9, 64, 67, 91, 137, 144, 152, 154, 167, 176, 239 n.68
    Act Without Words, 58
    Endgame, 58, 64, 66, 99, 154
    Happy Days, 81, 100, 167
    Krapp's Last Tape, 66
    Ohio Impromptu, 176
Beddoe, Jo, 185, 188, 197, 205
Behn, Aphra, 183
    The Lucky Chance, 183, 185
Belgrade Theatre, Coventry, 65, 72, 80
Bell, Tom, 167
Benham, Colin, 145–6
Bennett, Alan, 192–3, 195
    Kafka's Dick, 192, 194–5
Bentley, Eric, 52
Berkoff, Steven, 159
Berliner Ensemble, 52–3
Bessborough, Eric, 17, 19–20, 47, 77
Betti, Ugo, 37
Billington, Michael, 146
Birmingham Repertory Theatre, 165
Blacksell, J.E., 17–18, 20–1, 26, 47, 62, 65, 99, 101, 125, 142, 145
Blair, Betsy, 84
Blatchley, John, 77

Blin, Roger, 58
Blond, Elaine, 137, 156, 192
Blond, Neville, xix, 21–4, 26–7, 28, 30–1, 32, 36, 38–9, 40, 41, 47, 51, 53–4, 55–6, 58, 60, 61, 62–3, 64–5, 66, 67–8, 69, 70, 73–4, 77, 82, 83, 84–5, 86, 88, 89, 90–1, 95–6, 97, 99, 101, 106, 113, 114, 115, 117, 118–19, 120, 121, 123–5, 129, 133–8, 144, 229, 241 n.26
Bloom, Claire, 18–19
Bond, Edward, 63, 72, 91, 108–11, 117, 118, 121, 122, 128, 131, 139, 144, 148, 151, 152–3, 160, 162, 173–5, 179, 186–7, 222, 229
    Early Morning, 118–21, 123–5, 126, 128, 130
    The Fool, 153
    Lear, 131
    Narrow Road to the Deep North, 128
    The Pope's Wedding, 91, 175, 186
    Restoration, 173–5, 186, 229
    Saved, 91, 108–11, 112–13, 117, 122, 123, 128, 186, 222
    Summer, 175
Boyle, Danny, 186
Bradwell, Mike, 185
Brecht, Bertolt, 19–20, 29, 33–5, 37–9, 41, 52–3, 57, 64, 88, 102
    The Good Woman of Setzuan, 33, 37, 39, 52–5
    Happy End, 102
    Man is Man, 88
    Puntila and his Man Matti, 88
    The Resistible Rise of Arturo Ui, 92
    St Joan of the Stockyards, 90, 98
    The Threepenny Opera, 19–21, 29, 38
    'Brecht on Brecht', 91
Brenton, Howard, 115, 131, 137, 144, 159–60, 162, 182, 184, 195, 203–5, 211–12, 217
    Berlin Bertie, 217

The Genius, 181
Greenland, 204
Iranian Nights (with Tariq Ali), 205
Magnificence, 144
A Short Sharp Shock (with Tony
    Howard), 173
Brickman, Miriam, 108
Bride of Denmark Hill, The, 7
Brighton, Pam, 139–40, 142, 171
Bristol Old Vic, 34, 145
British Council, The, 9, 91
Britten, Benjamin, 17, 19, 29, 41, 47
    Let's Make An Opera, 17
Broadway, 79
Brome, Richard, 217
    A Jovial Crew, 217
Brook, Peter, 90, 101
Brown, Alan, 165–6, 182
    Panic, 182
    Wheelchair Willie, 166
Brown, Ian, 210
Brown, Pamela, 84
Browne, E. Martin, 17
Bruce, Brenda, 91
Brunner, Elaine, 6
Bryceland, Yvonne, 175
Bryden, Bill, 149, 224
Buckle, Dicky, 47–9
Büchner, Georg, 47
    Danton's Death, 47
Bullwinkle, Jean, 202
Burge, Stuart, xix, 79, 148, 155, 157–62,
    164, 165, 166–8, 177, 178–9, 185,
    198–9, 211, 212, 214–16
'Burning Boat, The', 28
Burrell, John, 1
Burton, Anthony, 176, 178, 192, 198,
    200, 216
Bush Theatre, 210
Butler, Richard, 110
Butterworth, Jez, 225–6
    Mojo, 225
Byam Shaw, Glen, 1–4, 5, 12, 42, 95

Byrne, John, 179, 217
    Colquhoun and Macbryde, 217
    The Slab Boys Trilogy, 179

Cadogan, Lord, 94
Calvert, Phyllis, 58
Cambridge Arts Scheme, 80, 88
Caplan, Isador, 19, 21, 146, 178
Carleton Greene, Hugh, 167
Carr, Marina, 226
    Portia Coughlan, 226
Carrington, Lord, 191
Cartwright, Jim 192–4
    Road, 192–4, 218
Casey, James, 119
Casson, Lewis, 7, 41
Catty, Jon, 154–5, 162
Central School of Speech and Drama,
    211
Cesarani, David, 196–7
Chagrin, Claude, 93
Changeling, The, 81, 86
Channon, Paul, 133
Chapman, Gerald, 171, 202
Chapman, Henry, 88
    That's Us, 88
Chaste Maid in Cheapside, A, 111
Chelsea Classic, 144
Chenalls, A.T. & Co., 21
Churchill, Caryl, 78, 144, 162, 171,
    176, 180, 182, 194–5, 198–9,
    201–2, 205, 207–9, 211, 228
    Cloud Nine, 166
    Fen, 182
    Icecream, 205
    Light Shining in Buckinghamshire,
        154
    Mad Forest, 211
    A Mouthful of Birds (with David
        Lan), 195
    Serious Money, 194–5, 199, 201–2,
        207, 218
    Top Girls, 180–2, 212, 218

Cilento, Diane, 84, 94
Citizens Theatre, Glasgow, 65, 157
Clark, Kenneth, 12
Cleopatra, 79, 87
'Club' performance, 103, 110–11, 121
Codron, Michael, 82, 137
Cole, Toby, 122
Collins, Norman, 112, 134, 150
Come Together, 138
Comedy of Errors, The, 8
'Coming on Strong', 221
Cookson, Harry, 75
   The Lily White Boys, 74–5
Cooper, Gladys, 38
Copeau, Jacques, 24, 42–3, 76
Corey, Giles, 46
Country Wife, The, 50, 52–3, 55–6, 62
Coveney, Michael, 172, 180, 213, 216
Coventry Cathedral Festival, 89
Cowley, Graham, 205, 207–9, 221–2
Cox, Peter, 186
   Up to the Sun and Down to the Centre, 186
Craig, Edward Gordon, 5, 42, 67, 235 n.56
Cregan, David, 63, 102, 116, 117, 120, 126
   Miniatures, 102
   Three Men for Colverton, 116
Crimp, Martin, 211, 218
   No One Sees the Video, 211
   The Treatment, 218
Criterion Theatre, 119
Crucible Theatre, Sheffield, 176, 210
Cruddas, Audrey, 81
Cruickshank, Harriet, 139, 215–16
Cudlipp, Hugh, 151, 187
Curtis, Simon, 185, 193–4, 199, 201, 213
Cuthbertson, Iain, 101, 107, 109, 110, 115, 116

D'Aguiar, Fred, 212

A Jamaican Airman Foresees his Death, 212
Daldry, Stephen, xiii, xix, 71, 213–17, 218, 219–20, 221–5, 226, 227, 228
Daniels, Sarah, 182, 194, 210
   Bedside Herself, 210
   Byrthrite, 194
   The Devil's Gateway, 182
   Masterpieces, 182–3
Darlington, W. A., 69, 90
Davies, Elidir, 94
Davies, Howard, 212
de Angelis, April, 217
   Hush, 217
Declaration, 62
de Jongh, Nicholas, 184, 215
Delaney, Sheila, 78, 80
   The Lion in Love, 78
   A Taste of Honey, 78
Dennis, Nigel, 33–4, 37, 41, 45, 51, 56, 61, 79, 87–8, 237 n.43
   August for the People, 79, 87–8
   Cards of Identity, 36–7, 41, 51–2
   The Making of Moo, 61, 81
Devine, George, xiii–xiv, xix, 1–16, 17–18, 21, 23–43, 45–7, 49–78, 79–104, 105, 106, 107, 109–10, 111–12, 114, 115, 118–19, 120, 121–2, 144, 151, 158, 159, 171, 173, 181, 189, 195, 209, 219–20, 221, 223–4, 227, 229, 243 n.17
George Devine Award, 112–13, 213–14
Devlin, Anne, 194
   Ourselves Alone, 194
Dexter, John, xix, 59, 72, 79, 88, 91–3, 168–9, 188
Diamond, Gillian, 139–40, 142, 162
Dixon, Doreen, 97, 108
Dodgson, Elyse, 193, 204
Doncaster, Stephen, 42
Dorfman, Ariel, 212
   Death and the Maiden, 212–13, 218

Drogheda, Earl of, 69
Druid Theatre, Galway, 226
Dublin Festival, 194
Duchess Theatre, 28
Dudley, William, 225
Duke of York's Theatre, 202, 220, 223,
   225–6
  Duke of York's Theatre (Holdings)
   Ltd, 220, 224–6
Dunbar, Andrea, 172, 176, 180, 192
  The Arbor, 172, 173
  Rita, Sue and Bob Too, 176, 218
  Shirley, 192
Duncan, Ronald, xix–xx, 16–25, 27–9,
   31, 33, 35–8, 40, 42, 46–7, 49–50,
   56, 59, 62, 64–6, 73–6, 81, 88, 101,
   114, 187, 233 n.16
  The Catalyst, 56, 64
  The Death of Satan, 17–19, 49–50
  Don Juan, 17–18, 49–50
Dunlop, Frank, 101, 145
Dury, Ian, 205
  Apples, 205, 207–8

Edgar, David, 166
  Mary Barnes, 166
Edinburgh Festival, 61, 79, 95
Eisenberg, Debbie, 194
  Pastoral, 194
Eleven Men Dead at Hola Camp,
  70
Eliot, T. S., 17, 28–9, 33, 37
  The Cocktail Party, 17
  The Family Reuinion, 29
  Sweeney Agonistes, 33
Elliott, Michael, 96
Embassy Theatre, 18–19, 21
English National Opera, 206
English Opera Group, 17–19, 114
'English Stage Guild Ltd', 20
English Stage Society, 58
'English Theatre Group', 19
'English Theatre Guild', 19, 21

Epstein, Jacob, 17
Esdaile, Alfred, xx, 7, 8, 11, 13, 18–20,
   22–3, 25–7, 28–30, 31–3, 36,
   38–40, 47, 54–5, 96, 110, 117,
   123–5, 137, 143, 153
Establishment Club, Greek Street, 92
Etherege, George, 220
  The Man of Mode, 220
Evans, Edith, 59, 112
Evans, Matthew, xx, 181, 185–94,
   197–204, 212
Everitt, Anthony, 211
Eyre, Richard, viii, 155, 157, 172, 218,
   226

Falkland Sound, 182, 210, 218
Farquhar, George, 203, 207
  The Recruiting Officer, 203–4, 207,
   218
Faulkner, William, 62
  Requiem for a Nun, 62, 237 n.44
Fearon, George, 21, 35–6, 48, 54
Field, Anthony, 154–5
Finch, Peter, 97
Findlater, Richard, 161, 164
Finney, Albert, 68, 79, 86, 92, 103, 112,
   142, 146–7
'First Results', 93
Forman, Denis, 185
Forsyte, Kerman & Phillips, 21
Fox, Robin, xx, 66, 73–4, 77, 85–6,
   122, 123, 124, 127, 129, 133, 135,
   137–9
Francis, Alfred, 145
Freud, Clement, 11, 92, 94
Friel, Brian, 144, 217, 220
  The Faith Healer, 217, 220
Frisch, Max, 79, 80
  Fire Raisers, 79, 80
Frost, David, 231 n.28
Fry, Christopher, 20, 28–9, 37, 39, 46,
   56, 74
  Curtmantle, 46, 74

Fugard, Athol, 144, 226
  Valley Song, 226

Garcia Lorca, Federico, 33
Garrick, The, 22
Gaskill, William, xx, 45, 59, 63, 66–7,
    72, 75–6, 80, 88–9, 92–4, 96,
    100–1, 105–28, 129–138, 141–4,
    152, 155, 157, 168, 171, 174, 175,
    177–8, 192, 198–201, 203–4,
    213–14, 224–5, 229, 241 n.41, 246
    n.46
Gate Theatre, 211, 213
Gay, Gordon Hamilton, 40
Gay, John, 17
  The Beggar's Opera, 17
Gay Sweatshop, 211
Gems, Jonathan, 187
  Susan's Breasts, 187–8
Genet, Jean, 79, 83–5
  The Balcony, 83
  The Blacks, 83–5
Gestetner, Henni, 209
Getting Attention, 212
Gielgud, John, 8, 15, 59, 184
Gilbert, Martin, 198
Gill, Peter, 101, 105, 108, 112, 118,
    125, 132, 138, 141–2, 224
  A Provincial Life, 118
  Over Gardens Out, 132
  The Sleeper's Den, 101, 112
Giraudoux, Jean, 61, 237 n.41
  L'Apollon de Bellac, 61
Glasgow Unity, 163
Globe Theatre, 140
Glory of the Garden, The, 182, 185,
    188
Goodman, Arnold, 10, 132–4, 165,
    184, 197
Gower, John, 111, 112
Gowrie, Lord, 188, 190–1
Gradwell, Leo, 112–13
Granada Television, 48, 69, 75

Granger, Derek, 185, 209
Granville Barker, Harley, 7, 9, 89, 114,
    228–9
  The Voysey Inheritance, 114, 116
Great Marlborough Street Magistrates
    Court, 110
Greater London Arts Board, 211
Greater London Council, 182–3
Green, Henry, 34
Grieve, Alan, 229
Grenfell, Joyce, 7
Griffiths, Trevor, 164, 179
  Oi for England, 179
Grimes, Frank, 151
Grosso, Nick, 220, 226
  Peaches, 220
  Sweetheart, 226
Guare, John, 217
  Six Degrees of Separation, 217
Guest Repertory Season, 64–5
Guinness, Alec, 61, 64, 66, 95, 112, 116
Gulbenkian Trust, 93
Gunter, John, 108
Guthrie, Tyrone, 2–4

Haigh, Kenneth, 84
Haggard, Piers, 101
Hale, Elvi, 77
Hales, Jonathan, 138, 139
Hall, Peter, 57, 70, 90–1, 145, 150, 156,
    158–9, 184, 190–1, 228–9, 231 n.34
Hall, Willis, 68
  The Long and the Short and the Tall,
    68–9, 74
Halliwell, David, 137
Hamilton, Julie, 54
Hamlet, 151, 172–4, 218
Hammersmith, 141
Hampstead Theatre Club, 75, 211
Hampton, Christopher, 114, 126, 131,
    137, 138, 144, 152–4
  The Philanthropist, 131
  Treats, 154

When Did You Last See My Mother?, 114

Hands, Terry, 184

Hanson, Barry, 149

Hare, David, viii, 129, 131, 137, 138, 152–4, 160, 168, 175–6, 184, 188, 209–11, 217–18, 228
   A Map of the World, 176
   Teeth 'n' Smiles, 154

Harewood, Countess of, 70

Harewood, Earl of, xx, 17–20, 23–7, 30–2, 35–8, 47–8, 50, 53, 55, 59–62, 64, 66, 68, 72, 73–4, 76, 81, 87, 89, 92, 97, 99–100, 101, 106, 109, 112, 114, 116, 119, 120, 123, 126, 127, 130, 135, 136, 137, 138, 142, 147, 150, 156, 233 n.22

Harris, Margaret 'Percy', 3–4, 25, 42–4, 55, 111

Harris, Richard and Anderson, Lindsay, 94
   The Diary of a Madman, 94

Harris, Sophie, 42, 46

Harrison, Rex, 77, 79, 87–8

Hartnell, Norman, 38

Harvey, Joanthan, 220
   Babies, 220

Harvey, Lawrence, 55, 59, 84

Hastings, Michael, 52, 56, 59, 98, 102, 165, 183, 195–6
   The Emperor (with Jonathan Miller), 194–5, 201–2, 218
   For the West, 165
   Tom and Viv, 183, 185, 187, 218
   The World's Baby, 98, 102
   Yes-and After, 59, 59

Hauptmann-Dessau, Elisabeth, 52–3

Hauser, Frank, 73

Havergal, Giles, 155, 157

Haworth Tompkins, 223

Haymarket Theatre, Leicester, 210

Haynes, Jim, 101

Heaton, Terry, 192

Short Change, 192

Hedley, Philip, 183

Heggie, Iain, 203, 205
   A Wholly Health Glasgow, 203

Helpmann, Robert, 17, 61, 99

Henry, Victor, 126

Herbert, Jocelyn, xx, 2–3, 5, 7, 10, 32, 42–4, 59, 61, 69, 81, 97, 100, 101, 111, 129, 143, 146, 147–9, 150, 155, 157–8, 159, 161, 168, 200, 208, 213–14, 216, 220–1, 224, 227

HRH Princess Margaret, 70

Heywood, Vikki, 222

Hiley, Jim, 170

Hilton, Frank, 92
   Day of the Prince, 92

Hobson, Harold, 75, 154

Hockney, David, 116

Hodgkinson, Jo, 27, 101, 119, 122, 128, 133–4, 234 n.32

Hoggart, Richard, 185

Holman, Robert, 144, 165, 176, 187, 191, 205, 211
   Other Worlds, 176, 179–82
   The Overgrown Path, 187, 191
   Rafts and Dreams, 211

Holroyd, Stuart, 64
   The Tenth Chance, 64

Howard, Trevor, 19, 61

Howarth, Donald, 63, 69, 119
   Sugar in the Morning, 69

Howell, Jane, 108, 118, 129, 171

Hughes, Dusty, 195
   Jenkin's Ear, 195

Hunt, Hugh, 2–4, 18–19

Hutchinson, Mary, 8

Hutchinson, Ron, 165, 186, 217, 226
   Pygmies in the Ruins, 217
   Rat in the Skull, 186–7, 218, 226

Ibsen, Henrik, 23
   Hedda Gabler, 23, 29–30
   Rosmersholm, 73

Independent Theatre Council, 184
Inge, William, 125
Institute of Jewish Affairs, 196–7
International Theatre Institute, 53
Ionesco, Eugene, 52, 56, 58, 61, 64, 75,
    79, 83–4, 95, 137
  The Bald Prima Donna, 84
  The Chairs, 52, 58, 61, 64
  Exit the King, 95
  Jacques, 83–4
  The Lesson, 61, 64
  Rhinoceros, 75–6, 118
Ivy Restaurant, 85
Izzard, Eddie, 225–6

Jackson, Leigh, 167
  Reggae Britannia, 167
Janiurek, Lenka, 165, 180
'Jazzetry', 69–70
Jeannetta Cochrane Theatre, 93
Jeffrey, Clare, 42, 44
Jeffrey, Stephen, 220
  The Libertine, 220
Jellicoe, Ann, 57, 63, 79, 108, 117, 137,
    146, 165, 209
  The Knack, 79, 90
  Shelley, 108, 111
  The Sport of My Mad Mother, 63,
    204
Jenkins, Anne, 154, 185
Jenkins, Hugh, 133
Jerwood Foundation, 220, 222, 228–9
Jerwood Theatre Downstairs, 228
Jerwood Theatre Upstairs, 228
John Lewis Partnership, 8, 10–11, 24,
    42, 230 n.16
Johnson, Judith, 225
  Uganda, 225
Johnson, Terry, 176, 183, 226
  Cries from the Mammal House, 183
  Hysteria, 226
  Insignificance, 176, 179, 218
Johnstone, Dennis, 37

The Golden Cuckoo, 37
Johnstone, Keith, 70, 72, 93, 107, 108,
    109, 115, 125
Johnstone, Lt-Col. J.F.D., 122
Joint Stock Theatre Company, 154,
    164, 166, 168, 170–1, 176, 179–80,
    183, 187, 195
Julius Caesar, 98–9

Kane, Sarah, 221–2
  Blasted, 221–2
Karge, Manfred, 203
  Man to Man, 203
Kellgren, Ian, 161, 163
Kelly, Jude, 212
Kember, Paul, 176
  Not Quite Jerusalem, 176, 181
Kempson, Rachel, 58
Keneally, Thomas, 203
  The Playmaker, 203
Kennedy-Cox, Reginald, 18–20, 36, 68
Kidd, Robert, xix, 142, 148–50, 151–8
Killick, Jenny, 215
Kilroy, Thomas, 173, 193
  Double Cross, 193
King Lear [the 'Noguchi' *Lear*], 31, 218
Kingsway Theatre, 22–8, 30–3, 35
Kiss for Adèle, A, 8
Kleeman, David, 206
Korder, Howard, 218, 226
  The Lights, 226
  Search and Destroy, 218
Korean War, 10–11
Kramer, Larry, 192
  The Normal Heart, 192–3
Kureishi, Hanif, 176, 193
  Borderline, 176

Laine, Cleo, 64
Lambert, J.W., 56
Lan, David, 144, 165, 167
  Sergeant Ola and His Followers, 167
  The Winter Dancers, 165

Lavery, Byrony, 211
  Kitchen Matters, 211
Lawrence, D.H., 101–2, 120, 220
  A Collier's Friday Night, 101
  The Daughter-in-Law, 118, 220
  The Trilogy, 125
Lawson, Nigel, 132–3
Lawson, Wilfred, 66, 238 n.57
Leatherhead Repertory Company, 65
Lee, Jennie, 244 n.35
Lehmann, John, 34, 53–4
Leigh, Vivien, 69, 72
Leighton, Margaret, 59
Lenya, Lotte, 91
Lessing, Doris, 62
  Each his own Wilderness, 64
Levy, Benn, 14, 41
Lewenstein, Oscar xx, 8, 11, 16, 18–20,
  22–3, 25, 27–9, 31, 33, 38–9, 42,
  50–1, 56–9, 66, 68, 74–5, 78,
  82–4, 86, 91, 97, 102, 105, 123,
  124, 125, 132, 133, 137, 138, 140,
  141–8, 150, 152, 154, 155, 160,
  162, 163, 179
Lewis, Spedan, 11
Lewis, Wyndham, 51
Lister, Laurier, 11, 39
  Airs on a Shoestring, 11, 13, 28, 32
Littlewood, Joan, 89
Liverpool Playhouse, 194
Living Theatre, The, 118
Livings, Henry, 92
  Kelly's Eye, 92
Lloyd, Selwyn, 83
Loach, Ken, 197, 199–200
Logue, Christopher, 69, 77
  The Trial of Cob and Leach, 69, 77
  Trials by Logue, 77
London Boroughs Grant Committee,
  226
London International Festival of
  Theatre, 187
London Magazine, 34

London Mask Theatre, 12, 19–20
London Theatre Studio, 1, 3, 42, 81,
  101
Look After Lulu, 50, 72
Lord Chamberlain, 20, 61, 65, 84, 90,
  93, 102–3, 108–11, 113, 120–1,
  122, 128, 242 n.56
Lousada, Anthony, 10
Lowe, Stephen, 173, 175
  Glasshouses, 173
  Tibetan Inroads, 175
Luce, Richard, 191
Lysistrata, 50, 62, 238 n.45

McBean, Angus, 54
Macbeth, 116–18, 133
McClure, Michael, 126
  The Beard, 126–7
McCullers, Carson, 57
  The Member of the Wedding, 57–8,
  61, 74
McDonagh, Martin, 226
  The Beauty Queen of Leenane, 226
Macdonald, James, 222
Macdonald, Sharman, 211
  All Things Nice, 211
McIndoe, Archibald, 21
McIntyre, Clare, 210, 226
  Low Level Panic, 210
  My Heart's a Suitcase, 210, 218
  The Thickness of Skin, 226
Mackintosh, Cameron, 226
McKellan, Ian, 166–7
McKenna, Siobhan, 98
McWhinnie, Donald, 91
Major Barbara, 65
Major, John, 217
Mamet, David, 218
  Oleanna, 218
Marcel, Gabriel, 29
Marchant, Tony, 187
  The Attractions, 187
Mary Poppins, 226

Massey, Anna, 58
Massey, Daniel, 98
Matura, Mustapha, 144
May, Val, 145
Maydays, 210
Meckler, Nancy, 165
Melchett, Sonia, 193, 197–8
Metropolitan Music Hall, Edgware
    Road, 75
Meyer, Marlane, 211
    Etta Jenks, 211
Midgely, Robin 101
Midsummer Night's Dream, A, 88
Millennium Fund, 221
Miller, Arthur, 19, 33, 35, 37, 38, 45–6,
    54
    The Crucible, 19, 33, 36, 37, 45–6,
    51
Miller, Charles, 47
Miller, Jonathan, 164
Miller, O.B., 10–11, 42
Mills, Jean, 171
Miss Hargreaves, 8
Montagu, Helen, 108, 119, 134, 142,
    162
Mongomerie, John, 137, 161
Monroe, Marilyn, 50–1, 54
Moore, Henry, 17
Morley, Christopher, 116
Morris, John, 154
    Tulloch, 154
Morris, Stephen, 206
Mortimer, John, xxi, 185, 210–16, 229
Mousetrap, The, 28
Much Ado About Nothing, 31
Mueller, Harald, 142
    Big Wolf, 142
Music Corporation of America, 47
Murdoch, Iris, 51

Nagy, Phyllis, 225
    The Strip, 225
Naming of Murderer's Rock, The, 75

Nathan, David, 197
National Lottery, 221–3, 225, 227
National Theatre, *see* Royal National
    Theatre
Negri, Richard, 42
Neville, John, 157
New Theatre, 68
New York Times, xi
Newby, Howard, xxi, 167–8, 171,
    176–7, 185–6, 188
Newman, G.F., 173, 176–8, 186
    An Honourable Trade, 186
    Operation Bad Apple, 176–8, 198
Nottingham Playhouse, 157
Nunn, Trevor, 184

Oakes, Meredith, 220
    The Editing Process, 220
O'Brien, Edna, 144
O'Brien, Richard, 152
    The Rocky Horror Show, 144, 152
O'Casey, Sean, 19, 33, 35, 38, 56, 72–3
    Cock-a-Doodle-Dandy, 19, 33, 72–3
O'Donovan, Desmond, 115
Old Vic Theatre, 1–3, 5, 8, 27, 42–3,
    67, 70, 85–6, 89–90, 101, 106, 141,
    145–7
    Old Vic Scheme, 145–6, 158
Olivier, Lawrence, 1, 5, 23, 54, 59–60,
    64, 70, 72, 74–5, 85, 93, 95, 101,
    112–13, 184
    Olivier Appeal, 204, 206, 222
O'Malley, Mary, 165
    Once A Catholic, 165
Open Hearted Enterprises, 183
Openheimer, Duncan, 10
Open Theatre, 120–1
Opera Factory, 183
Operation Countryman, 176
Orton, Joe, 115, 120, 144
Osborne, Helen, 221
Osborne, John, xi–xii, 30, 35, 39, 44,
    46–9, 54, 56, 60, 62, 63, 73, 77–8,

79–80, 90, 95, 99–100, 103–4,
112, 119, 120, 125, 137, 139–40,
145, 153, 157, 159, 160, 164–5,
166, 170–2, 221
The Entertainer, 54–5, 59–62, 118
Epitaph for George Dillon, 63
The Hotel in Amsterdam, 125
Inadmissible Evidence, 98–9, 166
Look Back in Anger, 30, 33, 37–8,
46–9, 51–2, 54, 57, 62, 70, 78, 120,
126–7, 131
Luther, 79, 86, 92
A Patriot for Me, 101, 103, 110–11
Plays for England, 90–1
Time Present, 125
West of Suez, 131, 139
Osborne, Thomas, 102
O'Toole, Peter, 68
Otway, Thomas, 118
The Soldier's Fortune, 118
Out of Joint Theatre Company, 218,
220, 226
Oxford Playhouse, 73

Page, Anthony, xxi, 59, 66, 75, 97–8,
99, 101, 103, 106, 108, 125, 126,
129, 132, 134–6, 141–2, 146
Page, Louise, 176, 179
Salonika, 176, 179
Palumbo, Peter, 206–7, 209, 211
Panter, Howard, 220, 226
Papp, Joe, 180, 188, 193, 212
Paris Festival, 86
Parker, Thane, 12, 19
Parry, Natasha, 95
Patterson, Bill, 212
Pears, Peter, 17
Penhall, Joe, 220, 225
Pale Horse, 225
Some Voices, 220
Pennington, Ann, 191–2
Pernak, Adam, 217
Killers, 217

Petzal, Tom, 202–4, 206
Phillips, Andy, 139, 142
Pinnock, Winsome, 194, 212, 226
A Hero's Welcome, 194
Mules, 226
Talking in Tongues, 212
Pinter, Harold, 69, 75, 212
The Dumb Waiter, 75
The New World Order, 212
The Room, 75
Piper, Ann, 114
Piper, John, 28–9
Pirandello, Luigi, 94
Naked, 94
Pirate Jenny, 165
Platonov, 77, 87
Playfair, Giles, 7–8
Plover, William, 51
Plowright, Joan, 50, 53, 55–6, 61, 91, 112
Poke, Greville, xxi, 17, 20–2, 27–9,
31–2, 35–6, 38, 40–2, 46–7, 51,
54–7, 61–6, 68, 72, 74, 76–7, 82,
88, 99, 101, 110, 112–13, 115, 117,
119, 123, 124, 126, 133–5, 137,
141, 142, 145, 146, 147, 148,
149–50, 151, 153, 156, 157–63,
165, 167, 168–9, 192, 217, 232 n.9,
247 n.2
Poke, Patricia, 112–13
Pollock, Ellen, 7
Poole, Gilly, 185
Pooley, Ernest, 4
Posner, Lindsay, 213
Pound, Ezra 17
Prichard, Rebecca, 221, 225
Essex Girls, 221
Pritchett, V.S., 34
Public Theater, New York, 180, 212
Pulford, Richard, 205

Quayle, Anthony, 4, 12–13, 85
Queen Victoria Hospital, East
Grinstead, 21

Queen's Theatre, 97, 102

Radin, Victoria, 170
Ramsay, Peggy, 84, 175
Rattigan, Terence, 18, 48–9, 51
Ravenscroft, Edward, 166
    The London Cuckolds, 166
Ray, Herbert, 30
Rayne, Jane, 200, 216
Lord Rayne, 197
    Rayne Foundation, 192
Reading, Bertice, 84
Reckord, Barry, 64, 92
    Flesh to a Tiger, 64
    Skyvers, 92–3
Redgrave, Corin, 88
Redgrave, Lynn, 88
Redgrave, Michael, 19, 23, 52
Redgrave, Vanessa, 88–9, 92, 93,
    97–8
    In the Interests of the State, 93–4
Reed, Dickon, 190
Rees-Mogg, William, 184–5, 190–1,
    204, 206
Reynolds, Simone, 154
Richardson, Ralph, 1, 139
Richardson, Tony, xxi, 5–7, 9–10, 18,
    21, 25, 27, 41–3, 46–7, 51, 53,
    55–7, 59, 61, 65, 67, 69, 74, 76–7,
    79, 81–2, 85–6, 88–9, 91–2, 94–5,
    97, 100, 103, 105, 126, 138, 141,
    146, 227, 242 n.45
Rickson, Ian, xiv, 217, 225, 227–8
Ritchie, Rob, viii, 164, 177, 181, 183,
    184–5, 188
Rix, Brian, 205
Robeson, Paul, 84–5
Robinson, Gerry, 227
Roose Evans, James, 75
Rose, David, 197
Roth, Stephen, 197
Roundhouse, 141
Rowntree, Jean, 10

Royal Academy of Dramatic Art, 27
Royal Ballet, 206
Royal Court Theatre Society, 178
Royal Court Young People's Scheme,
    202
Royal Court Young People's Theatre,
    193
Royal Court Young Writers' Festival,
    171–2, 176, 180, 193, 217, 220–1
Royal Court Young Writers' Group,
    171–2
Royal Exchange Theatre, Manchester,
    183, 205
Royal Lyceum Theatre, Edinburgh,
    154
Royal National Theatre, 1, 3, 12–13,
    70, 83, 85–6, 89–91, 93–5, 99,
    106, 115, 121, 141, 145, 150,
    157–9, 172, 175–6, 183–4, 206,
    211, 226
    Cottesloe Theatre, 190
    Royal National Theatre Studio, 205,
    221
Royal Opera House, 183, 306
Royal Shakespeare Company, 4, 8,
    12–13, 70, 85, 89–90, 97, 99, 106,
    116, 121, 175, 183, 206, 211, 217
Rudet, Jacqueline, 187
    The Basin, 187
Rushdie, Salman, 205
    The Satanic Verses, 205
Ruskin, John, 7

Sainsbury, Lord, 155
Saint-Denis, Michel, 1–4, 5, 6, 9,
    15–16, 42–3, 63, 76, 84, 91, 95,
    111–12
Salisbury Arts Theatre, 18, 65
Sartre, Jean-Paul, 37–8, 56, 58, 61, 79,
    83–4
    Altona, 83–5
    The Devil and the Lord, 37
    Nekrassov, 50, 52–3, 58, 61

Index

Saturday Night and Sunday Morning, 86

Schell, Maximilian, 103

Schools Scheme, 119

Scofield, Paul, 19, 146, 151

Seagull, The, 92, 97–8, 151, 173–4, 218

Second Mrs Tanqueray, The, 38

Selway, George, 18, 36

7:84 Scotland Theatre Company, 165

Shaftesbury Avenue, 139, 153

Shaw, George Bernard, 89, 220, 228–9

  John Bull's Other Island, 220

Shaw, Robert, 99

Shawn, Wallace, 187

  Aunt Dan and Lemon, 187, 218

Sheen, Martin, 192

Shepherd, Jack, 125

Shepard, Sam, 125, 165, 202, 225

  Curse of the Starving Class, 165

  A Lie of the Mind, 202

  Red Cross, 125

  Simpatico, 225

Sherman, Martin, 166

  Bent, 166–7

Sieff, Lois, 147, 148

Signoret, Simone, 116

Simpson, N.F., 59, 62–4, 74, 108, 109

  The Cresta Run, 108, 111

  One Way Pendulum, 73

  A Resounding Tinkle, 59, 62

Sinden, Donald, 19

Smith, Anna Devere, 218

  Fires in the Mirror, 218

Soho Poly, 165, 211

Soho Theatre Company, 211

Sons and Lovers, 167

Soyinka, Wole, 63, 70, 118, 243 n.21

  The Lion and the Jewel, 118

Spencer, David, 211

  Killing the Cat, 211

Spender, Stephen, 47

Spring Awakening, 93, 101–2

Spurling, Hilary, 114, 132–5, 137

Stafford-Clark, Max, xi–xii, xxi, 120, 142, 148–9, 162, 164–9, 170–82, 184, 186–94, 195–218, 219, 224, 251 n.23

Stephens, Robert, 93

Stevenson, Juliet, 212

Stoddard, Hugh, 210

  Gibraltar Strait, 210

Storey, David, 119–20, 128, 131, 140, 144, 146, 152, 188, 226

  The Changing Room, 131, 140, 188, 226

  The Contractor, 131

  Home, 131

  In Celebration, 128

  The Restoration of Arnold Middleton, 119–20

Strand Theatre, 76

Stratford Memorial Theatre, *see* Royal Shakespeare Company

Strauss, George, 122

Sulkin, David, 171, 180

Sully, Kathleen, 59

  The Waiting of Lester Abbs, 59

'Sunday Nights', 34, 58–9, 62, 65, 69–70, 73, 75, 80, 89, 92–4, 101, 102, 114–15, 118, 124–5, 131, 136, 220

Swash, Bob, 90

Tagg, Alan, 42, 69

Taming of the Shrew, The, 59

Taw and Torridge Festival of the Arts, 17–18, 20–1

Taylor, Gordon, 204, 206–7

Taylor, Joan, 123

Tennant, Cecil, 236 n.11

Tennant, H.M., 39, 65, 72

Thatcher, Margaret, 176, 181, 211

Theatre Royal, Stratford East, 55, 82, 183

Theatre Upstairs, 127–8, 130–1, 132, 136–7, 139, 141, 144, 149, 152–3, 165, 173, 176, 178–9, 182, 185–8, 190, 192–6, 202, 205, 210–13, 215, 217, 220–2, 225–6
Theatre Writers' Union, 200
Theatres Act, 111–13, 127
Thomas, Gwyn, 79, 88
  The Keep, 79, 88, 90
Thorndike, Sybil, 7, 11, 41
Thorpe, Jeremy, 17
Three Sisters, 118, 119, 211
Tickell, Dominic, 171–2
Tippett, Michael, 183
  The Knot Garden, 183
  La Calisto, 183
Tomkins, Steve, 223
Tony Kinsey Quintet, 69
Torch Song Trilogy, 192
Townsend, Sue, 183
  The Great Celestial Cow, 183
Travers, Ben, 98
  Cuckoo in the Nest, 98
Traverse Workshop, 170
Troubridge, St. Vincent, 20
Turner, Mark, 8
Twelfth Night, 123, 240, n.25
Twentieth-Century Fox, 79
Tynan, Kenneth, 48, 64, 101, 110, 126
Tyneside Theatre Company, 165

Ubu Roi, 116
'Uncertain Joy', 28
Uncle Vanya, 136
Unity Theatre, 61
Unwin, Paul, 215
Upton, Judy, 220
  Ashes and Sand, 220
Ustinov, Peter, 21, 29, 56

Vaudeville Theatre, 90, 120
Vedrenne, J.E., 7
Vedrenne-Barker Seasons, 63–4

Wain, John, 5
Wakelam, Stephen, 187
  Deadlines, 187
Walton, William, 23
  Troilus and Cressida, 23
Wardle, Irving, 170, 173, 175
Waterhouse, Keith and Hall, Willis, 91
  Billy Liar, 86
  The Sponge Room, 91
  Squat Betty, 91
Waugh, Evelyn, 51
Weidenfeld, Lord, 193, 198
Wiegel, Helen, 53
Welles, Orson, 41, 75
Wertenbaker, Timberlake, 187, 207, 212, 217
  The Grace of Mary Traverse, 187–8
  Our Country's Good, 203–4, 207, 218
  Three Birds Alighting on a Field, 212, 217, 218
Wesker, Arnold, 59, 63, 72, 76, 79–80, 86, 90, 107, 114, 144, 220
  Chicken Soup with Barley, 59, 65
  Chips with Everything, 90
  The Kitchen, 73, 79, 86, 220
  The Old Ones, 145
  Roots, 71–2, 118
  Their Very Own and Golden City, 114
West End, 3, 18, 64, 79, 88, 96, 107, 115, 125, 131, 139, 153–4, 163, 172, 180, 211, 225–6
Westminster Theatre, 12, 20–1, 23
West Yorkshire Playhouse, 212
White, Michael, 120, 126, 146, 148
Whitehead, E.A., 131, 139, 162
  Alpha Beta, 131, 142
Whitelaw, Billie, 167
Whiting, John, 15, 29, 33, 37, 39, 56
Wilkinson, Oliver, 61
  How Can We Save Father?, 61

Index

Willatt, Hugh, 135, 137, 157–9, 161–5, 189

Williams, Heathcote, 115, 137, 165
  The Local Stigmatic, 115

Williams, Nigel, 165, 226
  Class Enemy, 165
  Harry and Me, 226
  WC/PC, 166

Williams, Tennessee, 47, 90, 95
  Cat on a Hot Tin Roof, 47
  The Milk Train Doesn't Stop Here Any More, 95
  Orpheus Descending, 69
  Period of Adjustment, 90

Williams, W.E., 12, 14–15, 74, 90–1, 232 n.44

Williamson, Henry, 17

Williamson, Nicol, 98, 166

Wilson, Angus, 34, 37, 41, 45, 52, 56
  The Mulberry Bush, 37, 41, 44–8

Wilson, Cecil, 66

Wilson, Colin, 62

Wilson, Robert, 166
  I was Sitting on my Patio . . ., 166

Wilson, Snoo, 131, 144, 176

Winter, Ella, 52

Wolfe, George, 202, 212
  The Colored Museum, 202
  Spunk, 212

Wolfit, Donald, 18, 113

Women's Playhouse Trust, 183, 210

Wood, Charles, 109, 121
  Dingo, 120
  Fill the Stage with Happy Hours, 121
  Meals on Wheels, 101–3
  Veterans, 142

Worsley, T.C., 48, 90

Wright, Jules, 210

Wright, Nicholas, xxi, 79, 128, 131, 142, 143–4, 146, 148–50, 151–8, 162–3, 164, 165, 167, 171
  The Gorky Brigade, 167

Writers' Group, The, 63, 76, 118, 171

Wyndham's Theatre, 202

Wynne, Michael, 221, 225
  The Knocky, 221, 225

Yesterday's News, 154

Young Vic, 145